Rare Association Rule Mining and Knowledge Discovery:
Technologies for Infrequent and Critical Event Detection

Yun Sing Koh
Auckland University of Technology, New Zealand

Nathan Rountree
University of Otago, New Zealand

INFORMATION SCIENCE REFERENCE

Hershey · New York

Director of Editorial Content:	Kristin Klinger
Senior Managing Editor:	Jamie Snavely
Assistant Managing Editor:	Michael Brehm
Publishing Assistant:	Sean Woznicki
Typesetter:	Jamie Snavely
Cover Design:	Lisa Tosheff
Printed at:	Yurchak Printing Inc.

Published in the United States of America by
    Information Science Reference (an imprint of IGI Global)
    701 E. Chocolate Avenue
    Hershey PA 17033
    Tel: 717-533-8845
    Fax: 717-533-8661
    E-mail: cust@igi-global.com
    Web site: http://www.igi-global.com/reference

Library of Congress Cataloging-in-Publication Data

Rare association rule mining and knowledge discovery : technologies for
infrequent and critical event detection / Yun Sing Koh and Nathan Rountree,
editors.
    p. cm. -- (Advances in data warehousing and mining series)
  Includes bibliographical references and index.
  Summary: "This book provides readers with an in-depth compendium of current
issues, trends, and technologies in association rule mining"--Provided by
publisher.
  ISBN 978-1-60566-754-6 (hbk.) -- ISBN 978-1-60566-755-3 (ebook)
  1. Association rule mining. 2. Knowledge acquisition (Expert systems) 3.
Data mining. I. Koh, Yun Sing, 1978- II. Rountree, Nathan, 1974-
  QA76.9.D343R37 2010
  006.3'12--dc22
                    2009005260

British Cataloguing in Publication Data
A Cataloguing in Publication record for this book is available from the British Library.

All work contributed to this book is new, previously-unpublished material. The views expressed in this book are those of the authors, but not necessarily of the publisher.

Advances in Data Warehousing and Mining Series (ADWM)

ISBN: 1935-2646

Editor-in-Chief: David Taniar, Monash Univerisy, Australia

Research and Trends in Data Mining Technologies and Applications
David Taniar, Monash University, Australia

IGI Publishing • copyright 2007 • 340 pp • H/C (ISBN: 1-59904-271-1) • US $85.46 (our price)
• E-Book (ISBN: 1-59904-273-8) • US $63.96 (our price)

Activities in data warehousing and mining are constantly emerging. Data mining methods, algorithms, online analytical processes, data mart and practical issues consistently evolve, providing a challenge for professionals in the field. Research and Trends in Data Mining Technologies and Applications focuses on the integration between the fields of data warehousing and data mining, with emphasis on the applicability to real-world problems. This book provides an international perspective, highlighting solutions to some of researchers' toughest challenges. Developments in the knowledge discovery process, data models, structures, and design serve as answers and solutions to these emerging challenges.

The Advances in Data Warehousing and Mining (ADWM) Book Series aims to publish and disseminate knowledge on an international basis in the areas of data warehousing and data mining. The book series provides a highly regarded outlet for the most emerging research in the field and seeks to bridge underrepresented themes within the data warehousing and mining discipline.
The Advances in Data Warehousing and Mining (ADWM) Book Series serves to provide a continuous forum for state-of-the-art developments and research, as well as current innovative activities in data warehousing and mining. In contrast to other book series, the ADWM focuses on the integration between the fields of data warehousing and data mining, with emphasize on the applicability to real world problems. ADWM is targeted at both academic researchers and practicing IT professionals.

DISSEMINATOR of KNOWLEDGE

Hershey • New York

Order online at www.igi-global.com or call 717-533-8845 x 10 –
Mon-Fri 8:30 am - 5:00 pm (est) or fax 24 hours a day 717-533-8661

Table of Contents

Section 1
Beyond the Support-Confidence Framework

Section 2
Dealing with Imbalanced Datasets

Section 3
Rare, Anomalous, and Interesting Patterns

Section 4
Critical Event Detection and Applications

Detailed Table of Contents

Section 1
Beyond the Support-Confidence Framework

    Yun Sing Koh, Auckland University of Technology, New Zealand
    Nathan Rountree, University of Otago, New Zealand

The notion of finding rare association rules is like finding precious gems in an open field; it is a daunting task but, if successful, it is very rewarding. Association rule mining systems, such as Apriori, generally employ an exhaustive search algorithm. While these algorithms are in theory capable of finding rare association rules, they become intractable if the minimum level of support is set low enough to find rare rules. Such algorithms are therefore inadequate for finding rare associations, and also suffer from the rare item problem. Research to solve this problem has become more prevalent in recent times. The main goal of rare association rule mining is to discover relationships among sets of items in a transactional database that occur infrequently. This chapter presents a survey on the current trends and approaches in the area of rare association rule mining.

    Ling Zhou, University of Illinois at Chicago, USA
    Stephen Yau, University of Illinois at Chicago, USA

Association rule mining among frequent items has been extensively studied in data mining research. However, in recent years, there is an increasing demand for mining infrequent items (such as rare but expensive items). Since exploring interesting relationships among infrequent items has not been discussed much in the literature, in this chapter, the authors propose two simple, practical and effective schemes to mine association rules among rare items. Our algorithms can also be applied to frequent items with bounded length. Experiments are performed on the well-known IBM synthetic database. Their schemes compare favorably to Apriori and FP-growth under the situation being evaluated. In addition, they explore quantitative association rule mining in transactional databases among infrequent items by associating quantities of items: some interesting examples are drawn to illustrate the significance of such mining.

Rosa Meo, Università di Torino, Italy
Dino Ienco, Università di Torino, Italy

Association rules are an intuitive descriptive paradigm that has been used extensively in different application domains with the purpose to identify the regularities and correlation in a set of observed objects. However, association rules' statistical measures (support and confidence) have been criticized because in some cases they have shown to fail in their primary goal: that is to select the most relevant and significant association rules. In this paper the authors propose a new model that replaces the support measure. The new model, like support, is a tool for the identification of reliable rules and is used also to reduce the traversal of the itemsets' search space. The proposed model adopts new criteria in order to establish the reliability of the information extracted from the database. These criteria are based on Bayes' Theorem and on an estimate of the probability density function of each itemset. According to our criteria, the information that we have obtained from the database on an itemset is reliable if and only if the confidence interval of the estimated probability is low compared with the most likely value of it. The authors will see how this method can be computed in an approximate but satisfactory way, with the same algorithms that are usually adopted to select itemsets on support threshold.

Maybin Muyeba, Manchester Metropolitan University, UK
M. Sulaiman Khan, Liverpool Hope University, UK
Frans Coenen, University of Liverpool, UK

A novel approach is presented for effectively mining weighted fuzzy association rules (ARs). The authors address the issue of invalidation of downward closure property (DCP) in weighted association rule mining where each item is assigned a weight according to its significance with some user defined criteria. Most works on weighted association rule mining do not address the downward closure property while some make assumptions to validate the property. The authors generalize the weighted association rule mining problem with binary and fuzzy attributes with weighted settings. Their methodology follows an Apriori approach but employs T-tree data structure to improve efficiency of counting itemsets. Their approach avoids pre and post processing as opposed to most weighted association rule mining algorithms, thus eliminating the extra steps during rules generation. The chapter presents experimental results on both synthetic and real-data sets and a discussion on evaluating the proposed approach.

Section 2
Dealing with Imbalanced Datasets

Chapter 5

Huaifeng Zhang, University of Technology, Australia
Yanchang Zhao, University of Technology, Australia
Longbing Cao, University of Technology, Australia
Chengqi Zhang, University of Technology, Australia
Hans Bohlscheid, Projects Section, Business Integrity Programs Branch, Centrelink, Australia

In this chapter, the authors propose a novel framework for rare class association rule mining. In each class association rule, the right-hand is a target class while the left-hand may contain one or more attributes. This algorithm is focused on the multiple imbalanced attributes on the left-hand. In the proposed framework, the rules with and without imbalanced attributes are processed in parallel. The rules without imbalanced attributes are mined through a standard algorithm while the rules with imbalanced attributes are mined based on newly defined measurements. Through simple transformation, these measurements can be in a uniform space so that only a few parameters need to be specified by user. In the case study, the proposed algorithm is applied in the social security field. Although some attributes are severely imbalanced, rules with a minority of imbalanced attributes have been mined efficiently.

Chapter 6

Yun Sing Koh, Auckland University of Technology, New Zealand
Russel Pears, Auckland University of Technology, New Zealand

Rare association rule mining has received a great deal of attention in the past few years. In this paper, we propose a multi methodological approach to the problem of rare association rule mining that integrates three different strands of research in this area. Firstly, the authors make use of statistical techniques such as the Fisher test to determine whether itemsets co-occur by chance or not. Secondly, they use clustering as a pre-processing technique to improve the quality of the rare rules generated. Their third strategy is to weigh itemsets to ensure upward closure, thus checking unbounded growth of the rule base. Their results show that clustering isolates heterogeneous segments from each other, thus promoting the discovery of rules which would otherwise remain undiscovered. Likewise, the use of itemset weighting tends to improve rule quality by promoting the generation of rules with rarer itemsets that would otherwise not be possible with a simple weighting scheme that assigns an equal weight to all possible itemsets. The use of clustering enabled us to study in detail an important sub-class of rare rules, which we term absolute rare rules. Absolute rare rules are those are not just rare to the dataset as a whole but are also rare to the cluster from which they are derived.

The authors consider databases in which each attribute takes values from a partially ordered set (poset). This allows one to model a number of interesting scenarios arising in different applications, including quantitative databases, taxonomies, and databases in which each attribute is an interval representing the duration of a certain event occurring over time. A natural problem that arises in such circumstances is the following: given a database D and a threshold value t, find all collections of "generalizations" of attributes which are "supported" by less than t transactions from D. We call such collections infrequent elements. Due to monotonicity, they can reduce the output size by considering only minimal infrequent elements. The authors study the complexity of finding all minimal infrequent elements for some interesting classes of posets. They show how this problem can be applied to mining association rules in different types of databases, and to finding "sparse regions" or "holes" in quantitative data or in databases recording the time intervals during which a re-occurring event appears over time. Their main focus will be on these applications rather than on the correctness or analysis of the given algorithms.

Section 3
Rare, Anomalous, and Interesting Patterns

The paper presents an approach to mining patterns in numerical data without the need for discretization. The proposed method allows for discovery of arbitrary nonlinear relationships. The approach is based on finding a function of a set of attributes whose values are close to zero in the data. Intuitively such functions correspond to equations describing relationships between the attributes, but they are also able to capture more general classes of patterns. The approach is set in an association rule framework with analogues of itemsets and rules defined for numerical attributes. Furthermore, the user may include background knowledge in the form of a probabilistic model. Patterns which are already correctly predicted by the model will not be considered interesting. Interesting patterns can then be used by the user to update the probabilistic model.

In the context of anomaly detection, the data mining technique of extracting association rules can be used to identify rare rules which represent infrequent situations. A method to detect rare rules is to first infer the normal behavior of objects in the form of quasi-functional dependencies (i.e. functional dependencies that frequently hold), and then analyzing rare violations with respect to them. The quasi-functional dependencies are usually inferred from the current instance of a database. However, in several applications, the database is not static, but new data are added or deleted continuously. Thus, the anomalies have to be updated because they change over time. In this chapter, we propose an incremental algorithm to efficiently maintain up-to-date rules (i.e., functional and quasi-functional dependencies). The impact of the cardinality of the data set and the number of new tuples on the execution time is evaluated through a set of experiments on synthetic and real databases, whose results are here reported.

Chapter 10

Dong (Haoyuan) Li, LGI2P, École des Mines d'Alès, France
Anne Laurent, LIRMM, Université Montpellier II, France
Pascal Poncelet, LIRMM, Université Montpellier II, France

As common criteria in data mining methods, the frequency-based interestingness measures provide a statistical view of the correlation in the data, such as sequential patterns. However, when the authors consider domain knowledge within the mining process, the unexpected information that contradicts existing knowledge on the data has never less importance than the regularly frequent information. For this purpose, they present the approach USER for mining unexpected sequential rules in sequence databases. They propose a belief-driven formalization of the unexpectedness contained in sequential data, with which we propose 3 forms of unexpected sequences. They further propose the notion of unexpected sequential patterns and implication rules for determining the structures and implications of the unexpectedness. The experimental results on various types of data sets show the usefulness and effectiveness of our approach.

Chapter 11

Marco-Antonio Balderas Cepeda, Universidad de Granada, Spain

Association rule mining has been a highly active research field over the past decade. Extraction of frequency-related patterns has been applied to several domains. However, the way association rules are defined has limited our ability to obtain all the patterns of interest. In this chapter, the authors present an alternative approach that allows us to obtain new kinds of association rules that represent deviations from common behaviors. These new rules are called anomalous rules. To obtain such rules requires that we extract all the most frequent patterns together with certain extension patterns that may occur very infrequently. An approach that relies on anomalous rules has possible application in the areas of counterterrorism, fraud detection, pharmaceutical data analysis and network intrusion detection. They provide an adaption of measures of interest to our anomalous rule sets, and we propose an algorithm that can extract anomalous rules as well. Their experiments with benchmark and real-life datasets suggest that the set of anomalous rules is smaller than the set of association rules. Their work also provides evidence that our proposed approach can discover hidden patterns with good reliability.

Chapter 12

Strong symmetric association rules are defined as follows. Strong means that the association rule has a strong support and a strong confidence, well above the minimum thresholds. Symmetric means that X→Y and Y→X are both association rules. Common objective interestingness measures such as lift, correlation, conviction or Chi-square tend to rate this kind of rule poorly. By contrast, cosine is high for such rules. However, depending on the application domain, these rules may be interesting regarding criteria such as unexpectedness or actionability. In this chapter, the authors investigate why the above-mentioned measures, except cosine, rate strong symmetric association rules poorly, and show that the underlying data might take a quite special shape. This kind of rule can be qualified as rare, as they would be pruned by many objective interestingness measures. Then they present lift and cosine in depth, giving their intuitive meaning, their definition and typical values. Because lift has its roots in probability and cosine in geometry, these two interestingness measures give different information on the rules they rate. Furthermore they are fairly easy to interpret by domain experts, who are not necessarily data mining experts. The authors round off our investigation with a discussion on contrast rules and show that strong symmetric association rules give a hint to mine further rare rules, rare in the sense of a low support but a high confidence. Finally they present case studies from the field of education and discuss challenges.

Section 4
Critical Event Detection and Applications

Chapter 13

In this chapter, the authors discuss the characteristics of data collected by the New Zealand Centre for Adverse Drug Reaction Monitoring (CARM) over a five-year period. They begin by noting the ways in which adverse reaction data are similar to market basket data, and the ways in which they are different. They go on to develop a model for estimating the amount of missing data in the dataset, and another to decide whether a drug is rare simply because it was only available for a short time. They also discuss the notion of "rarity" with respect to drugs, and with respect to reactions. Although the discussion is confined to the CARM data, the models and techniques presented here are useful to anyone who is about to embark on an association mining project, or who needs to interpret association rules in the context of a particular database.

Chapter 14

Association rule mining produces a large number of rules but many of them are usually redundant ones. When a data set contains infrequent items, we need to set the minimum support criterion very low;

otherwise, these items will not be discovered. The downside is that it leads to even more redundancy. To deal with this dilemma, some proposed more efficient, and perhaps more complicated, rule generation methods. The others suggested using simple rule generation methods and rather focused on the post-pruning of the rules. This chapter follows the latter approach. The classic Apriori is employed for the rule generation. Their goal is to gain as much insight as possible about the domain. Therefore, the discovered rules are filtered by their semantics and structures. An individual rule is classified by its own semantic, or by how clear its domain description is. It can be labelled as one of the following: strongly meaningless, weakly meaningless, partially meaningful, and meaningful. In addition, multiple rules are compared. Rules with repetitive patterns are removed, while those conveying the most complete information are retained. They demonstrate an application of our techniques to a real case study, an analysis of traffic accidents in Nakorn Pathom, Thailand.

Markus Breitenbach, Northpointe Institute for Public Management, USA
William Dieterich, Northpointe Institute for Public Management, USA
Tim Brennan, Northpointe Institute for Public Management, USA
Adrian Fan, University of Colorado at Boulder, USA

In this chapter, the authors explore Area under Curve (AUC) as an error-metric suitable for imbalanced data, as well as survey methods of optimizing this metric directly. We also address the issue of cut-point thresholds for practical decision-making. The techniques will be illustrated by a study that examines predictive rule development and validation procedures for establishing risk levels for violent felony crimes committed when criminal offenders are released from prison in the USA. The "violent felony" category was selected as the key outcome since these crimes are a major public safety concern, have a low base-rate (around 7%), and represent the most extreme forms of violence. They compare the performance of different algorithms on the dataset and validate using survival analysis whether the risk scores produced by these techniques are computing reasonable estimates of the true risk.

Russel Pears, Auckland University of Technology, New Zealand
Raymond Oetama, Auckland University of Technology, New Zealand

Credit scoring is a tool commonly employed by lenders in credit risk management. However credit scoring methods are prone to error. Failures from credit scoring result in granting loans to high risk customers, thus significantly increasing the incidence of overdue payments, or in the worst case, customers defaulting on the loan altogether. In this research the authors use a machine learning approach to improve the identification of such customers. However, identifying such bad customers is not a trivial task as they form the minority of customers and standard machine learning algorithms have difficulty in learning accurate models on such imbalanced datasets. They propose a novel approach based on a data segmentation strategy that progressively partitions the original data set into segments where bad customers form the majority. These segments, known as Majority Bad Payment Segments (MBPS) are then used to train machine learning classifiers such as Logistic Regression, C4.5, and Bayesian Network to identify high risk customers in advance. They compare their approach to the traditional approach of under sampling the majority class of good customers using a variety of metrics such as Hit Rate, Coverage and the Area under the Curve (AUC) metrics which have been designed to evaluate classification performance on imbalanced data sets. The results of our experimentation showed that the MBPS generally outperformed the under sampling method on all of these measures. Although MBPS has been used in this research in the context of a financial credit application, the technique is a generic one and can be used in any application domain that involves imbalanced data.

Foreword

For more than a decade, researches on association rule mining have attracted a huge interest from the data mining communities. Many advances in association rule mining have been proposed in recent years, including more efficient algorithms to process association rules, new data structures to speed up processing, new compression techniques to overcome the memory limitation problem, and so on. Many issues surrounding association rules have been discussed, including security, privacy, and incomplete and inaccurate data. Association rules have also been applied in various domains, including mobile mining, social networking, graph mining, etc.

However, most of the existing research on association rules has been focusing on establishing common patterns and rules; these are patterns and rules based on the majority, some of which may be either obvious or irrelevant. Unfortunately, not enough attentions have been given to mining rare association rules; these are outlier rules and patterns.

Rare association rules are critically important as in many cases they represent outstanding patterns, which cannot be easily discovered by traditional association mining algorithms. This book presents an interesting collection of recent advances in rare association rule mining. This book is certainly an invaluable resource to data mining researchers, especially to those who have strong interest in association rules.

I am pleased to be able to recommend this timely reference source to readers, be they researchers looking for future directions to pursue research in data mining, or practitioners interested in applying data mining concepts in practical situations.

David Taniar
Monash University, Australia
January 2009

David Taniar holds Bachelor, Master, and PhD degrees - all in Computer Science, with a particular specialty in Databases. His current research areas are in mobile databases, parallel databases, web databases, GIS, and data mining. He publishes extensively every year, including his recent co-authored book: High Performance Parallel Database Processing and Grid Databases (John Wiley & Sons, 2008). His list of publications can be viewed at the DBLP server (http://www.informatik.uni-trier. de/~ley/db/indices/a-tree/t/Taniar:David.html). He is a founding editor-in-chief of a number of international journals, including Intl J of Data Warehousing and Mining, Intl J of Business Intelligence and Data Mining, Mobile Information Systems, Journal of Mobile Multimedia, Intl J of Web Information Systems, and Intl J of Web and Grid Services. He is currently an Associate Professor at the Faculty of Information Technology, Monash University, Australia. He can be contacted at David.Taniar@ infotech.monash.edu.au.

Preface

This is the third volume of the Advances in Data Warehousing and Mining (ADWM) book series. ADWM publishes books in the areas of data warehousing and mining. This special volume, *Rare Association Rule Mining and Knowledge Discovery: Technologies for Infrequent and Critical Event Detection*, presents cutting edge research in this newly emerging area. Techniques for rare association mining are quite different from that of traditional rule mining and this book fills an essential gap in this area.

The primary objective of this book is to give readers in-depth knowledge on the current issues in rare association rule mining and critical event detection. The book is designed to cover a comprehensive range of topics related to rare association rule mining and critical event detection: mining techniques, imbalanced datasets, interest metrics, and real-world application domains. We hope this book will highlight the need for growth and research in the area of rare association rule mining and critical event detection. This volume consists of sixteen chapters in four sections.

The first section, Beyond the Support-Confidence Framework, provides an introduction to the area of rare association rule mining, and looks at some of the current proposed techniques which have moved away from the traditional support and confidence measures. This section contains four chapters.

Chapter 1, "*Rare Association Rule Mining: Overview*", by Yun Sing Koh, Auckland University of Technology, New Zealand, and Nathan Rountree, University of Otago, New Zealand, introduces the problem faced in the area of rare association rule mining and the current trends in this area. They provide an extensive literature review on the currently available techniques when dealing with rare itemsets.

Chapter 2, "*Association Rule and Quantitative Association Rule Mining among Infrequent Items*", by Ling Zhou and Stephen Yau, University of Illinois at Chicago, proposes two new methods to mine infrequent items and find rare association rules. Their approach is versatile and can also be applied to frequent items with bounded length. In addition they explore quantitative association rule mining among infrequent items by associating quantities of items: some interesting examples are drawn to illustrate the significance of such mining.

Chapter 3, "*Replacing Support in Association Rule Mining*", by Rosa Meo and Dino Ienco, Università di Torino, Italy, proposes a new model which adopts criteria based on Bayes' Theorem and on an estimate of the probability density function of each itemset to establish the reliability of the information extracted from the database.

Chapter 4, "*Effective Mining of Weighted Fuzzy Association Rules*", by Maybin Muyeba, Manchester Metropolitan University, UK, M. Sulaiman Khan, Liverpool Hope University, UK, and Frans Coenen, University of Liverpool, UK, presents a novel approach for effectively mining weighted fuzzy association rules. They generalize the weighted association rule mining problem with binary and fuzzy attributes with weighted settings.

The second section, Dealing with Imbalanced Datasets, looks at algorithms and mining frameworks for dealing with datasets where there is uneven representation of various database objects. Imbalanced data is a key issue in rare association rule mining, because: a) it is a *necessary* condition of rare itemsets, and b) it affects the power and accuracy of the statistical models used to perform data mining. This section consists of three chapters, where we look at rare class association rule mining, sub-class association rule mining, and mining minimal infrequent elements.

Chapter 5, *"Rare Class Association Rule Mining with Multiple Imbalanced Attributes"*, by Huaifeng Zhang, Yanchang Zhao, Longbing Cao, Chengqi Zhang, University of Technology, Sydney, Australia, and Hans Bohlscheid, Projects Section, Business Integrity Programs Branch, Centrelink, Australia, proposes a framework for rare class association rule mining. In their approach, the rules without imbalanced attributes are mined through a standard algorithm while the rules with imbalanced attributes are mined based on newly defined measurements. In this chapter, they present a compelling case study applied in the social security field.

Chapter 6, *"A Multi-Methodological Approach to Rare Association Rule Mining"* by Yun Sing Koh, Auckland University of Technology, New Zealand, and Russel Pears, Auckland University of Technology, New Zealand, proposes a synthesis of material from three different methodologies to tackle the problem of rare association rule mining: itemset weighting, clustering, and statistical significance testing. They focus on the importance of sub-class rare rules or absolute rare rules. Absolute rare rules are those are not just rare to the dataset as a whole but are also rare to the cluster from which they are derived.

Chapter 7, *"Finding Minimal Infrequent Elements in Multi-Dimensional Data Defined over Partially Ordered Sets and its Applications"*, by Khaled M. Elbassioni, Max-Planck-Institut fur Informatik, Germany, studies the complexity of finding all minimal infrequent elements for some interesting classes of partially ordered set (poset). He looks at a general framework used to mine associations from different types of databases. The rules obtained under this framework are generally stronger than the ones obtained from techniques that use binarization.

In Section 3, Rare, Anomalous, and Interesting Patterns, we look at some of the techniques used to find interesting and unexpected patterns in the area of association rules. Section three consists of five chapters, discussing issues related to discovering interesting patterns in numerical data with background knowledge, discovering quasi-functional dependencies, mining unexpected patterns, and extracting anomalous rules.

Chapter 8, *"Discovering Interesting Patterns in Numerical Data with Background Knowledge"*, by Szymon Jaroszewicz, National Institute of Telecommunications, Warsaw, Poland, presents an approach to mining patterns in numerical data without the need for discretization. The proposed method allows for discovery of arbitrary nonlinear relationships where the user may include background knowledge in the form of a probabilistic model. The patterns that have been previously predicted by the model will not be considered interesting. Interesting patterns can then be used by the user to update the probabilistic model.

Chapter 9, *"Mining Rare Association Rules by Discovering Quasi-functional Dependencies: An Incremental Approach"*, by Giulia Bruno and Paolo Garza, Politecnico di Torino Corso Duca degli Abruzzi, Italy, and Elisa Quintarell, Politecnico di Milano Piazza Leonardo da Vinci, Italy, propose a method of detecting rare rules by first inferring the normal behaviour of objects in the form of quasi-functional dependencies (i.e. functional dependencies that frequently hold), and then analysing rare violations with respect to them. They propose an incremental algorithm to efficiently maintain up-to-date rules.

Chapter 10, *"Mining Unexpected Sequential Patterns and Implication Rules"* by Dong (Haoyuan) Li, LGI2P, École des Mines d'Alès, France, Anne Laurent and Pascal Poncelet, LIRMM, Université Montpellier II, France, presents an approach called USER for mining unexpected sequential rules in sequence databases. They propose a belief-driven formalization of the unexpectedness contained in sequential data.

Chapter 11, *"Mining Hidden Association Rules from Real-Life Data"* by Marco-Antonio Balderas Cepeda, Universidad de Granada, Spain, provides an adaptation of measures of interest to our anomalous rule sets, and proposed an algorithm that can extract anomalous rules as well. Their approach discovered hidden patterns with good reliability.

Chapter 12, *"Strong Symmetric Association Rules and Interestingness Measures"* by Agathe Merceron, University of Applied Sciences TFH Berlin, Germany, proposes a method to find strong symmetric association rules. This approach is slightly different from the conventional rare association rule mining. This kind of rule can be qualified as rare, as they would be pruned by many objective interestingness measures.

In Section 4, Critical Event Detection and Applications, we look at some of the applications of rare association rule mining and critical event detection. In this section, we provide two chapters which specifically look at the usage of association rule mining in different domains. The last two chapters look at a different data mining approach, namely classification techniques, for critical event detection. The areas of application discussed include adverse drug reaction monitoring, analysis of traffic accident, risk levels for violent felony crimes, and financial credit monitoring.

Chapter 13, *"He Wasn't There Again Today"*, by Richard O'Keefe and Nathan Rountree, University of Otago, New Zealand, discusses the characteristics of data collected by the New Zealand Centre for Adverse Drug Reaction Monitoring (CARM) over a five-year period. They discuss the notion of "rarity" with respect to drugs, and with respect to reactions.

Chapter 14, *"Filtering Association Rules by Their Semantics and Structures"* by Rangsipan Marukatat, Mahidol University, Thailand, introduces the filtering of association rules by their patterns and degrees of semantic redundancy. They applied their techniques to a real case study, an analysis of traffic accidents in Nakorn Pathom, Thailand.

Chapter 15, *Creating Risk-Scores in very Imbalanced Datasets: Predicting Extremely Violent Crime among Criminal Offenders Following Release from Prison* by Markus Breitenbach, William Dieterich, Tim Brennan, Northpointe Institute for Public Management, USA, and Adrian Fan, University of Colorado at Boulder, USA, explores the Area under Curve (AUC) as an error-metric suitable for imbalanced data, as well as survey methods of optimizing this metric directly. They conducted a study that examines predictive rule development and validation procedures for establishing risk levels for violent felony crimes committed when criminal offenders are released from prison in the USA.

Chapter 16, *"Boosting Prediction Accuracy of Bad Payments in Financial Credit Applications"*, by Russel Pears and Raymond Oetama, Auckland University of Technology, New Zealand, use a machine learning approach to improve the identification of such customers. They proposed a credit scoring approach to predict bad payments for credit risk management.

We hope that this book will provide readers some specific challenge that motivates the development and enhancement of rare association rule mining and critical event detection area. We also hope that this book will serve as an introductory material to the researchers and practitioners interested in this emerging area of research.

Yun Sing Koh and Nathan Rountree
January 2009

Section 1
Beyond the Support–Confidence Framework

Chapter 1
Rare Association Rule Mining:
An Overview

Yun Sing Koh
Auckland University of Technology, New Zealand

Nathan Rountree
University of Otago, New Zealand

ABSTRACT

The notion of finding rare association rules is like finding precious gems in an open field; it is a daunting task but, if successful, it is very rewarding. Association rule mining systems, such as Apriori, generally employ an exhaustive search algorithm. While these algorithms are in theory capable of finding rare association rules, they become intractable if the minimum level of support is set low enough to find rare rules. Such algorithms are therefore inadequate for finding rare associations, and also suffer from the rare item problem. Research to solve this problem has become more prevalent in recent times. The main goal of rare association rule mining is to discover relationships among sets of items in a transactional database that occur infrequently. This chapter presents a survey on the current trends and approaches in the area of rare association rule mining.

INTRODUCTION

The most popular pattern discovery method in data mining is association rule mining. Association rule mining was introduced by Agrawal, Imielinski, and Swami (1993). It aims to extract interesting correlations, frequent patterns, associations or casual structures among sets of items in transaction databases or other data repositories. The relationships are not based on inherent properties of the data themselves but rather based on the co-occurrence of the items within the database. The associations between items are commonly expressed in the form of *association rules*.

The original motivation for seeking association rules came from the need to analyse supermarket transaction data to examine customer behaviour in terms of the purchased products. This is known as market basket analysis. Market basket analysis begins by finding all *frequent itemsets*; that is, combinations of items that appear together in at least m transactions in the database, where m is specified by

DOI: 10.4018/978-1-60566-754-6.ch001

the analyst in advance. This user-specified parameter is called minimum support (minsup). Then association rules are derived in the form of X → Y where XY is a frequent itemset. Strong association rules are derived from frequent itemsets and constrained by another user-specified parameter: minimum confidence (minconf). Confidence is the percentage of transactions containing X that also contain Y. For example, suppose in a database 27% of all transactions contain both bread and milk, and 30% of all transactions contain bread. An association rule mining system might therefore derive the rule *bread → milk* with 27% support and 90% confidence. (Confidence can be treated as the conditional probability of a transaction containing bread also containing milk.) In classical association rule mining systems, the user must set minsup to 27% or lower, and minconf to 90% or lower for this rule to have been produced. For instance, if minconf had been set to 35%, the {*bread, milk*} itemset would never have been spotted by the system – and a rule of high confidence would have been missed.

Currently most association mining algorithms are dedicated to frequent itemset mining. These algorithms are defined in such a way that they only find rules with high support and high confidence. Most of these approaches adopt an Apriori-like approach (Agrawal & Srikant, 1994). A much less explored area in association mining is *infrequent* itemset mining. Intuitively, we can define rare itemsets as those that appear together in very few transactions, or some very small percentage of the transactions in the database. However, the key motivation of infrequent itemset mining is that, although two items may appear in very few transactions, it may be that when they do appear, they typically appear together. Therefore, it may be possible to form an association rule that has very low support, but very high confidence. For example, suppose that {espresso machine} appears in only 1% of a department store's transactions, and that {coffee grinder} appears in about 1.2%. Both items could be said to be rare. Furthermore,

suppose that {*coffee grinder, espresso machine*} appears in 0.8% of the store's transactions: even more rare. But with this information, we can derive the rule *espresso machine → coffee grinder* with a confidence of 80%.

A characteristic of frequent itemset mining is that it relies on there being a meaningful minimum support level that is sufficiently *high* to reduce the number of frequent itemsets to a manageable level. However, in some data mining applications relatively infrequent associations are likely to be of great interest as they relate to rare but crucial cases. Examples of mining infrequent itemsets include identifying relatively rare diseases, predicting telecommunication equipment failure, and finding associations between infrequently purchased (e.g. expensive or high-profit) retail items. Indeed, infrequent itemsets warrant special attention because they are more difficult to find using traditional data mining techniques.

This chapter introduces the current approaches to rare association rule mining. The chapter is divided into several sections that include an introduction to association rule mining, the rare item problem, current trends and approaches, and discussion on the future development of this area. Finally, we provide a section, Further Information, summarizing the key papers in the area of rare association rule mining.

Association Rule Mining

The following is a formal statement of association rule mining for a transaction database. Let $I = \{i_1, i_2, ..., i_m\}$ be the universe of items. A set $X \subseteq I$ of items is called an itemset or pattern. In particular, an itemset containing k items is called a k-itemset. Every transaction contains a unique transaction ID tid. A transaction $t = (tid, X)$ is a tuple where X is an itemset. A transaction $t = (tid, X)$ is said to contain itemset Y if $Y \subseteq X$. The main function of a unique transaction ID is to allow instances of an itemset to occur more than once in a database. Let $\{t_1, t_2, ..., t_n\}$ be the set of all possible transactions

T. A transaction database D is a set of transactions, such that $D \subseteq T$. In effect, D is really a multiset of itemsets. An association rule is an implication of the form $X \rightarrow Y$, where $X \subset I$, $Y \subset I$, and $X \cap Y = \varnothing$. Let sup(X) be the number of transactions containing all the items in itemset X. The rule $X \rightarrow Y$ has support of s in the transaction set D, if $s = \text{sup}(XY)$, where XY refers to an itemset that contains all of the items in X and all of the items of Y. Alternatively, sup(X) can be expressed in relative terms, as the percentage of transactions that contain X in the dataset. The rule $X \rightarrow Y$ holds in the transaction set D with confidence c where $c = \text{conf}(X \rightarrow Y)$, the *confidence* of the rule $X \rightarrow Y$. This may be expressed as sup(XY)/sup(X). Note that in the calculation of confidence, it does not matter whether support is absolute or relative.

The Apriori algorithm is the "classical" method of finding frequent k-itemsets, which may then be formed into rules. Its purpose is to avoid counting the support of every possible itemset derivable from I (since there are 2^m possible itemsets to be checked if there are m items). Apriori exploits the property of *downward closure*, which is that if any k-itemset is frequent, all of its subsets must be frequent too. Assume that the items in a k-itemset are always stored in lexicographic order. Apriori proceeds as follows:

1. Calculate the support of all 1-itemsets (this information is often readily available from the system anyway) and prune any that fall under minimum support. These are the frequent 1-itemsets.

    Loop

2. Form candidate k-itemsets by taking each pair *p, q* of itemsets in the (k-1)-itemsets where *all but* the last item match. Form each new k-itemset by adding the last item of *q* onto the items of *p*.
3. Prune the candidate k-itemsets by eliminating any itemset that contains a subset not in the (k-1)-frequent itemsets

4. Count the supports in the database of the remaining candidate k-itemsets and eliminate any that fall below minsup. The result is the frequent k-itemsets.

Until Step 2 fails to produce any candidates (which will also occur if Steps 3 or 4 resulted in an empty set of candidates).

It is clear that finding association rules with low support but high confidence using Apriori-like methods would face difficulties. To find these rules the minimum support threshold would need to be set quite low to enable rare items to be let in. The Apriori heuristic is only able to reduce the size of candidate itemsets if the minimum support is set reasonably high. However, in situations with abundant frequent patterns, long patterns, or a low minimum support threshold, an Apriori-like algorithm may still suffer from the following non-trivial cost: most of the items would be allowed to participate in itemset generation. This will have an effect on the scalability of the Apriori algorithm. It is costly to handle a huge number of candidate items. It is time consuming to repeatedly scan the database and check the support of each of the candidate itemsets generated. The complexity of the computation will increase exponentially with regard to the number of itemsets generated.

Let us consider the work that the Apriori algorithm does in terms of the specified minimum support and the number and length of frequent itemsets in the database. Apriori may be able to cut out a lot of candidates; however, it is still costly to handle a huge number of candidate itemsets in large transaction databases. For example, consider the case where there are 1 million items but only 1% (1000 items) are frequent 1-items. Apriori still has to generate more than 5×10^5 candidate 2-itemsets, and evaluate and store the support for the generation of candidate 3-itemsets. It is expensive to repeatedly scan the database and check a large set of frequent itemsets by pattern matching, especially if the length of the itemset is long. Apriori does a level-by-level candidate generation and test. If it has a frequent itemset $X = \{i^1 \ldots i^k\}$, Apriori has to scan the database k times. For example, if k is 100 we would have to scan the database 100 times for that particular itemset. Apriori encounters difficulty in mining long patterns. To find a frequent itemset $X = \{i^1 \ldots i^{100}\}$ it has to generate and test $2^{100} - 1$ candidate itemsets.

These drawbacks suggest that it would not be efficient to use Apriori to generate rare rules as rare itemsets have low frequencies in the database by definition. Hence if we use the Apriori algorithm we would need to lower the minimum support threshold close to 0. This would allow most of the items within the dataset to be extended and used in the next iteration. As Apriori will not be able to prune a lot of the candidate itemsets, the repeated scan through the database becomes very expensive.

RARE ITEM PROBLEM

Traditional association rule mining algorithms, such as Apriori, focus on mining association rules in large databases with a single minimum support (minsup) threshold. Since a single threshold is used for the whole database, it assumes that all items in the database are of the same nature and/or have similar frequencies. As such, Apriori works best when all items have approximately the same frequency in the data. Apriori exploits the downward closure property that states that if an itemset is frequent so are all its subsets. As such, it is not possible to use Apriori with multiple user-defined minsups without modification to the algorithm. Consider the case where the user-defined minsup of $\{A,B,C\}$ is 2% and the user-defined minsup of $\{A,B\}$, $\{A,C\}$, and $\{B,C\}$ is 5%. It is possible for $\{A,B,C\}$ to be frequent with respect to its minsup but none of $\{A,B\}$, $\{A,C\}$, $\{B,C\}$ to be frequent with respect to their minsup. Suppose $\{A,B\}$, $\{A,C\}$, $\{B,C\}$ have support of 4%, and $\{A,B,C\}$ has support of 3%. In this case itemset

$\{A,B,C\}$ should be considered frequent because the user has specified a minsup of 2% for it, and it is above that. However, Apriori will not generate it, because $\{AB\}$ and $\{AC\}$ fall below their user-specified minsup of 5%. In reality, some items may be very frequent while others may rarely appear. Hence minsup should not be fixed because deviation and exceptions generally have a much lower support than general trends. Note that support requirements vary as the support of items contained in an itemset varies. Given that the existing Apriori algorithm assumes a uniform support, rare itemsets can be hard to find. Rare items are by definition in very few transactions and will be pruned because they do not meet the minsup threshold. In data mining, rare itemsets may be obscured by common cases. Weiss (2004) calls this relative rarity. This means that items may not be rare in the absolute sense but are rare relative to other items. This is especially a problem when data mining algorithms rely on greedy search heuristics that examine one item at a time. Since rare cases may depend on the conjunction of many conditions, analysing any single condition alone may not be interesting (Weiss, 2004).

As a specific example of the problem, consider the association mining problem where we want to determine if there is an association between buying a food processor and buying a cooking pan (Liu et al., 1999a). The problem is that both items are rarely purchased in a supermarket. Thus, even if the two items are almost always purchased together, this association may not be found, because the 1-itemsets are pruned out before they can be used to generate 2-itemsets. Modifying the minsup threshold to take into account the importance of the items is one way to ensure that rare items remain in consideration. To find this association minsup must be set low. However setting this threshold low would cause a combinatorial explosion in the overall number of itemsets generated. Frequently occurring items will be associated with one another in an enormous number of ways simply because the items are so common that they cannot help but appear together. This is known as the rare item problem (Liu et al., 1999a). It means that, using the Apriori algorithm, we are unlikely to generate rules that may indicate rare events of potentially dramatic consequence. For example, we might prune out rules that indicate the symptoms of a rare but fatal disease due to the frequency of occurrence not reaching the minsup threshold. As rare rule mining is still an area that has not been well explored, there is some groundwork that needs to be established. A real dataset will contain noise, possibly at levels of low support. Normally, noise has low support. In Apriori, setting a high minimum support threshold would cut the noise out. Inherently we are looking for rules with low support that could make them indistinguishable from coincidences (that is, situations where items fall together no more often than they would normally by chance). Although Apriori is the most commonly used association mining technique, it is far from efficient when we try to find low support rules. Using Apriori, we would still need to wade through thousands of itemsets (often having high support) to find the rare itemsets that are of interest to us.

Although rare rule mining has many potential possibilities, like frequent pattern mining, there could be a large number of rules generated from a database. We would need to find ways to generate only the potentially useful rare rules.

Current Trends and Approaches

Classic association mining techniques, such as Apriori, rely on uniform minimum support. These algorithms either miss the rare but interesting rules or suffer from congestion in itemset generation caused by low support. Driven by such shortcomings, some research has been carried out in developing new rule discovery algorithms to mine rare rules. Currently there are several different approaches to deal with the shortcoming of using support threshold and the rare item problem. In this section we take a look at the mainstream research

effort in this particular area. There approaches to mining rare rules include using a variable support threshold, mining without support threshold, constraint-based mining, and structure-based mining. Here we take a look general idea behind these approaches.

There have been several approaches taken to ensure that rare items are considered during itemset generation. One of the approaches is association rule mining with variable support threshold. In this approach, each itemset may have a different support threshold. The support threshold for each itemset is dynamically lowered to allow some rare items to be included in the rule generation. Some of the research using this approach includes Multiple Supports Apriori (MSApriori) (Liu et al., 1999a), Relative Support Apriori (RSAA) (Wang et al., 2003), Weighted Association Rules (WARM) (Tao et al., 2003), Adaptive Apriori (Wang et al., 2003), LPMiner (Seno & Karypis, 2001), and NB model (Hashler, 2006). These approaches try to vary the support constraint in some fashion to allow some rare items to be included in frequent itemset generation. These approaches are exhaustive in their generation of rules, and so spend time looking for rules with high support and high confidence. If the varied minimum support value is set close to zero, they will take a similar amount of time to that taken by Apriori to generate low-support rules in amongst the high-support rules. These methods generate all rules that have high confidence and high support. To include truly rare items, the minsup threshold must be set very low, which consequently generates an enormous set of rules consisting of both frequent and infrequent items.

A fixed minimum support threshold is not effective for datasets with a skewed distribution because they tend to generate many trivial patterns or miss potential low-support patterns. Hence another approach uses association rule mining without support threshold, but it usually introduces another constraint to solve the rare item problem. We discussed some of the approaches that use a variable support threshold to include some rare items in rule generation. But to ensure each rare item is considered, the minimum support threshold must still be pushed low, resulting in a combinatorial explosion in the number of rules generated. To overcome this problem, some researchers have proposed to remove the support-based threshold entirely. Instead they use another constraint such as similarity or confidence-based pruning. Techniques in this area includes Min-Hashing and its variations (Cohen et al., 2001), Confidence-Based Pruning (Wang et al., 2001), and H-Confidence (Xiong et al., 2003). Similar to the techniques in the previous approach, these algorithms suffer from the same drawback of generating all the frequent rules as well as the rare rules. In both of these approaches we need post-pruning methods to filter out the frequent rules or the trivial rules produced.

Using a variable support threshold or no support threshold would generate frequent rules as well as rare rules. There are some approaches that try to generate only rare rules. For example, providing a list of those items that may or may not take part in a rule and then modifying the mining process to take advantage of that information. One of the restrictions that may be imposed is called consequent constraint-based rule mining. In this approach, an item constraint is used which requires mined rules to satisfy a given constraint. Techniques that use this approach include Dense-Miner (Bayardo et al., 2000), DS (Direction Setting) rules (Liu, Hsu & Ma, 1999b), EP (Emerging Pattern) (Li et al., 1999), and Fixed-Consequent ARM (Association Rule Mining) (Rahal et al., 2004). These algorithms are only useful when we have prior knowledge that a particular consequent is of interest. Since rare items occur infrequently by definition, they may go undetected by prior processes that seek to identify what itemsets *should* be participating in consequents. This makes it unsuitable for generating rare item rules efficiently because we want to generate rules without needing prior knowledge of which consequents ought to be interesting.

Another way to encourage low-support items to take part in candidate rule generation is by imposing structure constraints. Techniques in this approach usually use an extra boundary to only allow the generation of rare rules. Techniques in this approach includes Apriori-Inverse (Koh & Rountree, 2005), MIISR (Mining Interesting Imperfectly Sporadic Rules) (Koh et al., 2006), and Apriori-Rare (Szathmary et al, 2007). These approaches are reliant on the fixed upper-boundaries. Setting the correct boundaries is still an open research question in rare association rule mining.

Currently there are various techniques in the area of rare association rule mining. Nonetheless there is still room for expansion. The capability of current techniques is limited to particular types of rare rules. It is a difficult task to determine and generate all useful rare rules. This process is often bounded by the nature the dataset. Rare rules often consist of a combination of frequent items that separately have high support, but together have low support. Thus we can not rely on normal frequent mining techniques to detect rare rules. The low support of the itemsets also makes it difficult for us to tell apart rare rules from noise.

Discussion: Where is this Heading?

Mining rare association rule mining goes beyond techniques and approaches which generate the rules. Rare association rules require different pre-processing and post-pruning techniques as compared to frequent rule mining. Despite being in the same area, the properties of the rules are substantially different. Current pre-processing and post-pruning techniques which cater for frequent rule mining are designed to suit the characteristics of frequent rules. The development in this area of rare association rule mining has room for expansion in several different significant directions.

Rare Itemset Detection and Noise Detection. The first direction is to find a theoretically-sound way to find rare itemsets. While showing promise, current rare association rule mining (RARM) techniques use arbitrary thresholds for finding rare itemsets. While the current techniques are sound, many do not consider noise detection in the technique. One of the crucial factors in finding rare itemsets, is being able to differentiate valid itemsets from noise.

Rare Rule Generation. The second direction addresses the different types of rare rules that can be found. It has been commonly observed, especially in medical domains, that certain items might occur frequently on their own but rarely as a group (itemset). For instance, two common allergens combined can produce a rare allergic reaction. When such a situation arises, there are usually a few rare rules that one could have mined. Even recent developments only allow us to generate a subset of these rules. We acknowledge the fact that not all types of rare rules are interesting. However there still lacks a generic framework to produce all useful rare rules. One problem with rare rule mining is the possibility of generating too many rules many which are not useful. Real-world datasets contain noise. This part of the nature of rare rules means they are susceptible to being drowned out in the noise; or, maybe worse, that we incorrectly treat noise-rules as valid rules.

Post-pruning Metrics. The third direction focuses on developing post-pruning methods, i.e. interest measures, to examine rare rules. Existing interest measures are inaccurate when dealing with low support rules (i.e. rare rules). Given that there has not yet been a substantial amount of work carried out in this area of rare association rule mining, there is currently no method that can be used to rank or prune these rules. A complementary research line is devoted to mining a concise set of frequent association rules. Most interest measures, such as the Cosine, Jaccard, and Confidence measures, are biased towards high support rules. The current proposed techniques are designed for frequent association rule mining and are not suited for rare rule mining.

CONCLUSION

Rare rule mining is a fairly new area in association rule mining research and has gained some attention in the past few years. Rare association rule mining can be viewed as an extension in the area of association rule mining. However the properties of rare rules are inherently different to their counterpart, frequent rules, and warrants further research. Currently there is still no ideal solution that allows us to find all possible interesting rare association rules, and there is much room for expansion in this area.

FURTHER INFORMATION

Multiple Supports Apriori (MSApriori)

Liu et al. (1999a) deal with the rare item problem by using multiple minimum support thresholds. They note that some individual items can have such low support that they cannot contribute to rules generated by Apriori, even though they may participate in rules that have very high confidence. They overcome this problem with a technique whereby each item in the database can have its own minimum item support (MIS). By providing a different MIS for different items, a higher minimum support can be set for rules that involve frequent items and lower minimum support for rules that involve less frequent items. The minimum support of an itemset is the lowest MIS among those items in the itemset. For example, let MIS(i) denote the MIS value of item i. The minimum support of a rule R is the lowest MIS value of items in the rule. A rule, R: $AB \rightarrow C$ satisfies its minimum support if the rule has an actual support greater or equal to: min(MIS(A), MIS(B), MIS(C)). However consider four items in a dataset, A, B, C, and D with MIS(A) = 10%, MIS(B) = 20%, MIS(C) = 5%, and MIS(D) = 4%. If we find that {A,B} has 9% support at the second iteration, then it does not satisfy min(MIS(A), MIS(B)) and is discarded.

Then potentially interesting itemsets {A,B,C} and {A,B,D} will not be generated in the next iteration. By sorting the items in ascending order of their MIS values, the minimum support of the itemset never decreases as the length of an itemset grows, making the support a more general support constraint. In general, it means that a frequent itemset is only extended with an item having a higher (or equal) MIS value. The MIS for each data item i is generated by first specifying LS (the lowest allowable minimum support), and a value β, $0 \leq \beta \leq 1.0$. MIS(i) is then set according to the following formula:

MIS(i) = max(β.sup(i), LS)

The advantage of the MSApriori algorithm is that it has the capability of finding some rare-itemset rules. However, the actual criterion of discovery is determined by the user's value of β rather than the frequency of each data item.

Relative Support Apriori (RSAA)

Determining the optimal value for β could be tedious especially in a database with many items where manual assignment is not feasible. Thus Yun, Ha, Hwang and Ryu (2003) proposed the RSAA algorithm to generate rules in which significant rare itemsets take part, without any set number specified by the user. This technique uses relative support: for any dataset, and with the support of item i represented as sup(i), relative support (RSup) is defined as:

$$RSup(i_1, i_2, \ldots, i_k) = \frac{\sup(i_1, i_2, \ldots, i_k)}{\min(\sup(i_1), \sup(i_2), \ldots, \sup(i_k))}$$

Thus this algorithm increases the support threshold for items that have low frequency and decreases the support threshold for items that have high frequency. Using a non-uniform minimum support threshold leads to the problem of choosing a suitable minimum support threshold for a particular itemset. Each item within the itemset may have a different minimum support threshold. MSApriori and RSAA sort the items within the itemset in non-decreasing order of support. Here the support of a particular itemset never increases and the minimum support threshold never decreases as the itemset grows.

Adaptive Apriori

Wang, He and Han (2003) proposed Adaptive Apriori which has a variable minimum support threshold. Adaptive Apriori introduces the notion of support constraints (SC) as a way to specify general constraints on minimum support. In particular, they associate a support constraint with each of the itemsets. They consider support constraints of the form $SC_i(B_1, \ldots, B_s) \geq \theta_i$, where $s \geq 0$. Each B_j, called a bin, is a set of items that need not be distinguished by the specification of minimum support. θ_i is a minimum support in the range of $[0 \ldots 1]$, or a function that produces minimum support. If more than one constraint is applicable to an itemset, the constraint specifying the lowest minimum support is chosen. For example, given $SC_1(B_1, B_3) \geq 0.2$, $SC_2(B_3) \geq 0.4$, $SC_3(B_2) \geq 0.5$, and $SC_0() \geq 0.9$, if we have an itemset containing {B_1,B_2,B_3} the minimum support used is 0.2. However, if the itemset only contains { B_2,B_3} then the minimum support is 0.4. The key idea of this approach is to push the support constraint following the dependency chain of itemsets in the itemset generation. For example, we want to generate itemset {$B_0B_1B_2$}, which uses SC_3, which is 0.5. { $B_0B_1B_2$} is generated by using {B_0B_1} with SC_0 and {B_1B_2} with SC_3. This requires the minsup, which is 0.5 from { $B_0B_1B_2$}, to be pushed down to { B_0B_1}, and then pushed down to {B_0} and {B_1}. The pushed minimum support is 0.5, which is lower than the specified minsup for {B_0B_1}, {B_0}, or {B_1}, which is 0.9. The pushed minimum support of each itemset is forced to be equal to the support value corresponding to the longest itemset.

Weighted Association Rules (WARM)

We can determine the minimum support threshold of each itemset by using a weighted support measurement. Each item or itemset is assigned a weight based on its significance. Itemsets that are considered interesting are assigned a larger weight. Weighted association rule mining (WARM) (Tao, Murtagh and Farid, 2003) is based on a weighted support measurement with a weighted downward closure property. They propose two types of weights: item weight and itemset weight. Item weight w(i) is assigned to an item representing its significance, whereas itemset weight w(X) is the mean of the item weight.

$$w(X) = \frac{\sum_{k=1}^{X} w(i_k)}{|X|}$$

The goal of using weighted support is to make use of the weight in the mining process and prioritise the selection of targeted itemsets according to their significance in the dataset, rather than by their frequency alone. The weighted support of an itemset can be defined as the product of the total weight of the itemset (sum of the weights of the items) and the weight of the fraction of transactions that the itemset occurs in. In WARM, itemsets are no longer simply counted as they appear in a transaction. The change in the counting mechanism makes it necessary to adapt the traditional support to a weighted support. An itemset is significant if its support weight is above a pre-defined minimum weighted support threshold. Tao et al. (2003) also proposed a weighted downward closure property as the adjusted support values violate the original downward closure property in Apriori. The rules generated in this approach rely heavily on the weights used. Thus to ensure the results generated are useful, we have to determine a way to assign the item weights effectively.

LPMiner

Previous approaches vary the minimum support constraint by using a particular weighting method using either the frequency or significance of the itemsets. LPMiner (Seno & Karypis, 2001), also varies the minimum support threshold. It uses a pattern-length-decreasing support constraint that tries to reduce support so that we favour smaller itemsets which have higher counts over larger itemsets with lower counts. They propose a support threshold that decreases as a function of itemset length. A frequent itemset that satisfies the length-decreasing support constraint can be frequent even if the subsets of the itemset are infrequent. Hence the downward closure property does not hold. To overcome this problem, they developed a property called smallest valid extension (SVE). In this property, for an infrequent itemset to be considered it must be over a minimum pattern length before it can potentially become frequent. Exploiting this pruning property, they propose LPMiner based on the FP-tree algorithm (Han, Pei & Yin, 2000). This approach favours smaller itemsets; however, longer itemsets could be interesting, even if they are less frequent. In order to find longer itemsets, one would have to lower the support threshold, which would lead to an explosion of the number of short itemsets found.

Min-Hashing and its Variations

Variations on the Min-Hashing technique were introduced by Cohen et al. (2001) to mine significant rules without any constraint on support. Transactions are stored as a 0/1 matrix with as many columns as there are unique items. Rather than searching for pairs of columns that have high support or high confidence, the technique searches for columns that have high similarity, where similarity is defined as the fraction of rows that have a 1 in both columns when they have a 1 in either column. Although this is easy to do by brute force when the matrix fits into main memory, it is time-consuming when the matrix is disc-resident. Their solution is to compute a hashing signature for each column of the matrix in such a way that the probability that two columns have the same signature is proportional to their similarity. After signatures are calculated, candidate pairs are generated, and then finally checked against the original matrix to ensure that they do indeed have strong similarity. It should be noted that the hashing solution will produce many rules that have high support and high confidence, since only a minimum acceptable similarity is specified. It is not clear whether the method will extend to rules that contain more than two or three items, since $\binom{m}{k}$ checks for similarity must be done, where m is the number of unique items in the set of transactions, and k is the number of items that might appear in any one rule. Removing the support requirement entirely is an elegant solution, but it comes at a high cost of space: for n transactions containing an average of k items over m possible items, the matrix will require n × m bits, whereas the primary data structure for Apriori-based algorithms will require n × $\log_2$m× k bits. Note that itemsets with low similarity may still produce interesting rules.

Confidence-Based Pruning

Another constraint known as confidence-based pruning was proposed by Wang et al. (2001). It finds all rules that satisfy a minimum confidence, but not necessarily a minimum support threshold. They call the rules that satisfy this requirement "confident rules." The problem with mining confident rules is that, unlike support, confidence does not have a downward closure property. Wang et al. (2001) proposed a confidence-based pruning that uses the confidence requirement in rule generation. Given three rules R_1: A → B, R_2: AC → B, and R_3: AD → B, R_2 and R_3 are two specialisations of R_1, having additional items C and D. C and

D are exclusive and exhaustive in the sense that exactly one will hold up in each itemset but they will not appear together in the same itemset. The confidence of R_2 and R_3 must be greater than or equal to R_1. We can prune R_1 if neither R_2 nor R_3 is confident. This method has a universal existential upward closure. This states that if a rule of size k occurs above the given minimum confidence threshold, then for every other attribute not in the rule (C and D in the given example), some specialisation of size k+1 using the attribute must also be confident. They exploit this property to generate rules without having to use any support constraints.

H-Confidence

Xiong et al. (2003) try to improve on the previous confidence-based pruning method. They propose the h-confidence measure to mine hyperclique patterns. A hyperclique pattern is a type of association containing objects that are highly affiliated with each other, that is, every pair of objects in a hyperclique pattern is guaranteed to have a cosine similarity (uncentered correlation coefficient) above a certain level. They show that h-confidence has a cross-support property which is useful for eliminating candidate patterns having items with widely different supports. The h-confidence of an itemset $P = \{i_1, i_2, ..., i_m\}$ in a database D denoted by hconf(P, D), is a measure that reflects the overall affinity among items within the itemset.

$$\text{hconf}(P) = \begin{array}{l} \min(\ \text{conf}(\{i_1 \rightarrow i_2, ..., i_m\}), \\ \text{conf}(\{i_2 \rightarrow i_1, i_3, ..., i_m\}), \\ ... \\ \text{conf}(\{i_m \rightarrow i_1, i_2, ..., i_{m-1}\})) \end{array}$$

A hyperclique pattern P is a strong-affinity association pattern because the presence of any item x ∈ P in a transaction strongly implies the presence of P\{x} in the same transaction. To that end, the h-confidence measure is designed specifically for capturing such strong affinity relationships. Nevertheless, even when including hyperclique patterns in rule generation, we can also miss interesting patterns. For example, an itemset {A,B,C} that produces low confidence rules A → BC, B → AC, and C → AB, but a high confidence rule AB → C, would never be identified.

Dense-Miner

Bayardo et al. (2000) noted that the candidate frequent itemsets generated are too numerous in dense data, even when using an item constraint. A dense dataset has many frequently occurring items, strong correlations between several items, and many items in each record. Thus Bayardo et al. (2000) use a consequent constraint-based rule mining approach called Dense-Miner. They require mined rules to have a given consequent C specified by the user. They also introduce an additional metric called improvement. The key idea is to extract rules with confidence above a minimum improvement value greater than any of the simplifications of a rule. A simplification of a rule is formed by removing one or more items from its antecedent. Any positive minimum improvement value would prevent unnecessarily complex rules from being generated. A rule is considered overly complex if simplifying its antecedent results in a rule with higher confidence. The improvement of a rule A → C is defined as the minimum difference between its confidence and the confidence of any proper sub-rule with the same consequent.

$$\text{improvement}(A \rightarrow C) = \text{conf}(A \rightarrow C)$$
$$- \max\{\text{conf}(A' \rightarrow C) | A' \subset A\}$$

If the improvement of a rule is greater than 0, then removing any non-empty combination of items from the antecedent will lower the confidence by at least the improvement. Thus every item and every combination of items present in

the antecedent of a rule with a large improvement is an important contributor to its predictive ability. In contrast, it is considered undesirable for the improvement of a rule to be negative, as it suggests that the extra elements in the antecedent detract from the rule's predictive power.

Emerging Pattern (EP)

The Emerging Pattern (EP) method was proposed by Li et al. (1999). Given a known consequent C, a dataset partitioning approach is used to find top rules, zero-confidence rules, and μ-level confidence rules. The dataset, D, is divided into sub-datasets D_1 and D_2; where D_1 consists of the transactions containing the known consequent and D_2 consists of transactions which do not contain the consequent. All items in C are then removed from the transactions in D_1 and D_2. Using the transformed dataset, EP then finds all itemsets X which occur in D_1 but not in D_2. For each X, the rule $X \rightarrow T$ is a top rule in D with confidence of 100%. On the other hand, for all itemsets, Z, that only occur in D_2, all transactions in D which contain Z must not contain C. Therefore $Z \rightarrow C$ has a negative association and is a zero-confidence rule. For μ-level confidence rules $Y \rightarrow C$ the confidences are greater than or equal to $1 - \mu$. The confidences of μ-level rules must satisfy:

$$\frac{\sup(Y)|D_1|}{\sup(Y)|D_1| + \sup(Y)|D_2|} \geq 1 - \mu$$

Note that $\sup(Y)|D_1|$ is the number of times itemset YC appears together in dataset D and $\sup(Y)|D_1| + \sup(Y)|D_2|$ is the number of times itemset Y appears in dataset D. This approach is considered efficient as it only needs one pass through the dataset to partition and transform it. Of course, in this method one must supply C.

Fixed-Consequent Association Rule Mining

Rahal et al. (2004) proposed a slightly different approach. They proposed a method that generates the highest support rules that matched the user's specified minimum without having to specify any support threshold. Fixed-consequent association rule mining generates confident minimal rules using two kinds of trees (Rahal et al., 2004). Given two rules, R_1 and R_2, with confidence values higher than the confidence threshold, where R_1 is A → C and R_2 is AB → C, R_1 is preferred, because the antecedent of R_2 is a superset of the antecedent of R_1. The support of R_1 is necessarily greater than or equal to R_2. R_1 is referred to as a minimal rule ("simplest" in the notation of Bayardo et al. (2000)) and R_2 is referred to as a non-minimal rule (more complex). The algorithm was devised to generate the highest support rules that match the user specified minimum confidence threshold without having the user specify any support threshold.

Apriori-Inverse

Apriori–Inverse (Koh et al., 2005) is a variation of the Apriori algorithm that uses the notion of maximum support instead of minimum support to generate candidate itemsets. Candidate itemsets of interest to us fall below a maximum support value but above a minimum absolute support value. Given a user-specified maximum support threshold, maxsup, and a generated minabssup value, we are interested in a rule X if sup(X) < maxsup and sup(X) > minabssup. Rules above maximum support are considered frequent rules, which are of no interest to us, whereas we consider rules appearing below the minimum absolute support value as coincidence. Rare rules are generated in the same manner as in Apriori rule generation. Apriori-Inverse produces rare rules which do not consider any itemsets above maxsup.

Apriori-Rare

Szathmary et al (2007) presented an approach for rare itemset mining from a dataset that splits the problem into two tasks. The first task, the traversal of the frequent zone in the space, is addressed by two different algorithms, a naive one, Apriori-Rare, which relies on Apriori and hence enumerates all frequent itemsets; and MRG-Exp, which limits the considerations to frequent generators only. They consider computation of the rare itemsets that approaches them starting from the lattice bottom, from the frequent zone. They defined a positive and the negative border of the frequent itemsets, and a negative lower border and the positive lower border of the rare itemsets, respectively. An itemset is a maximal frequent itemset (MFI) if it is frequent but all its proper supersets are rare. An itemset is a minimal rare itemset (mRI) if it is rare but all its proper subsets are frequent.

REFERENCES

Agrawal, R., Imielinski, T., & Swami, A. (1993). Mining association rules between sets of items in large databases. In P. Buneman & S. Jajodia (Eds.), *Proceedings of the 1993 ACM SIGMOD international conference on management of data* (pp. 207–216). New York, NY: ACM Press.

Agrawal, R., & Srikant, R. (1994). Fast algorithms for mining association rules. In *Proceedings of the 20th International Conference on Very Large Databases* (pp. 487–499). San Francisco, CA: Morgan Kaufmann Publishers Inc.

Bayardo, R. J. (1998). Efficiently mining long patterns from databases. In *Proceedings of the 1998 ACM SIGMOD International Conference on Management of Data, SIGMOD '98* (pp. 85–93). New York, NY: ACM Press.

Bayardo, R. J., & Agrawal, R. (1999). Mining the most interesting rules. In *Proceedings of the Fifth ACM SIGKDD International Conference on Knowledge Discovery and Data Mining, KDD '99.*, (pp. 145–154). New York, NY: ACM Press.

Bayardo, R. J., Agrawal, R., & Gunopulos, D. (2000). Constraint-based rule mining in large, dense databases. *Data Mining and Knowledge Discovery, 4*(2/3), 217–240. doi:10.1023/A:1009895914772

Cohen, E., Datar, M., Fujiwara, S., Gionis, A., Indyk, P., & Motwani, R. (2001). Finding interesting association rules without support pruning. *IEEE Transactions on Knowledge and Data Engineering, 13*, 64–78. doi:10.1109/69.908981

Hahsler, M. (2006, September). A model-based frequency constraint for mining associations from transaction data. *Data Mining and Knowledge Discovery, 13*(2), 137–166. doi:10.1007/s10618-005-0026-2

Koh, Y. S., & Rountree, N. (2005). Finding sporadic rules using Apriori-Inverse. In *Advances in Knowledge Discovery and Data Mining, 9th Pacific-Asia Conference on Knowledge Discovery and Data Mining 2005* (pp. 97–106). Berlin / Heidelberg: Springer.

Koh, Y. S., Rountree, N., & O'Keefe, R. A. (2008, January). Mining interesting imperfectly sporadic rules. *Knowledge and Information Systems, 14*(2), 179–196. doi:10.1007/s10115-007-0074-6

Li, J., Zhang, X., Dong, G., Ramamohanarao, K., & Sun, Q. (1999). Efficient mining of high confidence association rules without support threshold. In *Proceedings of the 3rd European Conference on Principle and Practice of Knowledge Discovery in Databases, PKDD '99* (pp. 406 – 411).

Liu, B., Hsu, W., & Ma, Y. (1999a). Mining association rules with multiple minimum supports. In *Proceedings of the 5th ACM SIGKDD International Conference on Knowledge Discovery and Data Mining* (pp. 337–341). New York, NY: ACM Press.

Liu, B., Hsu, W., & Ma, Y. (1999b). Pruning and summarizing the discovered associations. In *Proceedings of the 5th ACM SIGKDD International Conference on Knowledge Discovery and Data Mining* (pp. 125–134). New York, NY: ACM Press.

Rahal, I., Ren, D., Wu, W., & Perrizo, W. (2004). Mining confident minimal rules with fixed-consequents. In *Proceedings of the 16th IEEE International Conference on Tools with Artificial Intelligence, ICTAI'04* (pp. 6–13). Washington, DC: IEEE Computer Society.

Seno, M., & Karypis, G. (2001). LPMINER: An algorithm for finding frequent itemsets using length-decreasing support constraint. In N. Cercone, T. Y. Lin, & X. Wu (Eds), In *Proceedings of the 2001 IEEE International Conference on Data Mining ICDM* (pp. 505–512). Washington, DC: IEEE Computer Society.

Szathmary, L., Napoli, A., & Valtchev, P. (2007). Towards Rare Itemset Mining. In *Proceedings of the 19th IEEE international Conference on Tools with Artificial intelligence - Vol.1 (ICTAI 2007) - Volume 01 (October 29 - 31, 2007). ICTAI. (pp. 305-312)*. Washington, DC: IEEE Computer Society

Tao, F., Murtagh, F., & Farid, M. (2003). Weighted association rule mining using weighted support and significance framework. In *Proceedings of the Ninth ACM SIGKDD International Conference on Knowledge Discovery and Data Mining, KDD '03* (pp. 661–666). New York, NY: ACM Press.

Wang, K., He, Y., & Cheung, D. W. (2001). Mining confident rules without support requirement. In *Proceedings of the Tenth International Conference on Information and Knowledge Management*, (pp. 89–96). New York, NY: ACM Press.

Wang, K., He, Y., & Han, J. (2003). Pushing support constraints into association rules mining. *IEEE Transactions on Knowledge and Data Engineering*, *15*(3), 642–658. doi:10.1109/TKDE.2003.1198396

Weiss, G. M. (2004). Mining with rarity: a unifying framework. *SIGKDD Exploration Newsletter*, *6*(1), 7–19. doi:10.1145/1007730.1007734

Xiong, H., Tan, P.-N., & Kumar, V. (2003). Mining strong affinity association patterns in data sets with skewed support distribution. In *Proceedings of the Third IEEE International Conference on Data Mining* (pp. 387 – 394). Washington, DC: IEEE Computer Society.

Yun, H., Ha, D., Hwang, B., & Ryu, K. H. (2003). Mining association rules on significant rare data using relative support. *Journal of Systems and Software*, *67*(3), 181–191. doi:10.1016/S0164-1212(02)00128-0

Chapter 2
Association Rule and Quantitative Association Rule Mining among Infrequent Items

Ling Zhou
University of Illinois at Chicago, USA

Stephen Yau
University of Illinois at Chicago, USA

ABSTRACT

Association rule mining among frequent items has been extensively studied in data mining research. However, in recent years, there is an increasing demand for mining infrequent items (such as rare but expensive items). Since exploring interesting relationships among infrequent items has not been discussed much in the literature, in this chapter, the authors propose two simple, practical and effective schemes to mine association rules among rare items. Their algorithms can also be applied to frequent items with bounded length. Experiments are performed on the well-known IBM synthetic database. The authors' schemes compare favorably to Apriori and FP-growth under the situation being evaluated. In addition, they explore quantitative association rule mining in transactional databases among infrequent items by associating quantities of items: some interesting examples are drawn to illustrate the significance of such mining.

INTRODUCTION

The main goal of association rule mining is to discover relationships among set of items in a transactional database. Association rules have been extensively studied in the literature since Agrawal et al. (1993; 1994) first introduced them. A typical application of association rule mining is the market basket analysis. An association rule is an implication of the form $A \Rightarrow B$, where A and B are frequent itemsets in a transaction database and $A \cap B = \varnothing$. The rule $A \Rightarrow B$ can be interpreted as "if itemset A occurs in a transaction, then itemset B will also likely occur in the same transaction". By such information, market personnel can place itemset A and B within close proximity which may encourage the sale of them together and develop discount strategies based on such association/correlation found in the data. Therefore, association rule mining has received a lot of attention. For

DOI: 10.4018/978-1-60566-754-6.ch002

example, Agrawal and Imielinski (1995; 1996) discussed mining sequential patterns, as well as mining quantitative association rules in large relational tables in [4], while Bayardo considered efficiently mining long patterns from databases and Dong and Li (1999) studied efficient mining of emerging patterns. On the other hand, Kamber et al. (1997) proposed to use data cubes to mine multi-dimensional association rules and Lent et al. (1997) used a clustering method. While most of the researchers focused on association analysis of rules (Agrawal, Imielinski & Swami, 1993; Chen, Han & Yu, 1996; Han, Pei & Yin, 2000; Mannila, Toivonen & Verkamo, 1994; Savasera, Omiecinski & Navathe, 1995; Srikant & Agrawal, 1995), Brin et al.(1997) analyzed the correlations of association rules. With the development of data mining technique, quite a few researchers worked on the alternative patterns, such as Padmanabhan et al.(2000) who discussed unexpected patterns, Liu et al. (1999) and Hwang et al.(1999) studied exception pattern in, and Savasere et al. (1998), Wu et al. (2004) and Yuan et al. (2002) discussed negative association respectively.

The traditional algorithms discover valid rules by exploiting support and confidence requirements, and use a minimum support threshold to prune their combinatorial search space. Two major problems may arise when applying such strategies. (1) If the minimum support is set too low, this may increase the workload significantly such as the generation of candidate sets, construction of tree nodes, comparisons and tests. It will also increase the number of rules considerably, which makes the traditional algorithms suffer from extremely poor performance problems. In addition, many patterns involving items with substantially different support levels are produced, which usually have a weak correlation and are not really interesting to users. (2) If the minimum support threshold is set too high, many interesting patterns involving items with low supports are missed. Such patterns are useful for identifying associations among rare but expensive items such as diamond necklace,

ring and earring, as well as the identification of identical or similar web documents, etc.

Recently, there is some growing interests in developing techniques for mining association patterns without support constraints. The algorithms proposed by Cohen et al. (2000) are limited to deal with identifying pairs of similar columns. The approaches presented by Wang et al. (2001) and Xiong et al. (2003) employ a confidence-based pruning strategy instead of support-based pruning adopted in traditional association rule mining. The mining of support-free association discovers rules in the patterns with high support, cross-support where items have widely differing support levels, and low supports. In fact, patterns with a high minimum support level are often obvious and well known; patterns with cross-support level have extremely poor correlation, and patterns with low support often provide valuable new insights. J. Ding (2005) discussed association rule mining among rare items. He designed a new disk-based data structure, called Transactional Co-Occurrence Matrix(TCOM) to store the data. This structure combines the advantages of transactional oriented (horizontal) layout and item oriented (vertical) layout of the database. So any itemsets could be randomly accessed and counted without a full scan of the original database or the TCOM. He also constructed a compressed matrix structure, called Reduced Transactional Co-Occurrence Matrix (RTCOM) which resides in memory. This matrix only contains the items which are of interest in application. Then the infrequent patterns and the valid association rules among infrequent items can be mined out. Although this is a significant theoretical advancement in the subject, it is quite costly to implement this algorithm. Due to the specialties of patterns with low support and the lack of practical and efficient methods for mining rules among rare items, we propose *two schemes* (Matrix-based Scheme and Hash-based Scheme) to explore interesting associations among infrequent items with memory-resident data structure. In our both schemes, only two passes over database are needed, pruning function, *interest(X, Y)*, is employed to improve mining efficiency, and new interestingness measures, *CPIR(Y|X)* and *correlation(X, Y),* are exploited to discover rules of strong interest. In addition, these two schemes can also be applied to discover association rules among frequent patterns with bounded length efficiently, which could be very useful for some special circumstances.

The main contributions of this chapter are as follows: (1) we devise two new algorithms to generate association rules and quantitative association rules among rare items. There are very few papers to discussing and the discovery of association rules and quantitative association rules among rare items. (2) New interesting measures are used to capture rules of strong interest. (3) Our two schemes can also be applied to discover rules among frequent items with bounded length efficiently comparing with the classical algorithms, Apriori and FP-growth. All of the traditional association rule mining algorithms explore rules of all lengths in database. Sometimes users could be quite interested in the relationship of certain items for some special cases, in which our methods could be very helpful.

In the following, we will introduce our two methods for mining association rules among infrequent items. To mine association rules among frequent items, we only need to make a little modification for the requirement of support threshold measure.

The rest of this paper is organized as follows. In section 2 we recall the basic concepts of association rule mining. In section 3 we present the pruning strategy. In section 4 we discuss the correlation analysis. In section 5 we present our two schemes MBS and HBS. In section 6 our experimental results are illustrated. In section 7 we discuss quantitative association rule mining among infrequent items in transactional database. And in section 8 conclusions and future work are described.

BASIC CONCEPTS AND TERMINOLOGY

Let I = {i1, i2…iN} be a set of N distinct literals called items. Let D be a set of database transactions where each transaction T is a set of items such that T⊆I. Each transaction is associated with a unique identifier, called TID. Let A, B be a set of items, an association rule is an implication of the form A⇒B, where A⊂I, B⊂I, and A∩B=∅. A is called antecedent of the rule, and B is called the consequent of the rule. The rule A⇒B holds in the transaction set D with support s, where s is the percentage of transactions in D that contain both A and B. In other words, the support of the rule is the probability P (A∪B). The rule A⇒B also has another measure called confidence c where c is the percentage of transactions in D containing A that also contain B. In other words, the confidence of the rule is the conditional probability P (B|A). The problem of discovering all association rules from transactional database D consists of generating the rules that have a support and confidence greater than predefined thresholds. Such rules are called valid (or strong) rules, and the framework is known as the support-confidence framework.

PRUNING STRATEGIES

Since there could exist a huge number of infrequent itemsets in a database, and only some of them are useful for mining association rules of interest, pruning is critical to efficient search for interesting itemsets. In this section, we design a pruning strategy using the idea discussed by Wu et al. in [21].

According to probability theory, X and Y are independent if P(X∪Y) =P(X) P(Y). So rule X ⇒Y is not interesting if supp(X ∪Y) ≈ supp(X) * supp(Y), which means that a rule is not interesting if its antecedent and consequent are approximately independent. Wu et al. introduces the function interest(X, Y)=|supp(X ∪Y) – supp(X)supp(Y)|

in [21]. If interest(X, Y) ≥ min_interest, where min_interest is predefined threshold, then itemset X ∪Y is referred to as a potentially interesting itemset.

In the following, we give the definition for infrequent itemset of potential interest, in this chapter; we only consider infrequent itemsets, which contain infrequent items.

Definition 1: *I is an infrequent itemset of potential interest if:* ∃X, Y: X∩Y=∅, X∪Y=I, *for* ∀ *ik∈X, jk∈Y, supp(ik) ≤ min_support, supp(jk) ≤ min_support, interest(X, Y) ≥min_interest.*

In the above definition, supp(*) constraints guarantee that all items are infrequent and interest(*) ensures the correlation strength between itemsets.

CORRELATION ANALYSIS

Most association rule mining algorithms employ a support-confidence framework for the discovery of interesting rules. Although these two parameters (minimum support and confidence thresholds) prune many associations discovered, many rules that are not interesting to the user may still be produced. For example, we want to study the purchase of Soy milk and Cow milk in a supermarket (Table 1), let Soy milk refer to the transactions containing Soy milk, and ¬ Soy milk refer to those not containing Soy milk. Let Cow milk refer to the transactions containing Cow milk and ¬ Cow milk refer to those not containing Cow milk. Use "support-confidence" framework, say, a minimum support of 30% and a minimum confidence of 60%. Rule Soy milk ⇒ Cow milk [supp = 40%,

conf = 67%] is discovered as a valid rule. However, "Soy milk ⇒ Cow milk" is misleading since the probability of purchasing Cow milk is 75%, which is even larger than 67%. In fact, Soy milk and Cow milk are negatively correlated since the purchase of one of these items actually decreases the likelihood of purchasing the other.

The above example indicates the weakness of support-confidence framework. Association rules mined using a support-confidence framework are useful for many applications. However, the support-confidence framework can be misleading if the occurrence of antecedent does not imply the occurrence of consequent. In this chapter we consider an alternative framework for finding interesting relationships between data itemsets based on correlation.

According to probability theory, the occurrence of itemset X is independent of the occurrence of itemset Y if P(X∪Y) = P(X) P(Y), otherwise itemsets X and Y are dependent and correlated as events. The correlation (dependence) between the occurrence of X and Y can be measured by *correlation(X, Y)*, which we shall introduce below.

$$correlation(X,Y) = \frac{P(X \cup Y)}{P(X)P(Y)} = \frac{P(Y \mid X)}{P(Y)} =$$

$$\frac{P(X \cup Y)}{P(X)P(Y)} \frac{P(Y \mid X)}{P(Y)} \frac{P(X \mid Y)}{P(X)} = \frac{P(Y \mid X)}{P(Y)} =$$

$$\frac{P(X \mid Y)}{P(X)}$$

Consider the relationship between P(Y|X) and P(Y) [or P(X|Y) and P(X)], *correlation(X, Y)* has

Table 1. Purchase of Soy milk and Cow milk in a supermarket

	Soy milk	¬Soy milk	Σ_{row}
Cow milk	400	350	750
¬ Cow milk	200	50	250
Σ_{col}	600	400	1000

the following three possible cases:

(1) If *correlation(X, Y)* = 1 or P(Y|X) = P(Y) [or P(X|Y) = P(X)], then Y and X are independent and there is no correlation between them.

(2) If *correlation(X, Y)* >1 or P(Y|X) >P(Y) [or P(X|Y) >P(X)], then X and Y are positively correlated, meaning the occurrence of one implies the occurrence of the other. In this case, one has $0 < P(Y|X)-P(Y) \le 1-p(Y)$, $0 < [P(Y|X)-P(Y)]/(1-P(Y)) \le 1$.

The bigger the ratio $(P(Y|X)-P(Y))/(1-P(Y))$, the stronger the Y is positively dependent on X.

(3) If *correlation(X, Y)* < 1 or P(Y|X) < P(Y) [or P(X|Y) <P(X)], then X and Y are negatively correlated, meaning the occurrence of one discourages the occurrence of the other. In this case, one has $-P(Y) < P(Y|X)-P(Y) < 0$, $-1 < [P(Y|X)-P(Y)]/P(Y) < 0$.

The smaller the ratio $(P(Y|X)-P(Y))/P(Y)$, the stronger the Y is negatively dependent on X.

Wu et al. defined *conditional-probability increment ratio* function for a pair of itemsets *X* and *Y*, denoted *CPIR* in Wu et al. (2004).

$CPIR(Y|X) = 0$, if P(Y|X) = P(Y)

= [P(Y|X) – P(Y)]/[1 – p(Y)], if P(Y|X)>P(Y) and P(Y) $\neq$ 1,

= [P(Y|X) – P(Y)]/P(Y), if P(Y|X)< p(Y), P(Y) $\neq$ 0

We employ *CPIR(Y|X)* as the confidence measure of an association rule between itemsets *X* and *Y*, i.e. we define *confidence(X⇒Y)* to be *CPIR(Y|X)*:

- If *P(Y|X) = P(Y)*, Y and X are independent and has no correlation. The confidence of the association rule X ⇒ Y would be *confidence(X⇒Y) = CPIR(Y|X) = 0*

- If *P(Y|X) > P(Y)*, Y is positively correlated on X. When *P(Y|X) = 1*, which reaches the strongest positive correlation, the confidence of the association rule X⇒Y would be confidence(X⇒Y) =CPIR(Y|X) = 1

- If *P(Y|X) < P(Y)*, Y is negatively correlated on X. When *P(Y|X) = 0*, which reaches the strongest negative correlation, and the confidence of the association rule X⇒Y would be *confidence(X ⇒ Y) =CPIR(Y|X) = -1*

In this chapter, we focus on only positive rules among infrequent items. So the confidence measure of rule $X \Rightarrow Y$ is defined as

$confidence(X \Rightarrow Y) = CPIR(Y|X) = [P(Y|X) - p(Y)]/[1 - P(Y)]$

$= [P(X \cup Y) - P(X)P(Y)]/[P(X)(1 - P(Y))]$

$= [supp(X \cup Y) - supp(X)supp(Y)]/[supp(X)(1 - supp(Y))]$

DISCOVERING ASSOCIATION RULES AMONG INFREQUENT ITEMS

Association Rules of Interest among Infrequent Items

Definition 2: *Let I be the set of items in a database D, J= A∪B be an itemset, A∩B=∅, supp(A)≠ 0, supp(B)≠0, and threshold min_support, min_confidence and min_interest > 0 be given by the user. Then, if supp(A) ≤ min_support, supp(B) ≤ min_support, interest(A,B) ≥min_interest, correlation(A,B)>1 and CPIR(B|A) ≥ min_confidence, then A⇒B is a rule of interest.*

In Definition 2, supp(*)≤min_support guarantees that an association rule describes the relationship between infrequent items; the interest(*) ≥ min_interest requirement makes sure that the association rule is of interest; correlation(*)>1 restricts rules that are positive and CPIR(*) $\geq$ min_confidence ensures the strength of correlation.

An example: A, B are itemsets in database D, supp(A) =0.4, supp(B)= 0.3, supp(A $\cup$ B)=0.3, min_support=0.5, min_confidence=0.5 and min_interest=0.05.

supp(A)=0.4 < 0.5, supp(B)=0.3<0.5

Interest(A,B)= |supp(A $\cup$ B) – supp(A) supp(B)|=|0.3 –0.4*0.3|=0.18>0.05

correlation(A,B)= supp(A $\cup$ B)/(supp(A) supp(B))=0.3/(0.4*0.3) >1

CPIR(B|A)=[supp(A $\cup$ B) – supp(A)supp(B)]/ [supp(A)(1 – supp(B))]

=(0.3 - 0.4 * 0.3)/[0.4 * (1 – 0.3)]= 0.64>0.5

Rule A$\Rightarrow$ B can be extracted as a rule of interest among infrequent items.

Association Rule Mining Process among Infrequent Items

Association rule mining among infrequent items consists of two phases*:*

Phase 1. Identify all infrequent itemsets of potential interest, i.e., I is an infrequent itemset of potential interest if: $\exists$A, B: A$\cap$B=$\varnothing$, A$\cup$B=I, for $\forall i_k \in$A, $j_{k\in}$B, supp(i_k)$\leq$ min_support,

supp(j_k)$\leq$ m in_support and interest(A,B) $\geq$min_interest.

Phase 2. Extract rules of interest from these itemsets, i.e., rule, A$\Rightarrow$B, is a rule of interest if supp(A) $\leq$min_support, supp(B)$\leq$min_support, interest(A,B)$\geq$min_interest, correlation(A,B)>1 and CPIR(B|A) $\geq$ min_confidence.

Matrix-Based Scheme (MBS)

In this approach, we construct matrices Infk to store information of infrequent k-itemsets and determine *support counts* (number of transactions containing this itemset) of all infrequent k-itemsets efficiently by employing index function, *I(x, y)*, introduced below. Then capture all itemsets of potential interest by exploiting pruning function, *interest(X, Y)*. Finally we extract association rules of strong interest using constraint functions, *correlation(X, Y)* and *CPIR(X|Y)*.(See Figure 1)

In the following, we will give a concrete example to illustrate the above algorithm design. In transaction database D (Table 2); there are 5 transactions and 6 items. Let min_support=50%.

Step 1: Scan database D, construct a matrix, Item, to store support counts of all items in D. Then identify infrequent items by comparing their supports with the predefined support threshold and map infrequent items into matrix Inf1. The first column of matrix Item is used to store all items in D, the second is the support count of all items and the third is the index (or position) of infrequent items in matrix Inf1, at the beginning, this column is initialized as –1. The detail is shown in Figure 2.

Step 2: Construct matrices Infk(k=2,3…) to store support counts of infrequent k-itemsets, where the k-itemsets are the k-combinations of infrequent items and stored in matrices Infk based on item-id ascending order. Support counts are initialized as 0. The detail is illustrated in Figure 3.

Step 3: Scan database D second time, for each transaction Ti, do the following: (1) Check index value of each item in matrix Item. If the item has an index value that is not –1, then map the index value into a matrix called Temp. (2) Count the total number of items stored in Temp. If the count is greater than 1, then sort all items in Temp based on item-id ascending order and find all combinations of these values, where the k-combinations are the infrequent k-itemsets. One

Figure 1. Algorithm design of MBS

> *Input D: database; minSupp: minimum support; minConf: minimum confidence; minInte: minimum interest*
> *Output AR: association rules*
> (0) scan the database D and find all infrequent 1-itemsets(Inf1)
> (1) **let** Item←{a matrix used to store information of all items in D}
> (2) **let** Item.index←the index value of infrequent item in Inf1, frequent items with a index value of −1;
> (3) **let** Infk←{matrixes used to store support counts of infrequent k-itemsets, where k>1};
> (4)scan database a second time
> (5) **for** each transaction Ti ∈D **do**
>   **for** each item i ∈transaction Ti **do**
>   **if** i.index ≠-1// identify infrequent items, **then** map i.index into Temp
>   **end**
>   **If** the number of items in Temp is greater than 1,**then** find all combinations of these values and increase support count of each combination
>   **end**
> (6) **for** each k-itemset I ∈ Infk **do**
>   **If** I.count≥1 **then**
>   **for** ∀itemsets X,Y, X∪Y=I and X∩Y=∅ **do**
>   **If** interest(X,Y)<minInte **then** Infk←Infk-{I};
>   **end**
>   **end**
> (7) **for** each infrequent k-itemset of interest {X∪Y} ∈Infk **do**
>   **If** Correlation(X,Y)>1 && CPIR(Y|X)≥minConf **then** AR←{X⇒Y}
>   **If** Correlation(X,Y)>1 && CPIR(X|Y)≥minConf **then** AR←{Y⇒Y}
>   **end**
> (8) **return** AR

example is given in Figure 4.

Step 4: Increase support counts of all infrequent k-itemsets found in step 3 by applying lemmas we shall introduce below.

Lemma 1. For a specific infrequent 2-itemset (a, b), if the indices of the two infrequent items a and b in matrix Inf1 are x and y respectively (x<y), then the index (or position) of the 2-itemset (a, b) in matrix Inf2 is

$$\mathbf{I(x, y)} = (2n\text{-}x\text{-}1) \ x/2 + y\text{-}x\text{-}1$$

Table 2. Transaction Database D

TID	ID of Items
T1	I2, I1, I0, I5
T2	I3, I1, I4
T3	I4, I3
T4	I2, I1
T5	I4, I0, I1

Where n is the total number of infrequent items in database D.

Lemma 2. For a specific infrequent 3-itemset (a, b, c), if the indices of the 3 infrequent items a, b and c in matrix Inf1 are x, y and z respectively (x<y<z), then the index of 3-itemset (a, b, c) in matrix Inf3 is

$$\mathbf{I(x, y, z)} = x \ (n\text{-}x\text{-}1) \ (n\text{-}x)/2 + (2n\text{-}2x\text{-}1) \ x(x\text{-}1)/4 + x(x\text{-}1) \ (2x\text{-}1)/12 + (y\text{-}x\text{-}1) \ (2n\text{-}x\text{-}y\text{-}2)/2 + z\text{-}y\text{-}1.$$

Where n is the total number of infrequent items in D.

Recall that the indices stored in matrix Temp are 0,1 and 3, all combinations of these index values are (0,1), (0,3), (1,3) and (0,1,3). So we have

-1-1=1;

Figure 2. Identification of infrequent items in database D

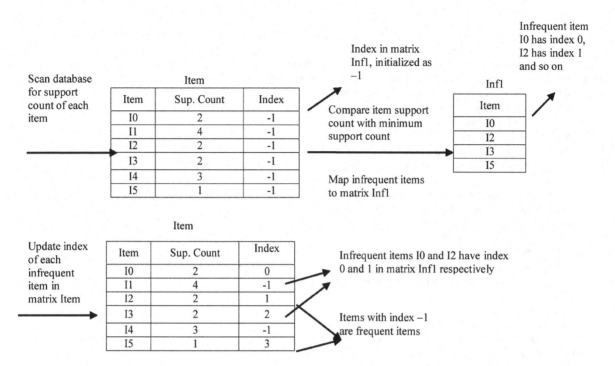

Since the Infk matrices would cause huge memory space consumption, in order to run the algorithm in a memory–resident data structure, we limit the length of association rules to 5 in our experimental studies, which is quite reasonable while working on infrequent items based on the fact that the probability of several infrequent items occurring in the same transaction is extremely low. We present the formulas for identifying the positions of infrequent 4-itemsets and 5-itemsets as follows.

Lemma 3. For a specific 4-itemset (a, b, c, d), if the indices of the 4 infrequent items a, b, c and d in matrix Inf1 are x, y, z and t respectively (x<y<z<t), then the index of 4-itemset (a, b, c, d) in a desired matrix Inf4 is

$$I(x,y,z,t)=x^2(2n-x-5)/24+x(n-x-2)^2/2+x(x-1)(n-x-2)/2+x(x-1)(2x-1)/12+x(2n-x-5)/6+(y-x-1)(2n-x-y-4)/4+(y-x-1)(n-y-1)^2/2+(n-y-1)(y-x-1)(y-x-2)/2+(y-x-1)(y-x-2)(2y-2x-3)/12+(z-y-1)(2n-y-z-2)/2+t-z-1$$

Where n is the total number of infrequent items in D.

Lemma 4. For a specific 5-itemset (a, b, c, d, e), if the indices of the 5 infrequent items a, b, c, d

Figure 3. Matrixes to store support counts of infrequent k-itemsets

Inf3

Inf2

2-itemsets	{I0, I2}	{I0, I3}	{I0, I5}	{I2, I3}	{I2, I5}	{I3, I5}
Sup. Count	0	0	0	0	0	0

Inf3

Figure 4. Updated support counts of k-itemsets

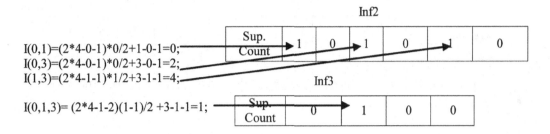

$I(0,1)=(2*4-0-1)*0/2+1-0-1=0;$
$I(0,3)=(2*4-0-1)*0/2+3-0-1=2;$
$I(1,3)=(2*4-1-1)*1/2+3-1-1=4;$

$I(0,1,3)=(2*4-1-2)(1-1)/2+3-1-1=1;$

and e in matrix Inf1 are x, y, z, t and h respectively (x<y<z<t<h), then the index of 5-itemset (a, b, c, d, e) in a desired matrix Inf5 is

$$I(x,y,z,t,h)=$$
$$\sum_{k=n-x-3}^{n-4}\sum_{j=1}^{k}\sum_{i=0}^{j-1}(1+j-i)(i-j)/2+\sum_{j=n-y-2}^{n-x-4}\sum_{i=0}^{j-1}(1+j-i)/(j-i)/2+$$
$$\sum_{i=n-z-1}^{n-y-3}i(1+i)/2+(2n-z-t-2)(t-z-1)/2+h-t-1$$

Where n is the total number of infrequent items in D.

Step 5: Identify all infrequent k-itemsets of potential interest by using pruning strategy, which applies interest function, *interest(X, Y), to* capture itemsets of potential interest. An example is given in Figure 4.

Assume minimum interest = 0.05

$Interest(I0,I2)=|supp(I0\cup I2)- supp(I0)supp(I2)|$
$=|0.2-0.4*0.4|=0.04<0.05$ [discard]

$Interest(I0,I5)=|supp(I0\cup I5)- supp(I0)supp(I5)|$
$=|0.2-0.4*0.2|=0.12>0.05$

$Interest(I2,I5)=|supp(I2 \cup I5)-supp(I2)supp(I5)|$
$=|0.2-0.4*0.2|=0.12>0.05$

Step 6: Compute value of *correlation(X,Y)*, if *correlation(X,Y)*>1, then employ interestingness measure, *CRIP(X,Y)*, to extract rules of strong interest.

Assume minimum confidence = 0.5. For infrequent 2-itemset {I0, I5}, we find

$correlation(I0, I5)= supp(I0 \cup I5)/(supp(I0)supp(I5))=0.2/(0.4*0.2) >1$

$CPIR(I0|I5)=[supp(I0 \cup I5) – supp(I0)supp(I5)]/[supp(I5)(1 – supp(I0))]$

$=(0.2– 0.4 * 0.2)/[0.2 * (1– 0.4)]= 1>0.5$

Hence rule I0$\Rightarrow$ I5 can be extracted as an association rule of interest

Figure 5. Generation of infrequent k-itemsets of interest

Infrequent 2-itemsets

Itemsets	Sup. Count
{I0,I2}	1
{I0,I5}	1
{I2,I5}	1

Identify itemsets of interest by exploiting function, interest(X, Y)

Infrequent 2-itemsets of interest

Itemsets	Sup. Count
{I0,I5}	1
{I2,I5}	1

Figure 6. Hash table generated to store support counts of all infrequent k-itemsets

	Bucket address	0	1	2	3	4	5	6
Create hash table using hash function h(x, y)	Bucket count	2	1	1	2	1	1	1
	Bucket contents	{I0,I1} {I0,I1}	{I0,I2}	{I0,I5}	{I1,I2} {I1,I2}	{I1,I5}	{I2,I5}	{I0,I2,I5}

CPIR(I5|I0)=[supp(I0 $\cup$ I5) – supp(I0) supp(I5)]/[supp(I0)(1 – supp(I5))]

=(0.2– 0.4 * 0.2)/[0.4 * (1 – 0.2)]= 3/8<0.5

Hence rule I5$\Rightarrow$ I0 is not a rule of interest

In MBS, he Infk matrices could be large number of size when the number of infrequent items is large, which causes too much memory space to be required. In order to process this algorithm in a main memory-resident data structure, the length of association rule must be limited. But, exploiting disk-resident implementation could substantially solve this problem. In fact, each combination of the index values of infrequent items must occupy a position in a particular matrix Infk even though some combinations do not exist in the database at all. To solve this problem, we present a Hash-Based Scheme below.

Hash-Based Scheme (HBS)

The Hash-Based Scheme has the same process as Matrix-Based Scheme for the first full scan of database. When the database is scanned for the second time, for each transaction Ti, identify all infrequent items by checking the corresponding index values stored in matrix Item, and then repeat the following:

Step 1: Find all combinations of the index values of these infrequent items, where the index values are the positions of infrequent items in matrix Inf1.

Step 2: Compute the hash value of each combination by exploiting hash function, h(x,y), provided by library, where the hash values are the indices of hash table. Then hash (i.e., map) them into different buckets of the hash table and increase the corresponding bucket counts (Figure 6). Hash collision occurs when different itemsets are assigned the same hash value.

Step 3: Use function, *interest(X,Y),* to prune uninteresting itemsets.

Step 4: Employ functions, *correlation(X,Y) and CPIR(X,Y),* to capture rules of strong interest.

We now present the algorithm implemented. Experiments show that this scheme is always better than the Matrix-based algorithm in terms of both running time and memory space while mining rules among infrequent items. However the Matrix-based scheme outperforms Hash-based scheme while working on the frequent items with bounded length. The reason is that the probability of hash collision is very high while mining rules among frequent items.(See Figure 7).

EXPERIMENTAL EVALUATION AND PERFORMANCE STUDY

Experimental Study

For evaluation purpose, we have conducted several experiments. We select the well-known IBM synthetic database generated by the generator (IBM).

Figure 7. Algorithm design of HMS

```
Input  D: database; minSupp: minimum support; minConf: minimum confidence; minInte: minimum interest
Output  AR: association rules
(0) scan the database D and find all infrequent 1-itemsets(Infl)
(1)create a hash table
(2)read database 2nd time
(3) for each transaction Ti ∈D do{
(4) identify all  infrequent items in this transaction;
(5) find all  combinations of these infrequent items;
(6) hash each combination to hash table and obtain a hash index&&  increase the value of hash index by 1
(7) for each k-itemset I in hash table do
      for ∀itemsets X,Y, X∪Y=I and X∩Y=∅ do
        If interest(X,Y)<minInte then Infk←Infk-{I};
      end
   end
(8) for each infrequent k-itemset of interest {X∪Y} ∈Infk do
  If  Correlation(X,Y)>1 && CPIR(Y|X)≥minConf then AR←{X⇒Y}
  If  Correlation(X,Y)>1 && CPIR(X|Y)≥minConf then AR←{Y⇒Y}
  end
(9) return  AR
```

This choice gives us the flexibility of controlling the size and dimension of database. The parameters for generating a synthetic database are the number of transactions D, the average transaction size T and the average length I of so-called maximal potentially large itemsets. The number of items in database is 1000. We conduct experiments on a varied average transaction size and different number of transactions to test our algorithm's efficiency and scalability. All of experiments are performed on computer with 3.4GHz processor and 2GB memory. The program is developed in the C++ language. In this chapter, the runtime includes both CPU time and I/O time. In all of the following experiments, we limit the length of association rules to 5.

Since our algorithms can be applied to mine association rules among frequent items with bounded length, we compare our schemes with the most influential algorithms for association rule mining, which are Apriori algorithm and FP-Growth. The implementation of Apriori and FP-Growth was downloaded from http://fuzy. cs.uni- magdeburg.de/ and http://www.csc.liv. ac.uk/~frans/KDD/ respectively.

In Figure 9, the experiment is performed on database T20I4D100K, and the minimum confidence threshold is set at 50%. Table 3 and Figure 9 show the mining result.

We also compare MBS/HBS against Apriori and FP-growth on database T20I4D(200K,400K,600K,800K, 1000K), which

Table 3. Runtime comparison on database T20I4D400K

Support(%)	Frequent itemsets	Runtime (seconds)			
		Apriori	FP-Growth	HBS	MBS
2	8997	2237	785	658	35.98
2.5	7486	2084.9	563.75	541.64	27.67
3	5038	1951.7	459.86	300.535	20.53
3.5	3926	1878.6	416.17	218.1	17.4
4	1879	1713.2	339.7	154	14.98

Figure 8. Performance comparison on database T20I4D(200K,400K,600K,800K,1000K)

```
Input D: database; minSupp: minimum support; minConf: minimum confidence; minInte: minimum interest
Output AR: association rules
(0) scan the database D and find all infrequent 1-itemsets(Inf1)
(1)create a hash table
(2)read database 2nd time
(3) for each transaction Ti ∈D do{
(4) identify all infrequent items in this transaction;
(5) find all combinations of these infrequent items;
(6) hash each combination to hash table and obtain a hash index&&  increase the value of hash index by 1
(7) for each k-itemset I in hash table do
      for ∀itemsets X,Y, X∪Y=I and X∩Y=∅ do
         If interest(X,Y)<minInte then Infk←Infk-{I};
      end
  end
(8) for each infrequent k-itemset of interest {X∪Y} ∈Infk do
  If Correlation(X,Y)>1 && CPIR(Y|X)≥minConf then AR←{X⇒Y}
  If Correlation(X,Y)>1 && CPIR(X|Y)≥minConf then AR←{Y⇒Y}
  end
(9) return AR
```

Table 4. Runtime comparison on database T20I4D(200K,400K,600K,800K, 1000K)

# of transactions(K)	Frequent itemsets	Runtime (seconds)			
		Aprori	FP-growth	HBS	MBS
200	10183	568	420	330	18.56
400	10238	2235	785	658	37.12
600	10165	4979	1127	1078	55.91
800	10192	8779	1472	1295	74.94
1000	10194	14870	1829	1664	93.22

Figure 9. Performance comparison on database I20I4D400K with different support level

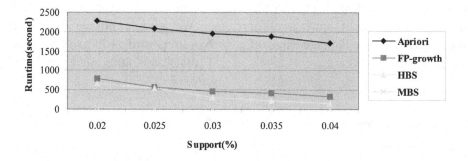

has a varied number of transactions. The minimum support threshold is 2% and minimum confidence is 50%. Table 4 and Figure 9 present the result.

From above performance studies, we can see our two algorithms outperform the classical al-

gorithms, Apriori and FP growth, while we limit the length of association rule to 5.

We also conducted an experiment to discover association rules among infrequent items by using our both our methods MBS and HBS. The database

Figure 10. Runtime comparison of our two schemes with different support level

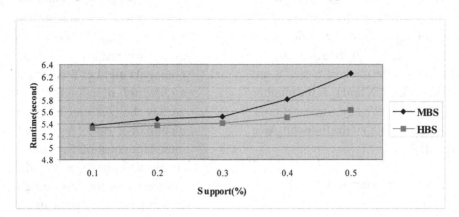

we used is T20I4D200K. We test the behaviors of our two algorithms at different support thresholds with a minimum confidence of 50%. Figure 10 shows the result.

From Figure 10, we see that HBS has a better performance than MBS when mining association rules among infrequent items.

QUANTITATIVE ASSOCIATION RULE MINING AMONG INFREQUENT ITEMS

Quantitative Association Rule Mining in Relational Database

Quantitative association rule mining is traditionally defined as describing associations between quantitative items or attributes. In such rules, quantitative values for items or attributes are partitioned into intervals. For example, the following rule is an example of a quantitative association rule:

Age("30...39")^ Income("40K...49K") $\Rightarrow$ Buys(new car)

where the quantitative attributes, age and income, are discretized.

In previous research (Sirant & Agarawal,

1996; Shragai & Schneider, 2001), the researchers studied the problem of mining quantitative association rules from relational databases. To process quantitative attributes in relational databases, each numeric attribute is discretized by partitioning the domain into intervals during the mining process, so as to satisfy some mining criteria, such as maximizing the confidence or compactness of the rules mined. In the following, we will discuss quantitative association rule mining based on transactional databases.

Quantitative Association Rule Mining in Transactional Database among Infrequent Items

P. Hsu et al. (2004) discussed quantitative association rules among frequent items in transactional databases. We will discuss quantitative association rules among infrequent items in transactional database.

Let I = $\{i_1, i_2 \ldots i_n\}$ be all distinct items in database D, where D consists of a set of database transactions. Each transaction T is a set of items such that T$\subseteq$I, each distinct item in transaction T is associated with a quantity. So, transaction T can be expressed as T=$\{(p_1, q_1), (p_2, q_2) \ldots (p_k, q_k)\}$, where $p_1, p_2 \ldots p_k$ are distinct items occurring in T and q_i is the number of occurrences of p_i in T. For example, if a customer bought 2 bottles of milk and 3 bags of bread, then we say this transaction Ti={(milk, 2), (bread, 3)}. Each transaction has a unique identifier, called TID. Let X={$(t_1, t_{q1}), (t_2, t_{q2})...(t_k, t_{qk})$} be a *quantitative itemset (Qitemset* for short), where $t_1, t_2... t_k$ are distinct items occurring in X and t_{qi} is the number of occurrence of t_i in X. We say a transaction T contains a *Qitemset* X (T⊇X) if the following two conditions are satisfied.

Every item t_i in X also appears in T

The number of occurrences of t_i in X, t_{qi}, is no greater than the number of occurrences of t_i in T, q_i.

For example, if X={(a, 1), (b, 2), (c, 1)}, T={(a, 1), (b, 3), (c, 2)}, then this satisfies T⊇X. But if X={(a, 2), (b, 2), (c, 1)}, then it does not satisfy T⊇X. In the transactional database D, the percentage of transactions containing *Qitemset* X is the support of X. Let *Qminsup* be the user-defined minimum support threshold for *Qitemset*. A *Qitemset* X is valuable if it satisfies support(X)≥*Qminsup*, and the rule derived from X is an interesting quantitative association rule.

We will mine quantitative association rules among infrequent items based on our above two algorithms, MBS and HBS. For each association rule mined by MBS (or HBS), we now reconsider each rule with a quantity involved for every item. For example, if we have a rule, {necklace⇒earring}, discovered from above methods the itemset, {(necklace, earring)}, is now a set of quantitative itemsets such as {{(necklace, 1), (earring, 2)}, {(necklace, 1), (earring, 1)} {(necklace, 1), (earring, 3)}}. Then we identify support of each quantitative itemset, which is the percentage of transactions containing that specific quantitative itemset. Based on the support information, we can identify interesting quantitative association rules as follows:

1. **Simple rule:** If quantitative itemset X={(A=q1), (B=q2)} satisfies *Qminsup*,

which is support(X)≥*Qminsup*, then we say the *Qitemset* X is valuable and the quantitative rule {A=q1} ⇒{B=q2} is an interesting quantitative rule.

2. **General rule:** Let Y={(A=q1), (B≥q2)} be a *Qitemset*, if support(Y) ≥*Qminsup*, then we say the *Qitemset* Y is valuable and the quantitative rule {A=q1}⇒{B≥q2} is an interesting quantitative rule.

3. **Semantic rule:** User may define some semantic terms for describing the quantities of items based on particular circumstance. For example, we may define "large quantity" for an item A if n(A)≥10, where n(A) stands for number of units of item A; "medium quantity" if 5≤n(A)<10, and "small quantity" if 0≤n(A)<5. We may also define semantic terms based on the percentage of transactions containing that item A, i.e., support of item A. For instance, define the number of units of item A as "large quantity" if support(A) ≥60%, "medium quantity" if 40%≤support(A)<60% and "small quantity" if support(A)<40%. Let Z={A= "large quantity", B= "small quantity"}. If support(Z) ≥*Qminsup*, then we say the *Qitemset* Z is valuable and the quantitative association rule, {A= "large quantity"}⇒{B= "small quantity"}, is an interesting quantitative rule. In the following, we will give examples to illustrate above algorithm.

Assume we obtain several interesting rules from MBS (or HBS), which are {necklace⇒earring}, {table⇒chair} and {water⇒beverage}. All of the rules have a support of 10% and a confidence of 60%: we now reconsider these rules with quantity involved. Assume there is a total of 10 transactions containing these three itemsets, {necklace, earring}, {table, chair} and {water, beverage}. For the convenience of comparison, we will compute the support of *Qitemset* based on the total number of transactions containing that itemset. Let quantitative minimum support, *Qminsup*, be 30%.

Table 5. Itemset {necklace, earring} with its quantitative itemsets

Itemset/Qitemset	# of transactions
{necklace, earring}	10
{necklace=1, earring=2}	6
{necklace=1, earring=1}	2
{necklace=1, earring=3}	2

(1) **Simple rule:** Let us re-analyze the association rule, {necklace⇒earring}, with quantity incorporated. Now the itemset, {necklace, earring}, is a set of quantitative itemsets as follows.

From Table 5, we have

Support(necklace=1,earring=2)=6/10=60%,

Support(necklace=1,earring=1)=2/10=20%

Support(necklace=1, earring=3)=2/10=20%

The quantitative itemset, {necklace=1,earring=2}, has a support of 60%, which is greater than Qminsup. So we say the quantitative association rule, {necklace=1}⇒{earring=2}, is an interesting quantitative association rule.

(2) **General rule:** We now consider association rule, {table⇒chair}, with quantity involved. Itemset, {table,chair}, is a set of quantitative itemsets as follows.

From Table 6, we have

support(table=1,chair=3)=1/10=10%, support(table=1,chair≥4)=9/10=90%.

The quantitative itemset, {table=1,chair≥4}, has a support of 90%, which is very high and significant. So we say the quantitative association rule, {table=1}⇒{chair≥4}, is an interesting quantitative association rule.

(3) **Semantic rule:** We now consider association rule, {water⇒beverage}, with quantity involved. Itemset, {water,beverage}, is now a set of quantitative itemsets as follows.

We will define semantic terms for water/beverage as follows. The number of units of water/beverage is considered as "large quantity" if $n(A) \geq 7$, where $n(A)$ is the number of units of water/beverage, "medium quantity" if $3 \leq n(A) < 7$, and "small quantity" if $n(A) < 3$.

From Table 7, we found that

support(small quantity of water ⇒ large quantity of beverage)=40%≥Qminsup

Table 6. Itemset {table, chair} with its quantitative itemsets

Itemset/Qitemset	# of transactions
{table, chair}	10
{table=1, chair=3}	1
{table=1, chair=4}	3
{table=1, chair=5}	3
{table=1, chair=6}	3

Table 7. Itemset {water, beverage} with its quantitative itemsets

Itemset/Qitemset	# of transactions
{water, beverage}	10
{water=1, beverage=8}	4
{water=4, beverage=4}	1
{water=7, beverage=2}	4
{water=5, beverage=4}	1

support(medium quantity of water $\Rightarrow$ medium quantity of beverage)=20% $\leq$ Qminsup

support(large quantity of beverage$\Rightarrow$small quantity of water)=40% $\geq$ Qminsup

So we say the quantitative association rules, {small quantity of water $\Rightarrow$ large quantity of beverage} and {large quantity of beverage$\Rightarrow$small quantity of water}, are interesting quantitative association rules.

CONCLUSION AND FUTURE WORK

In this chapter, we propose two novel algorithms called MBS and HBS for efficient discovery of association rules among infrequent items, which also can be applied to mine association rules efficiently among frequent items with limited length. In both of our methods, we only need to traverse the database twice, and we exploit pruning function *interest (X, Y)* to reduce the search space considerably, as well as use interestingness measures, *correlation(X,Y)* and *CPIR(X,Y)*, to extract rules of strong interest. In MBS, the index function, *I(x, y)*, is employed to identify the index values for any infrequent k-itemsets in a given transaction directly. The limitation of MBS is the restriction for the length of association rules due to the huge memory space consumption caused by the Infk matrices. In HBS, we introduce hash-based technique to overcome the drawback

of MBS. However, HBS is not a good option for mining association rules with any length among frequent items due to the expensive cost of hash collision. To further develop our research, the idea of using constraints proposed by Srikant et al. (1997) and Wang et al. (2000) can further help reduce the size of itemsets generated. Experiments have been conducted for the behavior analysis of our schemes, and the results show that our algorithms outperform the state-of-the-art algorithms under the situation being evaluated. Specially, we present two simple, practical and straightforward approaches to explore rules among rare items.

We also explore quantitative association rule mining among infrequent items in transactional databases. We reanalyze association rules with quantity incorporated, where the rules are discovered from method MBS (or HBS). Some interesting experiments are drawn to show that the quantitative association rules captured are more informative.

REFERENCES

Agrawal, R., Imielinski, T., & Swami, A. (1993). Mining association rules between sets of items in large databases. In *Proceedings of the Association for Computing Machinery- Special Interest Group on Management of Data (ACM-SIGMOD)* (pp. 207-216).

Agrawal, R., Imielinski, T., & Swami, A. (1993). Database mining: A performance perspective. *IEEE Transactions on Knowledge and Data Engineering, 5*(6), 914–925. doi:10.1109/69.250074

Agrawal, R., & Srikant, R. (1994). Fast algorithms for mining association rules. *In Proceedings of the 20th International Conference on Very Large Databases(VLDB)* (pp. 487-499).

Agrawal, R., & Srikant, R. (1995). Mining sequential patterns. In *International Conference on Data Engineering (ICDE)* (pp. 85-93).

Bayardo, R. J. (1998). Efficiently mining long patterns from database. In *Proceedings of the 1998 ACM SIGMOD International conference on Management of data* (pp. 85-93).

Brin, S., Motwani, R., & Silverstein, C. (1997). Beyond market basket: Generalizing association rules to correlations. In *Special Interest Group on Management of Data (SIGMOD)* (pp. 265-276).

Chen, M., Han, J., & Yu, P. (1996). Data mining: An overview from a database perspective. *IEEE Transactions on Knowledge and Data Engineering, 8*(6), 866–881. doi:10.1109/69.553155

Cohen, E., Datar, M., Fujiwara, S., Gionis, A., Indyk, P., Motwani, R., et al. (2000). Finding interesting associations without support pruning. In *Proceedings of the 16th International Conference on Data Engineering(ICDE)*, (pp. 489-500).

Ding, J. (2005). *Efficient association rule mining among infrequent items.* Ph.D. thesis. In University of Illinois at Chicago.

Dong, G., & Li, J. (1999). Efficient mining of emerging patterns: discovering trends and differences. In *Proceedings of ACM SIGKDD Conference on Knowledge Discovery and Data Mining (KDD)* (pp. 43-52).

Han, J., Pei, J., & Yin, Y. (2000). Mining frequent pattern without candidate generation. In *Proceeding of ACM SIGMOD International Conference Management of Data(ICMD)* (pp. 1–12).

Hsu, P., Chen, Y., & Ling, C. (2004). Algorithms for mining association rules in bag databases. *Information Sciences, 166*(1-4), 31–47. doi:10.1016/j.ins.2003.05.013

Hussain, F., Liu, L., Suzuki, E., & Lu, H. (2000). Exception rule mining with a relative interestingness measure. In *Pacific-Asia Conference on Knowledge Discovery and Data Mining(PAKDD)*, (pp. 86-97).

Hwang, S., Ho, S., & Tang, J. (1999). Mining exception instances to facilitate workflow exception handling. In *Proceedings of the Sixth International Conference on Database Systems for Advanced Applications* (DASFAA) (pp. 45-52).

Kamber, M., Han, J., & Chiang, J. Y. (1997). Metarule-guided mining of multi-dimensional association rules using data cubes. In *Proceeding of 3rd International Conference on Knowledge Discovery and Data Mining(KDD)* (pp. 207-210).

Lent, B., Swami, A., & Widom, J. (1997). Clustering association rules. In *Proceeding of International Conference Data Engineering (ICDE)* (pp. 220-231).

Liu, H., Lu, H., Feng, L., & Hussain, F. (1999). Efficient search of reliable exceptions. In *Proceedings of the Third Pacific-Asia Conference on Methodologies for Knowledge Discovery and Data Mining(PAKDD)*, (pp. 194-204).

Mannila, H., Toivonen, H., & Verkamo, A. (1994). Efficient algorithm for discovering association rules. In *Knowledge Discovery and Data Mining (KDD)* (pp. 181-192).

Padmanabhan, B., & Tuzhilin, A. (2000). Small is beautiful:discovering the minimal set of unexpected patterns. In *Proceeding of 6th ACM SIGKDD International Conference on Knowledge Discovery and Data Mining (KDD)* (pp. 54-63).

Savasere, A., Omiecinski, E., & Navathe, S. (1995). An efficient algorithm for mining association rules in large databases. *In Proceeding of the 21st International Conference on Very Large Databases (VLDB)*, (pp. 432-444).

Savasere, A., Omiecinski, E., & Navathe, S. (1998). Mining for strong negative associations in a large database of customer transactions. In *Proceedings of the Fourteenth International Conference on Data Engineering (ICDE)* (pp. 494-502).

Shragai, A., & Schneider, M. (2001). Discovering quantitative associations in databases. In Joint 9th *IFSA World Congress and 20th NAFIPS International Conferenc*e (pp. 423-42).

Srikant, R., & Agarawal, R. (1996). Mining quantitative association rules in large relational tables. In *Proceedings of the Association for Computing Machinery- Special Interest Group on Management of Data (ACM SIGMOD)* (pp. 1-12).

Srikant, R., & Agarawal, R. (1996). Mining quantitative association rules in large relational tables. In *Proceedings of the Association for Computing Machinery- Special Interest Group on Management of Data (ACM SIGMOD)* (pp. 1-12).

Srikant, R., & Agrawal, R. (1995). Mining generalized association rules. In *Proceedings of the 21th International Conference on Very Large Data Bases (VLDB)* (pp. 407-419).

Srikant, R., Vu, Q., & Agarawal, R. (1997). Mining association rules with item constraint. In *Proceeding of 3rd International Conference on Knowledge Discovery and Data Mining (KDD)* (pp. 67-73).

Wang, K., & He, Y. Cheung, D., & Chin, Y. (2001). Mining confident rules without support requirement. In *Proceedings of ACM International Conference on Information and Knowledge Management (CIKM),* (pp. 89-96).

Wang, K., He, Y., & Han, J. (2000). Pushing support constraints into frequent itemset mining. In *Proceeding of International Conference on Very Large Data Bases (VLDB),* (pp. 43-52).

Wu, X., Zhang, C., & Zhang, S. (2004). Efficient mining of both positive and negative association rules. *ACM Transactions on Information Systems*, 381–405. doi:10.1145/1010614.1010616

Xiong, H., Tan, P., & Kumar, V. (2003). Mining Strong Affinity Association Patterns in Data Sets with Skewed Support Distribution, In *Proceedings of the Third IEEE International Conference on Data Mining (ICDM)* (pp. 387-394).

Yuan, X., Buckles, B., Yuan, Z., & Zhang, J. (2002). Mining negative association rules. In *Proceedings of the Seventh International Symposium on Computers and Communications (ISCC),* (pp. 623-629).

Chapter 3
Replacing Support in Association Rule Mining

Rosa Meo
Università di Torino, Italy

Dino Ienco
Università di Torino, Italy

ABSTRACT

Association rules are an intuitive descriptive paradigm that has been used extensively in different application domains with the purpose to identify the regularities and correlation in a set of observed objects. However, association rules' statistical measures (support and confidence) have been criticized because in some cases they have shown to fail in their primary goal: that is to select the most relevant and significant association rules. In this chapter the authors propose a new model that replaces the support measure. The new model, like support, is a tool for the identification of reliable rules and is used also to reduce the traversal of the itemsets' search space. The proposed model adopts new criteria in order to establish the reliability of the information extracted from the database. These criteria are based on Bayes' Theorem and on an estimate of the probability density function of each itemset. According to our criteria, the information that we have obtained from the database on an itemset is reliable if and only if the confidence interval of the estimated probability is low compared with the most likely value of it. We will see how this method can be computed in an approximate but satisfactory way, with the same algorithms that are usually adopted to select itemsets on support threshold.

INTRODUCTION

The search for association rules in data mining has the aim of identifying the phenomena that are recurrent in a data set. The solution of this problem finds application in many fields, such as analysis of basket data of supermarkets, failures in telecommunication networks, medical test results, lexical features of texts, and so on. The extraction of association rules from very large databases has been solved by researchers in many different ways and the proposed solutions are embedded in as many powerful algorithms.

DOI: 10.4018/978-1-60566-754-6.ch003

An association rule X → Y is a pair of two sets of items (called itemsets), X and Y, which are often found together in a given collection of data. For instance, the association rule {milk, coffee} → {bread, sugar} extracted from the market basket domain, has the intuitive meaning that a customer purchasing milk and coffee together is likely to also purchase bread and sugar.

The validity of an association rule has been based on two measures: the support, the percentage of transactions of the database containing both X and Y; and the confidence, the percentage of the transactions in which Y occurs relative only to those transactions in which also X occurs.

For instance, with reference to the above example, a value of 2% of support and a value of 15% of confidence would mean that in 2% of all the transactions, customers buy together milk, coffee, bread and sugar, and that the 15% of the transactions in which customers have bought together milk and coffee contain also bread and sugar. In the original application domain of market basket analysis, support meant that only the association rules with decision making value were extracted.

Association rules are intuitive, and constitute a powerful and versatile conceptual tool that have been applied recently also to new types of problems, such as collaborative recommender systems for e-commerce (Lin, Alvarez & Ruiz, 2002), intrusion detection (Lee, Stolfo & Mok, 1998) and are extended to discover quasi-equivalent media objects in a distributed information system with the purpose of reducing the number of objects traversed by the queries (Shyu, Chen & Kashyap, 1999). However, in almost all the new and real-life applications the support-confidence framework reveals some limits. As a result, if itemsets are not validated by a statistical approach, non-significant itemsets could be extracted by frequent itemset algorithms and in turn non-significant rules. These problems are discussed in more detail in the section on related work.

Furthermore, Liu, Hsu & Ma (1999) provide evidence of the rare item problem consisting of the fact that the support-threshold constraint discards potentially meaningful association rules between items with low support. We can conclude that a unique value of support is not realistic: the various items present very different probability density distributions.

In this chapter we present a new statistical model whose purpose is to give a solid basis to the extraction of relevant itemsets from the database. In particular it provides a lower bound of the values of probability of occurrence of itemsets that can be observed in a given database. At the same time the new statistical model proposed, as any other model for data mining, must be implemented efficiently and allow pruning of the itemsets' search-space, which is one of the original motivations for the adoption of the support measure.

The new model allows for the replacement of the minimum support threshold imposed as a requirement by the user. According to the new model we are allowed to judge the relevance of the information obtained from the database with a criterion based on the Bayes' Theorem. This one allows us to make an estimate of the probability distribution function of an itemset (*a priori* probability) starting from the set of observations obtained by the database (*a posteriori* probability). The adopted criterion is very simple. We consider the probability of an itemset to be a random variable, and make an estimate of this probability on the basis of the observations (obtained a posteriori) from the database. If the most likely value of probability of occurrence of an itemset in the database is comparable with the error in this estimate we can conclude that the probability estimation is not reliable.

The rationale of the approach proposed here is motivated by the fact that the data mining analyst essentially uses the database to make an estimate of an unknown quantity: the probability of finding an itemset in a random observation of the database.

But the database itself is in turn a sample of all the possible outcomes. In general, if the sample is too little, then the probability estimation will not be reliable enough. This situation must be recognized and rejected by a correct statistical approach.

As we will see in the section entitled *Exploiting Bayes for a New Method of Itemsets Evaluation* this reliability property is again a downward-closed property that allows us to stop the lattice traversal in depth, in practice in an equivalent manner to the efficient algorithms based on a unique minimum support threshold. Thus, any standard algorithm for the extraction of frequent itemsets can be safely adopted with the only concern being to give the algorithm a statistical, reliable value of minimum support threshold. This can be computed by the proposed statistical model, knowing the size of the given database, the confidence level (chosen probability to make a correct estimation in the statistical inference process) and an error tolerance. As a result, the proposed statistical inference process gives the user the guarantee that the inferred values of probability of occurrence of itemsets are estimated with an error that is within an established error tolerance. According to the proposed inference framework, it is not possible to search for rare itemsets with arbitrarily low probability values. Instead, the domain of probability values must be suitably determined according to the size of the database and the precision in the estimates of the probability values that the user wants to achieve.

Another important contribution of this work consists in the elimination of the unique, minimum support threshold for all the itemsets. Indeed, a fixed and unique value of support threshold for all the patterns presents some drawbacks. First of all, it does not depend on the cardinality of the sets or on their PDF, which is not realistic. Second, the support threshold is given by the user who may not know how to set it. In contrast, he/she may well know the level of error tolerance he/she wishes to allow in the measure. Therefore, we allow the user

to set a different minimum threshold of probability for each itemset. We will see that each threshold is chosen on the basis of the estimated probability of occurrence of the itemset and of an error tolerance in this estimation given by the user.

This chapter is organized as follows. The section *Related Work* contains an overview of comparable approaches for the substitution of the support threshold or the adoption of statistical techniques that evaluate the relevance of an itemset. The subsequent section recalls the statistical theory used for the proposed approach and presents the new statistical model. In the same section a justification of the model is given in particular as regards its application to rare patterns and the rationale of it is presented. The section entitled *Experiments* presents the application of the theory in some experiments on real datasets. With these experiments we aim to show that with the aid of the proposed theory that the adopted support threshold in a given sample database allows the computation of a mean error in the estimation of the probabilities which is controlled by the user by a fixed error tolerance. Furthermore, this error is lower than the error committed with the same sample when the support threshold is established at too low a level, not compatible with the sample size and the error tolerance required by the user. Finally we will draw conclusions and present future work.

RELATED WORK

Siebes (1994), in a very early study on data mining from a statistical perspective, has the merit of studying the observed probability of an object. In this chapter the author studies a manner of extracting description clauses that represent a set of examples characterized by homogeneous features such that the descriptions are as general as possible. The notion of a description that represents an homogeneous set of examples is related to the concept of surprising patterns that Siebes formalizes in his work. It adopts Bernoulli's trials formulas but the paper has a different purpose, which is the achievement of a classifier that puts in a class the discovered homogeneous data.

Silverstein, Brin & Motwani (1998) have presented a critique of the concept of association rules and the related support-confidence framework. They have observed that the association rule model does not identify the correlation between the presence of an itemset and the absence of another one and between itemsets that are very frequent. In place of association rules and the support-confidence framework, Silverstein, Brin and Motwani propose a statistical approach based on the chi-squared measure and a new model of rules, called dependence rules. Similarly, Meo (2000) has proposed a new model that replaces association rules and the confidence measure with itemsets and the so-called dependence values; these values, computed maximizing an entropy function, reveal the dependency between the elements of the itemset, dependency that is not inherited by the ancestor itemsets in the lattice (like dependence rules) but is intrinsic to the itemset itself. The shown criticism is shared also by Aggarwal & Yu (1998), who provide evidence that in some cases there is no combination of support and confidence values that allows the extraction of more accurate association rules (with higher confidence) and at the same time discards the useless ones (rules that happen to have high support because of the high support of their items).

Furthermore, Liu, Hsu & Ma (1999) provide evidence of the rare item problem consisting of the fact that the support threshold constraint discards also potentially meaningful association rules between items with low support.

Aumann & Lindell (1999) apply statistical tests to recognize in the domain of quantitative association rules (association rules with a modifier attached to the antecedent and consequent) the more specific rules that effectively add some information to the more general rules.

The framework they introduce allows finding extraordinary and interesting phenomena in a subgroup of examples of the population. They use the mean and the variance of the values' distribution of the quantitative attributes. They compare these statistics computed on a subgroup with the statistics computed on the overall population. If the statistics differ from a user-defined amount they conclude that the difference is statistically significant. Again they rely on a user-defined threshold.

Webb (2006) proposes using statistical hypothesis tests in order to prevent the extraction of false discoveries occurring, for example, as an effect of the multiple comparisons problem, i.e., when it happens that the probability of a high number of independent rare events is high. The proposed statistical tests are the Fisher exact test and more advanced tests such as Bonferroni's adjustment and Holm procedure. This latter one is placed in a holdout evaluation strategy by dataset partitioning.

Mannila & Pavlov (1999) focus on a probabilistic framework to predict a global model of the joint probability distribution of all the items in the database given the observed distribution of the local patterns in the database. A local pattern is composed of a low number of items where an item is thought of as an attribute assuming a certain discrete value in the database. The global model is generated as a probabilistic model which is fitted by an iterative optimization algorithm constrained on the observed local patterns. The constrained optimization problem adopts Lagrangian multipliers and aims to reduce the cross-entropy between the probabilistic global model and a prior model. This prior is a uniform probability distribution of the single items. This work, has the merit of giving a criterion for defining a probabilistic model for itemsets but it does not deal with the problem of defining a reliable probability model for rare itemsets.

Morishita & Sese (2000) adopt chi-squared statistical measures to efficiently compute significant association rules with an algorithmic view-point (Apriori-like). This method allows the avoidance of the use of high support thresholds in the generation of the significant patterns, but it does not explain how we can statistically infer the support threshold from the data.

Roddick & Rice (2001) investigate various ways to set thresholds that define interestingness in rules, such as content-dependent and independent ones and links the interest in a pattern to its low probability of occurrence.

Wang, He, Cheung & Chin (2001) eliminate the problem of setting minimum support and find directly association rules with a minimum confidence threshold with the drawback that from some databases too many rules might be generated. In an analogous way, Omiecinski (2003) introduces some new measures based on confidence to replace support. Two of these measures are based on confidence and the third one is similar to the Jaccard Index. This work also studies some relationships that exist between the proposed measures and the support threshold, but it does not investigate how to set the threshold value of these statistics.

Tan, Kumar & Srivastava (2002) compare different evaluation measures and their effect in the ranking of patterns with different probability distributions. In their study they supply several key properties one should examine to select a good measure for its right application. In the paper an overview of some state-of-the-art statistics is presented. The behaviour of the different measures is compared with respect to different value distributions of two categorical variables represented by means of a contingency-table. The proposed measures instead have not been adopted with the purpose to obtain the domain of their values such that it represents the domain of validity of the patterns.

Steinbach, Tan, Xiong & Kumar (2004) define new aggregated measures of evaluation of a pattern in a vector form but the problem of setting the

threshold of the aggregated value still remains.

Hahsler & Hornik (2006) propose two new measures aimed to replace lift and confidence (hyper-lift and hyper-confidence) and test them against a null model based on independent Bernoulli trials.

Zhang, Wu, Zhang & Lu (2008) adopt polynomial and approximated functions to set the minimum support by a user-defined threshold requirement: this helps the user but still does not eliminate the problem of defining a threshold requirement.

Differently from the standard proposals, Jiang & Deogun (2007) propose a logical framework in which propositional logic and statistical discoveries are combined with a model based on Formal Concept Analysis. They aim to eliminate redundancies in rule discovery.

Differently from the above proposals, in this work we concentrate on the problem of establishing in a statistically sound way the minimum support threshold and in turn the reliability of the probability estimations from databases, viewed as sample collections. In our proposal the user sets parameters which are easier to set in a statistical perspective: the desired level of confidence in the inference of the value of probability, the error tolerance on the measured entities (pattern probabilities) and the cardinality of the sample.

Exploiting Bayes for a New Method of Itemsets Evaluation

In this Section we summarize the theoretical basis on which the contribution of this chapter is based. In the following sections, we will provide some details, present some examples and an experimental section in which the extraction of itemsets from some real datasets is conducted by the proposed framework with the aim to control and guarantee their statistical value.

In this chapter we present a new statistical model whose purpose is to give a solid basis to the extraction of relevant itemsets from the database.

At the same time the model must be implemented efficiently and allow pruning of the itemsets' search-space which is one of the motivations for the adoption of the support measure. Indeed, the satisfaction of the minimum support constraint is a downward-closed property with respect to the itemsets' containment relation: as soon as an itemset does not satisfy the minimum support constraint all the itemsets that contain the current one can be pruned from the search-space. This property can be usefully exploited in the implementation of algorithms that optimize the search for relevant itemsets in the database.

The new model allows the replacement of the support measure. It adopts new criteria to judge the relevance of the information obtained from the database. These criteria are based on the Bayes' Theorem. This allows us to make an estimate of the probability distribution function (PDF) of an itemset (*a priori* probability) starting from the set of observations obtained from the database (*a posteriori* probability). Our criteria are the following.

We consider the *unknown* probability p of an itemset I a random variable p and make an estimate of this probability p based on the observations (obtained *a posteriori*) from the database. The obtained most likely value of this probability p is not the true value, but the most probable value of it. According to Bayes' Theorem, the whole probability distribution function $P(x)$ of the probability of I is a curve centered around the expected value of probability p. The integral of that curve between two values p_1 and p_2 gives the overall probability P that the unknown value of probability p of I is between the two values p_1 and p_2. If, for instance, there is evidence that the most likely value of probability of occurrence of an itemset I in the database is comparable with the error in this estimate (width of the confidence interval of that value) we can conclude that the probability estimation that we have obtained from the database observation is not reliable and further work on it is useless. Furthermore, when the estimate of probability of the current itemset is not reliable, neither will be the estimate of the probability of the itemsets that contain this one because their probability is an even lower quantity. This reliability property is again a downward-closed property that allows us to stop the lattice traversal in depth.

In conclusion, on the basis of a more sound statistical theory with respect to the model based on support threshold, we propose an equivalent in methodology that allows the pruning of the depth of the lattice and retrieval of only the itemsets whose probability estimation is statistically reliable.

Evaluation of the Statistical Significance of Estimates

In this section the problem of verifying whether a given itemset has a sufficient support is discussed. In the introductory section we have discussed the problems regarding how this sufficiency could be established. Furthermore, we said we wish to eliminate the requirement that a unique minimum support threshold must be given to the algorithms of itemset extraction. Indeed, a fixed and unique value of support threshold for all the sets is not realistic: at least, it should depend on the cardinality of the sets or on their PDF. Furthermore, a suitable value for this threshold is expected by the user who may not know how to set it in the given dataset. The choice of a suitable support threshold could be very difficult and at least it requires a careful exploratory work of the distributions of the itemsets in the given dataset. In contrast, he/she may know the error tolerance he/she wants to allow. Therefore, the new model allows the setting of a different minimum threshold of probability for each itemset. This decision is taken automatically by the system on the basis of the most likely value of probability of occurrence of the itemset and of an error tolerance in this estimation given by the user.

In order to simplify presentation, assume, without loss of generality, that $I=\langle ABC\rangle$ is the considered itemset. The estimation of the unknown probability of $\langle ABC \rangle$, must be verified in order to avoid that $\langle ABC \rangle$ is accepted even when the probability of error is relatively large. A solution is here proposed.

The estimation of the unknown probability of $\langle ABC \rangle$, denoted as p, is $\dfrac{K}{N}$, with $K = n_{ABC}$ the absolute number of occurrences of $\langle ABC \rangle$ in the database and N the total number of observations contained in the database.

Let $f(p|K)$ denote the conditional *a posteriori* probability density function of the occurrence of $I = \langle ABC \rangle$, if $K = n_{ABC}$ is the observed number of occurrences of the same itemset I and p is the unknown value of probability of $\langle ABC \rangle$. That is, assuming that n_{ABC} occurrences of I have been observed, the probability that p is between p_1 and p_2 is given by

$$\int_{p_1}^{p_2} f(p|K) \, dp \tag{1}$$

By applying Bayes' Theorem it is possible to prove the following relationship:

$$f(\text{p}|\text{K}) = \frac{p^K (1-p)^{(N-K)} f(p)}{\int_0^1 p^K (1-p)^{(N-K)} f(p) dp} \tag{2}$$

where N is the total number of observations in the database and $f(p)$ is the a priori probability density function of p.

Equation (2) is equivalent to:

$$f(p \mid K) = Cp^K (1-p)^{(N-K)} f(p) \tag{3}$$

where C is a constant.

When the probability p of $\langle ABC \rangle$ is to be evaluated, in the level-wise algorithms, p_{AB}, p_{AC} and p_{BC} have already been determined. Therefore, $f(p)$ can be approximated with a uniform, constant

value between 0 and the minimum among p_{AB}, p_{AC} and p_{BC}. It follows that, by introducing another constant H, we can write:

$$f(p \mid K) = Hp^K (1-p)^{(N-K)} \tag{4}$$

where $f(p|K)$ has a single maximum for the most likely value of $p = K/N$.

$f(p|K)$ can be calculated as a function of p by applying Equation (4). Thus, we can determine two values p_1 and p_2 of p such that Equation (1) exceeds a given threshold given by the user (for example 0.9). This threshold is the probability that the true value of p lies effectively in the interval $[p_1, p_2]$. If $(p_1 - p_2)$, the size of the possible values of p, appears to be relatively large with respect to the estimation $\dfrac{K}{N}$, then such estimation cannot be accepted. In this case, the size N of the considered database used as a sample for this estimation is too small and not sufficient for a reasonable estimation from a statistical point of view. It follows that also the estimations of the probabilities of the itemsets that contain $\langle ABC \rangle$ (and that are descendants of $\langle ABC \rangle$ in the itemsets lattice) will not be acceptable as well. Indeed, since they are at least equal to (or lower than) p of $\langle ABC \rangle$ consequently the error on the estimation of these quantities will be proportionally greater.

A Simplified Criterion for the Test

From the viewpoint of the computational workload, the computation of Equation (4) is heavier than the minimum support test, that involves for each itemset only a simple comparison between the itemset support value and the support threshold. In order to simplify the test of Equation (4) a simplified criterion to establish when the itemset's probability estimation is reliable consists in performing a computation on the confidence interval for the inference on the proportions. Indeed, the probability p of occurrence of an itemset in a database of N transactions can be measured by the statistics on the proportion of K successful outcomes in a series of N trials (where the presence of the itemset in a transaction is a successful outcome and the transactions of the database, or equivalently, the number of database samples, are the trials).

We apply the theory for the inference of the proportion $\frac{K}{N}$ that gives the more likely value of the probability of an itemset. Since in data mining the sample size is always big, we can approximate the binomial distribution, that is the probability distribution function for the proportion estimation, with a normal distribution with mean $\frac{K}{N}$ and variance $\frac{K}{N}\left(1-\frac{K}{N}\right)$:

$$p_o - Z\sqrt{\frac{p_o(1-p_o)}{N}} \le p \le p_o + Z\sqrt{\frac{p_o(1-p_o)}{N}}$$

$$(5)$$

where we denote by p the real probability of the itemset, by p_O the observed proportion *(a posteriori* observation) that constitutes the estimation on the sample of this probability, by N the sample size and by Z the critical value in the normal distribution corresponding to the significance level imposed by the user (usually denoted by α). The usual values of Z are 1.96 or 2.58 corresponding to a probability of making an erroneous inference on the proportion with a dataset composed by a collection of random and independent samples equal respectively to 0.05 and 0.01. From the theory, we have that W, the width of the confidence interval, is the maximum error in the estimation of the proportion, and is given by:

$$W = 2Z\sqrt{\frac{p_o(1-p_o)}{N}}$$

$$(6)$$

Since we allow the user to set both Z and the maximum relative error in the probability estimation that he/she wants to allow, the relative error is given by $e_r = \frac{W}{p_o}$ and results equal to:

$$e_r = \frac{2Z}{\sqrt{N}}\sqrt{\frac{(1-p_o)}{p_o}}$$

$$(7)$$

Range of Observable Probabilities with a Relative Error

e_r is a monotonic decreasing function with the observable probabilities p_O. It means that we can set a certain value of e_r that is the error tolerance the user wishes to allow and we can set the confidence level in the inference of the proportion, that determines a critical Z value (usually set to Z=2.58 corresponding to α=0.01).

Given N, the number of samples that is fixed by the given database, the probabilities that are observable from the database within these constraints are higher than a threshold value, given by the diagram in Figure 1. It plots the lower bound to the observable probabilities in datasets of given size N, in correspondence to different values of e_r. It is evident that this methodology of setting the minimum support threshold is statistically reliable and provides the user a guideline to set this minimum value that usually is difficult to set. Above this support limit the observable probabilities are statistically reliable: it means that the probability of making an error greater than the error tolerance in this inference is controlled and it is lower than the significance level. Furthermore, the estimation error is within the user-established error tolerance. However, under this support limit, the estimation of itemsets probabilities is too risky and subjected to a too higher error (outside of the error tolerance).

Figure 1. Observable probabilities by relative error

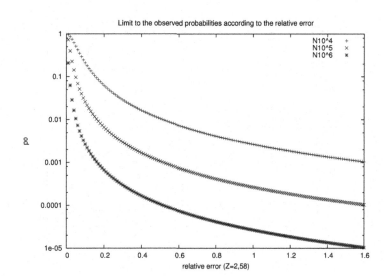

Limit to the Possibility of Observing Rare Patterns

This theory provides a limit to the observable probabilities. Given the database size, the relative error and the confidence level, there exists an intrinsic limit to the observable probabilities. This means that the rare itemsets that we wish to observe from the data are determined by the relative error and by the database size.

If we wish to push down the value of probability of rare itemsets that we want to estimate from the dataset, and we wish to keep the estimation error lower than a certain relative error, we need a dataset which is of progressively higher sizes. For instance, in a dataset of $N=10^5$ samples, with a relative error equal to 0.15 and a significance level equal to 0.01 (corresponding to $Z=2.58$) the observable rare itemsets cannot have a probability lower than 0.01. Instead, if the database size is $N=10^6$ we could observe rare itemsets characterized by probability values even 10 times lower (0.001). In Figure 2 we plot from Equation (7) the relationship between the relative error e_r and the sample size N that determines the observ-

able probabilities p_o. For instance, rare itemsets of probability equal to 10^{-2} are observable in a database of 10^5 samples with a relative error equal to 0.15 while in a database of size 10^6 are observable much more precisely, with a relative error equal to 0.05.

In Figure 3 we plot the function that returns the support limit to the observable probabilities p_O with respect to the database size n and the user desired error tolerance e_r. Again, we can observe that as soon as the database size increases, at the same level of error tolerance e_r, the observable probabilities can be progressively decreased. For instance, with a relative error equal to 5%, rare itemsets occurring with probability of 0.2 are observable even in a database of 10 thousand samples, while if we want to observe with the same relative error rare itemsets of probability equal to 0.025 we need a database of at least 100 thousand samples.

Computational Complexity

From the viewpoint of the computational complexity, the simplified criterion that we have proposed

Figure 2. Sample size necessary to observe rare patterns with a given relative error

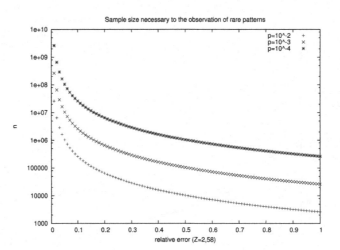

for the evaluation of the statistical significance of the probability estimates is computationally comparable to the classical support test. The difference in the two methods lies in the ability of our method to establish theoretically the support threshold in a significant, reliable way, taking into consideration the size of the database and the error tolerance in the probability estimates the user wishes to allow.

However, the statistical validity of this new test is superior than the classical test that involves a unique, constant support threshold for all the possible itemsets and is not aware of the real reliability of the outcome.

Rationale

The rationale of the approach described here is motivated by the fact that the data mining analyst essentially uses the database to make an estimate of an unknown quantity, the probability of finding an itemset I in a random observation

Figure 3. Observable probabilities in a given sample size

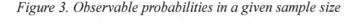

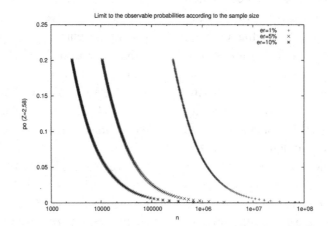

of the database. But the database itself is in turn a sample of all the possible outcomes and there is no certainty that the computed value of probability obtained from the database observations is near to the true value. In general, if the sample is too little, and the probability density function of an itemset is relatively large with respect to its most likely value, then the probability estimation will not be reliable enough. This situation must be recognized and rejected by a correct statistical approach.

Notice that there is a difference between the known algorithms such as *Apriori* and the technique proposed here. Indeed, in those algorithms the minimum support is heuristically defined as a constant, independently of the length of the itemsets, (and indeed, often the user has problems in finding a suitable value for it) whereas here the threshold for the support might be selectively chosen, by the statistical method itself, for any different itemset.

Finally, the proposed simplified test is a pragmatic way to test the sharpness of the probability density function $f(p|K)$ around its most likely value K/N.

Experiments

In this Section we present the application of the theory in some experiments on real datasets. We take two publicly available datasets that are well known in the literature because they have very different characteristics. The first one is *retail*, a sparse dataset provided by Tom Brijs (Hasselt University) available from the repository of the Frequent Itemset Mining competition (http://fimi.

cs.helsinki.fi/data/). It contains the anonymised transaction records of customers' purchases in a real retail store in Belgium. The second one is *connect-4*, a dense dataset coming from the Machine Learning Repository of University of Irvine (http://archive.ics.uci.edu/ml/). It contains all legal 8-ply positions in the game of connect-4 in which neither player has won yet, and in which the next move is not forced. These two datasets have a comparable number of samples but different number of items and average length of itemsets. Table 1 reports the characteristics of the two datasets as well as the number of closed itemsets with their average length obtained with the specified minimum support threshold. Closed itemsets have been defined as the itemsets whose supersets do not have the same support. Of course, it makes sense to consider only the closed itemsets, since the non-closed ones, by definition, have the same frequency and constitute a sort of redundancy in the set of itemsets extracted from a dataset.

Our experiments aim to highlight that when we estimate the probability of itemsets from a sample database and we set the support threshold in a safe zone, i.e., above the theoretical limit of observable probabilities given the sample size, error tolerance and confidence level, the mean error that we make in the estimation is lower than the mean error that we make in the non-safe zone, i.e., when the minimum support threshold is too low, under the theoretical limit, and the estimated probabilities are under the support limit.

In order to simulate the estimation of probabilities from a sample database, we took 100 random samples of 10% of each dataset (with replacement) and we ran on each sample the

Table 1. Datasets characteristics

Dataset Name	Number of samples (transaction)	Number of items	Number of (closed) itemsets	Average Itemsets Length	Minimum support threshold
connect-4	67557	129	758644	14.67	0.25
retail	88162	16470	160	1.78	0.01

algorithm of frequent itemsets mining with the same support threshold (in percentage) indicated in Table 1.

We computed the theoretical support limit in the two datasets, applying our model and obtained the values indicated in Table 2 (column *Observable probabilities limit*). We applied the error tolerance of 0.005 and of 0.06 respectively in *connect-4* and in *retail* and a confidence level of 99%. These two different values of error tolerance are due to the different values of typical support of itemsets observed in the two datasets (the sparse dataset has lower typical support values than the dense dataset). Thus Table 2 tells us that with a low error tolerance equal to 0.005, suitable for a dense dataset like *connect-4* with itemsets characterized by high support values, we cannot observe rare itemsets characterized by probability values lower than 0.81. Instead, in a sparse dataset like *retail*, with itemsets characterized by lower support values on average, it is meaningful to set a higher relative error: we set it equal to 0.06 in order to observe approximately the same number of itemsets observed in the other dataset, connect-4. In these conditions, it is possible to observe much more rare itemsets, occurring with lower probability values, but not lower than the limit to the observable probabilities which is 0.023.

We computed the absolute difference between the probability of each itemset i in the original dataset (denoted by $p(i)$) and the probability of the same itemset in each sample j (estimated probability $p_o(i|j)$). This difference allows us to compute the relative error that we commit in the estimation as follows:

$$e_r(i\mid j) = \frac{\mid p(i) - p_o(i\mid j)\mid}{p_o(i\mid j)} \qquad (8)$$

We normalized with respect to $p_o(i|j)$ and not with respect to $p(i)$ because several itemsets occurred in a sample but not in the original dataset and in this case their probability $p(i)$ would have been zero, leading to an infinite difference. Finally

we computed the mean of all the errors in each sample and then on all the samples as follows:

$$\overline{e_r} = \frac{1}{N_j}\frac{1}{N_i}\sum_j\sum_i \frac{\mid p(i) - p_o(i\mid j)\mid}{p_o(i\mid j)} \qquad (9)$$

where by i we denote the itemset, by j the sample and by N_i and N_j respectively the number of samples j and the number of itemsets in sample j.

We report the experimental results in Table 2.

1. First, it is evident that the probability estimation of the itemsets is contained within the error tolerance established by the user only in the safe zone determined by the theoretical limit to the observable probabilities. Outside this safe zone, the probability estimation is outside the error tolerance.
2. Second, but not less important, the mean error is lower in the safe zone than in the non-safe one.
3. Finally, we can observe that the difference between the mean error in the non-safe zone and in the safe zone is lower in the dense dataset than in the sparse one. This is expected since in dense data there is a huge number of itemsets, with similar support values. Thus it happens that both above and under the support limit many itemsets occur with similar values of support.

With these experiments we showed that with the aid of the proposed theory we were able to set a support limit to the observable rare itemsets in such as way that it allows the computation of a mean error in the estimation of the itemsets probabilities which is controlled by the user by a fixed error tolerance. Furthermore, this error is lower than the error committed on the same database sample when the support threshold is established at a too low level, not compatible with the sample size and the error tolerance required by the user.

Table 2. Experimental results on mean estimation error in different probabilities intervals (safe vs non).

Dataset Name	Error tolerance	Observable probabilities limit	Mean error in safe zone	Mean error in non-safe zone
connect-4	0.005	0.81	0.3063	0.3178
retail	0.06	0.023	0.0666	0.1869

CONCLUSION

In this chapter we have proposed a new model for the replacement of support in the evaluation of association rules. The proposed model, like support, is used to select reliable rules and also to prune the itemsets lattice. It is founded on criteria based on Bayes' Theorem. This powerful and well-known theorem allows us to make an estimation of the *a priori* probability density function of an itemset – an unknown curve centered around the most likely value, obtained according to the observations made on the database (*a posteriori* occurrence frequency of the itemset).

According to our criteria, the information we have obtained from the database on an itemset is reliable if and only if the size of the confidence interval of the estimated probability is low in comparison with the most likely value of probability. The rationale for this is that the narrower the *a posteriori* PDF around its expected value, the more probable will be the estimate. This criterion is implemented by the introduction of the relative error parameter e_r. We have shown an approximate technique based on the application of the normal probability density function for the inference of the probability of itemsets in sample databases. We verified these criteria in an experiment on two real datasets with different characteristics. We have shown that the technique not only is computationally comparable to the support threshold test but it is also statistically and empirically reliable because it results in a controlled and lower mean estimation error. Finally, with our model we are able to determine which rare itemsets a sample dataset allows us to observe safely, i.e., within the limits of the confidence interval for the inference validity.

In future work we plan to extract not only statistically significant itemsets but also significant association rules, by putting under control also the value of confidence.

REFERENCES

Aggarwal, C. C., & Yu, P. S. (1998). A new framework for itemset generation. In *Proceedings of the PODS Intl. Conference*, Seattle, WA, USA.

Agrawal, R., Imielinski, T., & Swami (1993, May). A. Mining association rules between sets of items in large databases. In *Proc. ACM SIGMOD Conference on Management of Data* (pp. 207–216), Washington, D.C., British Columbia.

Aumann, Y., & Lindell, Y. (1999). A statistical theory for quantitative association rules. In *Proceedings of ACM Intl. Conference KDD*, San Diego, CA, USA.

Hahsler, M., & Hornik, K. (2007). New Probabilistic Interest Measures for Association Rules. *Intelligent Data Analysis*, *11*(5), 437–455.

Jiang, L., & Deogun, J. (2007). SPICE: A New Framework for Data Mining based on Probability Logic and Formal Concept Analysis. *Fundam. Inf.*, *78*(4), 467–485.

Lee, W., Stolfo, S., & Mok, K. (1998). Mining audit data to build intrusion detection models. In *Proceedings of ACM Intl. Conference KDD*.

Lin, W., Alvarez, S., & Ruiz, C. (2002). Efficient adaptive-support association rule mining for recommender systems. *Data Mining and Knowledge Discovery, 6*(3), 83–105. doi:10.1023/A:1013284820704

Liu, B., Hsu, W., & Ma, Y. (1999a). Mining association rules with multiple minimum supports. In *Proceedings of ACM Intl. Conference KDD*, San Diego, CA, USA.

Liu, B., Hsu, W., Ma, Y., & Chen, S. (1999b). Mining interesting knowledge using DM-II. In *Proceedings of ACM Intl. Conference KDD*, San Diego, CA, USA.

Mannila, H., & Pavlov, D. (1999). Prediction with local patterns using cross-entropy. In *Proceedings of ACM Intl. Conference KDD*, San Diego, CA, USA.

Meo, R. (2000). Theory of dependence values. *ACM Transactions on Database Systems, 25*(3), September 2000.

Morishita, S., & Sese, J. (2000). Traversing itemset lattices with statistical metric pruning. In *Proceedings of the POD Intl. Conference*, Dallas, TX, USA.

Omiecinski, E. R. (2003). Alternative interest measures for mining associations in databases. *IEEE TKDE, 15*(1), 57–69.

Papoulis, A. (1965). *Probability, Random variables, and Stochastic Processes*. McGraw-Hill, Inc.

Park, J., Yu, P., & Chen, M.-S. (1997). Mining association rules with adjustable accuracy. In *Proceedings of the CIKM Intl. Conference*, Las Vegas, Nevada, USA.

Roddick, J., & Rice, S. (2001). What's interesting about cricket? – on thresholds and anticipation in discovered rules. *SIGKDD Explorations, 3*, 1–5. doi:10.1145/507533.507535

Shyu, M.-L., Chen, S.-C., & Kashyap, R. (1999). Discovering quasi-equivalence relationships from database systems. In *Proceedings of the CIKM Intl. Conference*, Kansas City, Mo, USA.

Siebes, A. (1994). *Homogeneous discoveries contain no surprises: Inferring risk-profiles from large databases*. Technical report, Computer Science Department/Department of Algorithmics and Architecture, CWI, The Netherlands.

Silverstein, C., Brin, S., & Motwani, R. (1998). Beyond market baskets: generalizing association rules to dependence rules. *Data Mining and Knowledge Discovery, 2*(1), 39–68. doi:10.1023/A:1009713703947

Steinbach, M., Tan, P., Xiong, H., & Kumar, V. (2004). Generalizing the notion of support. *Proc. ACM SIGKDD 2004* (pp. 689–694).

Tan, P., Kumar, V., & Srivastava, J. (2002, July). Selecting the right interestingness measure for association patterns. In *Proc. of the Eight ACM SIGKDD*.

Wang, K., He, Y., Cheung, D. W.-L., & Chin, F. (2001). Mining confident rules without support requirement. In *Proc. ACM CIKM*, (pp. 89–96).

Webb, G. I. (2006). Discovering significant rules. In *Proc. of the Twelfth ACM SIGKDD* (pp. 434-443).

Zhang, S., Wu, X., Zhang, C., & Lu, J. (2008). Computing the minimum-support for mining frequent patterns. *Knowledge and Information Systems, 15*(2), 233–257. doi:10.1007/s10115-007-0081-7

Chapter 4
Effective Mining of Weighted Fuzzy Association Rules

Maybin Muyeba
Manchester Metropolitan University, UK

M. Sulaiman Khan
Liverpool Hope University, UK

Frans Coenen
University of Liverpool, UK

ABSTRACT

A novel approach is presented for effectively mining weighted fuzzy association rules (ARs). The authors address the issue of invalidation of downward closure property (DCP) in weighted association rule mining where each item is assigned a weight according to its significance wrt some user defined criteria. Most works on weighted association rule mining do not address the downward closure property while some make assumptions to validate the property. This chapter generalizes the weighted association rule mining problem with binary and fuzzy attributes with weighted settings. Their methodology follows an Apriori approach but employs T-tree data structure to improve efficiency of counting itemsets. The authors' approach avoids pre and post processing as opposed to most weighted association rule mining algorithms, thus eliminating the extra steps during rules generation. The chapter presents experimental results on both synthetic and real-data sets and a discussion on evaluating the proposed approach.

INTRODUCTION

Association rules (ARs) (Agrawal, Imielinski & Swami, 1993) are a well established data mining technique used to discover co-occurrences of items mainly in market basket data. An item is usually a product amongst a list of other products and an itemset is a combination of two or more products.

The items in the database are usually recorded as binary data (present or not present). The technique aims to find association rules (with strong support and high confidence) in large databases. Classical Association Rule Mining (ARM) deals with the relationships among the items present in transactional databases (Agrawal & Srikant, 1994; Bodon, 2003). Typically, the algorithm first generates all large (frequent) itemsets (attribute sets) from which association rule (AR) sets are derived. A

DOI: 10.4018/978-1-60566-754-6.ch004

large itemset is defined as one that occurs more frequently in the given data set according to a user supplied support threshold. To limit the number of ARs generated, a confidence threshold is used to limit the number by careful selection of the support and confidence thresholds. By so doing, care must be taken to ensure that itemsets with low support but from which high confidence rules may be generated are not omitted. We define the problem as follows:

Given a set of items $I = \{i_1, i_2, ..., i_m\}$ and a database of transactions $D = \{t_1, t_2, ..., t_n\}$ where $t_i = \{I_{i1}, I_{i2}, ..., I_{ip}\}$, $p \leq m$ and $I_{ij} \in I$ if $X \subseteq I$ with $k = |X|$ is called a k-itemset or simply an itemset. Let a database D be a multi-set of subsets of I as shown. Each supports an itemset $X \subseteq I$ if $X \subseteq T$ holds. An association rule is an expression $X \Rightarrow Y$, where X, Y are item sets and $X \cap Y = \varnothing$ holds. Number of transactions T supporting an item X w.r.t D is called support of X, $Supp(X) = |\{T \in D \mid X \subseteq T\}| / |D|$. The strength or confidence (c) for an association rule $X \Rightarrow Y$ is the ratio of the number of transactions that contain $X \cup Y$ to the number of transactions that contain X, $Conf(X \rightarrow Y) = Supp(X \cup Y) / Supp(X)$.

For non-binary items, fuzzy association rule mining (firstly expressed as quantitative association rule mining (Srikant & Agrawal, 1996) has been proposed using fuzzy sets such that quantitative and categorical attributes can be handled (Kuok, Fu & Wong, 1998). A fuzzy rule represents each item as $< item, value >$ pair. Fuzzy association rules are expressed in the following form:

If X is A satisfies Y is B

For example,

if (age is young) $\rightarrow$ (salary is low)

Given a database T, attributes I with itemsets $X \subset I, Y \subset I$ and $X = \{x_1, x_2, ... x_n\}$ and $Y = \{y_1, y_2, ... y_n\}$ and $X \cap Y = \varnothing$, we can define fuzzy sets $A = \{fx_1, fx_2, ..., fx_n\}$ and $B = \{fx_1, fx_2, ..., fx_n\}$ associated with X and Y respectively. For example (X, A) could be *(age, young)*, *(age, old)* and (Y, B) as *(salary, high)* etc.

The semantics of the fuzzy rule is that when the antecedent "X is A" is satisfied, we can imply that "Y is B" is also satisfied, which means there are sufficient records that contribute their counts to the attribute fuzzy set pairs and the sum of these counts is greater than the user specified threshold.

However, the classical ARM framework assumes that all items have the same significance or importance.

In which case their weight within a transaction or record is the same (weight=1) which is not always the case. For example, from Table 1, the rule [printer $\rightarrow$ computer, 50%] may be more important than [scanner $\rightarrow$ computer, 75%] even though the former holds a lower support because those items in the first rule usually come with more profit per unit sale.

The main challenge in weighted ARM is validating the "downward closure property (DCP)" which is crucial for the efficient iterative process of generating and pruning frequent itemsets from subsets. The holding concept of DCP is that every frequent itemset means that their subsets are also frequent. In this chapter, we address the issue of DCP in Weighted ARM. We generalize and solve the problem of downward closure property for

Table 1. Weighted items database

ID	Item	Profit	Weight	...
1	Scanner	10	0.1	...
2	Printer	30	0.3	...
3	Monitor	60	0.6	...
4	Computer	90	0.9	...

Table 2. Transactions

TID	Items
1	1,2,4
2	2,3
3	1,2,3,4
4	1,3,4

databases with binary and quantitative items; use t-tree data structures to efficiently handle itemsets and then evaluate the proposed approach with experimental results.

This chapter is an amalgamation of the material presented in (Khan, Muyeba & Coenen, 2008) and (Muyeba, Khan & Coenen, 2008) with additional details provided on the structure and experimental results.

The chapter is organised as follows: section 2 presents background and related work; section 3 gives problem definition for weighted ARM with binary and fuzzy data and details weighted downward closure property; section 4 gives frameworks comparison; section 5 reviews experimental evaluation and section 8 concludes the chapter.

BACKGROUND AND RELATED WORK

In association rule mining literature, weights of items are mostly treated as equally important i.e. weight one (1) is assigned to each item until recently where some approaches generalize this and give item weights to reflect their significance to the user (Lu, Hu, & Li 2001). The weights may be as a result of particular promotions for such items or their profitability etc. There are two approaches for analyzing data sets with weighted settings: pre- and post-processing. Post processing handles firstly the non-weighted problem (weights=1) and then perform the pruning process later. Pre-processing prunes the non-frequent itemsets after each iteration using weights. The issue in post-processing weighted ARM is that first; items are scanned without considering their weights and later, the rule base is checked for frequent weighted ARs. By doing this, we end up with a very limited itemset pool to check weighted ARs and potentially missing many itemsets.

In pre-processed classical ARM, itemsets are pruned by checking frequent ones against weighted support after every scan. This results in less rules

being produced as compared to post processing because many potential frequent super sets are missed. In (Cai et al., 1998) a post-processing model is proposed with two algorithms proposed to mine itemsets with normalized and un-normalized weights. The authors use a k-support bound metric to ensure validity of the DCP but does not guarantee that every subset of a frequent set will be frequent unless the k-support bound value of (k-1) subsets was higher than (k).

An efficient mining methodology for Weighted Association Rules (WAR) is proposed in (Wang, Yang & Yu, 2000). A Numerical attribute was assigned for each item where the weight of the item was defined as part of a particular weight domain. For example, soda[4,6] → snack[3,5] means that if a customer purchases soda in the quantity between 4 and 6 bottles, he is likely to purchase 3 to 5 bags of snacks. WAR uses a post-processing approach by deriving the maximum weighted rules from frequent itemsets. Post WAR doesn't interfere with the process of generating frequent itemsets but focuses on how weighted AR's can be generated by examining weighting factors of items included in generated frequent itemsets.

Similar techniques for weighted fuzzy association rule mining are presented in (Lu, 2002; Wang & Zhang, 2003; Yue et al., 2000). In (Gyenesei, 2000), a two-fold pre processing approach is used where firstly, quantitative attributes are discretised into different fuzzy linguistic intervals and weights assigned to each linguistic label. A mining algorithm is applied then on the resulting dataset by applying two support measures for normalized and un-normalized cases. The downward closure property is addressed by using the z-potential frequent subset for each candidate set. An arithmetic mean is used to find the possibility of frequent k+1 itemset, which is not guaranteed to validate the valid downward closure property.

Another significance framework that handles DCP is proposed in (Tao, Murtagh & Farid, 2003). Weighting spaces were introduced as inner-transaction spaces, item spaces and transaction spaces, in which items can be weighted depending on different scenarios and mining focus. In this framework, however, support is calculated by only considering the transactions that contribute to the itemset. Further, no discussions were made on interestingness issue of the rules produced.

In this chapter, we present an approach to mine weighted binary and quantitative data (by fuzzy means) to address the issue of invalidation of DCP. We then show that using the proposed technique, rules can be generated efficiently with a valid DCP without any biases found in pre- or post-processing approaches.

PROBLEM DEFINITION

In this section, we define terms and basic concepts for item weight, itemset transaction weight, weighted support and weighted confidence for both binary (boolean attributes) and fuzzy (quantitative) data. The technique for binary data is termed as Binary Weighted Association Rule Mining (BWARM) and that for fuzzy data Fuzzy Weighted Association Rule mining (FWARM). Interested readers can see (Muyeba, Khan & Coenen, 2008) for formal definitions and more details.

Binary Weighted Association Rule Mining (BWARM)

Let the input data D with transactions $t = \{t_1, t_2,..,t_n\}$ have a set of items $I = \{i_1, i_2,.., i_{|I|}\}$ and a set of positive real numbered weights $W = \{w_1, w_2,.., w_{|I|}\}$ corresponding to each item i. Each ith transaction t_i is some subset of I and a weight w is attached to each item $t_i[i_j]$ (j^{th} item in the "i^{th}" transaction). A pair (i, w) is called a weighted item where $i \in I$ and the "" item's weight in the "" transaction is given by $t_i[i_j[w]]$.

We illustrate the terms and concepts using Tables 3 and 4. Table 3 contains 10 transactions of up to 5 items. Table 4 has corresponding weights

corresponding to each item i in T. We use sum of votes (counts) for each itemset by aggregating weights per item as a standard approach (Tao, Murtagh & Farid 2003).

Definition 1. Item Weight is a non-negative real value given to each item ranging [0..1] with some degree of importance, a weight .

Definition 2. Itemset Transaction Weight is the aggregated weight of all the items in the itemset present in a single transaction. Itemset transaction weight for an itemset X can be calculated as:

$$vote\ for\ t_i\ satisfying\ X = \prod_{k=1}^{|x|} \left(\forall [t[w]] \in X \right) t_i[i_k[w]]$$

(1)

Itemset transaction weight of itemset (A, B) from Table 4 is calculated as: $ITW(A, b) = 0.6 x 0.9 = 0.54$. We can use other aggregation operators other than product but we choose this for simplistic reasons and for easy compliance with the DCP property.

Definition 3. *Weighted Support WS* is the aggregated sum of itemset transaction weight *ITW* of all the transactions in which itemset is present, divided by the total number of transactions. It is calculated as:

$$WS(X) = \frac{\sum_{i=1}^{n} \prod_{k=1}^{|x|} \left(\forall [t[w]] \in X \right) t_i[i_k[w]]}{n}$$

(2)

Table 3. Transactional database

T	Items	T	Items
t_1	A B C D	t_6	A B C D E
t_2	B D	t_7	B C E
t_3	A D	t_8	D E
t_4	C	t_9	A C D
t_5	A B D E	t_{10}	B C D E

Table 4. Items with weights

Items i	Item Weights *(IW)*
A	0.60
B	0.90
C	0.30
D	0.10
E	0.20

WS of itemset (A, B) is calculated as:
$$\frac{0.54 + 0.54 + 0.54}{10} = 0.162$$

Definition 4.*Weighted Confidence WC is* the ratio of sum of votes satisfying both $X \cup Y$ to the sum of votes satisfying X. It is formulated (with $Z = X \cup Y$) as:

$$WC(X \rightarrow Y) = \frac{WS(Z)}{WS(X)} = \sum_{i=1}^{n} \frac{\prod_{k=1}^{|Z|} (\forall[z[w]] \in Z) t_i[z_k[w]]}{\prod_{k=1}^{|X|} (\forall[i[w]] \in X) t_i[x_k[w]]}$$

(3)

Weighted Confidence of itemset (A, B) is calculated with $WS(A) = \dfrac{5 * 0.6}{10} = 0.3$ as
$WS(A, B) = \dfrac{WS(A \cup B)}{WS(A)} = \dfrac{0.16}{0.30} = 0.54$

Fuzzy Weighted Association Rule Mining (FWARM)

A fuzzy dataset D' consists of fuzzy transactions $T' = \{t_1, t_2, .., t_n\}$ with fuzzy sets associated with each item in $I = \{i_1, i_2, .., i_{|I|}\}$, which is identified by a set of linguistic *labels* $L = \{l_1, l_2, .., l_{|I|}\}$ (for example $L = \{small, medium, l \arg e\}$). We assign a weight w to each l in L associated with i. Each attribute $t'_i[i_j]$ is associated (to some degree) with several fuzzy sets. The degree of association is given by a *membership value* in the range [0..1], which indicates the correspondence

between the value of a given $t'_i[i_j]$ and the set of *fuzzy linguistic labels*. The "k^{th}"weighted fuzzy set for the "j^{th}" item in the "i^{th}" fuzzy transaction is given by $t'_i[i_j[l_k[w]]]$.

We illustrate the fuzzy weighted ARM definition terms and concepts using Tables 5 and 6. Table 5 contains transactions for 2 quantitative items discretised into two overlapped intervals with fuzzy values. Table 6 has corresponding weights associated to each fuzzy item *i[l]* in *T*.

Definition 5. *Fuzzy Item Weight FIW is* a non-negative value in the range [0..1] attached to each fuzzy set wrt some degree of importance (Table 6). Weight of a fuzzy set for an item i_j is denoted as $i_j[l_k[w]]$

Definition 6.*Fuzzy Itemset Transaction Weight FITW is* the aggregated weights of all the fuzzy sets associated with items in the itemset present in a single transaction. Fuzzy Itemset transaction weight for an itemset (*X, A*) can be calculated as:

$$\text{vote for } t'_i \text{ satisfying } X = \prod_{k=1}^{|L|} (\forall[i[l[w]]] \in X) t'_i[i_j[l_k[w]]]$$

(4)

Let's take an example of itemset <(X, Medium), (Y, Small)> denoted by (X, Medium) as *A* and (Y, Small) as *B*. Fuzzy Itemset transaction weightof itemset (A, B) in transaction 1 is calculated as:

$$FITW(A, B) = (0.5x0.7)x(0.2x0.5) = 0.035$$

Table 5. Fuzzy transactional database

TID	X		Y	
	Small	Medium	Small	Medium
t_1	0.5	0.5	0.2	0.8
t_2	0.9	0.1	0.4	0.6
t_3	1.0	0.0	0.1	0.9
t_4	0.3	0.7	0.5	0.5

Table 6. Fuzzy items with weights

Fuzzy Items *i[l]*	Weights *(IW)*
(X, Small)	0.9
(X, Medium)	0.7
(Y, Small)	0.5
(Y, Medium)	0.3

Definition 7. *Fuzzy Weighted Support FWS* is the aggregated sum of *FITW* of all the transaction's itemsets present divided by the total number of transactions, represented as:

$$FWS(X) = \frac{\sum_{i=1}^{|L|} \left(\forall_{[i[l[w]]] \in X} \right) t_i{}'[i_j[l_k[w]]]}{n} \quad (5)$$

FWS of itemset (A, B) is calculated as:

$$FWS(A, B) = \frac{0.297}{4} = 0.074$$

Definition 8. *Fuzzy Weighted Confidence FWC* is the ratio of sum of votes satisfying both $X \cup Y$ to the sum of votes satisfying X with $Z = X \cup Y$ and given as:

$$FWC(X \to Y) = \frac{FWS(Z)}{FWS(X)} = \sum_{i=1}^{n} \frac{\prod_{k=1}^{|Z|} (\forall_{[z[w]] \in Z}) t_i{}'[z_k[w]]}{\prod_{k=1}^{|X|} (\forall_{[i[w]] \in X}) t_i{}'[x_k[w]]} \quad (6)$$

FWC of itemset (A, B) is calculated as:

$$FWC(A, B) = \frac{0.074}{0.227} = 0.325$$

Weighted Downward Closure Property (DCP)

In classical ARM algorithm, it is assumed that if the itemset is large, then all its subsets should be large, a principle called downward closure property (DCP). For example, in classical ARM using DCP, it states that if AB and BC are not frequent, then ABC and BCD cannot be frequent, consequently their supersets are of no value as they will contain non-frequent itemsets. This helps algorithm to generate large itemsets of increasing size by adding items to itemsets that are already large. In the weighted ARM where each item is given a weight, the DCP does not hold in a straightforward manner. Because of the weighted support, an itemset may be large even though some of its subsets are not large and we illustrate this in Table 7.

In Table 7, all frequent itemsets are generated using 30% support threshold. In column two, itemset {ACD} and {BDE} are frequent with support 30% and 36% respectively. And all of their subsets {AC}, {AD}, {CD} and {BD}, {BE}, {DE} are frequent as well. But in column 3 with weighted settings, itemsets {AC}, {CD} and {DE} are no longer frequent and thus violates the DCP.

We argue that the DCP with binary and quantitative data can be validated using the proposed approach. We prove this by showing that if an itemset is not frequent, then its superset cannot be frequent and $WS(subset) \geq WS(\sup erset)$ is always true (see Table 7, column 4, Proposed Weighted ARM, only the itemsets are frequent with frequent subsets). A formal proof and more detailed description of the weighted DCP is given in (Muyeba, Khan & Coenen, 2008).

Frameworks Comparison

In this section, we give a comparative analysis of frequent itemset generation between classical ARM, weighted ARM and the proposed binary and fuzzy ARM frameworks. In Table 7 all the possible itemsets are generated using Tables 3 and 4 (i.e. 31 itemsets from 5 items), and the frequent itemsets generated using classical ARM (column 2), weighted ARM (column 3) and proposed weighted ARM framework (column 4). Column 1 in Table 7 shows itemset's ids.

A support threshold for classical ARM is set to 30% and for classical WARM and proposed

Weighted ARM it is set to 0.3 and 0.03 respectively). Itemsets with a highlighted background indicate frequent itemsets. This experiment is conducted in order to illustrate the effect of item's occurrences and their weights on the generated rules.

Frequent itemsets in column 3 are generated using classical weighted ARM pre-processing technique. In this process all the frequent itemsets are generated first with count support and then those frequent itemsets are pruned using their weights. In this case only itemsets are generated from the itemset pool that is already frequent using their count support. Itemsets with shaded background and white text are those that WARM does not consider because they are not frequent using count support. But with weighted settings they may be frequent due to significance associated with them. Also, the generated itemsets do not hold DCP as described in sect. 3.2.

In column 4 frequent itemsets are generated using proposed weighted ARM framework. It is noted that the itemsets generated are mostly frequent using count support technique and interestingly included fewer rules like {AB→C} that is not frequent, which shows that the non-frequent itemsets can be frequent with weighted settings due to their significance in the data set even if they are not frequent using count support.

In column 4, itemsets {A→B} and {B→C} are frequent due to high weight and support count in transactions. It is interesting to have a rule {B→D} because D has very low weight (0.1) but it has the highest count support i.e. 80% and it appears more with item B than any other item i.e. with 50% support. Another aspect to note is that, B is highly significant (0.9) with high support count (60%). These kinds of rules can be helpful in "Cross-Marketing" and "Loss Leader Analysis" in real life applications.

Also the itemsets generated using our approach holds valid DCP as shown in sect. 3.2. Table 7 gives a concrete example of our approach and we now perform experiments based on this analysis.

Weighted Apriori-T Algorithm (WAT)

The proposed Weighted Apriori-T ARM (WAT) algorithm is developed using T-tree data structures (Coenen, Leng, & Goulbourne, 2004) and works in a fashion similar to the Apriori algorithm (Agrawal & Srikant, 1994). The WAT algorithm consists of two major steps:

1. Apply Apriori-T association rule mining algorithm using weighted support measures of the form described above to produce a set of frequent item sets F.
2. Process F and generate a set of weighted ARs R such that $\forall r \in R$ the interestingness threshold (confidence as desired by the end user) is above some user specified threshold.

The Fuzzy Apriori-T algorithm (Apriori-Total) is founded on a tree structure called the T-tree (Coenen, Leng & Ahmed 2004). This is a set enumeration tree structure in which to store frequent item set information. What distinguishes the T-tree from other set enumeration tree structures is:

1. Levels in each sub-branch of the tree are defined using arrays. This thus permits "indexing in" at all levels and consequently offers computational advantages.
2. To aid this indexing the tree is built in "reverse". Each branch is founded on the last element of the frequent sets to be stored. This allows direct indexing with attribute number rather than first applying some offset.

Thus given a data set of the form:
{ 1 3 4 }
{ 2 4 5 }
{ 2 4 6 } with weights: 1=0.6, 2=0.1, 3=0.3, 4=0.9, 5=0.2, 6=0.1, and assuming a support count of 0.01, we can identify the following frequent sets (weighted support counts in parenthesis):

1 (0.067)	1 3 (0.060)	4 5 (0.040)
2 (0.056)	1 4 (0.040)	4 6 (0.020)
3 (0.067)	2 4 (0.033)	1 3 4 (0.012)
4 (0.067)	2 5 (0.010)	2 4 5 (0.020)
5 (0.067)	3 4 (0.040)	
6 (0.033)	3 6 (0.030)	

These can be presented in a T-tree of the form given in Figure 1 (note the reverse nature of the tree). The internal representation of this "reverse" T-tree founded on arrays of T-tree nodes that can be conceptualised as shown in Figure 2.

Table 7. Frequent itemsets comparison

ID	Classical ARM	Classical Weighted ARM	Proposed Weighted ARM
1.	A (50%)	A (30%)	A (0.300)
2.	A→B (30%)	A→B (45%)	A→B (0.162)
3.	A→B→C (20%)	A→B→C (36%)	A→B→C (0.032)
4.	A→B→C→D (20%)	A→B→C→D (38%)	A→B→C→D (0.003)
5.	A→B→C→D→E (10%)	A→B→C→D→E (21%)	A→B→C→D→E (0.000)
6.	A→B→C→E (10%)	A→B→C→E (20%)	A→B→C→E (0.003)
7.	A→B→D (30%)	A→B→D (48%)	A→B→D (0.016)
8.	A→B→D→E (20%)	A→B→D→E (36%)	A→B→D→E (0.002)
9.	A→B→E (20%)	A→B→E (34%)	A→B→E (0.022)
10.	A→C (30%)	A→C (27%)	A→C (0.054)
11.	A→C→D (30%)	A→C→D (30%)	A→C→D (0.005)
12.	A→C→D→E (10%)	A→C→D→E (12%)	A→C→D→E (0.000)
13.	A→C→E (10%)	A→C→E (11%)	A→C→E (0.004)
14.	A→D (50%)	A→D (35%)	A→D (0.030)
15.	A→D→E (20%)	A→D→E (18%)	A→D→E (0.002)
16.	A→E (20%)	A→E (16%)	A→E (0.024)
17.	B (60%)	B (54%)	B (0.540)
18.	B→C (40%)	B→C (48%)	B→C (0.108)
19.	B→C→D (30%)	B→C→D (39%)	B→C→D (0.008)
20.	B→C→D→E (20%)	B→C→D→E (30%)	B→C→D→E (0.001)
21.	B→C→E (30%)	B→C→E (42%)	B→C→E (0.016)
22.	B→D (50%)	B→D (50%)	B→D (0.045)
23.	B→D→E (30%)	B→D→E (36%)	B→D→E (0.005)
24.	B→E (40%)	B→E (44%)	B→E (0.072)
25.	C (60%)	C (18%)	C (0.180)
26.	C→D (40%)	C→D (16%)	C→D (0.012)
27.	C→D→E (20%)	C→D→E (12%)	C→D→E (0.001)
28.	C→E (30%)	C→E (15%)	C→E (0.018)
29.	D (80%)	D (8%)	D (0.080)
30.	D→E (40%)	D→E (12%)	D→E (0.008)
31.	E (50%)	E (10%)	E (0.100)

The storage required for each node (representing a frequent set) in the T-tree is then 12 Bytes:

1. Reference to T-tree node structure (4 Bytes)
2. Support count field in T-tree node structure (4 Bytes)
3. Reference to child array field in T-tree node structure (4 Bytes)

Thus house keeping requirements are still 8 Bytes; however storage gains are obtained because it is not necessary to explicitly store individual attribute labels (i.e. column numbers representing instantiated elements) as these are implied by the indexing. Of course this approach must also require storage for "stubs" (4 Bytes) where nodes are missing (unsupported). Overall the storage advantages for this technique is thus, in part, dependent on the number of missing combinations contained in the data set.

We used a generalised version of T-tree data structure and it remains the same for binary and fuzzy data under the weighted settings. The only difference is the way the algorithm calculates support count and generates frequent sets for each binary weighted and the fuzzy weighted approaches.

The T-tree described above is built in an Apriori manner, as proposed in (Coenen, Leng & Goulbourne, 2004), starting with the one item sets and continuing until there are no more candidate N-itemsets. Thus, at a high level, a standard Apriori algorithm is used as shown in Figure 3.

In more detail the Apriori-T algorithm commences with a method createTotalSupportTree which is presented in Figure 4. The method starts by generating the top level of the T-tree (createTtreeTopLevel) and then generating the next level (generateLevel2) from the supported sets in level 1. Remember that if a 1-itemset is not supported none of its super sets will be supported. Once we have generated level 2 further levels can be generated (createTtreeLevelN).

The method to generate the top level of a T-tree is as presented in Figure 5. Note that the method includes a call to a general T-tree utility method pruneLevelN described later.

The generateLevel2 method loops through the

Figure 1. Conceptual example of the T-tree data structure

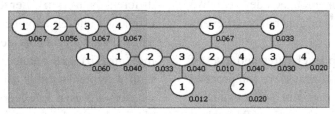

Figure 2. Internal representation of T-tree presented in Figure 1

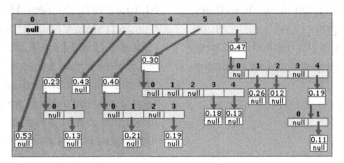

Figure 3. Apriori Algorithm

```
K <-- 1
nextlevelFlag=true;

generate candidate K-itemsets
Loop
    count support values for candidate K-itemsets
    prune unsupported K-itemsets
    K <-- 2
    generate candidate K2 itemsets from previous level
    if no K2 itemsets break
end Loop
```

Figure 4. The createTotalSupportTree method

```
Method: createTotalSupportTree
Arguments: none
Return: none
Fields: NA
------------------------------
createTtreeTopLevel()
generateLevel2()
createTtreeLevelN()
------------------------------
```

top level of the T-tree creating new T-tree arrays where appropriate (i.e. where the immediate parent nodes is supported). The method is outlined in Figure 6. Note that the method includes a call to a general T-tree utility method generateNextLevel() (also described later).

Once we have a top level T-tree and a set of candidate second levels (arrays) we can proceed with generating the rest of the T-tree using an iterative process, the createTtreeLevelN method presented in Figure 7. The createTtreeLevelN() method calls a number of other methods addSupportToTtreeLevelN(), pruneLevelN (also called by the createTtreeTopLevel() method) and generateLevelN() which are presented in Figures 8 and 9 respectively.

Experimental Evaluation

In this section we will test our algorithms with different datasets in order to evaluate the quality, efficiency and effectiveness of our approaches. The experiments are divided into two (i) Quality measures (ii) Performance measures, for datasets with weighted settings. Both synthetic and real datasets are used in experiments. Data sets are obtained as follows: retail (Brijs et al., 1999), T10I4D100K (Dataset 2), Poker Hand (Merz & Murph, 1998), Connect-4 (Merz & Murph, 1998), Connect (Merz & Murph, 1998; DataSet 1), Pumsb (Dataset 2) and Pumsb Star (Dataset 2).

Table 8 characterises the datasets in terms of the number of transactions, the number of distinct items, the average transaction size, and the maximum transaction size. It is worth mentioning that datasets contains sparse and dense data, since

Figure 5. The createTtreeTopLevel method

```
Method: createTtreeTopLevel
Arguments: none
Return: none
Fields: D number of attributes
        startTtreeRef start of T-tree
        dataArray 2D array holding input sets
---------------------------------------
Dimension and initialise top level of T-tree (length = D)

Loop from i = 0 to i = No. of records in dataArray
    Loop from j=0 to j= No. of attributes in dataArray[i]
        startTtreeRef[i][j]++
    End loop
End Loop

pruneLevelN(startTtreeRef,1)
---------------------------------------
```

most association rules discovery algorithms were designed for these types of problems. Weights were generated randomly and assigned to all items in the dataset to show their significance. Both Retail and T10I4D100K datasets (Table 8) were fuzzified to obtain fuzzy sets by using the approach described in (Khan, Muyeba & Coenen, 2008) to generate a fuzzy dataset where each attribute was divided into five different fuzzy sets.

Experiments were undertaken using four different association rule mining algorithms. Four algorithms were used for each approach, namely Binary Weighted Apriori-T (BWAT), Fuzzy Weighted Apriori-T (FWAT), standard ARM as Classical ARM and WARM as post processing weighted ARM algorithm.

For quality measures, we compared the number of frequent itemsets and the interesting rules generated using four algorithms described above. In the second experiment, we showed the scalability of the proposed BWAT and FWAT algorithms by comparing the execution time with BWARM, FWARM and WARM (Muyeba, Khan & Coenen, 2008) by varying user specified support thresholds and size of data (number of records).

Quality Measures

For quality measures, both synthetic and real retail datasets with binary and fuzzy extensions described above were used. Each item is assigned a weight range between [0..1] according to their significance in the dataset.

In Figures 10 and 11, the x-axis shows support thresholds from 2% to 10% and on the y-axis the number of frequent itemsets. Four algorithms are compared, BWAT (Binary Weighted Apriori-T) algorithm using weighted binary datasets; FWAT (Fuzzy Weighted Apriori-T) algorithm using fuzzy attributes and weighted fuzzy linguistic values; Classical ARM using standard ARM with binary dataset and WARM using weighted binary datasets and applying a post processing approach. Note that the weight of each item in classical ARM is 1 i.e. all items have equal weight.

The results show quite similar behavior of the three algorithms to classical ARM. As expected the number of frequent itemsets increases as the minimum support decreases in all cases. Number of frequent itemsets generated using the WARM algorithm are always less than the number of frequent itemsets generated by classical ARM

Figure 6. The createTtreeLevelN method

```
        Method: createTtreeLevelN
        Arguments: none
        Return: none
        Fields: startTtreeRef start of T-tree
                nextlevelFlag set to true if next level exists
        ---------------------------------------
        K <-- 2
        while (nextlevelFlag)
            addSupportToTtreeLevelN(K)
            pruneLevelN(startTtreeRef,K)
            nextlevelFlag <-- false
            generateLevelN(startTtreeRef,K,{})
            K <-- K+1
        End loop
        ---------------------------------------
```

Figure 7. The addSupportToTtreeLevelN method and its related addSupportToTtreeFindLevel method

```
    Method: addSupportToTtreeLevelN
    Arguments: K the current level
    Return: none
    Fields: startTtreeRef start of T-tree
            dataArray 2D array holding input sets
    ---------------------------------------
    Loop from i = 0 to i = number of records in dataArray
        length = number of attributes in dataArray[i]
        addSupportToTtreeFindLevel(startTtreeRef,K,length,
                    dataArray[i]
    End loop
    ---------------------------------------

    Method: addSupportToTtreeFindLevel
    Arguments: linkref reference to current array in T-tree
            K level marker
            length length of array at current branch in t-tree
            record input data record under consideration
    Return: none
    Fields: None
    ---------------------------------------
    if (K=1)
        Loop from i = 0 to i = length
            if (linkref[record[i]] != null)
                    calculate linkref[record[i]].support
            End if
        End Loop
    else
        Loop from i = K-1 to i = length
            if (linkref[record[i]] != null &&
                        linkref[record[i]].childRef != null)
                addSupportToTtreeFindLevel(linkref[record[i]].childRef,
                            K-1,i,record)
            End if
        End loop
    end if else
    ---------------------------------------
```

Figure 8. The pruneLevelN

```
Method: pruneLevelN
Arguments: linkref reference to current array in T-tree
        K level marker
Return: true if entire array pruned
Fields: minSupport the minimum support threshold
-------------------------------------
if (K=1)
    allUnsupported <-- true
    Loop from i = 1 to i = length of array
        if (linkref[i] != null)
            if (linkref[i].support < minSupport)
                        linkref[i] <-- null
            else allUnsupported <-- false
            End if else
        End if
    return allUnsupported
    End Loop
else
    Loop from i = K to i = length of array
        if (linkref[i] != null)
            if (pruneLevelN(linkref[i].childRef,K-1)
                linkref[i].childRef <-- null
            End if
        End if
    End loop
End if else
-------------------------------------
```

because WARM uses only generated frequent itemsets in the same manner as classical ARM. This generates less frequent itemsets and misses many potential ones (Muyeba, Khan & Coenen, 2008).

We do not use the classical ARM approach to first find frequent itemsets and then re-prune them using weighted support measures. Instead all the potential itemsets are considered from the beginning for pruning using Apriori approach (Agrawal & Srikant, 1994) in order to validate the DCP. Results of proposed approach are better than WARM because all possible frequent itemsets and rules are generated as we consider both itemset weights and their support count. Moreover, BWAT, classical ARM and WARM utilise binary data. FWAT generates more rules because of the extended fuzzy attributes, and it considers the degree of membership instead

of attribute presence only (count support) in a transaction. Figures 12 and 13 show the number of interesting rules generated using confidence measures. In all cases, the number of interesting rules is less because the interestingness measure generates fewer rules.

FWAT produces more rules because of the high number of initially generated frequent itemsets due to the introduction of more fuzzy sets for each quantitative attribute. Given a high confidence, BWAT outperforms classical WARM because the number of interesting rules produced is greater than WARM. This is because BWAT generates rules with items more correlated to each other and consistent at a higher confidence unlike WARM, where rules keep decreasing even at high confidence.

The experiments show that the proposed framework produces better results as it uses all

Figure 9. The generateLevelN method and its related generateNextLevel method

```
Method: generateLevelN
Arguments: linkref reference to current array in T-tree
           K level marker
           I the item set represented by the parent node
Return: None
Fields: None
-------------------------------------
if (K=1)
    Loop from i = 2 to i = length of array
        if (linkref[i] !=null)
            generateNextLevel(linkref,i,I union i)
        End if
    End loop
else
    Loop from i = K to i = length of array
        if (linkref[i] !=null && linkref[i].childRef !=null)
            generateLevelN(linkref[i].childRef,K-1,I union i
-------------------------------------

Method: generateNextLevel
Arguments: linkref reference to current array in T-tree
           i index to parent node in vurrent array
           I the item set represented by the parent node
Return: None
Fields: nextLevelExists flafg set to true or false
-------------------------------------
linkref[i].childRef <-- array of empty t-tree nodes of length i

Loop from j = 1 to j = i
    if (linkRef[j] !=null)
        newI <-- I union j
        if (all newI true subsets are all supported in the
                    T-tree sofar)
            linkRef[i].childRef[j] <-- new T-tree Node
            nextLevelExists <-- true
        else linkRef[i].childRef[j] <-- null
        End if else
    End if
End loop
-------------------------------------
```

Table 8. Data sets used for experiments

Dataset	# of Transactions	Distinct Items	Avg. Trans. Size	Max. Trans. Size
Retail	88,163	16,470	13	76
T10I4D100K	100,000	1000	10	30
Poker Hand	1000000	95	11	11
Connect-4	67557	129	42	42
Connect	67557	129	43	43
Pumsb	49046	7116	74	74
Pumsb Star	49046	7116	50	63

the possible itemsets and generates rules effectively using valid DCP. Further, the novelty is the ability to analyse both binary and fuzzy datasets with weighted settings.

Figure 10. No. of frequent itemsets generated using user specified support threshold

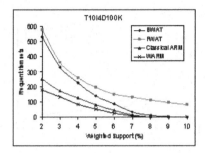

Figure 11. No. of frequent itemsets generated using user specified support threshold

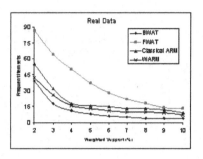

Figure 12. No. of interesting rules generated using user specified confidence

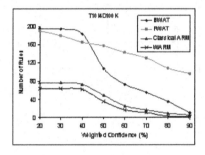

Figure 13. No. of interesting rules generated using user specified confidence

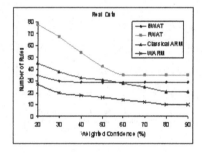

Performance Measures

Experiment two compares the execution time of BWAT and FWAT algorithms with BWARM, FWARM and WARM algorithms. We investigated the effect on execution time caused by varying the weighted support threshold with fixed data size (number of records) and by varying the data size with fixed support. In Figures 14 and 15, a support threshold from 2% to 10% is used.

We have showed in the experiments that proposed BWAT and FWAT algorithm outperform the previous weighted ARM approaches in terms of execution time.

Results show that BWAT has almost similar execution time to FWAT. The minor difference is due to the way it generates frequent sets i.e. it considers items weights and their count support. Similarly from Figure 10, it can be noted that BWAT and FWAT algorithms scale linearly with

increasing weighted support threshold, which is similar behavior to Classical ARM.

Finally the approach is tested on several real and synthetic datasets in order to show its applicability. Five different datasets were used to show the effect on execution time and the number of frequent sets generated using both sparse and dense datasets. Figure 18 shows the execution time of proposed algorithm by varying the support threshold for different datasets. It can be seen that the execution time increases as the threshold decreases in all cases irrespective of dataset type. Similarly in Figure 19 number of frequent sets increases as the support threshold decreases and it affects the execution time, again similar to the behavior of Classical ARM.

Figure 14. Performance measures: Varying weighted support (WS) threshold

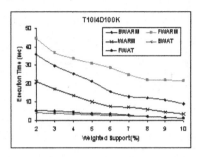

Figure 15. Performance measures: Varying weighted support (WS) threshold

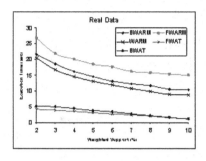

Figure 16. Performance measures: Varying data siz (num. of records)

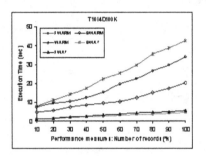

Figure 17. Performance measures: Varying data size (num. of records)

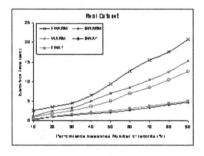

Figure 18. Execution time (different datasets)

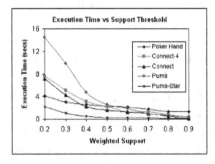

Figure 19. Frequent itemsets (different datasets)

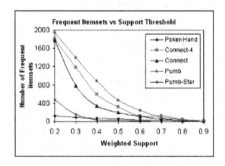

CONCLUSION

We have presented a generalised approach for effectively mining weighted fuzzy association rules from databases with binary and quantitative (fuzzy) data. A classical model of binary and fuzzy association rule mining is adopted to address the issue of invalidation of downward closure property (DCP) in weighted association rule mining. This was addressed using an improved model. We used classical and weighted ARM examples to compare support and confidence measures and evaluated the effectiveness of the proposed approach experimentally. We have demonstrated the validity of the DCP with formal comparisons to classical weighted ARM. It is notable that the approach as presented is effective in analysing databases with binary and fuzzy attributes with weighted settings. Moreover the proposed WAT algorithms (BAWT and FWAT with binary and fuzzy data) generate weighted association rules efficiently as compared to the previous weighted ARM approaches and is demonstrated experimentally. Further work will extend the framework to utility mining and how temporal features could be incorporated knowing for example the fact that weights and utilities can be dynamic entities in the life cycle of an item. Performance issues will then form the basis of the evaluation of such a framework.

REFERENCES

Agrawal, R., Imielinski, T., & Swami, A. (1993). Mining Association Rules Between Sets of Items in Large Databases. In *12th ACM SIGMOD on Management of Data* (pp. 207-216).

Agrawal, R., & Srikant, R. (1994). Fast Algorithms for Mining Association Rules. In *20th VLDB Conference* (pp. 487-499).

Bodon, F. (2003). A Fast Apriori implementation. *ICDM Workshop on Frequent Itemset Mining Implementations, vol. 90*, Melbourne, Florida, USA.

Brijs, T., Swinnen, G., Vanhoof, K., & Wets, G. (1999, August 15-18). The use of association rules for product assortment decisions: a case study. In *Proceedings of the Fifth International Conference on Knowledge Discovery and Data Mining* (pp. 254-260), San Diego, USA.

Cai, C. H., Fu, A. W.-C., Cheng, C. H., & Kwong, W. W. (1998). Mining Association Rules with Weighted Items. In *Proceedings of Intl. Database Engineering and Applications Symposium (IDEAS'98)* (pages 68-77). Cardiff, Wales, UK.

Coenen, F. P., Leng, P., & Ahmed, S. (2004). Data Structures for Association Rule Mining: T-trees and P-trees. *IEEE Transactions on Data and Knowledge Engineering, 16*(6), 774–778. doi:10.1109/TKDE.2004.8

Coenen, F. P., Leng, P., & Goulbourne, G. (2004). Tree Structures for Mining Association Rules. *Journal of Data Mining and Knowledge Discovery, 8*(1), 25–51. doi:10.1023/B:DAMI.0000005257.93780.3b

DataSet 1. http://hpc.isti.cnr.it/~palmeri/datam/sampling/simul/data/output/

Dataset 2. http://fimi.cs.helsinki.fi/data/

Gyenesei, A. (2000). Mining Weighted Association Rules for Fuzzy Quantitative Items. In *Proceedings of PKDD Conference* (pp. 416-423).

Khan, M. S., Muyeba, M., & Coenen, F. (2008). On Extraction of Nutritional Patterns (NPS) Using Fuzzy Association Rule Mining. In *Proc. of Intl. Conference on Health Informatics (HEALTHINF 08), INSTICC press Vol. 1* (pp. 34-42). Madeira, Portugal.

Kuok, C. M., Fu, A., & Wong, M. H. (1998). Mining Fuzzy Association Rules in Databases. *SIGMOD Record, 27*(1), 41–46. doi:10.1145/273244.273257

Lu, J.-J. (2002). Mining Boolean and General Fuzzy Weighted Association Rules in Databases. *Systems Engineering-Theory & Practice, 2*, 28–32.

Lu, S., Hu, H., & Li, F. (2001). Mining Weighted Association Rules. *Intelligent Data Analysis Journal, 5*(3), 211–255.

Merz & Murph. P. (1998). UCI repository of machine learning databases. http://www.ics.uci.edu/~mlearn/-MLRepository.html

Muyeba, M., Khan, M. S., & Coenen, F. (2008). Fuzzy Weighted Association Rule Mining with Weighted Support and Confidence Framework. In *PAKDD Workshop 2008, LNAI 5433* (pp. 49–61), Springer-Verlag, Berlin Heidelberg.

Srikant, R., & Agrawal, R. (1996). Mining Quantitative Association Rules in Large Relational Tables. In *Proceedings of ACM SIGMOD Conference on Management of Data* (pp. 1-12). ACM Press.

Tao, F., Murtagh, F., & Farid, M. (2003). Weighted Association Rule Mining Using Weighted Support and Significance Framework. In *Proceedings of 9th ACM SIGKDD Conference on Knowledge Discovery and Data Mining* (pp. 661- 666). Washington DC.

Wang, B.-Y., & Zhang, S.-M. (2003). A Mining Algorithm for Fuzzy Weighted Association Rules. In *IEEE Conference on Machine Learning and Cybernetics*, 4 (pp. 2495-2499).

Wang, W., Yang, J., & Yu, P. S. (2000). Efficient Mining of Weighted Association Rules (WAR). In *Proceedings of the KDD* (pp. 270-274). Boston.

Yue, S., Tsang, J., Yeung, E., & Shi, D. (2000). Mining Fuzzy Association Rules with Weighted Items, In *IEEE International Conference on Systems, Man, and Cybernetics, 3*, 1906-1911.

Section 2
Dealing with Imbalanced Datasets

Chapter 5
Rare Class Association Rule Mining with Multiple Imbalanced Attributes

Huaifeng Zhang
University of Technology, Australia

Yanchang Zhao
University of Technology, Australia

Longbing Cao
University of Technology, Australia

Chengqi Zhang
University of Technology, Australia

Hans Bohlscheid
Projects Section, Business Integrity Programs Branch, Centrelink, Australia

ABSTRACT

In this chapter, the authors propose a novel framework for rare class association rule mining. In each class association rule, the right-hand is a target class while the left-hand may contain one or more attributes. This algorithm is focused on the multiple imbalanced attributes on the left-hand. In the proposed framework, the rules with and without imbalanced attributes are processed in parallel. The rules without imbalanced attributes are mined through a standard algorithm while the rules with imbalanced attributes are mined based on newly defined measurements. Through simple transformation, these measurements can be in a uniform space so that only a few parameters need to be specified by user. In the case study, the proposed algorithm is applied in the social security field. Although some attributes are severely imbalanced, rules with a minority of imbalanced attributes have been mined efficiently.

DOI: 10.4018/978-1-60566-754-6.ch005

INTRODUCTION

Data imbalance is often encountered in data mining, especially in application-oriented data mining tasks. Conventional data mining algorithms always meet problems when applied on such imbalanced datasets. In the field of classification, when a prediction model is trained on an imbalanced data set, it could show a strong bias toward the majority class since typical learning algorithms intend to maximize the overall prediction accuracy. However, in most applications, the correct classification of samples in the minority class has a greater value than the contrary case. This problem is called class imbalance (Japkowicz, 2000), which has attracted considerable research attention in previous years (Akbani, 2004; Zhou, 2006; Cao, 2008). In the field of association rule mining, the rare item problem (Liu, 1999) is essentially the data imbalance problem on transactional datasets. In many applications, some items appear rarely but are very important. If the minimum support is set very low to find rules with rare items, a large amount of uninteresting rules will be found. Also the algorithm is extremely time-consuming.

Class association rule mining (Liu, 1998) is the integration of classification and association rule mining. In a class association rule, the right-hand side is a predefined target class while the left-hand side can be single or multiple attributes. Data imbalance on either side of the class association rule can cause severe problem.

In this chapter, we propose a novel algorithm to mine class association rules on datasets with multiple imbalanced attributes. The whole procedure includes four steps. Firstly, the association rules without imbalanced attributes are mined using the standard Apriori algorithm (Agrawal, 1994); secondly, with respect to one of the imbalanced attributes, the dataset is filtered so that the dominated part is removed; thirdly, on the filtered dataset, association rule mining is implemented based on new defined measurements; finally, the parameters of the rules with imbalanced attributes

are transformed so that the rules can be post-processed in a uniform space. In the case study, this algorithm is applied in the social security area. Many more rules with minorities of the imbalanced attributes have been mined, which is very interesting [to the business people].

The chapter is organized as follows. Section 2 presents some related work. Section 3 introduces class association rules. Section 4 gives the main procedure of our algorithm. Section 5 presents a case study. Section 6 is the conclusion and future work.

RELATED WORKS

The data imbalance problem has attracted more and more research interest in data mining and machine learning. The algorithms to tackle data imbalance problems can be categorized as data level and algorithm level. At data level, the solution is to resample the dataset, including oversampling the instances of minority, under-sampling the instances of majority (Liu, 2006), or a combination of the two techniques (Chawla, 2002). At algorithm level, the solutions are to adapt existing classifier learning algorithms to bias towards the minority, such as cost sensitive learning (Liu, 2006a; Sun, 2006; Sun, 2007) and recognition-based learning (Japkowicz, 2001).

Recently, there are some researchers working on the data imbalance in class association rule mining. In 2003, Gu et al. (2003) proposed an algorithm to deal with imbalanced class distribution in association rule mining. They defined a set of criteria to measure the interestingness of the association rules. Arunasalam and Chawla (2006) presented an algorithm for association rule mining in imbalanced data. Their paper studied the anti-monotonic property of the Complement Class Support (CCS) and applied it into the association rule mining procedure. Verhein and Chawla (2007) proposed a novel measure, Class Correlation Ratio (CCR), as the principal measure in association mining to tackle the data imbalance problem in class association rule mining. Their algorithm outperforms the previous algorithms on imbalanced datasets. However, the above three algorithms are focused on the data imbalance of the target class to improve the performance of so-called associative classifier (Liu, 1998).

In 1999, Liu et al. proposed the MSApriori algorithm (Liu, 1999) to deal with the rare item problem. Because the rare item problem is essentially the data imbalance problem, it is intuitive to apply MSApriori onto the data imbalance problem. In MSApriori, the author defined Minimum Item Support (MIS) to apply multiple minimum supports in the algorithm. However, MIS has to be assigned to every item by the user. Moreover, the discovered rules vary depending on the MIS values. Yun et al. (Yun, 2003) proposed an algorithm to mine association rule on significant rare data. In their algorithm, a number of supports also have to be specified by user. The performance of the algorithm heavily depends on the specified supports.

Class Association Rules

The algorithm proposed in this chapter is to tackle the multiple attribute imbalance problem when mining for class association rules on imbalanced datasets. In this section, we briefly introduce class association rule mining and its notations.

Let T be a set of tuples. Each tuple follows the schema $(A_1, A_2, ..., A_N, A_C)$, in which $(A_1, A_2, ..., A_N)$ are N attributes while A_C is a special attribute, the target class. The attributes may be either categorical or continuous ones. For continuous attributes, the value range is discretized into intervals. For the convenience of description, we call an attribute-value pair as an *item*. Suppose itemset $U \subseteq A$, A is the itemset of any items with attributes $(A_1, A_2, ..., A_N)$, c is 1-itemset of class attribute, a class association rule can be represented as

$$U \Rightarrow c.$$

Here, U may contain a single item or multiple items.

In this chapter, we represent the class association rules as

$$X \cup I \Rightarrow c,$$

where $X \subseteq A$ is the itemset of balanced attributes while $I \subseteq A$ is the itemset of the imbalanced attributes.

RULES WITH IMBALANCED ATTRIBUTES

Data Imbalance in Association Rule Mining

The data imbalance problem is characterized as having many more instances of certain attribute values than others. In most applications, the minority parts of an attribute are more interesting than the majority parts. For example, in a demographic dataset, the people who speak their native language are many more than the people who do not. However, the rules consisting of "Lang:native" are basically a common sense while the customers speaking other languages are more interesting to analysts. In routine medical examinations datasets, there are many more healthy cases than disease cases. Obviously, the rules consisting of "Status: Disease" are more important than the rules consisting of "Status: Healthy".

In most previous association rule mining algorithms, minimum support and minimum confidence are used to select interesting association rules from a large number of frequent patterns. In order to find rules that involve the minority part of an imbalanced attribute, minimum support has to be set very low, which will result in combinatorial explosion and huge amount of uninteresting rules.

Since there have been many algorithms dealing with the class imbalance problem, in this algorithm, we do not consider the imbalance problem of the target class. The algorithm will be focused on the multiple imbalanced attributes on the left-hand side of the class association rules.

Association Rule Mining Procedure

In our algorithm, association rule mining is done through two parallel parts. In one part, no imbalanced attributes are involved, and the standard Apriori algorithm is used to mine interesting rules. In the other part, the imbalanced attributes are mined on sub-datasets to achieve high efficiency. The detailed procedure is shown as follows (see Fig. 1).

1. Standard association rule mining on the balanced attributes. In the original dataset, the imbalanced attributes are excluded and all of the tuples are kept for association rule mining.
2. Filter the original dataset to obtain the tuples containing the minority part of one imbalanced attribute. In this step, only a small portion of the dataset is kept.
3. Mine the association rules on the filtered dataset using predefined minimum *confidence* and minimum *conditional support*. For every imbalanced attribute, repeat Step 2 and Step 3.
4. Transform the measurements into a uniform space and put all of the mined rules together. The final class association rule list is selected based on a set of criteria.

Interestingness Measures

In standard association rule mining algorithms, there are a number of interestingness measurements to be used to select interesting rules, for

Figure 1. The procedure of the proposed algorithm

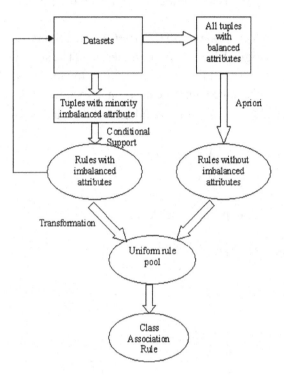

example, the minimum support *minsup*, minimum confidence *minconf*, the minimum lift *minlift*, and so on. In our algorithm, we modified some of the measurements for the processing of imbalanced attributes.

Conditional Support. In order to mine the rule consisting of imbalanced attributes, we extend the definition of support since the minority of an imbalanced attribute normally occurs in a small portion of the tuples. In this chapter, conditional support is defined to measure the interestingness of the rules with imbalanced attributes. If a class association rule is $X \cup I_m \Rightarrow c$, I_m is the minority part of one imbalanced attribute m, the conditional support of this rule is:

$$Supp_c = \frac{P\left(X \cup I_m \cup c\right)}{P\left(I_m\right)}$$

where X is an itemset of balanced attributes, I_m is a 1-itemset of imbalanced attribute m, c is a class ID.

Measurements on Original Dataset. Suppose the original dataset is represented as T. The subset T_m consists of the tuples containing the minority of imbalanced attribute m. If an association rule is $X \cup I_m \Rightarrow c$, the confidence of this rule is,

$$Conf = \frac{P\left(X \cup I_m \cup c\right)}{P\left(X \cup I_m\right)}$$

The expected confidence is

$$Conf_E = P\left(c\right)$$

And the lift is

$$Lift = \frac{Conf}{Conf_E} = \frac{\dfrac{P\left(X \cup I_m \cup c\right)}{P\left(X \cup I_m\right)}}{P\left(c\right)} = \frac{P\left(X \cup I_m \cup c\right)}{P\left(X \cup I_m\right) \cdot P\left(c\right)}$$

Measurements on Filtered Dataset. When an association rule $X \cup I_m \Rightarrow c$ is mined on the dataset T_m, the conditional support is

$$Supp'_c = P'\left(X \cup I_m \cup c\right) = \frac{P\left(I_m \cup \left(X \cup I_m \cup c\right)\right)}{P\left(I_m\right)}$$

Because T_m only has the tuples containing minority of the imbalanced itemset I_m,

$$P\left(I_m \cup \left(X \cup I_m \cup c\right)\right) = P\left(X \cup I_m \cup c\right)$$

Hence,

$$Supp'_c = P'\left(X \cup I_m \cup c\right) = \frac{P\left(I_m \cup \left(X \cup I_m \cup c\right)\right)}{P\left(I_m\right)} = Supp_c$$

Similarly, the confidence on the sub-dataset is

$$Conf = \frac{P'\left(X \cup I_m \cup c\right)}{P'\left(X \cup I_m\right)} = \frac{\dfrac{P\left(I_m \cup \left(X \cup I_m \cup c\right)\right)}{P\left(I_m\right)}}{\dfrac{P\left(I_m \cup \left(X \cup I_m\right)\right)}{P\left(I_m\right)}} = \frac{P\left(X \cup I_m \cup c\right)}{P\left(X \cup I_m\right)} = Conf$$

Obviously, either on the original dataset T or filtered dataset T_m, the conditional support and confidence of the mined rule keep invariant. However, on filtered dataset T_m, the expected confidence is

$$Conf'_E = P'\left(c\right) = \frac{P\left(I_m \cup c\right)}{P\left(I_m\right)}$$

So the lift on the filtered dataset T_m is

$$Lift' = \frac{Conf'}{Conf'_E} = \frac{\dfrac{P'\left(X \cup I_m \cup c\right)}{P'\left(X \cup I_m\right)}}{P'\left(c\right)} = \frac{P\left(X \cup I_m \cup c\right) \cdot P\left(I_m\right)}{P\left(X \cup I_m\right) \cdot P\left(I_m \cup c\right)} \neq lift$$

Transformation. Since the association rule mining in our algorithm is done through two parallel parts, we are trying to transform them into a uniform space so that as few as possible measurements are defined by user. From the above analysis, either on original dataset or filtered dataset, the conditional support and confidence of the rules are same. In order to use uniform criteria to select the rules, the lift on filtered dataset has to be transformed. On the original dataset T, the expected confidence with respect to c is known, which is $P(c)$. On the filtered dataset T_m, the confidence can be also obtained. So we may transform the lift obtained from filtered dataset.

$$L_{new} = \frac{Conf'}{Conf_E} = \frac{Conf'}{P\left(c\right)}$$

So far the confidence, lift and the conditional support of all the rules are on the same base. We can use a uniform criterion to select the final rules. In this chapter, minimum confidence, minimum lift and minimum conditional support are used to select the final class rule list.

Case Study

Our proposed algorithm has been tested with real-world data in Centrelink, Australia, which is an Australian government agency delivering a range of Commonwealth services to the Australian community.

Business Background and Problem Statement

When a customer has received public moneys to which he or she was not lawfully entitled, these funds become debts to be recovered. The purpose of the data mining in debt recovery is to profile the customers according to their capacity to pay off their debts in a shortened time frame. This enables targeting those customers with suitable arrangement to their own circumstances, and increases the frequency and level of repayment.

From a technical point of view, the objective is to mine association rules with respect to the demographic attributes and debt information of a customer, the arrangement between customer and Centrelink, and the target classes standing for whether the customer is a "Quick payer", "Moderate payer", or "Slow payer". If some customers have the same demographic attributes and the same debt information, under different arrangements, he/she belongs to different target classes, and Centrelink will recommend him/her to have an arrangement in order to make him/her be a "Quick Payer" or "Moderate Payer" rather than "Slow Payer".

In order to solve the above problems, we employ the combined pattern mining (Zhao, 2007) in our case study. The combined pattern is defined as

$$\begin{cases} X \cup Y_1 \Rightarrow c_1 \\ \quad\vdots \\ X \cup Y_i \Rightarrow c_j, \end{cases}$$

where c_j is class ID, Y_i is the itemset of actionable attributes. In this case study, Y_i is an arrangement pattern of a customer. From the above equation we can see that each association rule in the combined pattern is a class association rule. Hence we can apply the proposed algorithm to mine the class association rule in the combined pattern.

Datasets Involved

There are three kinds of datasets used for the association rule mining task: customer demographic data, debt data and repayment data. The first dataset keeps the demographic circumstances of customers, such as customer ID, gender, age, marital status, number of children, income, location, language, preferred language and so on. The second dataset stores the debt related information, such as the date of debt raised, the amount of debt, the outstanding balance of the debt, and the benefit type related to the debt. The repayment dataset includes the debt repayment amount, debt repayment date, the type of the repayment and the type of debt recovery arrangement. An arrangement is an agreement between a customer and Centrelink officer on the method, amount and frequency of repayments. The class IDs, which are defined by business experts, are included in the repayment dataset.

The data used are those debts raised in calendar year 2006 and the corresponding customers and repayments in the same year. Those debts raised in calendar year 2006 are first extracted, and then the customer data and repayment data in the same year related to the above debt data are extracted. Then the data are cleaned by removing noise, such as those repayments with zero or negative amount.

In the cleaned data, there are 479,288 customers in the demographic dataset and 2,627,348 repayments in the repayment dataset.

In the involved three datasets, the attributes in the debt dataset and repayment dataset are relatively balanced. However, in the demographic datasets, there are three attributes having imbalanced distributions: "Remote", "Lang", and "Indig". "Remote" stands for whether a customer lives in remote area. "Lang" stands for what language a customer speaks. "Indig" stands for whether a customer is indigenous or not. The distributions of these three attributes are shown in Figure 2.

Experimental Results

In the experiment, all the customers are grouped based on the arrangement patterns. Thus each arrangement is associated with a group of customers. Selected association rules on all the attributes but imbalanced ones are shown in Table 1.

On the filtered datasets, the rules with imbalanced attributes are mined. Selected rules are shown in Table 2.

The lifts of the above rules are transformed so that all the rules can be measured using uniform selection criteria. The final combined association rules are mined from the rule pool. Selected combined association rules are given in Table 3.

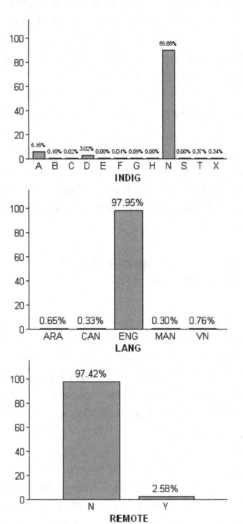

Figure 2. The distribution of the imbalance attributes

Table 1. Selected results with balanced attributes

Arrangement	Demographic Pattern	Class	$Conf_E$(%)	Conf(%)	Supp(%)	Lift	Count
C_A	Marital:SIN & Gender:F & Benefit:AAA	Slow Payer	51	60	6.4	1.2	33
CI_W	Benefit:BBB	Quick Payer	40.8	67	4.9	1.6	61
W_W	Weekly:0 & age:65y+	Quick Payer	72.4	88.7	8.9	1.2	110
WV_WC	Benefit:AAA	Quick Payer	72.4	88.4	8.7	1.2	107
V_V	Weekly:0 & Gender:M	Quick Payer	72.4	86	9	1.2	111
CI_W	Marital:SIN & Gender:F & Benefit:BBB	Moderate Payer	60.4	80.4	5.1	1.3	119
WI_W	Weekly:[$400, $600) & Marital:SEP & age:26y-50y	Moderate Payer	56.6	65.4	2.6	1.2	100

Table 2. Selected rules with imbalanced attributes caption style

Arrangement	Demographic Pattern	Class	$Conf_E$(%)	Conf(%)	$Supp_c$(%)	L_{new}	Count
W_W	Weekly:[$200 $400) & INDIG:A &GENDER:F	Moderate Payer	39	48.6	6.7	1.2	52
C_A	MARITAL:SEP & INDIG:A	Slow Payer	25.6	63.3	6.4	2.5	50
CI_A	Weekly:[$400 $600) & INDIG:D	Quick Payer	35.4	64.9	6.4	1.8	50
WV_W	MARITAL:SEP & INDIG:D & Children:0	Slow Payer	39	49.8	16.3	1.3	127
V_V	Weekly:0 & MARITAL:MAR & LANG:ARA	Moderate Payer	25.6	46.9	7.8	1.8	61
WV_WV	LANG:MAN & GENDER:F	Quick Payer	25.6	49.7	11.4	1.9	89
WI_CW	Weekly:[$200 $400) & REMOTE:Y & GENDER:F	Quick Payer	39	45.7	18.8	1.2	147

Table 3. Selected results of the combined association rules

Arrangement	Demographic Pattern	Class
C_A	Marital:SEP & Gender:F & Benefit:AAA	Slow Payer
V_V	Marital:SEP & Gender:F & Benefit:AAA	Quick Payer
W_A	Marital:SEP & Gender:F & Benefit:AAA	Moderate Payer
W_W	Marital:SEP & Gender:F & Benefit:AAA	Slow Payer
WI_CW	GENDER:F & Children:0 & Age:26y-50y	Moderate Payer
CI_C	GENDER:F & Children:0 & Age:26y-50y	Quick Payer
W_A	GENDER:F & Children:0 & Age:26y-50y	Slow Payer
WV_V	GENDER:F & Children:0 & Age:26y-50y	Moderate Payer
C_A	GENDER:F & Children:0 & Age:26y-50y	Slow Payer
WI_CW	Weekly:[$400, $600) & INDIG:D	Slow Payer
C_A	Weekly:[$400, $600) & INDIG:D	Quick Payer
WV_V	Weekly:[$400, $600) & INDIG:D	Quick Payer
CI_CW	Weekly:[$400, $600) & INDIG:D	Moderate Payer
WI_C	LANG:ARA & GENDER:F	Slow Payer
CI_C	LANG:ARA & GENDER:F	Moderate Payer
WI_C	Weekly:[$200, $400) & REMOTE:Y & GENDER:F	Quick Payer
C_A	Weekly:[$200, $400) & REMOTE:Y & GENDER:F	Slow Payer
WV_V	Weekly:[$200, $400) & REMOTE:Y & GENDER:F	Slow Payer
WI_W	Weekly:[$200, $400) & REMOTE:Y & GENDER:F	Moderate Payer

CONCLUSION

This chapter proposes an efficient algorithm to mine class association rules on the dataset with multiple imbalanced attributes. Unlike previous algorithms dealing with class imbalance, our algorithm processes the data imbalance on multiple attributes. Also different from the algorithms dealing with rare item problems, our algorithm employs uniform selection criteria to discover the final combined association rule, which makes the algorithm more robust. The experimental results show the effectiveness of our proposed algorithm.

ACKNOWLEDGMENT

We would like to thank Mr. Fernando Figueiredo and Mr. Peter Newbigin from Centrelink Australia for their support of domain knowledge. This work was supported by the University of Technology, Sydney (UTS) Early Career Research Grants (ECRG) 2007002448, Australian Research Council (ARC) Discovery Projects DP0449535, DP0667060 & DP0773412 and Linkage Project LP0775041.

REFERENCES

Agrawal, R., & Srikant, R. (1994). Fast algorithms for mining association rules in large databases. In *VLDB '94: Proceedings of the 20th International Conference on Very Large Data Bases* (pp. 487–499). San Francisco, CA, USA: Morgan Kaufmann Publishers Inc.

Akbani, R., Kwek, S., & Japkowicz, N. (2004, September 20-24). Applying support vector machines to imbalanced datasets. In *15th European Conference on Machine Learning (ECML2004), volume 3201 of Lecture Notes in Computer Science.* (pp. 39–50). Pisa, Italy.

Arunasalam, B., & Chawla, S. (2006). CCCS: a top-down associative classifier for imbalanced class distribution. In *KDD '06: Proceedings of the 12th ACM SIGKDD international conference on Knowledge discovery and data mining* (pp. 517–522). New York, NY, USA: ACM Press.

Cao, L., Zhao, Y., & Zhang, C. (2008). Mining Impact-Targeted Activity Patterns in Imbalanced Data. *IEEE Transactions on Knowledge and Data Engineering, 20,* 1053–1066. doi:10.1109/TKDE.2007.190635

Chawla, N. V., Bowyer, K. W., Hall, L. O., & Kegelmeyer, W. P. (2002). Smote: Synthetic minority over-sampling technique. *Journal of Artificial Intelligence Research, 16,* 321–357.

Japkowicz, N. (2000). Learning from imbalanced data sets: A comparison of various strategies. *AAAI workshop on Learning from Imbalanced Data Sets.*

Japkowicz, N. (2001). Supervised versus unsupervised binary-learning by feedforward neural networks. *Machine Learning, 42*(1), 97–122. doi:10.1023/A:1007660820062

Li Gu, L. J., He, H., Williams, G., Hawkins, S., & Kelman C. (2003). Association rule discovery with unbalanced class distributions. In *AI 2003: Advances in Artificial Intelligence* (pp. 221–232).

Liu, B., Hsu, W., & Ma, Y. (1998). Integrating classification and association rule mining. In *KDD98: Proceedings of the 4th International Conference on Knowledge Discovery and Data Mining* (pp. 80–86). New York City: AAAI Press.

Liu, B., Hsu, W., & Ma, Y. (1999). Mining association rules with multiple minimum supports. In *KDD '99: Proceedings of the fifth ACM SIGKDD international conference on Knowledge discovery and data mining,* (pp. 337–341). New York, NY, USA: ACM Press.

Liu, X.-Y., Wu, J., & Zhou, Z.-H. (2006). Exploratory under-sampling for class-imbalance learning. In *ICDM '06. Sixth International Conference on Data Mining* (pp. 965–969).

Liu, X.-Y., & Zhou, Z.-H. (2006). The influence of class imbalance on cost-sensitive learning: An empirical study. In *ICDM '06. Sixth International Conference on Data Mining* (pp. 970–974).

Sun, Y., Kamel, M. S., & Wang, Y. (2006). Boosting for Learning Multiple Classes with Imbalanced Class Distribution. In *ICDM '06. Sixth International Conference on Data Mining* (pp. 592-602).

Sun, Y., Kamel, M. S., Wong, A. K. C., & Wang, Y. (2007). Cost-sensitive boosting for classification of imbalanced data. *Pattern Recognition, 40*(12), 3358–3378. doi:10.1016/j.patcog.2007.04.009

Verhein, F., & Chawla, S. (2007). Using Significant, Positively Associated and Relatively Class Correlated Rules for Associative Classification of Imbalanced Datasets. In *ICDM'07: Seventh IEEE International Conference on Data Mining* (pp. 679-684).

Yun, H., Ha, D., Hwang, B., & Ryu, K. H. (2003). Mining association rules on significant rare data using relative support. *Journal of Systems and Software, 67*(3), 181–191. doi:10.1016/S0164-1212(02)00128-0

Zhao, Y., Zhang, H., Figueiredo, F., Cao, L., & Zhang, C. (2007). Mining for combined association rules on multiple datasets. In *DDDM07: KDD Workshop on Domain Driven Data Mining*, San Jose, CA, USA

Zhou, Z.-H., & Liu, X.-Y. (2006). Training cost-sensitive neural networks with methods addressing the class imbalance problem. *IEEE Transactions on Knowledge and Data Engineering, 18*(1), 63–77. doi:10.1109/TKDE.2006.17

Chapter 6
A Multi-Methodological Approach to Rare Association Rule Mining

Yun Sing Koh
Auckland University of Technology, New Zealand

Russel Pears
Auckland University of Technology, New Zealand

ABSTRACT

Rare association rule mining has received a great deal of attention in the past few years. In this chapter, the authors propose a multi methodological approach to the problem of rare association rule mining that integrates three different strands of research in this area. Firstly, the authors make use of statistical techniques such as the Fisher test to determine whether itemsets co-occur by chance or not. Secondly, they use clustering as a pre-processing technique to improve the quality of the rare rules generated. Their third strategy is to weigh itemsets to ensure upward closure, thus checking unbounded growth of the rule base. Their results show that clustering isolates heterogeneous segments from each other, thus promoting the discovery of rules which would otherwise remain undiscovered. Likewise, the use of itemset weighting tends to improve rule quality by promoting the generation of rules with rarer itemsets that would otherwise not be possible with a simple weighting scheme that assigns an equal weight to all possible itemsets. The use of clustering enabled us to study in detail an important sub-class of rare rules, which we term absolute rare rules. Absolute rare rules are those are not just rare to the dataset as a whole but are also rare to the cluster from which they are derived.

INTRODUCTION

The main goal of association rule mining is to discover relationships among sets of items in a transactional database. Association rule mining was introduced by Agrawal, Imielinski and Swami

DOI: 10.4018/978-1-60566-754-6.ch006

(1993). It aims to extract interesting correlations, frequent patterns, associations or causal structures among sets of items in transaction databases or other data repositories. The relationships are not based on inherent properties of the data themselves but rather based on the co-occurrence of the items within the database. The associations between items are also known as association rules. In the classical association rule mining process, all frequent itemsets are found, where an itemset is said to be frequent if it appears at least a given percentage of time in all transactions called minimum support s. Association rules are then generated in the form of A → B where AB is a frequent itemset. Strong association rules are derived from frequent itemsets and constrained by minimum confidence c (the percentage of transactions containing A that also contain B).

A much less explored area in association mining is infrequent itemset mining or rare association rule mining. Items that rarely occur are in very few transactions and are normally pruned out in the classical association mining process. One limitation of common association rule mining approaches, i.e. Apriori, are that they rely on there being a meaningful minimum support level that is reasonable (sufficiently strong) to reduce the number of frequent itemsets to a manageable level. However, in some data mining applications relatively infrequent associations are likely to be of great interest as they relate to rare but crucial cases. Examples of mining rare itemsets include identifying relatively rare diseases, predicting telecommunications equipment failure, and finding associations between infrequently purchased supermarket items. Indeed, infrequent itemsets warrant special attention because they are more difficult to find using traditional data mining techniques.

In this chapter we present a multi methodological approach to finding rare association rules. Our approach integrates three separate strands of research, each of which contributes in different ways to finding rules of interest which would not be discovered using conventional methods.

The first and most fundamental challenge that needs to be overcome in the rare mining context is to ensure that candidate itemsets do not occur together purely by chance. Various different schemes have been proposed to combat this problem, including the use of the Pearson correlation coefficient to measure the strength of

the relationship between co-occurring itemsets (Xiong, Shekhar, Tan, & Kumar, 2004). Our approach to this problem is to use an inverted Fisher test to find itemsets that co-occur together with a frequency greater than chance occurrence. The use of a rigorous statistical method such as the Fisher test was demonstrated in previous research (Koh, Rountree, & O'Keefe, 2006), (Koh, Rountree, & O'Keefe, 2008) to be superior to the use of subjective Pearson correlation coefficients.

We hypothesize that rare rules can manifest in only certain segments of a dataset and not appear across a dataset as a whole. Such rules can only be found by clustering transactions and then applying association mining on each of the clusters found. In previous research (Koh & Pears, 2008), we demonstrated that strong rules that were found in clusters could not be found by mining across the entire un-partitioned dataset due to contamination that occurs between different parts of the dataset.

Current methods in rare association rule mining do not discriminate between itemsets that have widely different levels of support. As long as an itemset meets the lower bound support threshold it is considered as a candidate itemset for rule generation. All such candidates can now be extended with other candidate itemsets to form composite itemsets which are guaranteed to have support lesser than or equal to the minimum of the individual itemsets. However, depending on the support threshold chosen, this could lead to a combinatorial explosion in the number of candidate itemsets, which in turn will lead to degradation in performance. Apart from this the number of rules generated could also grow exponentially, especially for dense datasets. We thus impose a control over the number of candidates by implementing a weighting scheme that associates a weight to each candidate itemset. A lower bound support threshold is initially chosen by the miner. As candidate generation progresses this threshold does not remain constant but is updated by the weight associated with an itemset that is being considered for inclusion in rule generation. Thus the support that a candidate itemset needs to satisfy is not a global constant but varies from itemset to itemset. For a given itemset I, the support threshold is given by $T_{curr} = T_{old} \times w_I$, where T_{old} is the threshold before the itemset was extended, T_{new} is the threshold after extension and w_I is the weight associated with itemset I. Candidates that have a higher proportion of high support items are given a higher weight, whilst those that have a lower proportion are given a correspondingly lower weight. This effectively means that as candidate itemsets become larger in size the support constraint becomes tighter, especially for those that have a higher proportion of items with high support. The net effect is to check unbounded growth of itemsets and ensure that the number of rules is kept to a manageable size.

The rest of the chapter is organized as follows. The next section discusses the major research that has previously being carried out in rare association rule mining. We discuss how the Fisher test has been being adapted to identify rare rules and the use of transaction clustering in improving the quality of the rules found. In the third section we discuss in detail an algorithm that we used in previous research to cluster transactions. The integrated approach that we use to mine association rules is presented in the fourth section. In the fifth section, we present the results of our experimentation on real-world and synthetic datasets. Our conclusions and directions for future research are presented in the last section.

RELATED WORK

We start by presenting the literature on rare association rule mining and then go on to discuss the various approaches used in clustering transactions. The body of work in the rare association mining arena is nowhere as extensive as in its frequent mining counterpart, but nevertheless substantial work has been done to advance this discipline.

We also discuss how clustering can be used as a pre-processing step to improve the quality of the association rules generated.

Rare Association Rule Mining

Rare association rules are characterized by rules that have low support but high confidence. Efficiently generating such rules is a difficult data mining problem. In order to find these rules with traditional approaches such as the Apriori algorithm, the upper bound support (minsup) threshold has to be set very low, which results in a large number of redundant rules. As a specific example of the problem, consider the association mining problem where we want to determine if there is an association between buying a food processor and buying a cooking pan (Liu, Hsu, & Ma, 1999a). The problem is that both items are rarely purchased in a supermarket. Thus, even if the two items are almost always purchased together, this association may not be found. Modifying the minsup threshold to take into account the importance of the items is one way of ensuring that rare items remain in consideration. To find this association minsup must be set very low. However setting this threshold low would cause a combinatorial explosion in the number of itemsets generated. Frequently occurring items will be associated with one another in an enormous number of ways simply because the items are so common that they cannot help but appear together. This is known as the rare item problem (Liu, Hsu, & Ma, 1999b). It means that using the Apriori algorithm, we are unlikely to generate rules that may indicate rare events of potentially dramatic consequence.

Liu et al. (1999a) note that some individual items can have such low support that they cannot contribute to rules generated by Apriori, even though they may participate in rules that have very high confidence. They overcome this problem by using multiple levels of support, depending on the item. The miner supplies a minimum item support (MIS) for each item. A higher minimum support is provided for items that are known from past experience to appear frequently, while those that are known to appear less frequently are given a lower threshold value. This enables the generation of rules involving items with low support. The drawback of this technique is that the burden is shifted to the miner to pre-judge the right threshold level for each and every item, which is a laborious and error-prone process. An improper threshold will either result in a rule explosion or a dearth in the number of rules, depending on whether the threshold value is underestimated or overestimated.

Yun, Ha., Hwang, & Ryu (2003) proposed the RSAA algorithm to generate rules in which significant rare itemsets take part, without any "magic numbers" specified by the user. This technique uses a relative support measure, RSup in place of support. The relative support Rsup is a measure that shows the relative support rate of a candidate itemset $\{i_1 i_2 \ldots i_k\}$ against each of the items $i_1, i_2, ., i_k$, which compose the candidate. The Rsup measure is given by: $Rsup(i_1, i_2, \ldots i_k)$ = max $(sup(i_1, i_2, \ldots, i_k)/sup(i_1), sup(i_1, i_2, \ldots, i_k)/sup(i_2), \ldots, sup(i_1, i_2, \ldots, i_k)/sup(i_k))$. The use of Rsup relieves the data miner from supplying support thresholds and thus this method represents a significant improvement over past work. The Rsup measure effectively decreases the support threshold for items that have low frequency and increases the support threshold for items that have high frequency. The scheme was shown to be faster than both Apriori and MSApriori and was able to discover rare items that these methods were unable to detect.

Koh and Rountree (2005) proposed an approach called Apriori Inverse to find rare rules with candidate itemsets that fall below a maxsup (maximum support) level but above a minimum absolute support value. The main contribution here was the use of the Fisher test to filter rare items that occur together purely by chance, thus excluding them from the rule generation phase. They later refined Apriori Inverse into the Mining

Interesting Imperfectly Sporadic Rules (MIISR) algorithm. MIISR concentrated on capturing rules with a single-item consequent below the maxsup threshold, while rule antecedents were allowed to have individual terms with support above maxsup, the antecedent as a whole had to have support below maxsup. Such types of rules are of interest in medical applications where individual disease symptoms on their own could occur frequently but their combination could be extremely rare, thus pointing to a specific and hard to diagnose disease.

Szathmary, Napoli, & Valtchev (2007) presented an approach for rare itemset mining from a dataset that splits the problem into two tasks. The first task, the traversal of the frequent zone in the space, is addressed by two different algorithms, a naïve one, Apriori-Rare, which relies on Apriori and hence enumerates all frequent itemsets; and MRG-Exp, which limits the considerations to frequent generators only. They consider computation of the rare itemsets that approaches them starting from the bottom of the itemset lattice and then moving upwards through the frequent zone. They defined a positive and the negative border of the frequent itemsets, and a negative lower border and the positive lower border of the rare itemsets, respectively. An itemset is a maximal frequent itemset (MFI) if it is frequent but all its proper supersets are rare. An itemset is a minimal rare itemset (mRI) if it is rare but all its proper subsets are frequent. Like Apriori and MSApriori, RSAA and Apriori-Rare, MRG-Exp is exhaustive in its generation of rules, so it spends time looking for rules which are not sporadic (i.e. rules with high support and high confidence). If the minimum-allowable relative support value is set close to zero, MRG-Exp takes a similar amount of time to that taken by Apriori to generate low-support rules due to having to sift through the high-support rules.

Thus it can be seen that current research falls into two categories: those that use ad-hoc methods to determine rare items (Liu et al., 1999a), (Yun et al., 2003) and (Szathmary et al., 2007) and others (Koh & Rountree, 2005) that utilize more rigorous methods such as the Fisher test to determine co-occurrence of rare items. The use of the Fisher test is appealing from a conceptual viewpoint as it takes subjectivity out of consideration. Coupled with the fact that rule quality was shown to be superior while having better execution times than it rivals, Apriori Inverse was the logical choice for further exploration. We now turn our attention to the important issue of transaction clustering and examine a number of different approaches for addressing this problem.

Transaction Clustering

In the recent past there has been an increasing level of interest in clustering transactions. All such approaches have employed methods quite different to traditional clustering methods. Wang et al. (1999) utilised the concept of large items (Agrawal et al., 1993) to cluster transactions. Their approach measures the similarity of a cluster based on the large items in the transaction dataset. Each transaction is either allocated to an existing cluster or assigned to a new cluster based on a cost function. The cost function measures the degree of similarity between a transaction and a cluster based on the number of large and small items shared between that transaction and the given cluster.

An item is considered as small if it does not occur with frequency above a certain threshold amongst the transactions in the cluster. For a clustering $C = \{C_1, ..., C_k\}$, the corresponding cost has two components, the intra-cluster cost Intra(C) and the inter-cluster cost, Inter(C). The intra-cluster cost represents the dissimilarity of items within a cluster and is measured by the set of small items in the cluster. It is defined by $\text{Intra}(\text{C}) = \bigcup_{i=1}^{k} Small_i$ where $Small_i$ is the set of small items in the cluster C_i. On the other hand, the inter-cost measure represents similarity

of the transactions within a cluster and is dependent on the duplication of large items across different clusters. More explicitly, they define inter-cost as: $\text{Inter}(\text{C}) = \Sigma_{i=1}^{k} | Large_i | - \bigcup_{i=1}^{k} Large_i$ where $Large_i$ is the set of large items in cluster C_i. The overall cost of C is: $\text{Cost}(\text{C}) = \omega.\text{Intra}(\text{C}) + \text{Inter}(\text{C})$, where ω is a weight that represents the relative importance of intra-cluster cost over inter-cluster cost and by default ω is set to 1. Given a collection of transactions and a specified minimum support, their approach aims to find a cluster configuration C with minimum cost.

To speed-up the method proposed above, Yun, Chuang, and Chen (2001) introduced a method called *SLR* (Small-Large Ratio). Their method essentially uses the measurement of the ratio between small to large items to cluster transactions. Both the large item (Wang, Xu, & Liu, 1999) and *SLR* (Yun et al., 2001) methods suffer a common drawback. In some cases, they may fail to give a good representation of the clusters. Suppose that *A* and *B* are large items in a transaction dataset, with *A* and *B* occurring 60% of the time and *AB* occurring together 40% of the time. If the support threshold is set at 40%, then it follows that the cluster configuration that minimises the cost function Cost(*C*) results in two clusters, one having transactions that contain the item A and the other that contains item *B*. However it is clear that the optimal cluster configuration requires an additional cluster containing the itemset *AB*. Their approach thus discourages splitting large items between clusters. This in turn forces transactions to choose between sub-optimal clusters.

Xu et al. (2003) proposed a method using the concept of a caucus. The basic idea of introducing a caucus to cluster transactions is motivated by the fact that cluster quality is sensitive to the initial choice of cluster centroids (Xu et al., 2003). Fundamentally different from most other clustering algorithms, their approach attempts to group customers with similar behavior. In their approach they first determine a set of background attributes from the dataset that are significant. A set of caucuses, consisting of different subsets of items is then constructed to identify the initial cluster centroids.

The main drawback of this method is that it requires the user to define the initial centroids which is difficult as it requires some form of prior knowledge about the dataset. To overcome this problem Koh and Pears (2008) proposed a method based on cluster seeding. The cluster seeding method overcomes the two main issues with the current approaches in that it copes well with overlapping centroids and does not require background information on domain specific knowledge. These properties make it attractive to us in our quest to pre-process a given dataset into homogenous clusters with the expectation of yielding higher quality rules from homogenously segmented data. We describe in detail the cluster seeding method later in this review. We now consider the benefits of combining clustering with association mining.

Combining Clustering and Association Rule Mining

Plasse et al (2007) presents a method of analysing links between binary attributes in a large sparse data set. Initially the variables are clustered to obtain homogeneous clusters of attributes. Association rules are then mined from each cluster. They used several clustering methods and compared the resulting partitions. Clusters generation was based on hierarchical methods which are divided in two groups: ascendant methods based on an agglomerative algorithm and descendant methods performed by a divisive algorithm. The similarity coefficients used in their clustering technique includes Russel and Rao, Jaccard, Ochiai, and Dice. Once clusters are generated with each of the different techniques, association rules were then generated based on each of the clusters obtained. While their method did suc-

ceed in finding association rules that could not be discovered without clustering, the inherent weakness was in the clustering algorithms that they employed. None of the methods proposed offered a good solution to scenarios where large items overlap across clusters.

A further limitation with some of the existing transaction clustering algorithms is that they rely on some form of domain specific knowledge, thus limiting their range of applicability. Executing numerous different clustering methods and then generating rules based on each of the clusters produced is prohibitively expensive in certain cases. This is especially true when clustering is employed over a variety of datasets from different domains.

Transaction Clustering By Seeding

We now present the cluster seeding algorithm in detail. This algorithm does not require any prior domain-specific knowledge nor does it artificially force large items to belong to only a single cluster; rather, it replicates items as and when necessary amongst different clusters.

Clustering is the process of finding naturally occurring groups in data. Clustering is one of the most widely studied techniques in the context of data mining and has many applications, including disease classification, image processing, pattern recognition, and document retrieval. Traditional clustering techniques deal with horizontal segmentation of data, whereby clusters are formed from sets of non-overlapping instances. Many efficient algorithms exist for the traditional clustering problem (Jain, Murty, & Flynn, 1999; Ganti, Gehrke, & Ramakrishnan, 1999; Gibson, Kleinberg, & Raghavan, 1998; Guha, Rastogi, & Shim, 2000). In contrast, transaction clustering has fundamentally different requirements, and has been gaining increasing attention in recent years. Unlike traditional clustering, transaction clustering requires that transactions be partitioned across clusters in such a manner that instances within a cluster share a common set of large items, where the concept of large follows the same meaning attributed to frequent items in association rule mining (Agrawal, Imielinski, & Swami, 1993). Thus it is clear that transaction clustering requires a fundamentally different approach from the traditional clustering techniques. Compounding the level of difficulty is the fact transaction data is known to have high dimensionality, sparsity, and a potentially large number of outliers (Xu, Xiong, Sung, & Kumar, 2003).

Current research in both data mining and information retrieval suggests that transaction clustering functionality needs to extend well beyond a near neighbourhood search for similar instances (Wang, Xu, & Liu, 1999; Cutting, Pedersen, Karger, & Tukey, 1992). This form of clustering provides a natural solution to many applications such as targeted marketing/advertising, discovering causes of diseases, and others. A new clustering approach tailored to transaction clustering was first introduced by Wang et al. (1999). They used a similarity measure based on the occurrence of large items. The underlying criterion of this clustering technique is that there should be a high degree of instances sharing large items within a cluster and that there should be little overlap in large items across clusters. Their approach forces transactions containing the same large items to stick together. While their approach was shown to perform better than traditional clustering algorithms, it does not cope well with data where a natural solution consists of clusters that require the same large items to be present in two or more clusters.

In this chapter we present an approach based on an initial seeding of cluster centroids to the problem of transaction clustering. This approach uses two phases: a seed generation phase followed by a transaction allocation phase. In the seed generation phase seeds are generated based on the candidate generation process used in Apriori (Agrawal et al., 1993). We allow large items to be extended in precisely the same manner as Apriori.

The items are extended to itemsets if they fulfill a significance test requirement and an improvement constraint. We use the chi square significance testing to ensure that only strongly associated items are joined together into an itemset. The improvement constraint restricts the growth of a seed to ensure that it only consists of items that increase the value of an improvement function which we define later in this paper. Once seeds are generated, the next phase assigns transactions to clusters. Each transaction is allocated to a cluster centroid with the highest similarity. Once all transactions have been allocated, we recalculate the centroid for each cluster. The new centroid consists of large items that reside in the cluster. Transactions are then reallocated to clusters on the basis of proximity to the new centroids that were defined. In order to determine the optimal value for the number of clusters, we repeat the allocation phase until the value of a fitness function reaches a plateau.

Let $D = \{t_1, \ldots t_n\}$ be a set of transactions. Each transaction is a set of items $\{i_1, \ldots i_m\}$. C is a partition of the transaction, $\{C_1, \ldots C_k\}$ of $\{t_1, \ldots t_n\}$. Each C_i is called a cluster. Overall the clustering is divided into two main phases: seed generation and allocation phases.

Seed Generation Phase

We start by describing a method for finding the optimal number of clusters. Our initial choice of seeds is the large items in the dataset and we thus begin by setting a minimum support threshold, θ, where, $0 < \theta < 1$. Any item in the dataset that has support above $|D| \times \theta$ is considered a large item. Let L_i denote the set of large items or large itemsets. We now allow the items L_i to be extended to itemsets L_{i+1} in the same way as Apriori generates candidate frequent itemsets. For example, $L_1 = \{\{a\}, \{b\}, \{c\}\}$ may be extended to $L_2 = \{\{ab\}, \{ac\}, \{bc\}\}$. For a large itemset to be considered a cluster seed the frequency of

Figure 1. Seed Generation Phase

Input: Transaction database D, θ value, σ value, universe of items I
Output: Cluster Seeds, $S = \{s_1 \ldots s_k\}$
$k \leftarrow 1$
$s_k \leftarrow \{\{i\}|i \in I,\ \text{count}(\{i\}) \geq |D| * \theta\}$
while $l_k \neq \emptyset$ **do**
   $k \leftarrow k + 1$
   $l_k \leftarrow \{x \cup y | x, y \in s_{k-1}, |x \cap y| = k - 2\}$
   $s_k \leftarrow \{x \cup y | x \cup y \in l_k, \phi(x \cup y) \geq \chi_c^2, RS(x \cup y) - RS(y) > \sigma,$
        $RS(x \cup y) - RS(x) > \sigma\}$
end while
return $\bigcup_{t=1}^{k-1} s_t$

co-occurrence of all pairs of subsets within the seed must occur together with a frequency above a threshold value at a given significance level. This effectively ensures that cluster seeds of size ≥ 2 have items that co-occur together at a frequency that is statistically significant. In addition, we require that all cluster seeds satisfy an improvement constraint when they are extended. We first define the concept of relative support.

Definition 1 (Relative Support). The relative support of an itemset X_k of size k is defined to be the ratio of the support of X_k to the support of Y_{k-1} which is that (k−1)-sized subset of X_k with the maximum support.

$$RS(X_k) = \frac{\sup(X_k)}{\sup(Y_{k-1})}$$

We are now in a position to determine if a seed should be extended.

Definition 2 (Extension of a Seed). Given two existing seeds, X_{k-1} and Y_{k-1}, X_{k-1} is extended to a new seed $X_{k-1} \cup Y_{k-1}$ if and only if:

$$\varphi(X_{k-1}, Y_{k-1}) > \chi_c^2,$$
$$RS(X_{k-1} \cup Y_{k-1}) - RS(X_{k-1}) > \sigma, \text{and}$$
$$RS(X_{k-1} \cup Y_{k-1}) - RS(Y_{k-1}) > \sigma$$

where φ denotes the chi square correlation coefficient, χ_c^2, the chi square cut-off threshold at the c% confidence level and σ is a user-defined threshold.

The rationale behind extension lies in the fact that the new itemset to be added to the seed has a statistically strong correlation with the existing seed and that the inclusion of the new itemset will improve the relative support of the seed above a user defined minimum threshold. The algorithm for the seed clustering phase is shown below. In the next section, we formulate an algorithm for allocating transactions to clusters based on the seeds constructed in the algorithm above.

Allocation Phase

The seeds produced in the initial phase are considered as the initial centroids for the clusters. In this phase, transactions are assigned to clusters on the basis of similarity to cluster centroids. In order to measure similarity we use a modified version of the Jaccard similarity coefficient (Ivchenko & Honov, 2006). For each transaction, t, we calculate the similarity between t and the existing centroid, c_k. The similarity, sim, is between t and the c_k is calculated as:

$$sim(t, c_k) = \frac{|\, t \cap c_k\, |}{|\, t \cup c_k\, | - |\, t \cap c_k\, | + 1}$$

$$J = \frac{1}{k} \sum_{j=1}^{k} \frac{\sum_{t \in C_j} sim(t, c_j)}{|\, C_j\, |}$$

Given $t_1 = \{\{a\}, \{b\}, \{c\}, \{d\}, \{e\}\}$ and $c_1 = \{\{b\}, \{c\}\}$, here $t_1 \cap c_1 = \{\{b\}, \{c\}\}$ and $t_1 \cup c_1 = \{\{a\}, \{b\}, \{c\}, \{d\}, \{e\}\}$. Using our measure, the similarity between t_1 and c_1 is calculated as $2/(5 - 2 + 1) = 0.5$. The greater the overlap between t and C_k, the greater the value of sim coefficient.

Once all transactions are allocated to clusters, further refinement is accomplished by re-computing the centroids which may need to be updated with large items belonging to transactions allocated to a given cluster but not presently part of its centroid. The updating of centroids will result in the need for reorganization of the clusters, thus the process of centroid update and cluster reorganization will need to be repeated in tandem until a suitable point of stabilization is reached.

In order to determine the point of which stabilization is reached, we use a fitness function adapted from the particle swarm optimization approach (Xiao, Dow, Eberhart, Miled, & Oppelt, 2003) was proposed to find the optimal clusters. For all cluster $\{C_1, ... C_k\}$, the fitness function is calculated as:

Typically, we want to maximize the fitness value generated. The fitness measure calculates the average similarity between every transaction in a cluster to its centroid. We show the algorithm for allocation phase in Figure 2.

Evaluation of Transaction Clustering

In order to evaluate the effectiveness of our seed based approach to transaction clustering, seven different real world datasets taken from the UCI Machine Learning Repository (Newman, Hettich, Blake, & Merz, 1998) were used. A full analysis of the Cluster Seeding algorithm's performance, including a comparative study with the Large Item approach is in (Koh and Pears, 2007). We reproduce a summary here to illustrate its effectiveness as a pre-processing tool for rare association mining.

We first examine the quality of the clusters produced and cluster creation time. The quality metric that we used is the Root Mean Square Standard Deviation or RMSSTD index (Sharma,

Figure 2. Allocation Phase

Input: Transaction database, $D = \{t_1, \ldots, t_n\}$, Cluster Seed, $S = \{s_1, \ldots, s_k\}$
Output: Cluster, $C = \{C_1, \ldots C_k\}$
$J_{prev} \leftarrow 0$
$C \leftarrow \{C_k \leftarrow \emptyset | k \in S\}$
/* Assign transactions to clusters with the highest similarity */
$C \leftarrow \{C_k \cup t |\arg\max\{k \mapsto sim(t, s_k) | s_k \in S\}, t \in D\}$
$C \leftarrow \{C_k | C_k \neq \emptyset, C_k \in C\}$ /* Removes the empty clusters */
$J_{curr} \leftarrow \frac{1}{|C|} \sum_{j=1}^{|C|} \frac{\sum_{t \in C_j} sim(t, m_j)}{|C_j|}$
while $J_{prev} < J_{curr}$ **do**
    /* Refine clusters */
    $J_{prev} \leftarrow J_{curr}$
    $c \leftarrow \{c_k | \{i | i \in C_k, \text{count}(\{i\}, D) \geq |D| * \theta\}, C_k \in C$
    $C \leftarrow \{C_k \cup t |\arg\max\{k \mapsto sim(t, c_k) | c_k \in c\}, t \in D\}$
    $C \leftarrow \{C_k | C_k \neq \emptyset, C_k \in C\}$
    $J_{curr} \leftarrow \frac{1}{|C|} \sum_{j=1}^{|C|} \frac{\sum_{t \in C_j} sim(t, c_j)}{|C_j|}$
end while
return C

Table 1.Experiment results

Dataset	No Trans	Cluster Seeding		Large Item	
		RMSSTD Index	Time(s)	RMSSTD Index	Time(s)
Zoo	101	21.2	4.4	24.9	13.7
Hepatitis	155	25.9	3.6	26.5	23.1
Spect Heart	267	27.7	13.1	29.2	46.9
Flag	194	40.8	16.7	41.7	188.3
Heart-Cleveland	303	20.4	14.4	21.4	66.5
Soybean-Large	307	44.8	15.1	45.2	239.2
Congressional Votes	435	19.9	15.8	20.6	155.6
Mushroom	8124	26.9	4042.1	30.0	28684.0

1996), a commonly used metric for this purpose. RMSSTD measures the variance within a cluster, which in turn indicates the degree of homogeneity in a cluster. Since the main objective of cluster analysis is to form homogeneous groups, we chose to use the RMSSTD index. The RMSSTD should be as small as possible. In the case that the values of RMSSTD are higher than of another approach, we have an indication that the clustering solution is worse. Table 1 below shows that our Cluster Seeding approach outperforms Large Items across all datasets tested.

In terms of cluster quality the cluster seeding algorithm consistently returned lower RMSSTD values than its Large Item counterpart. With respect to processing time the Cluster Seeding approach returned run times that were generally lower, with the difference in timing between the two approaches widening with increasing da-

tabase size, as evidenced with the soybean and mushroom dataset. This suggests that the cluster seeding approach scales better with respect to dataset size.

We next examine cluster homogeneity from a different perspective, i.e. support. We use both real-world and synthetic data for this purpose. We consider the Zoo, Congressional Votes, Hepatitis and Mushroom datasets and measure the percentage of homogeneous attributes across each of them. For each cluster we record the support received by each attribute; if this support exceeds 80% then we consider the attribute to be homogeneous. Table 2 gives the degrees of homogeneity for the Cluster Seeding and Large Item approaches.

It is evident from Table 2 that Cluster Seeding once again outperforms its Large Item counterpart on this measure of cluster quality as well. We now turn our attention to the synthetic data. To assess

Table 2. Comparison between seed clustering and large items on real-world data

Dataset	Cluster Seeding	Large Item
	% of Homogeneous Attributes	% of Homogeneous Attributes
Zoo	94	50
Votes	77	50
Hepatitis	66	40
Mushroom	57	16

Table 3. Synthetic datasets

Dataset	|C|	|T|	|L|	|R|	|D|
C4.T10.L16.R16.D1K	4	10	16	16	1000
C4.T10.L16.R32.D10K	4	10	16	32	10000

the performance of our algorithm in discovering rare rules, we used a synthetic data generator. Table 3 summarizes the characteristics of several of the datasets generated during our tests. To create a dataset D, our synthetic data generation program takes the following parameters: number of clusters |C|, number of transactions |D|, average size of transactions |T|, number of large itemsets |L|, average size of large itemsets |I|, number of rare itemsets |R|, and average size of rare itemsets |r|. Each itemset has a weight associated with it, which corresponds to the probability that this itemset will be picked. Each cluster is assigned a set of large and rare itemsets. Only itemsets which belong to a cluster can be assigned to a specific transaction. The itemsets are randomly assigned to the transaction based on a Poisson distribution.

We first determine the size of the next transaction. The transaction in the dataset is randomly assigned a cluster number based on a Poisson distribution. We then fill the transactions with items. Each transaction is assigned a series of potential frequent itemsets and/or a rare itemset. The rare itemsets are only injected into the particular cluster that was randomly assigned by the Poisson distribution. Typically, in the datasets generated the clusters may consist of large clusters which have more transactions, as well as clusters which are relatively smaller and may contain a lesser number of transactions than the maximum support threshold set for the dataset. This formulation is to ensure that we are able to produce rules that are not just rare to the dataset, but also to the cluster.

For each value of the number of rare itemsets parameter which ranged from 4 to 64 we generated 10 datasets at random and measured the average degree of homogeneity. In all cases it turned that the average was 100%. In fact each and every run resulted in a value of 100% for each value of the rare itemsets parameter, once again confirming the degree of purity gained with the Cluster Seeding approach.

In this section we have established the purity of the clusters produced by the Cluster Seeding algorithm. Purity is the ideal platform on which to build a rare association rule miner as a high degree of purity ensures that cross-cluster contamination is kept to a minimum, thus facilitating the discovery of association rules that would not otherwise be discovered, either with a sub-optimal cluster configuration or on an un-partitioned dataset.

Rare Association Rule Mining via Transaction Clustering

We start by presenting the basic version of the Apriori Inverse algorithm and in the next section we discuss how it can be used in a clustered setting. We also discuss the extensions required to incorporate a weighting scheme to prune the rule base to a manageable size. In the experimental results section we will see that the weighting scheme has the added benefit of increasing rule precision.

The Basic Apriori Inverse Algorithm

We first give a formal statement of the rare association rule mining problem. Let I = {i_1, i_2, ..., i_m} be the universe of items and D be a set of transactions, where each transaction T is a set of items such that $T \subseteq I$. An association rule is an

Figure 3. Apriori Inverse Algorithm

```
Input: Transaction Database D, universe of items I, maxsup value
Output: Rare Itemsets
N ← |D|
Idx ← invert(D, I)
k ← 1
S_k ← {{i}|i ∈ dom Idx, count({i}, Idx) < N.maxsup}
while S_k ≠ ∅ do
    k ← k + 1
    C_k ← {x∪y|x, y ∈ S_{k-1}, |x∩y| = k - 2}
    S_k ← {c|c ∈ C_k, count(c, Idx) > minabssup, count(c, Idx) < N.maxsup}
end while
return ∪_{i=2}^{k-1} S_i
```

implication of the form: $A \rightarrow B$, where $A \subset I$, $B \subset I$, and $A \cap B = \varnothing$. A is referred to as the antecedent of the rule, and B as the consequent. The rule $A \rightarrow B$ holds in the transaction set D with confidence c% if c% of transactions in D that contain X also contain Y. The rule $A \rightarrow B$ has support s% in the transaction set D, if s% of transactions in D contains AB (Agrawal & Srikant, 1994). In the rare mining context, all rules R such as: $A \rightarrow B$ need to satisfy:

C(R) ≥ CLower, where CLower is the lower bound confidence threshold, and

S(R) ≤ SUpper, where SUpper is the upper bound support threshold

Figure 3 below gives the pseudo code for the Apriori Inverse algorithm. As can be seen from Figure 3 above, the algorithm also imposes another support constraint, called the MinAbsSup which is minimum number of times that itemsets (A,B) need to co-occur in order for them to be considered for rule generation. This constraint is derived from the Fisher test for significance of co-occurrence. Because we are dealing with candidate itemsets with low support, the chance that an itemset appears due to noise or just by coincidence is higher than for candidate itemsets with higher support. Itemsets that occur within the dataset due to co-incidence should therefore be pruned out during candidate itemset generation. Apriori-Inverse thus inverts the downward-closure principle of the Apriori algorithm; rather than all subsets of candidate itemsets being over minsup, all subsets

are under maximum support threshold (maxsup). Since making a candidate itemset longer cannot increase its support, all extensions are viable except those that fall under the minimum absolute support requirement. Those exceptions are pruned out, and are not used to extend itemsets in the next round. We now describe how MinAbsSup is calculated from the Fisher test.

Suppose that we have N transactions in which antecedent A occurs in a transactions and consequent B occurs in b transactions, we can calculate the probability that A and B will occur together exactly c times by chance. We refer to this as "probability of chance collision". We can calculate this probability using Pcc in (1). The probability that A and B will occur together exactly c times is:

$$\mathrm{Pcc}\left(c \mid N, a, b\right) = \frac{\binom{a}{c}\binom{N-a}{b-c}}{\binom{N}{b}}$$

This equation is the usual calculation for exact probability of a 2×2 contingency table. Now, we want the least number of collisions above which Pcc is smaller than some small value p (usually 0.001). This is:

$$\text{MinAbsSup}\big(N, a, b, p\big) = \min\left\{ m \mid \sum_{i=0}^{i=m} \text{Pcc}\big(i \mid N, a, b\big) \geq 1.0 - p \right\}$$

This formula amounts to inverting the usual sense of Fisher's exact test (Weisstein, 2005). Usually a 2×2 contingency table is provided and a p-value calculated however here we are providing two of the four values and a p-value and calculating the minimum value to complete the table. For instance, $\text{Pcc}\big(100 \mid 10000, 1000, 1000\big) = 0.044$.

Similar to Apriori, the algorithm is based on a level-wise search. On the first pass through the dataset, an inverted index is built using the unique items as keys and the transaction IDs as data. At this point, the support of each unique item (the 1-itemsets) in the dataset is available as the length of each data chain. To generate k-itemsets under maxsup, the (k − 1)-itemsets are extended in precisely the same manner as Apriori to generate candidate k-itemsets. That is, a (k − 1)-itemset i_1 is turned into a k -itemset by finding another (k − 1)-itemset i_2 that has a matching prefix of size (k − 2), and attaching the last item of i_1 to i_2. For example, the 3-itemsets {1, 3, 4} and {1, 3, 6} can be extended to form the 4-itemset {1, 3, 4, 6}, but {1, 3, 4} and {1, 2, 5} will not produce a 4-itemset due to their prefixes failing to match at the second item.

Rare Association Rule Mining via Transaction Clustering

Initially we cluster the transactions into different partitions and then mine each of the partitions for rare association rules. We then apply the basic Apriori Inverse algorithm against each of the partitions. Our approach, called AICLuster, is able to produce interesting rules which may not be detected in Apriori-Inverse. For example, consider a case where we are looking at a diagnosis which leads to mortality in a medical scenario. When we partition the datasets into clusters, a trend we may

notice is that the treatment leads to a much higher mortality rate in the cluster corresponding to the intensive care section when compared to the rest of the dataset. This is however not very interesting. On the other hand, if we detect rules in clusters from the outpatient unit which refer to mortality, this instead would be considered more interesting as this represents relatively rare and unexpected events which deserve closer examination as to the circumstances that led to the fatalities. These types of rules may never have manifested with Apriori-Inverse on the un-partitioned dataset. We now offer a formal proof of AICluster's rule coverage vis-a-vis the Apriori-Inverse algorithm.

Theorem: AICluster together with traditional frequent mining has a coverage that is greater than a combination of Apriori-Inverse with traditional association rule mining.

Proof: Refer (Koh and Pears, 2008) for a full proof.

The theorem compares the rule coverage of operating the Apriori Inverse rule generator in an un-partitioned dataset as opposed to a dataset that has been clustered with the Cluster Seeding algorithm. In a real-world setting we envisage that rare association rule mining will be done in conjunction with frequent rule mining and thus any rule discovered on the unclustered data set will be picked up by AICluster under association rule mining as a whole. The importance of this theorem is that AICluster's rule base is larger than that of the basic Apriori Inverse algorithm. In the experimental results section, we show that AICluster discovers certain rules that Apriori Inverse is unable to identify. At the same time, certain itemsets that are rare across the entire dataset become frequent within a cluster thus inhibiting rule discovery by AICluster. However, with suitable adjustment of the upper bound support threshold that will take the mining from the rare to the frequent realm, it will be possible to identify the rules that were missed by AICluster with settings suitable for frequent association mining.

Weighted Apriori Inverse

With the standard Apriori Inverse algorithm, any itemset I_1 can be freely extended to I_1I_2 without hindrance as $\sup(I_1I_2) \leq \text{supp}(I_1)$ is guaranteed. In other words there is no upward closure property in rare mining analogous to the downward closure property in traditional frequent mining. The only constraint that is faced is the minabsupp constraint. However, this constraint is not effective at enforcing upward closure as its only role is to prevent noise from entering the rule generation process.

Upward closure is desirable as the rule base in dense datasets can grow in an unbounded manner, with a large number of rules consisting of long strings of terms containing itemsets which are not rare on their own but are rare in combination with each other, thus diminishing the effectiveness of the rule mining process. We extend Apriori Inverse by using a weighted maximum support value that is unique to each itemset. The weights are to enable itemsets containing rare items to have a higher maximum support threshold, while those itemsets having a relatively high proportion of more frequent itemsets are assigned a lower support threshold. A higher support threshold for an itemset i_1 means that in the next round of combination, itemsets i_2 whose support is smaller in relation to i_1 will be needed to meet the tighter support threshold that has been set. This effectively favors rare terms over those that are frequent.

We implement the weighting scheme through a weight factor β_k that is updated at each combination round k. Suppose that at round k the itemset $i_1i_2.....i_{k-1}$ is being considered for extension with itemset i_k. The candidate itemset $i_1i_2...i_k$ is given a weighted support $ws(i_1i_2....i_k) = \beta_k$, where β_k is defined by:

$$\beta_k = \frac{\sup(i_1i_2...i_{k-1}) \times \min(\sup(i_1), \sup(i_2), ..\sup(i_{k-1}), \sup(i_k))}{\sup(i_k)}\beta_{k-1}$$

$$ws(i_1i_2....i_k) = \beta_k$$

Thus whenever a new itemset i_k has a lower support than any of the individual items $i_1, i_2, ..., i_k$ comprising the composite itemset $i_1i_2....i_{k-1}$ the result will be to multiply the existing value of β by $\sup(i_1i_2....i_{k-1})$. The itemset $i_1i_2....i_k$ is considered for rule generation only if $\sup(i_1i_2....i_k) \leq ws(i_1i_2.... i_k)$. We illustrate the use of the weighting scheme through an example. Suppose that the miner sets the initial value of β at $\beta_0 = 0.8$. Now suppose that we have itemset i_1 with $\sup(i_1) = 0.6$ being considered for extension with itemset i_2 with $\sup(i_2) = 0.6$. Thus at round 1 we have $\beta_1 = \frac{0.6 \times 0.6}{0.6}\beta_0$ $= 0.48$. This means that the weighted support for itemset i_1i_2, is given by $ws(i_1i_2)=0.48$. Thus itemset i_1 is extended to itemset i_2 if $\sup(i_1i_2) \leq ws(i_1i_2)=0.48$. Suppose that $\sup(i_1i_2) = 0.4$. Thus itemset i_1 is extended with itemset i_2 to form the composite i_1i_2. Now consider round 2; suppose that we have itemset i_3 with $\sup(i_3) = 0.2$. We now have $\beta_2 = \frac{0.4 \times 0.2}{0.2}\beta_1 = 0.4 \times 0.48 = 0.192$. The weighted support for itemset $i_1i_2i_3$ is given by $ws(i_1,i_2,i_3)=0.192$. Thus itemset i_1i_2 is extended to $i_1i_2i_3$ if $\sup(i_1i_2i_3) \leq ws(i_1i_2i_3)=0.192$.

Thus we can see the effect of introducing the weighted support scheme in the above example. In round 1, the support of the itemset to be introduced (i_2) did not have support less than the existing itemset i_1, so a relatively low support threshold of 0.48 was imposed in order for them to be combined together. This represents a steep drop in support by a factor of 0.6. The opposite happens in round 2 where the new itemset i_3 has a lower support than the composite i_1i_2 which resulted in a support threshold of 0.192. In this case the drop in support is not as steep, dropping by a factor of only 0.4. We now present the pseudo code for the Weighted Apriori Inverse algorithm in Figure 4.

Thus it can be seen from Figure 4 above that Weighted Apriori Inverse method is algorithmically very similar to the Apriori Inverse with two exceptions: the use of clusters as the unit of data

Figure 4. Weighted Apriori Inverse

```
Input: Transaction Database D, universe of items I, maxsup value
Output: Weighted Rare Itemsets
N ← |D|
Idx ← invert(D, I)
k ← 1
S_k ← {{i}|i ∈ dom Idx, count({i}, Idx) < N.maxsup}
while S_k ≠ ∅ do
    k ← k + 1
    C_k ← {x∪y|x, y ∈ S_{k-1}, |x∩y| = k − 2}
    ws(i_1, i_2, ..., i_k) ← β_k
    S_k ← {c|c ∈ C_k, ws(c, Idx).N > minabssup, ws(c, Idx) < maxsup}
end while
return ⋃_{t=2}^{k-1} S_t
```

on which the rules are generated and the use of the weighting scheme.

Experimental Results

In this section we conduct a three-way analysis between Apriori Inverse (henceforth known as API), Apriori Inverse with Clustering (henceforth known as APIC) and weighted Apriori Inverse (henceforth known as APICW) algorithms. As API has been tested extensively for the quality of rare rules that it generates (Koh and Rountree, 2005), we decided to restrict the analysis to a particular sub class of rare rules which we refer to as *absolute rare* rules.

With absolute rare rules, each term is in itself rare to the unit in which it resides. In terms of the un-partitioned dataset, absolute rules are those containing terms that are rare to the dataset as a whole. On the other hand, with respect to a cluster, absolute rare rules are those with terms that are rare to the cluster itself, thus imposing a much severer constraint on them passing the upper bound support threshold, maxsup. Thus certain rules R that hold on the un-partitioned dataset may no longer hold on a given cluster, particularly if that cluster happens to be small in relation to the other clusters generated. This tends to boost the Recall value for API vis-à-vis APIC. Likewise certain rare rules R' that are discovered by AP on the un-partitioned dataset may not be rare in the absolute sense as

they may contain itemsets that are frequent, but are rare in combination with each other.

We summarize below the conditions that need to be met for a rule R (X→Y) to qualify as an absolute rare rule.

Un-Partitioned Dataset

$$sup(X) < maxsup \qquad (1)$$

$$sup(Y) < maxsup \qquad (2)$$

$$conf(R) > minconf \qquad (3)$$

$$Lift(R) > L \qquad (4)$$

where $sup(X) = freq(X)/N$; N is the total number of transactions in the dataset; $sup(Y) = freq(Y)/N$.

Cluster

Rule R needs to satisfy all 4 constraints above as for the un-partitioned dataset, except that $sup(X) = freq_C(X)/N_c$, where $freq_C$, N_c are the frequency of occurrence of itemset X in cluster C and the size of cluster C respectively.

Table 4. Rule bases for the AIC and AI algorithms

Dataset	APIC		API					
	maxsup(0.30)		maxsup(0.10)		maxsup(0.20)		maxsup(0.30)	
	Rules	Avg Rule Support	Rules	Avg Rule Support	Rules	Avg Rule Support	Rules	Avg Rule Support
Zoo	2	4	1	8	10	11	72	13
Hepatitis	1	3	0	0	11	6	11	6
Flag	20	4	3	4	27	6	135	9
Heart	2	6	0	0	0	0	0	0
Soybean-Large	1803	6	166	7	6446	7	6975	8
Congressional Votes	3	3	0	0	0	0	0	0
Mushroom	765	27	10772	12	27505	17	39543	17

Experimentation on Real World Data

We start by presenting results for the real world data. We first conduct a two-way comparative analysis of the API and APIC algorithms on real-world data.

Our experimentation used the same real-world data and synthetic data that we used to illustrate the performance of the Cluster Seeding algorithm. We did not include the weighted schema in this experimentation as we wanted to first investigate from both a quantitative and qualitative viewpoint the effect that clustering has on the rule base produced by the basic Apriori Inverse algorithm.

Table 3 represents the rules found by the APIC and API algorithms. For APIC we set the maximum support threshold (maxsup) to 0.30 for all datasets except for the mushroom dataset. For six of the datasets, we ran API at three different maxsup values of 0.10, 0.20, and 0.30. This was done in order to obtain a bench-mark for comparison with APIC on the all important rule support measure. In all of the experiments, we set the minimum threshold values for confidence and lift to 0.90 and 1.0 respectively.

We now compare the number of rules generated using APIC with maxsup at 0.30 and API with maxsup at 0.10. From Table 4 above we can clearly

see that comparable levels of actual rule support occur at a maxsup of 0.3 for AIC and 0.1 for AI, the only exception being the mushroom dataset. As we expected, the maxsup threshold for APIC had to be set higher, due to the greater degree of homogeneity in the un-partitioned dataset. At these support thresholds we can see from Table 3 that the rule coverage for APIC is consistently greater than that of API for the first six datasets in Table 3 (once again, with the exception of mushroom). In the case of the mushroom dataset, the average rule support for APIC at 27 was much higher than that of API at 12 and so the number of rules generated with the latter was much bigger.

Table 5 gives a more in-depth view of the rule bases covered by the two algorithms. The most striking feature is the very low degree of overlap between the two algorithms. The degree of overlap ranged from 0% (for mushroom) to 10% (for the much smaller Flag dataset) across the range of datasets tested. Coupled with the fact that APIC on its own covers a very large percentage of the total rule base in the rare mining mode, this shows once again its superiority over API in terms of rule coverage. As shown by the Theorem above this percentage will rise to 100% when frequent

Table 5. Summary of rule counts for the APIC and API algorithms

Dataset	No of Rules with API	No. of Rules with APIC	No of Rules on the Complete Set	No. of Rules Overlapping
Zoo	1	2	3	0
Hepatitis	0	1	1	0
Flag	3	20	21	2
Heart	0	2	2	0
Soybean-Large	166	1862	1993	35
Congressional Votes	0	3	3	0
Mushroom	10772	765	11537	0

association rule mining is done in conjunction with rare mining via APIC.

Next we analyze the information content of the rules produced by these techniques by taking an in-depth look at the rare rules produced by APIC which could not be discovered by API.

Rule Analysis on Congressional Votes

The APIC algorithm identified 4 rare rules from the set of clustered transactions in Congressional Votes dataset using a maximum support threshold of 0.3. Clustering on this dataset produced a total of 4 clusters. Two of the rules were from cluster 0 and the other 2 rules came from cluster 3.

Cluster 0:
  physician-fee-freeze:y → Class:republican, (Conf:1.00, Lift:31.0)
  Class:republican → physician-fee-freeze:y, (Conf:1.00, Lift:31.0)

Cluster 3:
  anti-satellite-test-ban:y → export-administration-act-south-africa: y, (Conf:0.94, Lift:1.54)
  physician-fee-freeze:n → Class:democrat, (Conf:1.00, Lift:16.83)

However the API algorithm failed to produce any rare rules at the upper bound support threshold

that we set. This is due to the groupings contaminating each other and preventing candidate rules from meeting the minimum confidence threshold.

Rule Analysis on Zoo

Using APIC we were able to find 2 rules from the set of clustered transactions in Zoo Dataset.

Cluster 0:
  fins:1 → aquatic:1 (Conf =1.00, Lift =6.33)
  legs:0 → fins:1 (Conf =1.00, Lift =9.50)

These two rules are particularly interesting, as the class of animals in the cluster was Type 1 which is mammal. In this instance, we only had three transactions (seal, dolphins, porpoise) which have fins, are aquatic, and are mammals. Finding these rules within this cluster is indeed interesting. In the case of API we were able to detect only 1 rule with maxsup at 0.10.

API (maxsup =0.10)
  type:6 → legs:6 (Conf:1.00, Lift:10.10)

With a maximum support value of 0.30, we were able to find 2 more rules with APIC. Using APIC we were not able to find the specific rule which API had found. This is because we are looking for absolute rarity in using APIC as to

Figure 5. Precision vs. number of rules injected for APC and APCW

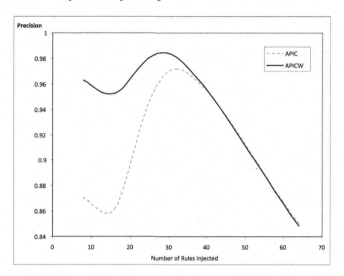

relative rarity when we use API. In the general sense the rule produced by API is indeed interesting however it is a relative rare rule as compared to the dataset, whereas, in the rules generated by APIC are considered absolute rare rules.

Rule Analysis on Heart Cleveland Dataset

Using APIC we were able to find 2 rules from the Heart Cleveland Dataset.

Cluster 0:
num:3 → ca:2 (Conf =1.00, Lift =11.22)

Cluster 1:
num:0 → thal:normal (Conf =0.92, Lift =2.08)

However we were not able to detect any rules with API alone on the un-partitioned dataset. This is because these rules were contaminated from other sub groupings.

Experimentation on Synthetic Data

In this section we conduct an analysis on all three algorithms using synthetic data that we gener-

ated as described earlier in this chapter. With synthetic data we are able to measure important metrics such as Precision and Recall as we inject a known number of rules into the dataset. Unlike with the experimentation on the real-world data, we set the upper bound support threshold, maxsup to 0.1 for all three algorithms. Equalizing the support threshold to 0.1 tends to favor API over APIC (and also APICW) in terms of the Recall metric as shown by the results on the Mushroom dataset in the previous section. Our first experiment compared the effect of varying the number of rules injected on the Precision metric.

Comparison of APIC and APICW on Precision

We ran the two algorithms for a given value of the "number of rules" variable for 10 different datasets that were generated at random and measured the average value of Precision across the 10 runs. Figure 5 below shows the variation of Precision against the number of absolute rare rules injected. The settings that we used for this experiment were maxsup = 0.1, minconf = 0.9 and Lift = 1.0.

Figure 6. Recall vs. number of rules injected for API, APIC and APICW

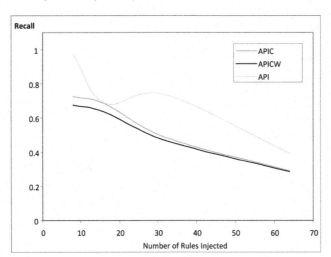

Figure 5 shows that the Precision values are high for both algorithms in the range tested. However, it is clear that the weighting scheme has succeeded in improving Precision. This is due to the fact that APICW tends to impose tighter upper bound support constraints whenever itemsets with relatively high support are absorbed into an existing itemset during itemset extension, thus reducing the probability of a frequent itemset being generated.

Comparison on Recall

In this experiment we tested the effect of varying the number of rules injected on the Recall metric. We expected API to outperform both its clustering variants (APIC and APICW) due to the fact that the support thresholds was set at the identical value for all three algorithms and this was borne out in by Figure 6.

Figure 6 shows that the two cluster based algorithms perform very similarly with respect to Recall with APIC having a slight advantage due to the pruning scheme used by APICW that sometimes has a tendency to prune legitimate (i.e. absolute rare) rules in addition to rules that are rare to the dataset as a whole. As the number

of rules injected becomes large it is evident that both algorithms find it increasingly difficult to find legitimate rules. This is due to the manner in which we generated the datasets. We increased the number of rare rules injected by increasing the number of rare itemsets allocated to a cluster, while holding the number of frequent itemsets constant. As the number of rare itemsets increases, the transactions in small clusters become increasingly dense thus making it more difficult for the algorithms to meet the maxsup constraint.

It is also clear that API outperforms the other two algorithms in the entire range tested. At the same time it is also evident that API copes better with the increasing number of rare itemsets injected as it does not face the problem of fragmentation of the dataset into clusters of uneven size.

Result Summary

The results presented above have clearly shown the effectiveness of clustering data prior to performing rare association rule mining. Rare rules which would never manifest with an un-partitioned dataset were discovered with both cluster based variations of the Apriori Inverse algorithm. At the same time both cluster-based algorithms displayed high levels of Precision with the synthetic data that we used. Although the Apriori Inverse algorithm outperformed its cluster-based variants on Recall with respect to absolute rare rules, empirical evidence from real world data suggests that with the right setting of upper bound support threshold that the cluster-based algorithms would hold their own against the Apriori Inverse algorithm.

CONCLUSIONS AND DIRECTIONS FOR FUTURE WORK

In this chapter we proposed a comprehensive approach to the problem of rare association rule mining. The novelty of the approach derives from the integration of two well established approaches, namely the use of a rigorous approach in determining genuinely rare items and the use of clustering as a pre-processing tool. We also proposed and demonstrated the effectiveness of a novel weighting scheme in implementing the upward closure property, a line of research that has hitherto not been explored. We also took advantage of the clustering scheme to study the behaviour of absolute rare rule in a systematic manner.

One area that has remain untouched, and this is also true of frequent itemset mining, is the setting of support thresholds that take into account data density in the underlying dataset to be mined. With respect to rare itemset mining, we would like the initial value of our β coefficient, β_0 to be related to density, thus decreasing the value to be low for a dense dataset while proportionately increasing the value for sparse data. This would take the guess work out of setting the value by the miner and effectively place both dense and spare datasets on a more equal footing in terms of size of the rule base generated.

We also anticipate that with advances in transaction clustering, the quality of rules generated would improve as a result. One of the biggest challenges faced by a clustering algorithm, particularly when it is employed in conjunction with rule generation is to ensure that clusters do not split off into small sub-clusters of their own in a bid to increase homogeneity. This is of course a challenge in the traditional clustering arena as well, but it assumes greater importance in the rare association rule mining realm, as the smaller a cluster gets, the greater the chances of itemsets not meeting the upper bound support threshold. What this means in essence is that our loose integration between clustering and rare mining should be replaced by a tightly integrated strategy where different cluster configurations are evaluated in terms of rare rule generation capability and the best configuration is then submitted to a detailed rule mining module that will implement details such as filtering noise, weighing itemsets, and so on.

REFERENCES

Agrawal, R., Imielinski, T., & Swami, A. (1993). Mining association rules between sets of items in large databases. In P. Buneman & S. Jajodia (Eds.), *Proceedings of the 1993 ACM SIGMOD international conference on management of data* (pp. 207 – 216).

Agrawal, R., & Srikant, R. (1994). Fast algorithms for mining association rules. In Proceedings *of the 20th International Conference on Very Large Databases* (pp. 487–499).

Cutting, D. R., Pedersen, J. O., Karger, D., & Tukey, J. W. (1992). Scatter/gather: A cluster-based approach to browsing large document collections. In *Proceedings of the fifteenth annual International ACM SIGIR conference on research and development in information retrieval* (pp. 318–329).

Ganti, V., Gehrke, J., & Ramakrishnan, R. (1999). CACTUS: Clustering categorical data using summaries. In *KDD '99: Proceedings of the fifth ACM SIGKDD International conference on knowledge discovery and data mining* (pp. 73–83). New York, NY, USA: ACM Press.

Gibson, D., Kleinberg, J. M., & Raghavan, P. (1998). Clustering categorical data: An approach based on dynamical systems. In *VLDB '98: Proceedings of the 24rd international conference on very large data bases* (pp. 311– 322). San Francisco, CA, USA: Morgan Kaufmann Publishers Inc.

Guha, S., Rastogi, R., & Shim, K. (2000). ROCK: A robust clustering algorithm for categorical attributes. *Information Systems, 25*(5), 345–366. doi:10.1016/S0306-4379(00)00022-3

Ivchenko, G. I., & Honov, S. A. (2006). On the Jaccard similarity test. *Journal of Mathematical Sciences, 88*(6), 789–794. doi:10.1007/BF02365362

Jain, A. K., Murty, M. N., & Flynn, P. J. (1999). Data clustering: a review. *ACM Computing Surveys, 31*(3), 264–323. doi:10.1145/331499.331504

Koh, Y. S., & Pears, R. (2008). Transaction Clustering Using a Seeds Based Approach. *Advances in Knowledge Discovery and Data Mining, 12th Pacific-Asia Conference on Knowledge Discovery and Data Mining* (pp. 916-922). Springer-Verlag.

Koh, Y. S., Rountree, N., & O'Keefe, R. A. (2006). Finding Non-Coincidental Sporadic Rules using Apriori-Inverse. *International Journal of Data Warehousing and Mining, 2*(2), 38–54.

Koh, Y. S., Rountree, N., & O'Keefe, R. A. (2008, January). Mining interesting imperfectly sporadic rules. *Knowledge and Information Systems, 14*(2), 179–196. doi:10.1007/s10115-007-0074-6

Liu, B., Hsu, W., & Ma, Y. (1999a). Mining association rules with multiple minimum supports. In *Proceedings of the 5th ACM SIGKDD International Conference on Knowledge Discovery and Data Mining* (pp. 337–341).

Liu, B., Hsu, W., & Ma, Y. (1999b). Pruning and summarizing the discovered associations. In *Proceedings of the 5th ACM SIGKDD International Conference on Knowledge Discovery and Data Mining* (pp. 125–134).

Newman, D., Hettich, S., Blake, C., & Merz, C. (1998). *UCI repository of machine learning databases*. http://www.ics.uci.edu/~mlearn/ ML-Repository.html.

Plasse, M., Niang, N., Saporta, G., Villeminot, A., & Leblond, L. (2007). Combined use of association rules mining and clustering methods to find relevant links between binary rare attributes in a large data set. *Computational Statistics & Data Analysis, 52*(1), 596–613. doi:10.1016/j.csda.2007.02.020

Sharma, S. (1996). *Applied multivariate techniques*. John Wiley & Sons Inc.

Szathmary, L., Napoli, A., & Valtchev, P. (2007, October 29-31). Towards Rare Itemset Mining. In *Proceedings of the 19th IEEE international Conference on Tools with Artificial intelligence - Vol. 1 (ICTAI 2007) - Volume 1. ICTAI. IEEE Computer Society, Washington, DC,* (pp. 305-312)

Wang, K., Xu, C., & Liu, B. (1999). Clustering transactions using large items. In *CIKM '99: Proceedings of the eighth international conference on information and knowledge management* (pp. 483–490). New York, NY, USA: ACM Press.

Xiao, X., Dow, E. R., Eberhart, R., Miled, Z. B., & Oppelt, R. J. (2003). Gene clustering using self-organizing maps and particle swarm optimization. In *IPDPS'03: Proceedings of the 17th international symposium on parallel and distributed processing*. Washington, DC, USA: IEEE Computer Society.

Xiong, H., Shekhar, S., Tan, P., & Kumar, V. (2004). Exploiting a support-based upper bound of Pearson's correlation coefficient for efficiently identifying strongly correlated pairs. In *Proceedings of the Tenth ACM SIGKDD international Conference on Knowledge Discovery and Data Mining* (Seattle, WA, USA, August 22 - 25, 2004). (pp.334-343). KDD '04. ACM, New York, NY, Xu, J., Xiong, H., Sung, S. Y., & Kumar, V. (2003). A new clustering algorithm for transaction data via caucus. In *Proceedings Advances in knowledge discovery and data mining: 7th Pacific-Asia conference, PAKDD 2003*, (pp. 551–562) Seoul, Korea.

Yun, C.-H., Chuang, K.-T., & Chen, M.-S. (2001). An efficient clustering algorithm for market basket data based on small large ratios. In *Compsac '01: Proceedings of the 25th international computer software and applications conference on invigorating software development* (pp. 505–510). Washington, DC, USA: IEEE Computer Society.

Yun, H., Ha, D., Hwang, B., & Ryu, K. H. (2003). Mining association rules on significant rare data using relative support. *Journal of Systems and Software*, *67*, 181–191. doi:10.1016/S0164-1212(02)00128-0

Chapter 7
Finding Minimal Infrequent Elements in Multi-Dimensional Data Defined over Partially Ordered Sets and its Applications

Khaled M. Elbassioni
Max-Planck-Institute für Informatik, Saarbrücken, Germany

ABSTRACT

The authors consider databases in which each attribute takes values from a partially ordered set (poset). This allows one to model a number of interesting scenarios arising in different applications, including quantitative databases, taxonomies, and databases in which each attribute is an interval representing the duration of a certain event occurring over time. A natural problem that arises in such circumstances is the following: given a database D and a threshold value t, find all collections of "generalizations" of attributes which are "supported" by less than t transactions from D. They call such collections infrequent elements. Due to monotonicity, they can reduce the output size by considering only minimal infrequent elements. We study the complexity of finding all minimal infrequent elements for some interesting classes of posets. The authors show how this problem can be applied to mining association rules in different types of databases, and to finding "sparse regions" or "holes" in quantitative data or in databases recording the time intervals during which a re-occurring event appears over time. Their main focus will be on these applications rather than on the correctness or analysis of the given algorithms.

INTRODUCTION

The problem of mining association rules from large databases has emerged as an important area of research since their introduction in (Agrawal et

al., 1993). Typically, the different data attributes exhibit certain correlations between them, which can be summarized in terms of certain rules, provided that enough transactions or records in the database agree with these rules. For a few examples, in a database storing sets of items purchased by different customers in a supermarket, it may be interesting to

DOI: 10.4018/978-1-60566-754-6.ch007

observe a rule of the from "most customers that purchase bread and butter tend also to purchase orange juice"; in a database storing personal data about individuals, it may be interesting to observe that "most individuals who are married and with age in the range 28-34 have at least 2 cars"; and in a database storing data about the time periods a given service is used by different customers, an interesting observation may take the form: "customers who make full use of the service between 2:00-3:00 on Friday tend also to use the service between 2:00-3:00 on Saturday". Such information could be useful, for example, for placing items next to each other on supermarket shelves or providing better services for anticipated customers.

Most of the work on finding association rules divides the task into two basic steps: the first one is to identify those collections of items or attribute values that appear together frequently in the database, the so-called *frequent* itemsets; the second step is to generate association rules from these. While the first step has received considerable attention in the literature, with many algorithms proposed, the second step seems to be somehow overlooked. In this chapter, we will have a more careful look at this latter step, and show in fact that a lot of redundancy can be eliminated from the generated rules by solving the somewhat complementary problem of finding *infrequent sets*, i.e., those collection of items that *rarely* appear together in any transaction. This gives one important motivation for studying the problem of finding infrequent collections of values that can be assumed by the attributes of the given database. But apart from that, finding such collections is a problem of independent interest, since each infrequent collection of attribute values indicates rare associations between these values. For instance, in the database of personal data above one can observe a rule like "no individuals with age between 26 and 38 have a single car", and in the database recording service usage, one may observe that ``Fewer than 40% of the customers occupy the service on Friday between 2:00-3:00 and on

Saturday between 2:00-4:00". Another application will be given in Section 4.2, in which the objective is to discover the so-called *rare association rules*, which are informally rules that result from data appearing rarely in the database.

Rather than using *binarization*, as is common in the literature (see e.g. Srikant et al., 1995; Srikant et al. 1996), to represent the different ranges of each attribute by binary values, we shall consider more generally databases in which each attribute assumes values belonging to a *partially ordered set* (poset). This general framework will allow us to model a number of different scenarios in data mining applications, including the mining of association rules for databases with quantitative, categorical and hierarchical attributes, and the discovery of missing associations or ``holes'' in data (see (Agrawal et al., 1996; Liu et al., 1997; Mun et al., 1998)). One important feature of this framework is that it allows us to find *generalized associations*, which are obtained by generalizing some attribute values, for which otherwise there exist no enough support from the database transactions. As an example on the supermarket data above, it may be the case that most customers who purchase milk products tend also to purchase bread, but in the database only "cheese" and "butter" appear as items. In this case generalizing both these items to "milk products" allows us to discover the above rule.

We begin our exposition in the next section with recalling some definitions and terminologies related to partially ordered sets and give some examples of databases defined over products of posets. In Section 3, we define the main object of interest in this chapter, namely minimal infrequent elements in products of posets, describe the associated enumeration problem, and discuss how to measure its complexity. Section 4 gives some applications of such enumeration problems to finding association rules in different types of databases and to finding sparse regions on quantitative data. In Section 5, we discuss briefly the complexity of finding infrequent/minimal infrequent elements.

Figure 1. Lattices, forests and chains

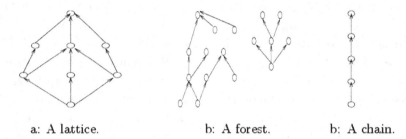

a: A lattice.   b: A forest.   b: A chain.

We conclude in Section 6 with pointers to implementation issues and some open problems.

DATABASES DEFINED ON PRODUCTS OF PARTIALLY ORDERED SETS

Recall that a partially ordered set (poset) is defined by a pair $(P, \leq)$, where P is a finite set and $\leq$ is a binary relation satisfying the following three properties:

1. reflexivity: $a \leq a$ for all $a \in P$;
2. anti-symmetry: if $a \leq b$ and $b \leq a$ then $a = b$;
3. transitivity: if $a \leq b$ and $b \leq c$ then $a \leq c$.

Let P be (the ground set of) a poset. Two elements x,y in P are said to be comparable if either $x \leq y$ or $y \leq x$ and otherwise are said to be incomparable. A chain (anti-chain) of P is subset of pairwise comparable (respectively, incomparable) elements. For an element x in P, we say that $y \in P$ is an immediate successor of x if $y \geq x$ and there is no $z \in P_i$ such that $y > z > x$. Immediate predecessors of x are defined similarly. The precedence graph of a poset P is a directed acyclic graph with vertex set P, and set of arcs $\{(x,y): y$ is an immediate successor of $x\}$. We say that poset P is a forest (or a tree) if the underlying undirected graph of the precedence graph of P is a forest (respectively, a

tree). For two elements $x,y \in P$, z is called an upper (lower) bound if $z \geq x$ and $z \geq y$ (respectively, $z \leq x$ and $z \leq y$). A join semi-lattice (meet semi-lattice) is a poset in which every two elements x,y have a unique minimum upper-bound, called the join, $x \vee y$ (respectively, a unique maximum lower-bound, called the meet, $x \wedge y$). A lattice is a poset which is both a join and a meet semi-lattice. For a poset P, the dual poset P* is the poset with the same set of elements as P, but such that $x < y$ in P* whenever $x < y$ in P. The unique class of posets in the intersection of forests and lattices is the class of totally ordered sets, in which every two elements are comparable. Since the precedence graphs of such posets is a path, we shall refer also to them as chains. (See Figure 1 for an example.) For a good introduction to the theory of posets, we refer the reader to (Schroder 2003).

Let $P = P_1 \times \ldots \times P_n$ be the Cartesian product of n partially ordered sets. We will overload notation and denote by $\leq$ the precedence relation in P and also in $P_1, \ldots, P_n$, i.e., if $p = (p_1, \ldots, p_n) \in P$ and $q = (q_1, \ldots, q_n) \in P$, then $p \leq q$ in P if and only if $p_1 \leq q_1$ in P_1, $p_2 \leq q_2$ in $P_2, \ldots,$ and $p_n \leq q_n$ in P_n.

We consider a database $D \subseteq P$ of transactions, each of which is an n-dimensional vector of attribute values over P. This gives a fairly general framework that allows us to model many interesting scenarios. Let us look at some examples.

Table 1. Supermarket data

TID	Bread	Butter	Cheese	Milk	Orange Juice	Yogurt
T^1	1	1	1	1	1	1
T^2	1	1	1	0	0	0
T^3	1	1	0	1	1	1
T^4	1	1	1	0	1	0
T^5	1	1	1	0	0	1
T^6	1	0	0	0	1	0
T^7	1	1	1	1	1	1
T^8	0	1	1	1	0	0
T^9	1	1	0	0	1	0
T^{10}	1	1	1	1	1	1

Binary Databases

Perhaps, the simplest example is when the database is used to store transactions representing subsets of items purchased by different customers in, say, a supermarket. Formally, we have a set I of n items, and each record in the database is a 0/1-vector representing a subset of I. Thus, each factor poset $P_i = \{0,1\}$ and the product P is the Boolean cube $\{0,1\}^n$. Table 1 shows an example of a binary database D.

Quantitative Databases

This is the direct generalization of binary databases to the case when each attribute can assume integer or real values instead of being only binary. In a typical database, most data attributes can be classified as either categorical (e.g., zip code, make of car), or quantitative (e.g., age, income). Categorical attributes assume only a fixed number of discrete values, but typically, there are no precedence relations between these. For instance, there is no obvious way to order zip codes, and therefore, each such attribute a_i assumes values from an antichain, which can be equivalently, represented by different binary attributes each corresponding to one value of a_i. Quantitative attributes, on the other hand, are real-valued attributes which are

totally ordered, but for which there might not exist any bound. However, given a database of m transactions, the number of different values that a given quantitative attribute can take is at most m. As we shall see later, for our purposes, we may assume without loss of generality that the different values of each quantitative attribute a_i are in one-to-one correspondence with some totally ordered set (chain) P_i. Thus a database D with Boolean, categorical, and quantitative attributes can be represented as a subset of a poset $P = P_1 \times \ldots \times P_n$, where each poset P_i is a chain or an antichain. Table 2 gives an example of a quantitative database (taken from (Srikant et al. 1996)).

Taxonomies

This is yet another generalization of binary databases, in which each attribute can assume values belonging to some hierarchy. For instance, in a store, items available for purchase can be classified into different categories, e.g., clothes, footwear, etc. Each such type can be further classified, e.g., clothes into scarfs, shirts, etc. Then further classifications are possible, and so on. Figure 2 gives an example of two such taxonomies. Typically, a database of transactions D is given where each transaction represents the set of items purchased by some customer. Each such item is a top-level

Table 2. Quantitative Data

ID	Age	Married	NumCars
I[1]	23	No	1
I[2]	25	Yes	1
I[3]	29	No	0
I[4]	34	Yes	2
I[5]	38	Yes	2

element in a certain hierarchy (e.g., scarfs, jackets, ski pants, shirts, shoes, and hiking boots, in Figure 2). To obtain generalized association rules which have enough support from the database, it may be necessary to generalize some items as described by the hierarchy (more on this later in the chapter). This can be done by having each attribute a_i in the database assume values belonging to a tree poset P_i. To account for transactions that do not contain any element from a certain taxonomy, a minimum element called "Item" is assumed to be at the lowest level in each taxonomy. For instance, in Table 3, transaction T^6 corresponds to the element (Jacket,Item). Then $D \subseteq P = P_1 \times \ldots \times P_n$, where n is the number of different attributes. Table 3 shows an example taken from (Srikant et al., 1995), where n=2 and the two posets P_1 and P_2 correspond to the two taxonomies shown in Figure 2.

Databases of Events Occurring Over Time

Consider the situation when each attribute in the database can assume an interval of time. For instance, a service provider may keep a log file containing the start and end times at which each customer has used the service (A more specific example, given in (Lin 2003), is a cellular phone company which records the time and length for each phone call made by each Customer). To analyze the correlation between the usage of the service at different points of time, one discretizes the time horizon into n regions. Naturally, these could be the days of the week (n=7) or the days of the year (n=365). For each such region, we get a collection of intervals I_i, i=1,…,n, which represent the usage of the service during that region of time. We shall need the following definition.

Definition 1 (Lattice of intervals). Let I be a set of real closed intervals. The lattice of intervals P defined by I is the lattice whose elements are all possible intersections and spans defined by the intervals in I, and ordered by containment. The meet of any two intervals in P is their intersection, and the join is their span, i.e., the minimum interval containing both of them.

Consider for instance the database shown in Table 4. It shows the times of 3 days of the week

Figure 2. Example of taxonomy

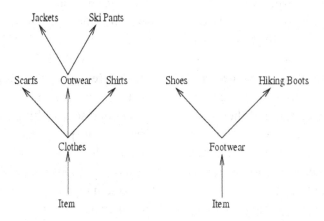

Table 3. A hierarchical database

	Clothes				Footwear	
TID	**Jacket**	**Scarf**	**Shirt**	**Ski Pants**	**Hiking Boots**	**Shoes**
T¹	*0*	*0*	*1*	*0*	*0*	*0*
T²	*1*	*0*	*0*	*0*	*1*	*0*
T³	*0*	*0*	*0*	*1*	*1*	*0*
T⁴	*0*	*0*	*0*	*0*	*0*	*1*
T⁵	*0*	*0*	*0*	*0*	*0*	*1*
T⁶	*1*	*0*	*0*	*0*	*0*	*0*

Table 4. A database of intervals: "-" indicates no usage of the service

TID	Friday	Saturday	Sunday
T¹	*2:00-3:00*	*2:00-3:00*	*1:00-2:00*
T²	*1:00-3:00*	*1:00-3:00*	*1:00-3:00*
T³	*2:00-4:00*	*2:00-4:00*	*1:00-4:00*
T⁴	*1:00-2:00*	*1:00-4:00*	*-*
T⁵	*3:00-4:00*	*-*	*1:00-3:00*

at which a set of customers have visited a certain web server. Figure 3 gives the set of intervals defined by the first column of the database, and the corresponding lattice of intervals defined by them.

Infrequent Elements

Definitions and Notation

In the following sections, we let $P = P_1 \times \ldots \times P_n$ be a product of n posets and $D \subseteq P$ be a database defined over P.

Definition 2 (Support). For an element $p \in P$, let us denote by

$S(p) = S_D(p) := \{q \in D \mid q \geq p\}$,

the set of transactions in D that support $p \in P$.

Note that the function $|S_D(p)|$ is monotonically non-decreasing in $p \in P$, i.e., if $p \leq q$, then $|S_D(p)| \geq |S_D(q)|$.

Definition 3 (Frequent/infrequent element). Given $D \subseteq P$ and an integer threshold t, let us say that an element $p \in P$ is t-frequent if it is sup-

Figure 3. The lattice of intervals

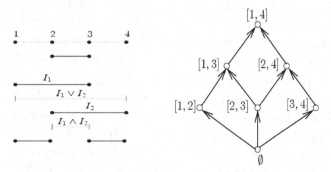

a: A set of intervals $\mathbb{I}_1$. b: The corresponding lattice of intervals $\mathcal{P}_1$.

ported by at least t transactions in the database, i.e., if $|S_D(p)| \geq t$. Conversely, $p \in P$ is said to be t-infrequent if $|S_D(p)| < t$.

Note that the property of being infrequent is monotone, i.e., if x is t-infrequent and $y \geq x$, then y is also t-infrequent. This motivates the following definition.

Definition 4 (Minimal infrequent/maximal frequent element). An element $p \in P$ is said to be minimal t-infrequent (maximal t-frequent) with respect to a database $D \subseteq P$ and an integer threshold t, if p is t-infrequent (respectively, t-frequent), but any $q \in P$ such that $q < p$ (respectively, $q > p$) is t-frequent (respectively, t-infrequent).

Example 1. Consider the binary database in Table 1. The set of items X={Bread,Butter} has support $|S(X)| = 8$. For t=4, X is t-frequent but not maximal as it is contained in the maximal t-frequent set {Bread,Butter,Cheese,Orange Juice}. The set {Bread,Butter,Cheese,Milk,Orange Juice, Yogurt} is t-infrequent but not minimal since it contains the minimal t-infrequent set {Bread,Butter,Cheese,Milk,Orange Juice}.

Example 2. Consider the database in Table 3. The element x=(Outwear,Footwear) has support $|S(x)| = 2$. For t=2, x is t-frequent but not maximal as it precedes the maximal t-frequent element (Outwear,Hiking Boots). The element (Jacket, Hiking Boots) is t-infrequent but not minimal since it is above the minimal t-infrequent element (Jacket,Footwear).

Given a poset P, and a subset of its elements $A \subseteq P$, we will denote by $A^+ = \{x \in P \mid x \geq a, \text{ for some } a \in A\}$ and $A^- = \{x \in P \mid x \leq a, \text{ for some } a \in A\}$, the so-called ideal and filter defined by A.

Definition 5 (independent/maximal independent element). Let P be a poset and A be an arbitrary subset of P. An element in $p \in P$ is called independent of A if p is not above any element of A, i.e., $p \notin A^+$. p is said further to be a maximal independent element if there is no $q \in P$, such that $q > p$ and q is independent of A.

Throughout we will denote by I(A) be the set of all maximal independent elements for A. Then

one can easily verify the following decomposition of P:

$$A^+ \cap I(A)^- = \varnothing, \quad A \cup I(A)^- = P. \tag{1}$$

Given a database $D \subseteq P$, and an integer threshold t, let us denote by $F_{D,t}$ the set of minimal t-infrequent elements of P with respect to D and t. Then $I(F_{D,t})$ is the set of maximal t-frequent elements:

$$I(F_{D,t}) = \text{Min } \{x \in P : |S_D(x)| < t\}, \quad I(F_{D,t}) = \text{Max } \{x \ x \in P : |S_D(x)| \geq t\},$$

where for a set $A \subseteq P$, we denote by Min(A) (respectively, Max(A)), the smallest cardinality (with respect to the relation $\leq$) set $B \subseteq P$ such that $B^+ = A^+$ (respectively, $B^- = A^-$). Using the above notation, the sets $F_{D,t}^+$ and $I(F_{D,t})^-$ will denote respectively the set of t-infrequent and t-frequent elements.

Associated Enumeration Problems

The problem of finding all frequent/infrequent elements in a database has proved useful in data mining applications (Gunopulos et al. 1997) (see also the examples below). As mentioned earlier, the property of being infrequent is monotone, and hence a lot of redundancy can be removed by considering only minimal t-infrequent elements. This motivates us to study the complexity of the problem finding the sets $F_{D,t}$ and $I(F_{D,t})^-$ of all minimal t-infrequent elements and all t-frequent elements, respectively. The generic generation problem we will consider is the following:

GEN_H **(P, D,t):** Given a database D defined over in a poset product *P*, and a threshold t, find all elements of *H* with respect to D and t.

In the above definition if $H = F_{D,t}$ then we are considering the generation of minimal infrequent elements, and if $H = I(F_{D,t})^-$ ($H = F_{D,t}^+$) then we are considering the generation of frequent (respectively, infrequent) elements. Clearly, the whole set H can be generated by starting with $X=\varnothing$ and performing $|H|+1$ calls to the following incremental generation problem (with $k=1$):

INC-GEN$_H$ (P, D,t,X,k): Given a database D defined over a poset product P, a threshold t, a subset $X \subseteq H$, and an integer k, find $\min\{k,|H\backslash X|\}$ elements of $H\backslash X$, or state that no such element exists.

Before we talk about the complexity of the enumeration problems we are interested in, we should remark on how to measure this complexity, since typically the complete output size is exponentially large in the size of the input database. One can distinguish different notions of efficiency, according to the time/space complexity of such generation problem:

Output polynomial or Total polynomial: Problem GEN$_H$ (P, D,t) can be solved in poly($\Sigma_{i=1}^{n}$ $|P_i|,|D|$) time.

Incremental polynomial: Problem INC-GEN$_H$(P, D,t,X,1) can be solved in poly($\Sigma_{i=1}^{n}$ $|P_i|,|D|,|X|$) time, for every $X \subseteq H$, or equivalently, INC-GEN$_H$(P,D,t,$\varnothing$,k) can be solved in poly($\Sigma_{i=1}^{n}$ $|P_i|,|D|$, $\min\{k, |H|\}$) time, for every integer k.

Polynomial delay: INC-GEN$_H$(P, D,t,X,1) can be solved in poly($\Sigma_{i=1}^{n}$ $|P_i|,|D|$) time. In other words, the time required to generate a new element of H is polynomial only in the input size. If the time required to solve INC-GEN$_H$(P, D,t,X,1) is poly($\Sigma_{i=1}^{n}$ $|P_i|,|D|$)$|X|$, then the problem is said to be solvable with amortized polynomial delay.

Polynomial space: The total space required to solve GEN$_H$ (P, D,t) is bounded by a poly($\Sigma_{i=1}^{n}$ $|P_i|,|D|$). This is only possible if the algorithm looks at no more than poly($\Sigma_{i=1}^{n}$ $|P_i|,|D|$) many outputs that it has already generated.

NP-hard: The decision problem associated with INC-GEN$_H$(P, D,t,X,1) (i.e., deciding if H = X) is NP-hard, which means that is coNP-complete, since it belongs to coNP.

We will see that, generally, the generation of infrequent elements can be done with amortized polynomial delay, using an Apriori-like algorithm,

while the currently best known algorithm for generating minimal infrequent elements runs in quasi-polynomial time.

The general framework suggested in this section allows us to model a number of different scenarios in data mining applications. We consider some examples in the next section.

APPLICATIONS

Mining Association Rules

Boolean Association Rules

Consider a binary database D each record of which represents a subset of items from a large set V of n items. In our terminology, we have $P_i = \{0,1\}$ for $i=1,\ldots,n$, and $D \subseteq P = 2^V$, the binary cube of dimension n. We recall the following central definition from (Agrawal et al., 1993):

Definition 6 (Association rules). Let $D \subseteq 2^V$ be a binary database, and s, $c \in [0,1]$ be given numbers. An association rule, with support s and confidence c, is a pair of disjoint subsets $X,Y \subseteq [n]$ such that,

$$\frac{|S_D(X \cup Y)|}{|S_D(X)|} \geq c, \qquad \frac{|S_D(X \cup Y)|}{|D|} \geq s, \quad (1)$$

and will abbreviated by $X \Rightarrow Y |(c,s)$. (That is, at least c fraction of the transactions that contain X also contain Y (confidence condition), and at least a fraction s of all transactions contain both X and Y (support condition).)

Each such rule $X \Rightarrow Y$ roughly means that transactions which contain all items in X tend also to contain all items in Y. Here X is usually called the antecedent of the rule, and Y is called the consequent. Generating such association rules has received a lot of attention since their introduction in (Agrawal et al., 1993).

Note that the anti-monotonicity of the support

function implies the following.

Proposition 1. Let $X,Y,X',Y' \subseteq V$ be such that $X' \subseteq X$ and $X' \cup Y' \subseteq X \cup Y$, and suppose that the rule $X \Rightarrow Y \mid (c,s)$ holds. Then the rule $X' \Rightarrow Y' \mid (c,s)$ also holds.

Proof. Set $Z = X \cup Y$ and $Z' = X' \cup Y'$. Then $|S_D(Z)| \geq s|D|$ and $|S_D(X)| \leq |S_D(Z)|/c$ since the rule $X \Rightarrow Y \mid (c,s)$ holds. Since $X' \supseteq X$ and $Z' \subseteq Z$, we get,

$$
\begin{aligned}
|S_D(Z')| &\geq |S_D(Z)| \geq s|D| \\
|S_D(X')| &\leq |S_D(X)| \leq \frac{|S_D(Z)|}{c} \leq \frac{|S_D(Z')|}{c}.
\end{aligned}
$$

Clearly, one should be interested only in generating rules that are not implied by others. This motivates the following definition.

Definition 7 (Irredundant association rules). Let $D \subseteq 2^V$ be a binary database, and $s,c \in [0,1]$ be given numbers. An irredundant association rule $X \Rightarrow (Z \backslash X) \mid (c,s)$, with support s and confidence c, is determined by a pair of a (inclusion-wise) minimal subset X and a maximal subset Z, such that $X \subseteq Z$, and,

$$|S_D(Z)| \geq s|D| \tag{2}$$

$$|S_D(X)| \leq \frac{|S_D(Z)|}{c} \tag{3}$$

Example 3. Consider the binary database in Table 1. Using $s=0.4$ and $c=0.5$, one can verify that the rule {Bread, Butter, Cheese} $\Rightarrow$ {Orange Juice} holds. However, this a redundant rule since it is implied by the irredundant rule {Bread, Butter} $\Rightarrow$ {Cheese, Orange Juice}.

It follows from Definition 7 that, in order to generate irredundant association rules, one needs to perform two basic steps (see Figure 4):

1. *Generate all subsets Z satisfying (2); these are the elements of the family $I(F_{D,})^{-}$ (t-frequent sets) where $t=s|D|$, which can be obtained by solving problem $GEN_H(2^V, D, t)$ for $H=I(F_{D,})^{-}$. This can be done using the Apriori algorithm; see Section 5.*

2. *For each such t-frequent set Z, generate all minimal t'-infrequent subsets of Z, where $t' = |S_D(Z)|/c + 1$. To avoid generating redundant rules, we maintain a list $X(Z)$ of already generated t'-infrequent subsets of Z. For each set Z, we compute the set $X(Z)$ by solving problem $INC\text{-}GEN_H(2^Z, D[Z], t', X', |F_{D[Z],t'} \backslash X'|)$, where $H = F_{D[Z],t'}$, and $D[Z] = \{T \cap Z : T \in D\}$, and X' is the set of minimal infrequent subsets of Z that are contained in some $X \in X(Z')$ for some $Z' \subseteq Z$. The set X' can be computed easily once we have computed $X'(Z')$ for all $Z' \supseteq Z$, and in particular all subsets Z' that have one more item than Z. That is why the procedure iterates from larger frequent sets to small ones.*

We leave it as an exercise for the reader to verify that the procedure outputs all irredundant rules without repetition.

The number of sets generated in the first step might be exponential in the number of irredundant rules. This is because some set Z maybe frequent, but still there exist no new minimal infrequent elements in $X(Z)$. However, this seems unavoidable as the problem of generating the irredundant rules turns out to be NP-hard. To see why this is the case, we note first that in (Boros et al., 2003) it was proved that generating maximal frequent sets is hard.

Theorem 1 (Boros et al., 2003). Given a database $D \subseteq 2^V$ of binary attributes, and a threshold t, problem $INC\text{-}GEN_H(2^V, D, t, X, 1)$, where $H = I(F_{D,t})$, is NP-hard.

This immediately implies the following.

Corollary 1. Given a database $D \subseteq 2^V$ of binary attributes, and a threshold t, the problem

Figure 4. Generating irredundant association rules

```
Procedure GEN-RULES(D, c, s):
    Input: A binary database D, and c, s ∈ [0, 1]
    Output: The list of irredundant association rules from D with confidence c and support s

1.  R := ∅
2.  t := s|D|, G := GEN_{I(F_{D,t})}-(2^V, D, t)
3.  for i = n downto 1, do
4.      foreach Z ∈ G with |Z| = i do
5.          X(Z) := Min{X ∈ ∪_{j∉Z} X(Z ∪ {j}) : X ⊆ Z}
6.          t' := |S_D(Z)|/c + 1
7.          X(Z) := X(Z) ∪ GEN-INC_{F_{D[Z],t'}}(2^Z, D[Z], t', X(Z), |F_{D[Z],t'} \ X(Z)|)
8.          R := R ∪ {(X, Z) : X ∈ X(Z) \ ∪_{j∉Z} X(Z ∪ {j})}
9.  return R
```

of generating all irredundant association rules is NP-hard.

Proof. Consider the problem of generating maximal t-frequent sets. Set s=t/|D| and c=1/|D|. Then irredundant association rules are in one-to-one correspondence with minimal X⊆ V and maximal Z⊆V satisfying (2) and (3), and such that X⊆ Z. By our choice of c any such X will be empty and thus the irredundant rules are in one-to-one correspondence with maximal sets Z such that |S(Z)|≥ t. Thus Theorem 1 implies that the problem of generating these rules is NP-hard.

Another framework to reduce redundancy, based on the concept of closed frequent itemsets, is proposed in (Zaki 2000).

Generalized Association Rules

We assume that each poset P_i has a minimum element 1_i. Following Definition 7, we can generalize binary association rules to more general databases as follows.

Definition 8 (Irredundant generalized association rules). Let $D⊆ P = P_1×…× P_n$ be a database over a poset product, and s,c∈ [0,1] be given numbers. An irredundant association rule x⇒z |(c,s), with support s and confidence c, is determined by a pair of a minimal element x∈P and a maximal element z∈P, such that x≤ z, $x_i ∈$ {$z_i, 1_i$} for all i, and

$$\frac{|S_D(z)|}{|D|} \geq s, \quad \frac{|S_D(z)|}{|S_D(x)|} \geq c \quad (4)$$

The rule x⇒z is interpreted as follows: With support s, at least c fraction of the transactions that dominate x also dominate z (i.e., t≥ x implies t≥ z for all t∈ D). From the pair (x,z), we can get a useful rule by letting R={i: z_i=1_i} and S={i: x_i=z_i}, and inferring for a transaction t∈ D that

$$(t_i \geq z_i)\forall i \in S \setminus R \Rightarrow (t_i \geq z_i)\forall i \notin S \cup R. \quad (5)$$

As in the binary case, the generation of such rules can be done, by first generating frequent elements from D (working on a product of posets), then generating minimal frequent elements on a binary problem, defined by setting each P_i ={1_i, z_i}. We can do this by a straightforward extension of the Apriori Algorithm (Agrawal et al. 1994) to finding frequent elements in a database defined over a product of posets.

As we shall see in the examples below, this generalization allows us to discover association rules in which antecedents and consequents are generalizations of the individual entries appearing in the database, and which might otherwise lack enough support.

Example 4 (Association rules derived from taxonomies). Consider the database in Table 3. Using s=0.3 and c=0.6, we get z=(Outwear,Hiking Boots) as a frequent element, and x=(Outwear,Item) as a minimal infrequent element with x≤ z and x∈ {Item,Outwear}×{Item,Hiking Boots}. According to (5), this gives rise to the rule Outwear⇒Hiking Boots. Note that both rules Ski Pants⇒Hiking Boots and Jackets⇒Hiking Boots

Figure 5. The 3 factor posets in Example 5

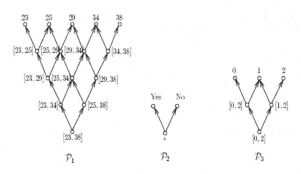

lack minimum support, and hence the generalized association rule was useful.

In (Srikant et al. 1996), a method was proposed for mining quantitative association rules by partitioning the range of each quantitative attribute into disjoint intervals, and thus reducing the problem into the Boolean case. However, as mentioned in (Srikant et al., 1996), this technique is sensitive to the number of intervals selected for each attribute: if the number of intervals is too small (respectively, too large), some rules may not be discovered since they lack minimum confidence (respectively, minimum support); see (Srikant et al., 1996) for more details.

An alternative approach, which avoids the need to impose a certain partitioning on the attribute ranges, is to consider each quantitative attribute as defined on a semi-lattice of intervals. More precisely, suppose that a_i is a quantitative attribute, and consider the set of possible values assumed by a_i in the database, say, $S_i := \{t_i \mid t \in D\}$. Let P_i be the dual of the lattice of intervals whose elements correspond to the different intervals defined by the points in S_i, and ordered by containment. The minimum element $\bar{1}_i$ of P_i corresponds to the interval spanning all the points in S_i. The maximum element is not needed and can be deleted to obtain a meet semi-lattice P_i. A 2-dimensional example is shown in Figure 5. Let $P = P_1 \times \ldots \times P_n$. Then each element x of P corresponds to an n-dimensional box, and those elements can be used to produce association rules derived form the data. Using a

similar reduction as the one that will be used in Section 4.2.1, the situation can be simplified since each semi-lattice P_i can be decomposed into the product of two chains.

For categorical attributes, each attribute value can be used to introduce a binary attribute. However, this imposes that each generated association rule must have a condition on this attribute, which restricts the sets of rules generated. For example, in the database in Table 2, the categorical attribute "Married" can be replaced by two binary attributes "Married: Yes" and "Married: No" and an entry of "1" is entered in the right place in each record. But since each record must have a "1" in exactly one of these locations, this means that any association rule generated from this database must contain a condition on the marital status of the individual. Here is a way to avoid this restriction. For a categorical attribute a_i which assumes values $\{v_1, \ldots, v_r\}$, we introduce an artificial element l_i (corresponding essentially to a "don't care") and define a tree poset on $\{l_i, v_1, \ldots, v_r\}$ in which the only precedence relation are $l_i < v_j$, for j=1,…,r (see Figure 5).

Let us look at an example.

Example 5 (Quantitative association rules). Consider the database in Table 2. This database can be viewed as a subset of the product of the 3 posets shown in Figure 5. Using s=0.4 and c=1.0, we get z=([34,38], Yes,[2,2]) as a frequent element, and x=([34,38],*,[0:2]) as a minimal infrequent element with x≤z and x∈{[23,38],[

30,38]} $\times$ {*,Yes} $\times$ {[0,2],[2,2]} (assuming Age is integer-valued). According to (3), this gives rise to the rule: <Age: 34..38> $\Rightarrow$ <Married: Yes> and <NumCars: 2>. Note that the rule (<Age: 34..38> and <Married: Yes>) $\Rightarrow$ <NumCars: 2> is also valid but it is redundant since it is implied by the first rule.

Note that, using this approach, we consider overlapping two-sided intervals for each attribute a_i, i.e., intervals of the form $x_i \le a_i \le y_i$, but we do not set, a priori, the boundaries of these intervals. Instead, these boundaries are determined by the minimum support requirements and the values of the transactions in the database.

We refer the reader to (Han et al., 1993; Han et al., 1995; Hipp, et al., 1998; Huang et al., 2002; Nanavati et al., 2001; Srikan, et al., 1995; Srikant et al., 1996; Thomas et al., 1998; Tong et al., 2005) for more algorithms for mining generalized and quantitative association rules.

Negative Correlations

Consider a binary database $D \subseteq 2^V$. It may be interesting to generate association rules in which the antecedent or the consequent has a negated predicate. For instance, in Example 1, we may be interested in generating also rules of the form: (Bread, Butter, Milk) $\Rightarrow \neg$ Yogurt, that is, customers who purchase Bread, Butter, and Milk tend not to buy Yogurt.

Several techniques have been proposed in the literature for mining negative correlations, see e.g. (Antonie et al,.2004; Brin et al,. 1997; Koh, et al. 2007; Sharma et al,. 2005; Yuan et al., 2002). Interestingly, such association rules can be found by embedding the database into the product of tree posets as follows. For each item we introduce a tree poset {*,+,−}, where "+" stands for the item being present and "−" stands for the item being absent, and "*" stands for a "don't care". The only relations in this poset are * < + and * < −.

Example 6 (Negative association rules). Consider the database in Table 1. To allow for negative

correlations, we view this database as a subset of the product P of 6 tree posets, as described above. Using this representation, transaction T_8 in the table, for instance, corresponds to the element x=(−,+,+,+,−,−) of P. Using s=0.3 and c=0.75, we get z=(+,+,*,−,*,−) (corresponding to {Bread, Butter, No Milk, No Yogurt}) as a frequent element, and x=(*,+,*,−,*,*) as a minimal infrequent element with x $\le$ z. According to (5), this gives rise to the rule: (Butter, $\neg$ Milk) $\Rightarrow$ (Bread, $\neg$ Yogurt).

Generating Rare Associations and Rare Association Rules

In the examples we have seen above, our objective was to discover correlations that might exist between data attributes. In some situations, it may be required to discover correlations in which some attributes are unlikely to assume certain values together. This is a direct application of finding infrequent elements. Given a database $D \subseteq P_1 \times \ldots \times P_n$, an infrequent element is a collection of generalizations of items that do not tend to appear together in the database. For instance, consider the database in Table 3. For t=2, the element (Jacket, Hiking Boots) is t-infrequent and we can conclude that in less than 34% of the transactions these two items are purchased together. However, this is not the strongest conclusion we can make, since the minimal t-infrequent element (Jacket, Footwear) tells us that less than 34% of the customers purchase jackets and footwear in a single transaction.

One important application of finding rare associations is in mining the so-called rare association rules. These are rules that appear with low support but high confidence. This happens when some of the items appear rarely in the database, but they exhibit enough association between them to generate useful rules. The problem in discovering such rules is that one needs to set the minimum support parameter s at a low value to be able to detect these rules, but this on the other hand, may introduce many other meaningless rules, resulting from other frequent itemsets, that would lack enough support otherwise (this dilemma is called the rate item problem in (Mannila 1998)).

A number of methods have been proposed for dealing with such rare rules, see e.g. (Liu et al. 1999, Koh 2008). One approach that can be used here is based on finding minimal infrequent elements. Consider for simplicity a binary database $D \subseteq 2^V$. We choose two threshold values $0 < s_1 < s_2 < 1$ for the support: A subset of items $X \subseteq V$ will qualify if its support satisfies $s_1|D| \leq |S_D(X)| \leq s_2|D|$. Such sets will have enough support but still are infrequent. Once these sets are generated, the discovery of the corresponding association rules can be done by looking at the confidence as before. The generation of these sets can be done as follows. First, we find the family X of all minimal sets X such that $S_D(X)| \leq s_2|D|$, which is an instance of problem $GEN_H(2^V, D, t)$ with $H = F_{D,t}$ and $t = s_2|D|$. Next, for each such $X \in X$, we find the frequent sets containing X, by solving an instance of problem $GEN_H(2^V, D', t')$ with $H = I(F_{D',t'})^-$, $D' = \{T \in D: T \supseteq X\}$, and $t' = s_1|D|$. A related approach was used in (Mustafa et al. 2006).

We look at two more examples of this kind in the next two subsections.

Maximal k-Boxes

As another example (taken from (Edmonds et al., 2001)), consider a database of tickets, car registrations, and drivers' information. Interesting observations that can be drawn from such tables could be: "No tickets were issued to BMW Z3 series cars before 1997", or "No tickets for $1000 were issued before 1990 for drivers born before 1956", etc.

To model these scenarios, we let S be a set of points in R^n, representing the quantitative parts of the transactions in the database. We would like to find all regions in R^n which contain no, or a few, data points from S. Moreover, to avoid redundancy we are interested in finding only maximal such regions. This motivates the fol-

lowing definition.

Definition 9 (Maximal k-boxes). Let $S \subseteq R^n$ be a set of n-dimensional points and $k \leq |S|$ be a given integer. A maximal k-box is a closed n-dimensional box which contains at most k points of S in its interior, and which is maximal with respect to this property (i.e., cannot be extended in any direction without strictly enclosing more points of S).

Example 7. Consider again the database in Table 2. In Figure 6, we represent (Age,NumCars) as points in 2-dimensional space. The corresponding two products of chains are shown on the right.

The box $B_1 = [(25,0),(39,2)]$ is a maximal empty box, and box $B_2 = [(23,0),(39,2)]$ is a maximal 1-box. The box B_1 tells us that no individuals with age between 26 and 38 have 1 car.

Let $F_{S,k}$ be the set of all maximal k-boxes for a given pointset S. Then we are interested in generating the elements of $F_{S,k}$. Let us note that without any loss of generality, we could consider the generation of the boxes $\{B \cap D \mid B \in F_{S,k}\}$, where D is a fixed bounded box containing all points of S in its interior. Let us further note that the i-th coordinate of each vertex of such a box is the same as p_i for some $p \in S$, or the i-th coordinate of a vertex of D, hence all these coordinates belong to a finite set of cardinality at most $|S|+2$. Thus we can view $F_{S,k}$ as a set of boxes with vertices belonging to such a finite grid. More precisely, let $C_i = \{p_i \mid p \in S\}$ for $i=1,\dots,n$ and consider the family of boxes $B = \{[a,b] \subseteq R^n \mid a,b \in C_1 \times \dots \times C_n, a \leq b\}$. For $i=1,\dots,n$, let $u_i = \max\{C_i\}$, and let $C_i^* := \{u_i - p \mid p \in C_i\}$ be the chain ordered in the direction opposite to C_i. Consider the 2n-dimensional box $C = C_1 \times \dots \times C_n \times C_1^* \times \dots \times C_n^*$, and let us represent every n-dimensional box $[a,b] \in B$ as the 2n-dimensional vector $(a,u-b) \in C$, where $u = (u_1,\dots, u_n)$. This gives a monotone injective mapping $B \to C$ (not all elements of C define a box, since $a_i > b_i$ is possible for $(a,u-b) \in C$).

It is not difficult to see that our problem reduces to solving problem $GEN_H(C^*, D, k+1)$,

Figure 6. A maximal empty box and two factor posets used for representing such boxes

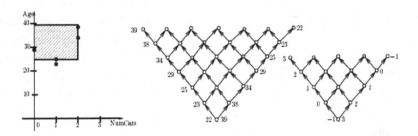

where $H=F_{S,k+1}$, $D = \{(p, u-p): p \in S\}$, and where we redefine support to be $S_D(p) := \{q \in D \mid q > p\}$ (ignoring a small number (at most $\Sigma_{i=1}^n |C_i|$) of additionally generated elements, corresponding to non-boxes), see (Khachiyan et al,. 2007) for more details.

Minimal Infrequent Multi-Dimensional Intervals

Consider the database of intervals given in Section 2.4. An interesting observation, that may be deduced from the database, can take the form ``Fewer than 40% of the customers occupy the service on Friday between 2:00-3:00 and on Saturday between 2:00-4:00'', or "With support 60%, all customers who make full use of the service between 2:00-3:00 on Friday tend also to use the service between 2:00-3:00 on Saturday and between 1:00-2:00 on Sunday". These examples illustrate the requirement for discovering correlations or association rules between occurrences of events over time. As in the previous examples, a fundamental problem that arises in this case is the generation of frequent and minimal infrequent multi-dimensional intervals.

More formally, given a database of n-dimensional intervals D, and $i \in [n]$, let $P_i = \{p_i^1, p_i^2, \ldots, p_i^{k(i)}\}$ be the set of end-points of intervals appearing in the i-th column of D. Clearly $k(i) \le 2|D|$, and assuming that $p_i^1 < p_i^2 < \ldots < p_i^{k(i)}$, we obtain a set $I_i = \{[p_i^1, p_i^2], [p_i^2, p_i^3], \ldots, [p_i^{k(i)-1}, p_i^{k(i)}]\}$ of at most $2|D|$ intervals. Let P_i be the lattice of intervals defined by the set I_i (recall Definition 1), for $i=1,\ldots,$ n, and let $P = P_1 \times \ldots \times P_n$. Then, each record in D appears as an element in P, i.e., $D \subseteq P$.

Now, it is easy to see that the t-frequent elements of P are in one-to-one correspondence with the t-frequent intervals defined by D, in the obvious way: if $x=(x_1,\ldots,x_n) \in P$ is a frequent element, then the corresponding interval $(I_1,\ldots,I_n)$ (where I_i corresponds to x_i, for $i=1,\ldots,n$) is the corresponding frequent interval. The situation with minimal infrequent intervals is just a bit more complicated: if $x=(x_1,\ldots,x_n) \in P$ is a minimal infrequent element then the corresponding minimal infrequent interval $(I_1,\ldots,I_n)$ is computed as follows. For $i=1,\ldots,n$, if $x_i = 1_i$ is the minimum element of P_i, then $I_i = \emptyset$. If x_i represents a point $x_i \in R$ then $I_i = [p_i, p_i]$. Otherwise, let $[a_i, b_i]$ and $[c_i, d_i]$ be the two intervals corresponding to the two immediate predecessors of x_i in P_i, where we assume $a_i < c_i$. If $a_i = b_i$ and $c_i = d_i$ then x_i corresponds to the interval $[a_i, c_i]$ and we have an infinite number of minimal infrequent intervals defined (uniquely) by I_i, namely $I_i = [p_i, p_i]$ for all points p_i in the open interval (a_i, c_i). Finally, if $a_i < b_i$ and $c_i < d_i$, then $I_i = [c_i - \varepsilon, b_i + \varepsilon]$ for a sufficiently small constant ε (which can be taken as the smallest precision used in the representation of intervals, e.g., 1 minute). Consequently, in all cases, our problems reduce to finding t-frequent/minimal t-infrequent elements in the lattice product P.

COMPLEXITY

Minimal Infrequent Elements

We will illustrate now that, for all the examples considered above, the problem of finding minimal t-infrequent elements, that is, problem GENH (P, D,t, X) for H=FD, t can be solved in incremental quasi-polynomial time.

Central to this is the notion of *duality testing*. Call two subsets $A, B \subseteq P$ *partially dual* if the following condition holds:

$$a \text{ not} \leq b, \quad \text{for all} \quad a \in A, b \in B. \qquad (6)$$

For instance if $X \subseteq F_{D,t}$ and $Y \subseteq I(F_{D,t})$ then X, Y are partially dual. The duality testing problem on P is the following:

DUAL(P, *A*, *B*): Given two partially dual sets $A, B \subseteq P$, check if there exists an element x∈P, such that

$$x \text{ not} \geq a \text{ for all } a \in A \text{ and } x \text{ not} \leq b \text{ for all } b \in B \qquad (7)$$

Let m=|*A*| +|*B*|. The main result that we need here is the following.

Theorem 2 ((Boros et al. 2002, Elbassioni 2008))

(i)   If each P_i is a chain, then DUAL(P, A, B) can be solved in $n.m^{o(\log m)}$ time.

(ii) If each P_i is tree poset, then DUAL(P, A, B) can be solved in $poly(n, \mu(P)). m^{o(\log m)}$ time, where $\mu(P)=\max\{|P_i|: i \in [n]\}$.

(iii) If each poset P_i is a lattice of intervals then DUAL(P, A, B) can be solved in $k^{O(\log^2 k)}$ time, where $k=m+\Sigma_{i=1}^{n}|P_i|$.

We also note that a mixture of posets of the three types can be taken in the product and the running time will be the maximum of the bounds in (i), (ii) and (iii). Thus the duality testing problem can be solved in quasi-polynomial time for the classes of posets that arise in our applications. To apply this result to the generation of minimal infrequent elements, we need another important ingredient. Namely, that the number of all maximal t-frequent elements is polynomially small in the number of minimal t-infrequent elements. In fact the following stronger bound holds.

Theorem 3 (*Boros* et al. 2002). For any poset product $P = P_1 \times ... \times P_n$ in which each two elements of each poset P_i have at most one join, the set $F_{D,t}$ is *uniformly dual-bounded* in the sense that

$$|I(A) \cap I(F_{D,t})| \leq (|D|-t+1)|A|, \qquad (8)$$

for any non-empty subset $A \subseteq F_{D,t}$.

To generate the elements of $F_{D,t}$ we keep two lists $X \subseteq F_{D,t}$ and $Y \subseteq I(F_{D,t})$, both initially empty.

Given these partial lists, we call the procedure for solving DUAL (P, X, Y). If it returns an element x satisfying (7), we obtain from x a vector x' in $F_{D,t}$ or $I(F_{D,t})$, depending respectively on whether x is t-infrequent or t-frequent element. This continues until no more such elements x can be returned. Clearly, if this happens then all elements of P have been classified to either lie above some x∈X or below some x∈ Y, i.e., $X = F_{D,t}$ and $Y=I(F_{D,t})$. By (8), the time needed to produce a new element of $F_{D,t}$ is at most a factor of |D| times the time needed to solve problem DUAL(P, X, Y). A Pseudo-code is shown in Figure 7.

Theorem 4. Let $P = P_1 \times ... \times P_n$ where each P_i is either a chain, a lattice of intervals, or a meet semi-lattice tree poset. Then for any $D \subseteq P$, and integer t, problem $GEN_H (P, D,t)$ for $H=F_{D,t}$ can be solved in incremental quasi-polynomial time.

We refer the reader to (Elbassioni, 2008) for more details and for dualization algorithms on products of meet semi-lattice tree posets, and of lattices of intervals.

Figure 7. A procedure for enumerating minimal infrequent elements

Procedure GenerateInfrequent$(\mathcal{P}, \mathcal{D}, t)$:
  Input: A database $\mathcal{D} \subseteq \mathcal{P}$ and a integer threshold t.
  Output: The t-minimal infrequent elements.

1. $\mathcal{X} := \emptyset;\ \mathcal{Y} := \emptyset.$
2. **while** DUAL$(\mathcal{P}, \mathcal{X}, \mathcal{Y})$ returns a vector x
3.   If $|S_{\mathcal{D}}(x)| < t$, **then**
4. $x' :=$ a minimal vector such that $x' \leq x$ and $|S_{\mathcal{D}}(x)| < t.$
5. $\mathcal{X} := \mathcal{X} \cup \{x'\}.$
6.   **else**
7. $x' :=$ a maximal vector such that $x \leq x'$ and $|S_{\mathcal{D}}(x)| \geq t$
8. $\mathcal{Y} := \mathcal{Y} \cup \{x'\}.$
9. **return** $\mathcal{X}.$

Infrequent/Frequent Elements

If we are interested in finding all infrequent elements rather then the minimal ones, then the problem seems to be easier. As we have seen in the applications above, one basic step in finding association rules is enumerating all frequent elements. Those can be typically found by a straightforward generalization of the Apriori algorithm. Since one can regard the problem of finding infrequent elements as of that finding frequent elements on the dual poset, we can conclude that the infrequent elements can also be found by the algorithm Apriori, and hence the problem can be solved in incremental polynomial time. We leave the details an exercise for the interested reader.

Theorem 5. Let $P = P_1 \times \ldots \times P_n$, $D \subseteq P$, and t be an integer. Then all t-frequent (t-infrequent) elements can be computed with amortized delay.

CONCLUSION

In this chapter, we have looked at a general framework that allows us to mine associations from different types of databases. We have argued that the rules obtained under this framework are generally stronger than the ones obtained from techniques that use binarization. A fundamental problem that comes out from this framework is that of finding minimal infrequent elements in a given product of partially ordered sets. As we have seen, this problem can be solved in quasi-polynomial time, while the problem becomes easier if we are interested in finding all infrequent/frequent elements. On the theoretical level, while the complexity of enumerating minimal infrequent elements is not known to be polynomial, the problem is unlikely to be NP-hard unless every NP-complete problem can be solved in quasi-polynomial time.

Finally, we mention that a number of implementations exist for the duality testing problem on products of chains (Bailey, 2003; Kavvadias, 2005; Khachiyan et al., 2006), and for the generation of infrequent elements (Khachiyan et al., 2006) on such products. Experiments in (Khachiyan et al., 2006) indicate that the algorithms behave practically much faster than the theoretically best-known upper bounds on their running times, and therefore may be applicable in practical applications. Improving these implementations further and putting them into practical use, as well as the extension to more general products of partially ordered sets remain challenging issues that can be the subject of interesting future research.

REFERENCES

Agrawal, R., Imielinski, T., & Swami, A. (1993). Mining association rules between sets of items in large databases. In *SIGMOD '93: Proceedings of the 1993 ACM SIGMOD international conference on Management of data* (pp. 207-216), New York, NY, USA.

Agrawal, R., Mannila, H., Srikant, R., Toivonen, H., & Verkamo, A. I. (1996). Fast discovery of association rules. In *Advances in knowledge discovery and data mining* (pp. 307-328). American Association for Artificial Intelligence Menlo Park, CA, USA.

Agrawal, R., & Srikant, R. (1994). Fast algorithms for mining association rules in large databases. In *VLDB '94: Proceedings of the 20th International Conference on Very Large Data Bases* (pp. 487-499), San Francisco, CA, USA. Morgan Kaufmann Publishers Inc.

Antonie, M.-L., & Zaiane, O. R. (2004). Mining positive and negative association rules: An approach for confined rules. In *PKDD '04: Proceedings of the 8th European Conference on Principles and Practice of Knowledge Discovery in Databases* (pp. 27-38). New York: Springer-Verlag New York, Inc.

Bailey, J., Manoukian, T., & Ramamohanarao, K. (2003). A fast algorithm for computing hypergraph transversals and its application in mining emerging patterns. In *ICDM '03: Proceedings of the Third IEEE International Conference on Data Mining* (pp. 485-488). Washington, DC, IEEE Computer Society.

Boros, E., Elbassioni, K., Gurvich, V., Khachiyan, L., & Makino, K. (2002). Dual-bounded generating problems: All minimal integer solutions for a monotone system of linear inequalities. *SIAM Journal on Computing, 31*(5), 1624–1643. doi:10.1137/S0097539701388768

Boros, E., Gurvich, V., Khachiyan, L., & Makino, K. (2002). On the complexity of generating maximal frequent and minimal infrequent sets. In *STACS '02: Proceedings of the 19th Annual Symposium on Theoretical Aspects of Computer Science* (pp. 133-141), London, UK: Springer-Verlag.

Boros, E., Gurvich, V., Khachiyan, L., & Makino, K. (2003). On maximal frequent and minimal infrequent sets in binary matrices. *Annals of Mathematics and Artificial Intelligence, 39*(3), 211–221. doi:10.1023/A:1024605820527

Brin, S., Motwani, R., & Silverstein, C. (1997). Beyond market baskets: generalizing association rules to correlations. In *SIGMOD '97: Proceedings of the 1997 ACM SIGMOD international conference on Management of data* (pp. 265-276), New York, NY: ACM.

Edmonds, J., Gryz, J., Liang, D., & Miller, R. J. (2001). Mining for empty rectangles in large data sets. In *ICDT '01: International conference on database theory* (pp. 174-188), London, UK: Springer Berlin / Heidelberg.

Elbassioni, K. (2008). Algorithms for dualization over products of partially ordered sets. To appear In *SIAM J. Disctere Math.*

Gunopulos, D., Mannila, H., Khardon, R., & Toivonen, H. (1997). Data mining, hypergraph transversals, and machine learning (extended abstract). In *PODS '97: Proceedings of the 16th ACM SIGACT-SIGMOD-SIGART symposium on Principles of database systems* (pp. 209-216), New York: ACM Press.

Han, J., Cai, Y., & Cercone, N. (1993). Data-driven discovery of quantitative rules in relational databases. *IEEE Transactions on Knowledge and Data Engineering, 5*(1), 29–40. doi:10.1109/69.204089

Han, J., & Fu, Y. (1995). Discovery of multiple-level association rules from large databases. In *VLDB '95: Proceedings of the 21th International Conference on Very Large Data Bases* (pp. 420-431), San Francisco, CA, USA: Morgan Kaufmann Publishers Inc.

Hipp, J., Myka, A., Wirth, R., & Guntzer, U. (1998). A new algorithm for faster mining of generalized association rules. In *PKDD '98: Proceedings of the Second European Symposium on Principles of Data Mining and Knowledge Discovery* (pp. 74-82). London, UK: Springer-Verlag.

Huang, Y.-F., & Wu, C.-M. (2002). Mining generalized association rules using pruning techniques. In *ICDM '02: Proceedings of the 2002 IEEE International Conference on Data Mining* (pp. 227-234). Washington, DC: IEEE Computer Society.

Kavvadias, D. J., & Stavropoulos, E. C. (2005). An efficient algorithm for the transversal hypergraph generation. *J. Graph Algorithms Appl.*, *9*(2), 239–264.

Khachiyan, L., Boros, E., Elbassioni, K., & Gurvich, V. (2006). An efficient implementation of a quasi-polynomial algorithm for generating hypergraph transversals and its application in joint generation. *Discrete Applied Mathematics*, *154*(16), 2350–2372. doi:10.1016/j.dam.2006.04.012

Khachiyan, L., Boros, E., Elbassioni, K., Gurvich, V., & Makino, K. (2007). Dual-bounded generating problems: Efficient and inefficient points for discrete probability distributions and sparse boxes for multidimensional data. *Theoretical Computer Science*, *379*(3), 361–376. doi:10.1016/j.tcs.2007.02.044

Koh, Y. S. (2008). Mining non-coincidental rules without a user defined support threshold. In *PAKDD: Proceedings of the 12th Pacific-Asia Conference on Advances in Knowledge Discovery and Data Mining*, (pp. 910-915). Springer.

Koh, Y. S., & Pears, R. (2007). Efficiently finding negative association rules without support threshold. In *Australian Conference on Artificial Intelligence* (pp. 710-714). Springer Berlin / Heidelberg.

Lin, J.-L. (2003). Mining maximal frequent intervals. In *SAC '03: Proceedings of the 2003 ACM symposium on Applied computing* (pp. 426-431), New York: ACM.

Liu, B., Hsu, W., & Ma, Y. (1999). Mining association rules with multiple minimum supports. In *KDD '99: Proceedings of the fifth ACM SIGKDD international conference on Knowledge discovery and data mining* (pp. 337-341), New York: ACM.

Liu, B., Ku, L.-P., & Hsu, W. (1997). Discovering interesting holes in data. In *IJCAI '1997* (2): *Proceedings of Fifteenth International Joint Conference on Artificial Intelligence* (pp. 930-935).

Mannila, H. (1998). Database methods for data mining, tutorial. In *KDD '98: Proceedings of the fifth ACM SIGKDD international conference on Knowledge discovery and data mining*. ACM.

Mun, L.-F., Liu, B., Wang, K., & Qi, X.-Z. (1998). Using decision tree induction for discovering holes in data. In *PRICAI '98: Proceedings of the 5th Pacific Rim International Conference on Artificial Intelligence* (pp. 182-193), London, UK: Springer-Verlag.

Mustafa, M. D., Nabila, N. F., Evans, D. J., Saman, M. Y., & Mamat, A. (2006). Association rules on significant rare data using second support. *International Journal of Computer Mathematics*, *83*(1), 69–80. doi:10.1080/00207160500113330

Nanavati, A. A., Chitrapura, K. P., Joshi, S., & Krishnapuram, R. (2001). Mining generalised disjunctive association rules. In *CIKM '01: Proceedings of the tenth international conference on Information and knowledge management* (pp. 482-489), New York: ACM.

Schroder, B. S. W. (2003). *Ordered Sets: An Introduction.* Birkhauser, Boston.

Sharma, L. K., Vyas, O. P., Tiwary, U. S., & Vyas, R. (2005). A novel approach of multilevel positive and negative association rule mining for spatial databases. In *MLDM '05: Proceedings of* the 4th International Conference on Machine Learning and Data Mining in Pattern Recognition (pp. 620-629). Springer.

Srikant, R., & Agrawal, R. (1995). Mining generalized association rules. In *VLDB '95: Proceedings of the 21th International Conference on Very Large Data Bases* (pp. 407-419), San Francisco, CA, USA. Morgan Kaufmann Publishers Inc.

Srikant, R., & Agrawal, R. (1996). Mining quantitative association rules in large relational tables. In *SIGMOD '96: Proceedings of the 1996 ACM SIGMOD international conference on Management of data* (pp. 1-12), New York: ACM.

Thomas, S., & Sarawagi, S. (1998). Mining generalized association rules and sequential patterns using SQL queries. In *KDD '98: Proceedings of the Fourth International Conference on Knowledge Discovery and Data Mining* (pp. 344-348).

Tong, Q., Yan, B., & Zhou, Y. (2005). Mining quantitative association rules on overlapped intervals. In *ADMA '05: Proceedings of the* 1st International Conference on *Advanced Data Mining and Applications* (pp. 43-50). Springer.

Yuan, X., Buckles, B. P., Yuan, Z., & Zhang, J. (2002). Mining negative association rules. In *Computers and Communications, IEEE Symposium on* (pp. 0-623).

Zaki, M. J. (2000). Generating non-redundant association rules. In *KDD '00: Proceedings of the sixth ACM SIGKDD international conference on Knowledge discovery and data mining* (pp. 34-43). ACM, New York, NY, USA.

Section 3
Rare, Anomalous, and Interesting Patterns

Chapter 8
Discovering Interesting Patterns in Numerical Data with Background Knowledge

Szymon Jaroszewicz
National Institute of Telecommunications, Poland

ABSTRACT

The paper presents an approach to mining patterns in numerical data without the need for discretization. The proposed method allows for discovery of arbitrary nonlinear relationships. The approach is based on finding a function of a set of attributes whose values are close to zero in the data. Intuitively such functions correspond to equations describing relationships between the attributes, but they are also able to capture more general classes of patterns. The approach is set in an association rule framework with analogues of itemsets and rules defined for numerical attributes. Furthermore, the user may include background knowledge in the form of a probabilistic model. Patterns which are already correctly predicted by the model will not be considered interesting. Interesting patterns can then be used by the user to update the probabilistic model.

INTRODUCTION

Association rule mining (Agrawal, Imielinski & Swami, 1993) is one of the most important data mining tasks. Initially only simple conjunctions of items were allowed as patterns, but generalizations of the framework to other pattern types such as sequences, trees, graphs etc. have been developed, significantly expanding its applicability. Curiously there has been relatively little effort devoted to gen-eralizing association rules to numerical attributes, despite the practical ubiquity of numerical data.

The main approach to mining numerical data has been discretization (Srikant & Agrawal, 1996). In this approach numerical attributes are split into a number of discrete intervals, after which the data can be mined using standard techniques. Discretization however has several problems. First, discretizing the attributes leads to information loss. Second, each interval contains only a small portion of the data which can lead to statistical estimation problems. The third problem is that relationships between at-

DOI: 10.4018/978-1-60566-754-6.ch008

tributes are split among several intervals, so the underlying patterns are harder to spot. Increasing the number of intervals alleviates the first problem, but makes the two remaining ones more acute, so it is not a completely satisfactory solution.

In recent years important progress has been made in the area of mining association rules in numerical data without discretization (Steinbah, Tan, Xiong, Kumar, 2004; Rückert, Richter, Kramer, 2004; Rückert, Kramer, 2006; Achtert, Böhm, Kriegel, Kröger, Zimek, 2006; Besson, Robardet, De Raedt, Boulicaut, 2006; Jaroszewicz 2006; Claders, Goethals, Jaroszewicz 2006; Jaroszewicz, Korzeń 2007; Jaroszewicz, 2008). Those works will be discussed in more detail in the following section.

This chapter presents a method for mining numerical data in the style of association rule mining without discretization. It is possible to discover arbitrary nonlinear relationships through the use of polynomial approximations. Furthermore it extends the method such that the user can provide background knowledge in the form of a probabilistic model. Patterns which are correctly modeled by background knowledge are considered uninteresting and will not be ranked highly. This is a very important improvement as association rule mining algorithms typically produce thousands of patterns which then have to be searched manually. Including background knowledge in the process gives a solid framework for handling interestingness related issues. After interesting patterns have been presented to the user, he/she can update background knowledge based on those patterns, after which a new set of patterns will become interesting. This interactive approach has several advantages such as the understandability of constructed probabilistic models.

BACKGROUND

We will now discuss previous work related to mining association rules in numerical data with-

out discretization. In Rückert, Richter, Kramer, (2004), Georgii, Richter, Rückert, Kramer (2005), Rückert, Kramer (2006) an approach is presented based on finding rules of the type "if a linear combination of some set of attributes exceeds some threshold a, than another linear combination of another set of attributes is likely to exceed some threshold b". As sharp thresholds are used, the approach cannot represent functional relationships between attributes, contrary to the approach presented in this Chapter. In Achtert, Böhm, Kriegel, Kröger, Zimek (2006) a method for summarizing clusters of numerical data using linear equations is described. The authors use a clustering algorithm to do the actual pattern discovery, and their approach does not follow the association rule framework.

The idea of Steinbah, Tan, Xiong & Kumar (2004) is closer to our approach. They present a definition of support for numerical data, which does not require discretization. Unfortunately the presented definition of support is not very intuitive, although some interpretation in terms of a lower bound on scalar products is proposed. In similar spirit Calders, Goethals, Jaroszewicz (2006) and Jaroszewicz (2006) presented definitions of support for numerical data based on ranks and polynomials which are easier to interpret.

This work is based on the work Jaroszewicz (2008) where so called minimum variance associations were proposed for mining arbitrary nonlinear relationships in data without discretization. This Chapter extends the method by including background knowledge in the process of selecting interesting patterns. The method will be described in detail in the following section.

There is some similarity between this approach and equation discovery (Dzeroski, Todorovski, 1995), however our approach is much more efficient (see (Jaroszewicz, 2008) for a comparison with the Lagrange equation discovery system) as only a single eigenvalue computation per pattern is required instead of a combinatorial search.

One problem faced by most approaches to

association rule mining is the huge number of discovered patterns. The user is then faced with a secondary mining problem, where now not the amount of data, but the amount of patterns is the hindrance. Typical solutions involve sorting discovered rules based on some interestingness measure and/or pruning those rules which can be derived from others, see *e.g.* (McGarry, 2005) for an overview. Those methods however only discover highly correlated patterns which are often already known to specialists in the field. In fact Ohsaki, Kitaguchi, Okamoto, Yokoi, Yamaguchi (2004) and Carvalho, Freitas, Ebecken (2005) have shown that in many cases human interest is negatively correlated with interestingness measures.

In Jaroszewicz, Simovici (2004), Jaroszewicz, Scheffer (2005) Jaroszewicz, Scheffer, Simovici, 2009) a solution to this problem has been proposed by the use of background knowledge. The user specifies the background knowledge as a (possibly initially empty) probabilistic model such as a Bayesian network. Patterns whose probabilities in data diverge most strongly from what the model predicts are considered most interesting. Discovered patterns are shown to the user, whose task is then to update the probabilistic model, such that it predicts those patterns correctly. After such a correction is made, new patterns become interesting and the cycle is repeated. In Jaroszewicz, Scheffer, Simovici (2009) it is demonstrated that such an interactive approach gives models which are much more understandable and better reflect the underlying causal structure than models built automatically.

This chapter applies interestingness based on background knowledge to the minimum variance approach to pattern discovery in numerical data. It thus becomes possible to discover interesting (with respect to user provided background knowledge) patterns in data without the need for discretization.

Minimum Variance Associations

In this section the minimum variance associations, first proposed in Jaroszewicz (2008) will be summarized and discussed. The following section will extend the framework with the possibility of including background knowledge.

Let us begin with two simple motivating examples. Suppose we have a dataset D with attributes x and y. Suppose further that there is a relationship between x and y which can be described as $x = y$. Such a pattern can be represented by a function $F(x,y) = x\text{-}y$ which is always close to zero in the given data. Similarly if x and y represent random points on a unit circle, the function F describing their relationship is given by $F(x,y) = x^2\text{-}y^2\text{-}1$. It is thus tempting to define patterns on numerical data as "*sets of attributes for which there exists a function F whose value is close to zero for all data points*".

A weakness of this first formulation is easily observed. Dividing F by 2 brings function's values closer to zero without providing any new information. Worse, taking F to be the constant zero function leads to considering all sets of attributes to be patterns. Function F thus needs to be restricted in some way in order to prevent such cases. The restriction must guarantee that the function F would have high values, were the relationships given in the dataset D not present. In (Jaroszewicz, 2008) is has been argued that a suitable restriction was to require that the function should have high values, were the attributes in D statistically independent.

Another problem is, which family of functions to choose for F. In (Jaroszewicz, 2008) polynomials of given degree were used and we continue this convention here. A more formal statement of the problem will now be given.

Given a set of attributes $I = x_1, x_2, ..., x_n$ and a function $F(I) = F(x_1, x_2, ..., x_n)$, the *variance* of F on D is defined as $\sum_{t \in D} F^2\left(t\left[I\right]\right)$. Thus the variance is low if the values of F are close to zero on D. Notice that this is different from the statistical notion of variance unless function's mean is zero on D. This is an intended abuse of terminology.

Let us now assume that F is represented by a polynomial where each variable has degree at most d:

$$F_c\left(x_1,\ldots,x_n\right) = \sum_{\alpha_1=0}^{d} \cdots \sum_{\alpha_n=0}^{d} c_{(\alpha_1,\ldots,\alpha_n)} x_1^{\alpha_1} \cdots x_n^{\alpha_n}.$$

By grouping the coefficients and variables into vectors $c = [c(0, \ldots, 0), c(0, \ldots, 1), \ldots, c(d, \ldots, d)]^T$ and $x = [x_0^{\,0}\cdots x_n^{\,0}, x_0^{\,0}\cdots x_n^{\,1}, \ldots, x_0^{\,d}\cdots x_n^{\,d}]^T$ respectively, we can succinctly write $F_c = c^T x = x^T c$, and $F_c^{\,2} = c^T(xx^T)c$, where xx^T is a matrix whose entries are monomials in $x_1, x_2, \ldots, x_n$, in which each variable's power is at most $2d$. Let x_t denote the value of vector x at record t. Notice now that the variance of F_c can be expressed as:

$$\sum_{t\in D} F_c^2\left(t[x_1,\ldots,x_n]\right) = \sum_{t\in D} c^T\left(x_t \cdot x_t^T\right)c = c^T\left(\sum_{t\in D} x_t \cdot x_t^T\right)c = c^T S_D c,$$

where S_D is a matrix computed based on the dataset D only, independent of c. Thus, once S_D has been computed, variances for all functions F_c can be computed without accessing the data. This property is extremely important as it allows for fast variance evaluation without the need to access the potentially huge database. This property has been explored for other types of problems in (Jaroszewicz, Korzeń, 2007)

As stated above, since the constant zero function trivially minimizes the variance in every case, we need to restrict the space of the functions considered. Formally it will be required that the variance of the function F_c be equal to 1 if all attributes of D were independent. We need to define the matrix S_I which will be analogous to

S_D but correspond to the case when all attributes in D are independent.

While constructing the matrix S_I we will make use of the fact that the expectation of the product of independent random variables is the product of their expectations. Consider for example an entry in the matrix S_D corresponding to a monomial $x_1^{\,\alpha 1}\cdots x_n^{\,\alpha n}$. The corresponding entry in the matrix S_I, based on the independence assumption, and the abovementioned property of expectation of independent variables, becomes

$$\left(\sum_{t\in D} t.x_1^{\alpha_1}\right)\cdots\left(\sum_{t\in D} t.x_n^{\alpha_n}\right).$$

In the following sections of this Chapter we will present a more general approach, which uses background knowledge to construct S_I, with independence being a special case. Once the matrix S_I is computed, the variance of F_c under independence assumption can be expressed as $c^T S_I c$.

We are now ready to formally state the minimization problem which will allow for finding the best function F_c for a given set of attributes $I = x_1, x_2, \ldots, x_n$:

It has been shown in Jaroszewicz (2008) that the problem is equivalent to the so called Generalized Eigenvalue Problem. Solvers for this problem are readily available in numerical algebra packages such as LAPACK (Anderson et al. 1999). The best value of c is the generalized eigenvector corresponding to the smallest eigenvalue, and the variance of the best F_c is equal to the smallest eigenvalue. The problem is thus easy to solve in time linear in the number of data records (from computing the S_D matrix).

The approach can be seen as multivariate polynomial regression without the target variable. Including target variables will be considered in the next section when rules are introduced. Also note, that the use of eigenvalues is similar to the Total Least Squares regression.

An Example Calculation

Suppose that the dataset D over attributes x and y consists of three records: (-2,4), (1,-2), (-1,2). Assume, for clarity of presentation, that the maximum degree is $d = 1$. The x vector is $[1,x,y,xy]^\mathrm{T}$. The full S_D and S_I matrices are

$$S_D = \begin{bmatrix} 3 & -2 & 4 & -12 \\ -2 & 6 & -12 & 16 \\ 4 & -12 & 24 & -32 \\ -12 & 16 & -32 & 72 \end{bmatrix} \quad S_I = \begin{bmatrix} 9 & -6 & 12 & -8 \\ -6 & 6 & -8 & 24 \\ 12 & -8 & 24 & -48 \\ -8 & 24 & -48 & 144 \end{bmatrix}.$$

For example, entry (4,4) of the S_D matrix corresponds to the monomial x^2y^2 and is equal to $(-2)^24^2 + 1^2(-2)^2 + (-1)^22^2 = 64+4+4 = 72$. The same entry of the S_I matrix is computed as $((-2)^2+1^2+(-1)^2)(4^2+(-2)^2+2^2) = 144$.

The generalized eigenvector corresponding to the smallest generalized eigenvalue is $c = [0, -0.5, -0.25, 0]^\mathrm{T}$. The minimum variance function F_c becomes $c^\mathrm{T}x = [0, -0.5, -0.25, 0]^\mathrm{T}[1,x,y,xy] = -0.5x -0.25y$. Thus the relationship $y = 2x$ has been recovered.

Relation to Association Rule Mining

We will now discuss how minimum variance patterns fit into the association rule framework: the minimum variance sets of attributes will play the role of itemsets, on top of which two types of rules will be defined. While the analogy with association rule mining is not perfect, the most important properties, such as the possibility to first mine itemsets, and then find rules from 'good' itemsets only are preserved.

Let us begin by discussing monotonicity properties. First notice that a function of n variables is a special case of a function of $n+1$ variables (constant in one variable). Thus adding attributes to a pattern always increases the space of possible functions, and can thus only reduce the pattern's variance. The proposed patterns thus exhibit a monotonicity property, such that if a set of attributes is a low variance pattern, so are all of its supersets. This property is opposite to the standard association rules, but nevertheless allows for efficient mining algorithms in the style of the well known Apriori algorithm (Agrawal, Imielinski, Swami, 1993). A minimum variance threshold is set by the user; patterns with variance below this threshold are considered sufficiently correlated. Once a pattern has been found, its supersets are not explored further; the pattern represents the *smallest* set of attributes with given strength of the relationship. The mining algorithm is a trivial modification of the Apriori algorithm with the itemset support counting replaced by minimum variance calculations described in the previous section.

The extension of the framework with rules will now be discussed. As patterns described above are not always easy to interpret, it is necessary to define rules which may further help the user in identifying the nature of discovered relationships. Two types of rules: *equality rules* and *regression rules* are proposed (see Jaroszewicz, 2008).

Equality rules have the form $F(I) = G(J)$, where I and J are disjoint sets of attributes. Equality rules capture a situation where a pattern can be decomposed into two *disjoint* sub-patterns with a functional constraint between them. Such rules are obviously much easier to interpret than a full pattern on the union of I and J. For example if x and y lie on a unit circle, the equality rule would be $y^2 = x^2-1$. Regression rules have the form $x = F(I)$, where I is a set of attributes, and x a single attribute not in I. Such rules correspond to standard polynomial regression. Of course regression rules are easier to interpret than equation rules which in turn are easier to interpret than minimum variance sets of attributes. However there are cases when a set of attributes can have low variance but no equality rule is present, as well as cases when only equality rules, and not regression rules can be found.

The variance of an equality rule $F(I) = G(J)$

is defined as the sum on a dataset D of $(F(I) - G(J))^2$. For regression rules analogously as the sum of $(x - F(I))^2$. For regression rules the variance thus becomes the standard least squares error. It is easy to see that the variance of an equality rule can be computed using the same approach as described in the previous section. Minimum variance pattern is found for the union of I and J with an additional restriction that all elements of the vector c corresponding to interactions between variables in I and J are forced to have the value of zero. In practice those elements are simply omitted from the computation. It follows that the minimum variance of an equality rule $F(I) = G(J)$ has to be higher than the minimum variance of the pattern on the union of I and J. A similar argument shows that regression rules on a set of attributes must have higher variance than equality rules on that set of attributes.

This allows for the following discovery strategy: first find all minimal sets of attributes satisfying the given minimum variance threshold, then find equality rules within those patterns. For those patterns which have equality rules, regression rules should also be found. This strategy is a direct analogue of standard association rule mining, where first frequent itemsets are found (minimum variance sets of attributes in our case), and, during a later stage, association rules (equality and regression rules in our case) are found based on frequent itemsets only.

Background Knowledge – Bayesian Networks

In the next section we will discuss how to include background knowledge in the above process, which is the main contribution of this Chapter.

Let us first discuss how the user provided background knowledge will be represented. The proposed approach needs a representation which is capable of expressing arbitrary joint probability distributions on the attributes, while at the same time, is easy to understand and update by the user. Those conditions are satisfied by Bayesian networks (Pearl, 1998; Pearl, 2000).

A Bayesian network is a directed acyclic graph, whose nodes correspond to attributes (random variables) and edges correspond to influences between variables. Often it is assumed that an edge from A to B means that A *directly*, causally influences B. Satisfying this assumption is advantageous from the point of view of model understandability and usability, but is not strictly necessary, and the proposed method works when it is not satisfied. In addition, nodes are labeled with conditional distributions of the node's variable on its parents in the graph.

The joint probability distribution represented by the network is simply a product of conditional distributions of all nodes. An example Bayesian network is shown in Figure 1. In the network both a break-in and an earthquake can cause an alarm sound, which in turn can cause the neighbor to call. The joint probability distribution of the network is $P(BEAN) = P(B)P(E)P(A|B,E)P(N|A)$.

Traditionally Bayesian networks are defined for discrete attributes, but they work equally well for numerical attributes too. The usual assumption in this case is that all distributions are normal, and conditional distributions are modeled using linear regression. In practice this assumptions are often too restrictive and arbitrary distributions need to be allowed.

Inference (*i.e.* finding marginal distributions from the joint distribution) from a Bayesian network can be done in two ways: exact and approximate (see Pearl, 1998 for details). As inference from Bayesian networks is NP-complete, approximate methods are more useful. Also there are no exact methods for inference from Bayesian networks with numerical attributes, unless only normal distributions are allowed. Approximate approaches are usually based on sampling, and in this work we will use a sampling based method. To sample from a Bayesian network its nodes are visited in a topological sort order. When a node is visited, values of its parents are already

Figure 1. An example Bayesian network

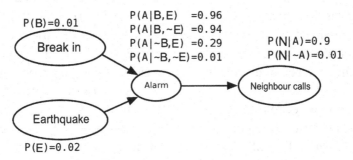

known so its value can simply be drawn from an appropriate probability distribution. Full details can be found in (Jaroszewicz, Scheffer, 2005; Jaroszewicz, Scheffer, Simovici, 2009).

Mining Interesting Patterns from Numerical Data with Background Knowledge

This section presents the main contribution of the Chapter, the extension of the minimum variance framework with a possibility of inclusion of background knowledge. Overall the idea is to replace the independence assumption (matrix S_I) with the assumption that the data comes from the distribution specified by the background knowledge (a probabilistic model such as a Bayesian network). Patterns which will now be discovered will have variance of 1 according to the background knowledge, but will have low variance in the actual dataset D. This represents relationships present in data, which are not present in the background knowledge.

The actual implementation of the scheme is easy. A large sample B of a given size is taken from the Bayesian network and used to estimate the variance of F according to background knowledge. To achieve this a matrix S_B is constructed in exactly the same way as the matrix S_D, but based on the sample B used in place of the dataset D. The calculations proceed in exactly the same way as for the case without background knowledge, except that the matrix S_I is replaced with the matrix

S_B. For example, the variance of F_c according to background knowledge now becomes $c^T S_B c$.

Notice that when the Bayesian network has no edges, its joint probability distribution corresponds to an independence assumption. Thus the minimum variance associations without background knowledge are a natural special case of minimum variance associations with background knowledge.

Currently the choice of the size of the sample B taken from the network is left to the user (in the experiments shown in this Chapter the value of 10000 was chosen) but a framework with formal guarantees, such as in (Jaroszewicz, Scheffer, 2005; Jaroszewicz, Scheffer, Simovici, 2009) can also be developed.

The concepts of equality and regression rules can be directly carried over to the case with background knowledge. They will now represent restricted classes of patterns which are present in data but not modeled well by the user supplied background knowledge.

Unfortunately, when the background knowledge models some part of the data very closely, the generalized eigenvalue problem can become numerically unstable. This issue has been solved by regularizing the coefficient vector c. More precisely, it is additionally required that the square of the norm of the vector c, which can be expressed as $c^T c$, be small. The optimization problem updated for inclusion of background knowledge and regularization becomes:

Here w is the regularization parameter which decides on the trade-off between minimizing the variance and the norm of c. Notice that $c^T S_D c + w c^T c = c^T S_D c + w c^T I c = c^T (S_D + wI) c$, where I is a unit matrix of appropriate size. So the inclusion the regularization factor is very easy and can be done by simply adding constants to the diagonal of the matrix S_D. In our applications, the regularization parameter w was typically very small, in the range of 10^{-3} to 10^{-5} which proved sufficient to prevent numerical instability. The regularization approach is analogous to that used in ridge regression, see (Rao, Toutenburg, 1997) or most other multivariate statistical analysis textbooks.

We are now ready to describe the discovery procedure at a high level. The user provides background knowledge in the form of a Bayesian network. The minimum variance associations with background knowledge are discovered, and the best of them (those with smallest variance) are presented to the user. Using his/her understanding of the domain, the user then updates the background knowledge (Bayesian network) such that it explains the new patterns. This is usually done by simply adding new edges to the network. Conditional distributions are estimated from the dataset D automatically. Note that even though the conditional distributions are estimated from data, the joint distribution of the network will not in general match that found in data, as an incomplete network structure introduces statistical independencies some of which may not be present in the D (Jaroszewicz, Scheffer, Simovici, 2009).

Providing a full Bayesian network may seem to be a very demanding requirement, however, if the user does not know the domain well, it is always possible to provide a Bayesian network with no edges. Such a network naturally corresponds to the assumption that all variables are statistically independent, which is a reasonable initial assumption when nothing is known. As interesting patterns are discovered, the user will be able to update the network by adding more edges.

The following section presents experimental evaluation of the proposed approach.

Experimental Evaluation

In (Jaroszewicz, 2008) a thorough experimental evaluation of the minimum variance approach to pattern discovery without background knowledge has been presented. It has been demonstrated that the approach successfully discovers various types of functional relationships, as well as other patterns, such as 'holes in data' which are not always discovered by traditional regression analysis.

We will now present an experimental evaluation involving user supplied background knowledge to find interesting patterns. We will use the well known UCI dataset on housing in Boston. The dataset contains about 500 descriptions of several housing offers from the Boston area including data about the town in which the building is located. Full list of attributes is given in Table 1.

As the author did not know what to expect from the data, the initial network had no edges, corresponding to the independence assumption. The regularization parameter w was set to 10^{-5}. An important issue is representing arbitrary conditional probability distributions for numerical variables (as it was mentioned before, normality assumption is often insufficient in practice). It has been decided to represent the distributions using histograms. Each histogram bucket contains the number of the values in D falling into it as well as the mean of those values. Conditional probabilities are simply represented as multidimensional histograms. To generate a random value, the histogram bucket is chosen at random, and the mean of values of D in that bucket is returned. The probability of each bucket being selected is proportional to the number of data points which fall into this bucket. The problem is thus reduced to sampling from a discrete distribution, which can be done in constant time (Knuth, 1997). While this method of approximation is quite coarse, it was sufficient in practice. It is not difficult to replace it with other density estimation methods such as kernel density estimation.

Initially, the Bayesian network had no edges,

Table 1. Attributes of the Boston housing data

Attribute name	Description
CRIM	per capita crime rate by town
ZN	proportion of residential land zoned for lots over 25,000 sq.ft.
INDUS	proportion of non-retail business acres per town
CHAS	Charles River dummy variable (= 1 if tract bounds river; 0 otherwise)
NOX	nitric oxides concentration (parts per 10 million)
RM	average number of rooms per dwelling
AGE	proportion of owner-occupied units built prior to 1940
DIS	weighted distances to five Boston employment centres
RAD	index of accessibility to radial highways
TAX	full-value property-tax rate per $10,000
PTRATIO	pupil-teacher ratio by town
LSTAT	% lower status of the population
MEDV	median valu of owner-occupied homes in $1000's

and histograms with ten buckets have been used for all attributes. Initial analysis revealed that distributions for ZN and RAD attributes are not modeled well due to big spread to their values, the number of buckets in their histograms has been increased to 100. Additionally, since CHAS is a zero-one variable, its distribution has been changed to a Bernoulli distribution with the probability of CHAS=1 being about 0.07 (estimated from data).

The first application of the algorithm yielded a pattern {RAD, TAX}, which had the lowest variance. Inspection revealed that in most cases there was no visible relationship between the attributes, however some values were sticking out. Out of the total of 506 records, 132 had value 24 for RAD and 666 for TAX. The value of 24 for RAD (accessibility to highways) was much higher than all other values for this attribute, which suggested (although this is not stated explicitly in the data) that all those records represent listings in Boston proper. Since it is the biggest city in the region, its characteristics are expected to be different, and since a large percentage of listings (apparently around a quarter) comes from Boston it heavily skews the data.

To improve the model's behavior, it was decided to replace it with a mixture of two models, one corresponding to Boston, and one corresponding to the remaining cases. Actually only attributes ZN, INDUS, RAD, TAX, PTRATIO needed separate (curiously exactly those values were constant for all Boston listings) distributions, all others shared histograms between the two models as their distributions within Boston didn't differ from other towns.

After performing the above change, {RAD, TAX} was no longer the most interesting set of attributes, which shows that the dependency has been accounted for.

The most interesting pattern now became {AGE, ZN}. Figure 2 shows the scatterplot for those two attributes. The cross symbols mark the actual data points. It can be seen that towns with high proportion of old houses have small percentage of large residential lots. An important thing to notice is that the relationship depicted in the Figure is not functional, it can be easily seen however that towns with higher proportion of older houses *never* have a high percentage of large lots. One might think that minimum variance patterns are not well suited for discovering such relationships, but the

Figure 2. Scatterplot showing the relationship between the proportion of households built before 1940 (AGE) and the proportion of large residential lots (ZN) in a town together with the contourplot illustrating the minimum variance itemset discovered.

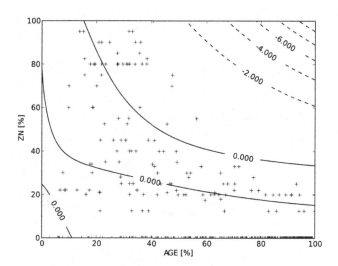

example proves that this is not the case. Figure 2 also shows the contour plot for the function *F(AGE, ZN)* which had the smallest variance (with respect to background knowledge of course, but at current stage background knowledge assumes the attributes are independent). It can be seen that the function had low, close to zero, values in the region where the actual points are concentrated, and high absolute values in the empty regions. The minimum variance itemset thus captures the nature of the dependency well. The background knowledge distributed points evenly throughout the chart (not shown due to clarity) including the area where data points in *D* did not occur.

Note, that such relationships in data are usually not modeled well by standard regression analysis, but appear commonly in practice. In fact most of the relationships discovered in this study are of that type.

To account for the dependency, the distribution of ZN has been changed into a distribution conditional on AGE. This corresponds to adding an edge from AGE to ZN in the Bayesian network. This direction was chosen, as it is the age of the

town that is the *cause* of the way it is zoned, and not vice versa.

After making the modification to the model, the attribute set {AGE, ZN} was no longer interesting, which its the expected behavior. It was now possible to focus on other, not yet explained, dependencies.

The next most interesting attribute set was {ZN, INDUS}. The scatterplot looks similar to Figure 2 and is thus omitted. Essentially, towns with large lots are less likely to have a lot of industry. A possible explanation is that towns with large residential lots are inhabited by wealthy people who do not want to have industry close to their homes. An edge was added from ZN to INDUS, to indicate the influence. After the modification, the attribute set was no longer interesting, which again shows that the approach is good at removing known dependencies.

The next most interesting pattern turned out to be {ZN, NOX}. Towns with big residential lots (and supposedly wealthy inhabitants) have lower nitric oxide levels. However, one might expect that INDUS would be a better indicator, as nitric

Figure 3. The relationship between town's poverty rate (LSTAT) and house values (MEDV) for Boston housing data.

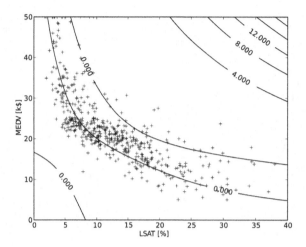

oxides are a major industrial pollutant. We have decided that this is indeed the case, and INDUS is the direct cause of NOX. The relationship between ZN and NOX can be explained by the correlation between ZN and INDUS. Towns with large lots are less industrialized, and as a consequence, less polluted with nitric oxides.

We have added and edge between INDUS and NOX, and as a result the relationship between ZN and NOX became much less interesting. Thus the transitive dependency has correctly been taken into account. This dependency also shows the importance of using human intelligence in explaining statistical relationships. The strongest dependency does not necessarily correspond to a true causal relationship.

Another relationship discovered was between INDUS and DIS. This is quite natural, as employment centers are clearly correlated with industry. Yet another example was CHAS and CRIM. Indeed average crime rate was more than twice lower for properties close to the Charles river (supposedly attractive locations). This shows that the approach does not break down for binary attributes, even though it was designed with numerical attributes in mind.

The last example which will be shown here is the set of attributes {LSTAT, MEDV} shown in Figure 3. This relationship is pretty close to being functional. The poverty rate in an area is an excellent predictor for house prices. Indeed the equality and regression rules for this case had much lower variances (around 0.15) than in all other presented cases (around 0.5).

CONCLUSION

A method for discovering arbitrary nonlinear relationships in numerical data without discretization presented in Jaroszewicz (2008) has been extended to include interestingness of patterns based on user supplied background knowledge. An interactive framework in style of (Jaroszewicz, Scheffer, Simovici, 2009) has thus been obtained for numerical attributes.

The practical usefulness of the framework has been demonstrated experimentally. Several interesting relationships have been discovered in an example dataset on Boston housing data. Various types of dependencies: functional, nonfunctional and discrete have been discovered, showing the versatility of the approach.

REFERENCES

Achtert, E., Böhm, C., Kriegel, H.-P., Kröger, P., & Zimek, A. (2006). Deriving quantitative models for correlation clusters. In *Proceedings of the ACM SIGMOD Conference on Management of Data (KDD)*, (pp. 4–13), Philadelphia, PA.

Agrawal, R., Imielinski, T., & Swami, A. (1993). Mining association rules between sets of items in large databases, In *Proceedings of the ACM SIGMOD Conference on Management of Data (KDD)*, (pp. 207–216).

Anderson, E., et al. (1999). *LAPACK Users' Guide*. SIAM.

Besson, J., Robardet, C., De Raedt, L., & Boulicaut, J.-F. (2006). Mining bi-sets in numerical data. In *Proceedings of the 5th International Workshop on Knowledge Discovery in Inductive Databases (KDID'06) at PKDD'06*, (pp. 9–19), Berlin, Germany.

Calders, T., Goethals, B., & Jaroszewicz, S. (2006). Mining Rank-Correlated Sets of Numerical Attributes. In *Proceedings of the 12th ACM SIGKDD International Conference on Knowledge Discovery and Data Mining (KDD)*, (pp. 96 - 105).

Carvalho, D., Freitas, A., & Ebecken, N. (2005). Evaluating the correlation between objective rule interestingness measures and real human interest. In: *Proceedings of the 9th European conference on principles of data mining and knowledge discovery (PKDD)*, (pp. 453–461).

Dzeroski, S., & Todorovski, L. (1995). Discovering dynamics: from inductive logic programming to machine discovery. *Journal of Intelligent Information Systems*, 4, 89–108. doi:10.1007/BF00962824

Georgii, E., Richter, L., Rückert, U., & Kramer, S. (2005). Analyzing microarray data using quantitative association rules. *Bioinformatics (Oxford, England)*, *21*(2), ii1–ii8. doi:10.1093/bioinformatics/bti1121

Jaroszewicz, S. (2006). Polynomial Association Rules with Applications to Logistic Regression. In *Proceedings of the ACM SIGKDD International Conference on Knowledge Discovery and Data Mining (KDD)*, (pp. 586 - 591).

Jaroszewicz, S. (2008). Minimum Variance Associations–Discovering Relationships in Numerical Data, In *Proceedings of the Pacific-Asia Conference on Knowledge Discovery and Data Mining (PAKDD)*, (pp. 172-183), Osaka, Japan.

Jaroszewicz, S., & Korzeń, M. (2007). Approximating Representations for Large Numerical Databases. In *Proceedings of the 7th SIAM International Conference on Data Mining (SDM)*, (pp. 521-526), Minneapolis, MN.

Jaroszewicz, S., & Scheffer, T. (2005). Fast Discovery of Unexpected Patterns in Data, Relative to a Bayesian Network. In *Proceedings of the 11th ACM SIGKDD International Conference on Knowledge Discovery and Data Mining (KDD)*, (pp. 118-127), Chicago, IL.

Jaroszewicz, S., Scheffer, T., & Simovici, D. (2009). Scalable pattern mining with Bayesian networks as background knowledge. *Data Mining and Knowledge Discovery*, *18*(1), 56-100.

Jaroszewicz, S., & Simovici, D. (2004). Interestingness of Frequent Itemsets Using Bayesian Networks as Background Knowledge. In *Proceedings of the 10th ACM SIGKDD International Conference on Knowledge Discovery and Data Mining (KDD)*, (pp. 178-186), Seattle, WA.

Knuth, D. (1997). *The Art of Computer Programming*, vol. 2, *Seminumerical Algorithms*, Addison-Wesley, Reading, MA.

McGarry, K. (2005). A survey of interestingness measures for knowledge discovery. *The Knowledge Engineering Review, 20*, 39–61. doi:10.1017/S0269888905000408

Ohsaki, M., Kitaguchi, S., Okamoto, K., Yokoi, H., & Yamaguchi, T. (2004). Evaluation of rule interestingness measures with a clinical dataset on hepatitis. In *Proceedings of the 8th European conference on principles of data mining and knowledge discovery (PKDD)*, (pp. 362–373).

Pearl, J. (1998). *Probabilistic reasoning in intelligent systems.* Morgan Kaufmann, Los Altos, CA.

Pearl, J. (2000). *Causality: models, reasoning, and inference.* Cambridge University Press, Cambridge, UK.

Rao, C. R., & Toutenburg, H. (1997). *Linear Models: Least Squares and Alternatives*, Springer Verlag, Heidelberg.

Rückert, U., & Kramer, S. (2006). A statistical approach to rule learning. In *Proceedings of the International Conference on Machine Learning (ICML)*, (pp. 785–792), Pittsburgh, PA.

Rückert, U., Richter, L., & Kramer, S. (2004). Quantitative association rules based on half-spaces: An optimization approach. *In Proceedings of the IEEE International Conference on Data Mining (ICDM)*, (pp. 507–510).

Srikant, R., & Agrawal, R. (1996). Mining quantitative association rules in large relational tables. In *Proceedings of the ACM SIGMOD Conference on Management of Data*, (pp. 1–12).

Steinbach, M., Tan, P.-N., Xiong, H., & Kumar, V. (2004). Generalizing the notion of support. In *Proceedings of the ACM SIGKDD International Conference on Knowledge Discovery and Data Mining (KDD)*, (pp, 689–694), Seattle, WA.

Chapter 9
Mining Rare Association Rules by Discovering Quasi-Functional Dependencies:
An Incremental Approach

Giulia Bruno
Politecnico di Torino, Italy

Paolo Garza
Politecnico di Torino, Italy

Elisa Quintarelli
Politecnico di Milano, Italy

ABSTRACT

In the context of anomaly detection, the data mining technique of extracting association rules can be used to identify rare rules which represent infrequent situations. A method to detect rare rules is to first infer the normal behavior of objects in the form of quasi-functional dependencies (i.e. functional dependencies that frequently hold), and then analyzing rare violations with respect to them. The quasi-functional dependencies are usually inferred from the current instance of a database. However, in several applications, the database is not static, but new data are added or deleted continuously. Thus, the anomalies have to be updated because they change over time. In this chapter, we propose an incremental algorithm to efficiently maintain up-to-date rules (i.e., functional and quasi-functional dependencies). The impact of the cardinality of the data set and the number of new tuples on the execution time is evaluated through a set of experiments on synthetic and real databases, whose results are here reported.

INTRODUCTION

Mining rare events is a critical task in several research areas such as database, machine learning, knowledge discovery, fraud detection, activity monitoring, and image analysis. In all these situations the main goal is to identify objects of a given population whose behavior is anomalous with respect to a set of rules part of the knowledge base, usually expressed by means of some statistical kind of computation on the given population. These exceptional situations

DOI: 10.4018/978-1-60566-754-6.ch009

are usually referred as outliers in the literature. Indeed, "an outlier is an observation that lies an abnormal distance from other values in a random sample from a population" ("NIST/SEMATECH" 2007). In this work, we define such infrequent situations as anomalies.

Anomalies indicate abnormal conditions, such as anomalous objects in an image, intruders inside a system, and faults on a factory production line (Hodge & Austin, 2004). It is imperative to detect sudden changes in the patterns which may indicate problems or exceptions in the behaviours. Anomaly detection methods can monitor individual shares or markets and detect novel trends which may indicate buying or selling opportunities. In a database, anomalies may indicate fraudulent cases or they may denote an error by the entry clerk or a misinterpretation of a missing value code; apart from the method, the detection of the anomaly is vital for database consistency and integrity.

The problem of analyzing anomalies is interesting, since they represent errors or semantically correct, albeit infrequent, situations. In both cases, detecting anomalies is a challenging task either to allow one to correct erroneous data or to investigate the meaning of exceptions. In the database research field and in real applications, the problem of identifying and correcting anomalies has received a lot of attention in recent years (Angiulli et al., 2007; Angiulli & Pizzuti, 2005; Ceri et al., 2007). The outlier detection problem is considered in order to examine a target database to derive more complex forms of constraints, with respect to those that are imposed during the design phase. This task is of great importance also in a variety of application fields, especially for biological, financial, and clinical data, where it is important to detect anomalies in order to clean errors or discover exceptions needing a further investigation by specialists (Apiletti et al., 2006).

A method to detect rare rules, which represent anomalies, is to first infer the normal behavior of objects by extracting frequent rules from a given dataset, and then analyzing rare violations to what has been inferred as a normal behaviors (Bruno et al., 2007 (b)).

The frequent rules are described in the form of quasi-functional dependencies and mined from the dataset by using association rules. A quasi-functional dependency is an approximate functional dependency derived from data (Baralis et al., 2004), and represents an implication among attributes (in the context of relational databases) or among elements (with respect to XML documents), which frequently holds in the analyzed dataset. Each quasi-functional dependency is characterized by a dependency degree value that represents the strength of the dependency. For each mined quasi-functional dependency, the set of association rules that involve the same attributes is queried in order to detect anomalies. In particular, the rare association rules (i.e., with a confidence lower than a fixed threshold) are selected, and further investigated in order to distinguish interesting anomalies from erroneous data.

Quasi-functional dependencies, which are a priori unknown, are usually inferred from the current instance of the considered database. However, in several applications anomalies have to be promptly detected, but the instance continuously changes (i.e., augment) over time (e.g., financial data). A more recent scenario where dynamicity is fundamental is the one where high level information processing tasks, like environmental monitoring, tracking, and classification, are performed with wireless sensor networks, where sensors must process a continuous (possibly fast) stream of data (Mozafari et al., 2008). When monitoring time critical activities, outlier detection problems have to be considered, in order to isolate erroneous or significant, but infrequent, streams of data. In this dynamic scenario all the inferred quasi-functional and functional dependencies, their dependency degree value, and the set of anomalies can potentially change over time.

Goals and Contributions

The interest in data mining applications is due to the growing amount of applications using large datasets; indeed data mining algorithms allow one to gain implicit knowledge from datasets, and to improve the quality of data when erroneous outliers are inferred.

When datasets continuously change and anomalies or outliers have to be promptly detected for application reasons (e.g., in medical or environmental applications), mining algorithms have to be adapted in order to efficiently mine current rules.

Therefore, the main contribution of this chapter is to extend the approach described in (Bruno et al., 2007(b)) by proposing an incremental algorithm to efficiently maintain up-to-date quasi-functional dependencies and their dependency degree value, in particular when large append-only databases are used. By using this algorithm we are able to maintain up-to-date the current set of mined quasi-functional dependencies and association rules, and consequently also the set of anomalies (outliers). The incremental version of the algorithm can be exploited in real time contexts, where anomaly detection must be performed immediately on append-only databases.

Chapter Outline

The chapter is organized as follows. In Section Background some preliminary notions of functional dependencies, association rules and quasi-functional dependencies are described. In Section Outlier Detection we discuss how to find the rare association rules by analyzing the dependency degree between quasi-functional dependent attributes, and thus identify anomalies. In Section Incremental Outlier Detection the incremental algorithm to update the association rules and the quasi-functional dependencies without performing again the extraction is described. Section Experimental Results compares the performances of the

original algorithm and the incremental version, shows the gain in term of computation time when using the incremental one and the conditions under which it is useful to use it. Finally, conclusions and possible lines for future work are presented in Section Conclusions and Future Work.

BACKGROUND

In the context of relational databases, functional dependencies are constraints among sets of attributes. Given a relation R, a functional dependency between two sets of attributes X and Y of a relation R imposes the following constraint on an instance r of R. Any two tuples t_1 and t_2 of r that agree on the value of X (i.e., $t_1[X] = t_2[X]$) must agree on the value of Y (i.e., they must also have $t_1[Y] = t_2[Y]$). The functional dependency between the two sets of attributes X and Y of R is denoted by $X \rightarrow Y$ (Elmasri, 2005).

Functional dependencies for XML have been defined in (Arenas, 2004) by using tree tuples, which describe the paths of an XML document whose schema is expressed by a DTD (Document Type Definition).

Let us assume the following disjoint sets El of element names, Att of attribute names, Str of possible values of string-valued attributes, and Vert of node identifiers. All attribute names start with the symbol @, whereas symbols ε and S represent element type declarations EMPTY and #PCDATA.

In Arenas (2004) a DTD is defined to be D = (E, A, P, R, r), where:

- E $\subseteq$ El is a finite set of element types,
- A $\subseteq$ Att is a finite set of attributes,
- P is a mapping from E to element type definitions: given $\tau \in$ E, P(τ) = S or P(τ) is a regular expression α defined as $\alpha ::= \varepsilon \mid \tau' \mid \alpha \mid \alpha, \alpha \mid \alpha^*$, where ε is the empty sequence, $\tau' \in$ E, and "|", ",", and "*" denote union, concatenation, and the Kleene

closure, respectively.

- R is a mapping from E to the powerset of A. If $@m \in R(\tau)$, $@m$ is defined for τ.
- $r \in E$ and is called the element type of the root; without loss of generality, it is assumed that r does not occur in $P(\tau)$ for any $\tau \in E$.

Given a DTD $D = (E, A, P, R, r)$, a string $w = w_1 \ldots w_n$ is a path in D if $w_1 = r$, w_i is in the alphabet of $P(w_{i-1})$, for each $i \in [2, n-1]$, and w_n is in the alphabet of $P(w_{n-1})$ or $w_n = @m$ for some $@m \in R(w_{n-1})$. The notation paths(D) stand for the set of all paths in D and EPaths(D) for the set of all paths that end with an element type (rather than an attribute or S).

A tree tuple t in a DTD D is a function that assigns to each path in D a value that represents a node identifier, or a string (for the content of leaf elements), in such a way that t represents a finite tree with paths from D containing at most one occurrence of each path.

Formally, given a DTD $D=(E, A, P, R, r)$, a tree tuple t in D is a function from paths(D) to $Vert \cup Str \cup \{\bot\}$ such that:

- for $p \in$ EPaths(D), $t(p) \in Vert \cup \{\bot\}$, and $t(r) \neq \bot$
- for $p \in$ paths(D) - EPaths(D), $t(p) \in Str \cup \{\bot\}$
- if $t(p_1) = t(p_2)$ and $t(p1) \in Vert$, then $p_1 = p_2$
- if $t(p_1) = \bot$ and p_1 is a prefix of p_2, then $t(p_2) = \bot$
- $\{p \in$ paths(D) $| t(p) \neq \bot \}$ is finite.

Given a DTD D, a functional dependency over D is an expression of the form $S1 \rightarrow S2$, where S1, S2 are finite nonempty subsets of paths(D). Given an XML tree T valid w.r.t. D, T satisfies $S1 \rightarrow S2$, if for every tree tuple t_1 and t_2 in T, $t_1[S1] = t_2[S1]$ and $t_1[S1] \neq \bot$ imply $t_1[S2] = t_2[S2]$.

Association rules describe the co-occurrence of data items (i.e., couples of the form (attribute, value)) in a large amount of collected data (Agrawal & Srikant 1994). Rules are usually represented as implications in the form $A \Rightarrow B$, where A and B are two arbitrary sets of data items, such that $A \cap B = \emptyset$. The quality of an association rule is usually measured by means of support (s) and confidence (c). Support corresponds to the frequency of the set $A \cup B$ in the dataset, while confidence corresponds to the conditional probability of finding B, having found A and is given by

$$c = \frac{s(A \cup B)}{s(A)}$$

As demonstrated in Baralis et al. (2004), a functional dependency can be detected from data by analyzing all the previously mined association rules (with a significant support) determining the correlation between the values of the attributes X and Y, and computing the dependency degree between them.

The dependency degree of a mined functional dependency between the sets X and Y is computed according to the following formula:

$$p = \sum_{i \in AR} s_i \cdot c_i$$

where AR is the set of all association rules relating attributes X and Y. s_i and c_i are respectively the support and confidence values of each rule. If the dependency degree is equal to one, we can state that a functional dependency has been mined. If the degree is close to one (does not decrease below a specific threshold), we define the involved attributes as quasi-functional dependent. In (Baralis et al., 2004), the authors show that the dependency degree is equal to one if and only if all the rules have a confidence equal to 100%. If at least one of the rules relating attributes X and Y has a confidence lower than 100% the value of the dependency degree is lower than one, because there are some tuples (related to the rules with

Table 1. A portion of the Vehicle Table

RegN	Brand	Category	...	Wheels	City	Province
A001	Kymco	Scooter	...	2	Verona	Verona
A002	Fiat	Car	...	4	Verona	Verona
A003	Piaggio	Scooter	...	2	Piobesi	Torino
A004	Aprilia	Scooter	...	2	Piobesi	Cuneo
A005	Toyota	Car	...	4	Recetto	Milano
A006	Possl	Auto caravan	...	4	Recetto	Novara
...	...	...	...	...	...	...

a confidence lower than 100%) that violate the functional dependency constraint. The support of the rules also impact on the dependency degree value. If a rule is characterized by a low confidence and a low support, its impact is negligible on the dependency degree value (it represents few tuples violating the functional dependency constraint). Differently, a rule with a low confidence and an high support impacts heavily on the dependency degree value (the value of p significantly decreases), because it represents a large set of tuples violating the dependency degree constraint.

Example

The notion of quasi-functional dependency is explained by using a simple example. Considering a relational database storing information about vehicle registrations of a private retailer, a partial view of the vehicle table is (RegN, Brand, Category, Wheels, City, Province), as reported in Table 1. RegN is the registration number (i.e., the key attribute), Brand and Category are the vehicle brand and category, Wheels is the number of wheels, City and the Province are the places where the vehicle has been registered.

All the association rules relating RegN and Brand have a support of one, because there is only a tuple with a specific RegN, and thus a confidence of 100%. Examples of rules that involve RegN and Brand are reported in Table 2. Thus, a functional dependence between RegN and Brand is inferred,

i.e. the dependency RegN → Brand holds, with p=1. Similarly, functional dependencies between RegN and every other attribute hold, because they are key constraints.

On the contrary, by mining association rules between City and Province attributes, association rules with confidence lower than 100% are found, because there are several cities which have the same name but different province value (e.g., there is a city named Piobesi in the Torino province and one in the Cuneo province).

Table **3** reports examples of those rules that are used to infer a quasi-function dependency between City and Province.

By analyzing every couple of attributes (i.e., by considering all the extracted rules and not only those that are reported in Table 2 and Table **3**), a list of functional and quasi-functional dependencies with their dependency degree value is built. A partial list of functional and quasi-functional dependencies is reported in Table 4.

Table 2. Examples of association rules between RegN and Brand

Body	Head	Sup	Conf
RegN=A001	Brand=Kymco	1	100%
RegN=A002	Brand= Fiat	1	100%
RegN=A003	Brand= Piaggio	1	100%
RegN=A004	Brand= Aprilia	1	100%

Table 3. Examples of association rules between City and Province

Body	Head	Sup	Conf
City=Verona	Province=Verona	19.5%	100%
City=Piobesi	Province=Torino	45.1%	75.2%
City=Piobesi	Province=Cuneo	14.9%	24.8%
City=Recetto	Province=Novara	28.7%	99.7%
City=Recetto	Province=Milano	0.1%	0.3%

After choosing an appropriate threshold value for the dependency degree, only the quasi- functional dependencies with a p value greater than the threshold (i.e., only the quasi- functional dependencies representing a frequent behavior) are considered.

Related Work

In literature, different types of relations among data similar to quasi-functional dependencies have been proposed. Even if the formal names of such relations are different, they have almost the same meaning.

In Ceri et al. (2007) the authors introduce the notion of pseudo-constraints, which are predicates having significantly few violations. The authors use this pattern to identify rare events in databases. Thus, the aim of the work is similar to the main purpose of the approach based on quasi-functional dependencies. However, it differs for two reasons. Firstly, the notion of pseudo-constraint is defined on the Entity-Relationship (ER) model, whereas association rules are used to define a quasi-functional constraint. Then, the focus is on cyclic pseudo-constraints and authors propose an algorithm for extracting this kind of cyclic pattern. On the contrary, for the quasi-functional dependencies approach, the notion of dependency is an implication between sets of elements and is not related to the structure of the data source used to mine the pattern.

Kivinen & Mannila (1992) define the ap-

proximate functional dependencies, which are functional dependencies that almost hold, i.e. with an error lower than a threshold. Authors define various measures for the error of a dependency in a relation (e.g. the number of tuples not satisfying the dependency); approximate functional dependencies are retrieved by random sampling of relations, and not with data-mining algorithms. In Huhtala et al. (1999) an algorithm to discover approximate functional dependencies is described.

In Bohannon et al. (2007) authors define the conditional functional dependencies. They are a sort of functional dependencies which are conditioned to the specific value of other attributes, i.e. which are valid only for certain values of other attributes. For example, in a citizen database, if two tuples have the same Address, they must have also the same Zip code, but only for a particular value of the City attribute. It can happen if all the tuples with such City value respect the constraints, but some tuples that have other City values do not respect it. Thus, there is not a functional dependency between Address and Zip code, but it is conditioned by the value of the City. Then authors define a method to detect violations of conditional functional dependencies to perform data cleaning. They do not consider the problem of anomalies, but they are mainly interested in the detection of inconsistencies in data.

Two techniques for discovering frequent association rules from significant rare data (i.e.

Table 4. Dependency degree between attributes

Dependency	P
RegN → Brand	1.00
RegN → Category	1.00
...	...
Category → Wheels	1.00
City → Province	0.95
City → Category	0.60
...	...
Category → City	0.05

Figure 1.

```
RULE (ID, Sup, Conf, NumItemHead,NumItemBody)
ITEMR (IDRule, DataElement, Value, Head_Body)
CONSTR (ID, P_Degree, NumItemHead, NumItemBody)
ITEMD (IDDep, DataElement, Head_Body)
```

data that appear infrequently in the database) are presented in Yun et al. (2003) and Szathmary et al. (2007): the authors propose two different algorithms to mine frequent correlations that are present in specific (but no frequent) data, i.e. data with a low support. We differ from this proposal because we first mine frequent association rules with the standard A-priori algorithm; as a second step, we gain knowledge both from such rules (we discover frequent correlations) and from violations to the mined rules. Indeed, the violations represent unexpected rare events that must be considered as error or interesting exceptions.

A work considering the problem of mining association rules from temporal data is described in Böttcher et al. (2007): the authors mine trends from data that change over time in order to discover interesting segments in data. Our proposal differs from the one described in Böttcher et al. (2007) because we are not interested in mining trends; our main focus is on mining association rules and efficiently maintaining them up-to-date when datasets are dynamic.

OUTLIER DETECTION

As described in Bruno et al. (2007)(a), once the association rules and the related quasi-functional dependencies have been mined from a dataset, they are stored either in a relational database or as XML documents ("XML" 1998) depending on the analyzed data sources.

The following tables form the relational databases of rules (RULE and ITEMR) and quasi-functional dependencies (CONSTR and ITEMD). (Figure 1)

In particular, each tuple of the table RULE keeps trace of the identifier (ID) of an extracted association rule, and stores its support (Sup), confidence (Conf), the number of item appearing in the head (NumItemHead) and in the body (NumItemBody) of the rule itself. The table ITEMR stores the structure of each extracted association rule. In particular, IDRule is the identifier of a rule, DataElement and Value describe the name and the value of an attribute/element that appears in the considered rule, and Head_Body is a flag attribute that denotes if the considered attribute/element appears in the head or in the body of the current rule.

Analogously, the table CONSTR stores the identifier of a quasi-functional dependency (ID), its dependency degree (P_Degree), and the number of attributes that appear in the head (NumItemHead) and in the body (NumItemBody) of the dependency itself. The tuples of ITEMD table store the structures of quasi-functional dependencies.

After having stored the association rules and the quasi-functional dependencies, the anomalies are retrieved. For each quasi-functional dependency relating the sets X and Y, the rare association rules that involve X and Y, i.e. with a confidence lower that a fixed threshold, are considered.

For investigating the nature of detected anomalies, the confidence of each rule is further analyzed. If it is very low (compared to the confidence value of the other rules), it is likely to be an error, otherwise, a correct exception. Another possibility to distinguish semantically correct anomalies from errors, with a semi-automatic procedure, is to apply the query to detect anomalies to other databases in the same application domain. By comparing the results of the distributed query, an anomaly can be considered an error if it does not occur in more than one data source. Otherwise, if the same anomaly is discovered more times, it is an admissible situation, which is different from the normality of cases for some reasons.

With respect to the relation Vehicle introduced previously, if the rare association rules (i.e., with a confidence lower than 50%) that involve City and Province are investigated, the following rules are retrieved.

1. City=Piobesi $\Rightarrow$ Province=Cuneo [s=14.9%, c=24.8%]
2. City=Recetto $\Rightarrow$ Province=Milano [s=0.1%, c=0.3%]

Both of them represent interesting cases. The first one is a correct, albeit infrequent, relationship, since there are two cities with the same name (Piobesi) in two different provinces (Cuneo and Torino). The second one is an error, since there is only a city named Recetto in the Novara province. By analyzing the confidence value, it is possible to distinguish between the two cases. The value of the second rule (0.3%) is at least one order of magnitude smaller than the average confidence values of the other rules, hence, it is an error.

We first retrieve all the quasi-functional dependencies with a dependency degree value greater than a threshold, and then we identify the rare association rules related to each of them. To this aim, we can use a SQL query if data are in a relational database, or an XQuery ("XQuery, 2002) if they are in a XML database.

In the former case, for each selected quasi-functional dependency X → Y, the rare association rules with body X, head Y, and confidence lower than a threshold are extracted from tables RULE and ITEMR. The applied SQL query is reported in Figure 2.

When dealing with XML-based data sources, in order to have a homogeneous representation of data and queries, the set of association rules can be represented as an XML document with the DTD reported in Figure 3.

A subset of the functional dependencies defined for XML in Arenas & Libkin (2004) is adopted. In particular, only dependencies between sets of paths that reach leaf nodes of the considered XML document are considered. The quasi-functional dependencies are represented by an XML documents with the DTD reported in Figure 4.

Finally, the XQuery ("XQuery", 2002) expression to retrieve the anomalies from the document of association rules (i.e., the rare association rules with a low confidence) is reported in Figure 5.

The above XQuery expression is a FLWOR expression with a syntax similar to select statements of SQL. The For part is used for iteration, in the Where part the conditions on the documents to be retrieved are specified and the Return expression is used to generate the result.

Figure 2.

```
SELECT IDRule, DataElement, Value, Head_Body, Conf
FROM ITEMR
WHERE IDRule IN
  (SELECT ID FROM RULE JOIN ITEMR ON ID=IDRule
  WHERE Conf<Threshold AND NumItemHead=1 AND NumItemBody=1
  AND DataElement='X' AND HEAD_BODY='body'
  INTERSECT
  SELECT ID FROM RULE JOIN ITEMR ON ID=IDRule
  WHERE Conf<Threshold AND NumItemHead=1 AND NumItemBody=1
   AND DataElement='Y' AND HEAD_BODY='head')
ORDER BY IDRule
```

The described SQL and XML queries can be generalized when dependencies with more that two items are mined. Indeed, they allow domain experts to retrieve anomalies with respect to quasi-functional dependencies and consequently to concentrate on a small portion of data (the anomalies) to find out interesting outlier situations, by manually or semi-automatically discarding errors.

INCREMENTAL OUTLIER DETECTION

The described outlier detection method produces a set of anomalies by analyzing the tuples of a database. However, when data are not static, but new tuples are inserted or deleted over time, also the anomalies have to be extracted periodically. The iterative application of an extracting algorithm is unfeasible, because of the waste of time when few data are modified. Thus, a procedure

Figure 3.

```
<?xml version="1.0" encoding="UTF-8"?>
<!ELEMENT RuleSet (AssRule+)>
<!ELEMENT AssRule (RuleBody, RuleHead)>
<!ATTLIST AssRule NumberItemHead CDATA #REQUIRED
                  NumberItemBody CDATA #REQUIRED
                  support CDATA #REQUIRED
                  confidence CDATA #REQUIRED>
<!ELEMENT RuleBody (item+)>
<!ELEMENT RuleHead (item+)>
<!ELEMENT Item (#PCDATA)>
<!ATTLIST Item DataElement CDATA #REQUIRED>
```

Figure 4.

```
<?xml version="1.0" encoding="UTF-8"?>
<!ELEMENT DepSet (Constraint+)>
<!ELEMENT Constraint (Body, Head)>
<!ATTLIST Constraint NumItemHead CDATA  #REQUIRED
                     NumItemBody CDATA #REQUIRED
                     P_degree CDATA #REQUIRED>
<!ELEMENT Body (item+)>
<!ELEMENT Head (item+)>
<!ELEMENT Item (#PCDATA)>
```

Figure 5.

```
FOR $r IN  doc("AssociationRule.xml")
WHERE $r[@confidence<Threshold] AND
$r[@NumberItemHead=1] AND $r[@NumberItemBody=1] AND
$r/RuleBody/item/@DataElement='X' AND
$r/RuleHead/item/@DataElement='Y'
return $r
```

Table 5. The Vehicle temporal relation

RegN	Brand	Category	...	Wheels	City	Province	T_s	T_e
A001	Kymco	Scooter	...	2	Verona	Verona	0	Now
A002	Fiat	Car	...	4	Verona	Verona	1	Now
A003	Piaggio	Scooter	...	2	Piobesi	Torino	1	5
A004	Aprilia	Scooter	...	2	Piobesi	Cuneo	2	Now
A005	Toyota	Car	...	4	Recetto	Milano	6	Now
...	...	...	...	...	...	...	...	...

is needed to update the anomalies without extract them again from the whole dataset.

When data are dynamic, two attributes are added to the database structure, to represent the transaction time interval of each tuple. Such interval is system-generated, and represents the time when the fact described by the tuple is current in the database and may be retrieved (Jensen et al. 1998). More formally, in the context of relational databases, we suppose each tuple has associated two timestamps, start time (T_s) and end time (T_e), which indicate that the tuple is current in the database from instant T_s to T_e.

For example, the new instance of the Vehicle relation with time attributes is reported in Table 5. The tuples with T_e equal to "Now" are current in the database. When a tuple is deleted at time t, its T_e changes from Now to t (see for example the tuple related to the registration number A003; it has been deleted at time instant 5).

For representing temporal information in XML format, we use the proposal described in Rizzolo et al. (2008), where elements have two special attributes named Time:From and Time:To, which represent the start and end time of the time interval when the element is current in the document. A special element, denoted <ATTRIBUTE> is introduced to make no difference between elements and no-temporal attributes.

A portion of XML document representing temporal information about vehicles is reported in Figure 6. Note that the transaction time interval of attributes is not reported explicitly because is

the same interval of the ancestor element <VE-HICLE>.

The aim of the incremental outlier detection technique is to avoid computing all the association rules and the quasi-functional and functional dependencies at each tuple insertion or removal, but update them and report only changes in the previously stored data.

We analyze only the insertion and deletion operations, but every update can be seen as a composition of these basic operations.

Our algorithm takes as input the time interval in which the changes have been done $[T_1, T_2]$, the relations R and D which contain the association rules and the quasi-functional dependencies previously found, which could be updated. Then, for each tuple with a start time greater than T_1 or an end time less than T_2 (but not the two condition contemporaneously) it performs the following steps.

Given a quasi-functional dependency $X \rightarrow Y$ (or a functional dependency), the incremental approach considers all the association rules which involve the two attributes X and Y, i.e., in the form $X = * \Rightarrow Y = *$ (the asterisk symbol indicates every value), and analyses the following three conditions.

1. If there is a rule in the form $X = V_X \Rightarrow Y = V_Y$, where V_x and V_y are the X and Y attribute values of the new tuple, the support and the confidence of the rule have to be modified, because a tuple

Figure 6. A portion of XML document representing temporal information of vehicles.

```
<VEHICLE Time:From="0"  Time:To="Now">
     <ATTRIBUTE>
          <RegN>A001</RegN>
          <Brand>Kymco</Brand>
          <Category>Scooter</Category>
               . . .
          <Wheels>2</Wheels>
          <City>Verona</City>
          <Province>Verona</Province>
     </ATTRIBUTE>
</VEHICLE>
<VEHICLE Time:From="1"  Time:To="Now">
     <ATTRIBUTE>
          <RegN>A002</RegN>
          <Brand>Fiat</Brand>
          <Category>Car</Category>
               . . .
          <Wheels>4</Wheels>
          <City>Verona</City>
          <Province>Verona</Province>
     </ATTRIBUTE>
</VEHICLE>
...
```

that involves the same values is inserted or deleted.

- If it is inserted, i.e., the start time is greater than T_1, the new support and the confidence value are computed by using the following formulas:

$$s_{new} = s_{old} + 1$$

$$c_{new} = \frac{s_{new}}{\dfrac{s_{old}}{c_{old}} + 1}$$

- If the tuple is deleted, i.e., the end time is less than T_2, the new support and the confidence value are computed by using the following formulas:

$$s_{new} = s_{old} - 1$$

$$c_{new} = \frac{s_{new}}{\dfrac{s_{old}}{c_{old}} - 1}$$

After this update, if the support reaches the zero value, the association rule is deleted from the list.

If there is not any rule in the form $X = V_X \Rightarrow Y = V_Y$, such rule is added to the list of rules, with a support of 1 and a confidence of 100%.

2. For each rule in the form $X = V_X \Rightarrow Y \neq V_Y$ only the confidence of the rule has to be modified.

   - If the tuple is inserted, i.e., the start

time is greater than T_1, the new confidence value is

$$c_{new} = \frac{s_{old}}{\frac{s_{old}}{c_{old}} + 1}$$

○ If the tuple is deleted, i.e., the end time is less than T_2, the new confidence value is

$$c_{new} = \frac{s_{old}}{\frac{s_{old}}{c_{old}} - 1}$$

Finally, the quasi-functional dependency $X \rightarrow Y$ (or the functional dependency) is considered and its dependency degree is updated in D. Let n be the number of association rules which involve X and Y. If there is a tuple insertion, the new value of n is $n_{new} = n_{old} + 1$, if there is a tuple deletion, $n_{new} = n_{old} - 1$. The new value of p is computed according to the following formula:

$$p_{new} = \frac{p_{old} \cdot n_{old} + \sum_{\{updated\ rules\}} (c_{new} \cdot s_{new} - c_{old} \cdot s_{old})}{n_{new}}$$

Once every tuple has been processed, the new values of support, confidence and dependency degree of association rules and quasi-functional dependencies are stored in R (the relation containing all the association rules) and D (the relation containing all the quasi-functional dependencies). Then, the procedure of outlier detection described in Section Outlier Detection can be applied to the new relations, either in SQL or XQuery.

As an example, we can consider the situation reported in Figure 7. The start time and end time of five tuples (A, B, C, D, and E) are reported. For simplicity we suppose that the interval in which we want to consider the database change is [3,15], thus T_1=3 and T_2=15. According to our algorithm, the tuple A is not considered, because its end time is less then T1, i.e., it has been already considered in the previous computation at time T_1.

Tuple B is not considered either, because starts before T_1 and is current after T_2, so it is current through the whole time interval. Tuple C represents a tuple deletion, because begins before T_1 and its end time is 8. Thus, for each attribute pair of the tuple our algorithm updates in a proper way the value of support, confidence and dependency degree of the stored association rules and the

Figure 7. Start time and end time of five tuples

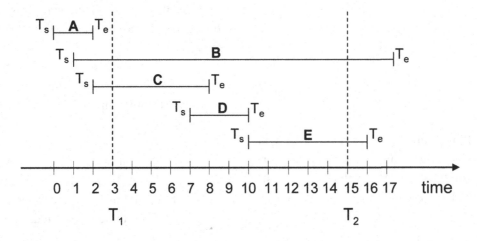

Table 6. Five tuples of vehicle temporal relation

	RegN	Brand	Category	Wheels	City	Province	T_s	T_e
A	A001	Kymco	Scooter	2	Verona	Verona	0	2
B	A002	Fiat	Car	4	Verona	Verona	1	Now
C	A003	Toyota	Car	4	Recetto	Milano	2	8
D	A004	Aprilia	Scooter	2	Piobesi	Cuneo	7	10
E	A005	Piaggio	Scooter	4	Piobesi	Cuneo	10	Now

quasi-functional dependencies. Tuple D is not considered, because it is inserted and deleted in the considered interval, and, thus, provides no change in the result. Finally, tuple E represents an insertion, because the start time is inside the interval, but the end time is outside. Hence, for each pair of attributes our algorithm updates the values of support, confidence and dependency degree of the rules and the quasi-functional dependencies. Tuple updates can be represented as a composition of a delete operation followed by an insert operation referred to the same tuple (with the same key attribute).

Referring to the vehicle relation, we can associate the previous example to the tuples in Table 6. We analyze the two quasi-functional dependencies in Table 7. Tuples A and B are not considered by our algorithm, because they have been already analyzed at time T_1. Similarly, tuple D is not considered because brings no change in the result.

Tuple C represents a delete operation, so for each couple of attributes our algorithm update the support, confidence and dependency degree values of the related association rules and quasi-functional dependencies. In particular, association rules that involve RegN as body (e.g. RegN=A003 $\Rightarrow$ Brand=Toyota, RegN=A003 $\Rightarrow$ Category=Car, etc.) are deleted because their support fall to zero.

Tuple D represents a tuple insertion that modifies both association rules and quasi-functional and functional dependencies. In fact, it represents the sale of a particular model of scooter, which contains four wheels instead of two. It causes the introduction of the rule Category =Scooter $\Rightarrow$ Wheels=4, with a support of one and a confidence computed according to the formula previously described. Furthermore, it causes the decrease of the confidence of the rule Category =Scooter $\Rightarrow$ Wheels =2, which previously had a confidence of 100%. It causes a change also in the dependency degree between Category and Wheels, which becomes less than one. Hence, the functional dependency becomes a quasi-functional dependency, and when the procedure of outlier detection will be executed, the rule Category =Scooter $\Rightarrow$ Wheels=4 will be considered a rare association rule and tuple D will be reported as an anomaly.

EXPERIMENTAL RESULTS

We performed a set of experiments to compare the incremental approach proposed in this paper with respect to the standard version of the outlier detection algorithm proposed in (Bruno et al., 2007 (a)). We first analyze the efficiency of our algorithm with respect to the number of association rules, by showing that the execution time depends on the number of involved rules. Then,

Table 7. Dependency degree between attributes

Quasi-functional dependency	P
Category $\rightarrow$ Wheels	1.00
City $\rightarrow$ Province	0.95

we varied both the cardinality of the initial data set and the number of tuple updates (insertion/deletion) applied on the initial data set, with the aim of analyzing the impact of the cardinality of the data set and the number of new tuples on the execution time.

Datasets

The experiments were executed on the synthetic TPC-H database ("TPC benchmark") and 7 real databases from the UCI repository (Newman et al., 2007). TPC-H is a suite of synthetic databases generated by using the TPC-H data generator. We performed scalability experiments by using the ORDER table of the TPC-H database. Each tuple in the ORDER table represents a selling order and it is characterized by the following attributes: ORDERKEY, CUSTKEY, ORDERSTATUS, TOTALPRICE, ORDERDATE, ORDERPRIORITY, CLERK, SHIPPRIORITY, and COMMENT. The selected 7 UCI databases cover a wide range of different real life domains (census data, solar flare data, etc.) and, thus, they allow us to validate the efficiency of our approach on real data sets. The main characteristics of the selected databases are reported in Table 8.

We performed our experiments on structure databases. However, analogously to the non-incremental version, the incremental approach proposed in this paper can also be applied to XML data collections.

All the experiments have been performed on a 3.2GHz Pentium IV system with 2GB RAM, running Kubuntu 6.10.

Update Time per Tuple

Since our algorithm considers a pair of attributes at time, as explained in Section Incremental Outlier Detection, we performed experiments by considering three pairs of attributes, involved in the three dependencies reported in Table 9.

Each dependency (indifferently quasi-functional or functional dependency) is characterized by a different number of rules associated to it (i.e., the number of rules involving the attributes of the dependency). In particular, the first dependency is associated to a number of rules that is comparable to the cardinality of the database, the second one is associated to few thousands of rules, and the third one is associated to a number of rules that is almost always equal to 3, independently of the size of the database. Figure 8 reports the number

Table 8. Databases characteristics

Dataset	Size (MB)	Tuples	Attributes	Description
TPC-H order table	Variable	1500000* *ScaleFactor*	9	Order table, where *ScaleFactor* is a parameter of the TPC-H data generator
Census	3.8	30162	15	Census data
Flare	0.028	1066	13	Solar flare data
Mushroom	0.365	8124	23	Mushroom records drawn from the Audubon Society Field Guide to North American Mushrooms
Nursery	1.1	12960	9	Nursery-school application ranking
Tic-tac-toe	0.026	958	10	Complete set of possible board configurations at the end of tic-tac-toe games
Voting	0.018	435	17	1984 United Stated Congressional Voting Records
Zoo	0.004	103	18	Classification of animals

Table 9. Analyzed dependencies

Dependency	P	Number of rules
ORDERKEY → CUSTKEY	1	Large (comparable to the cardinality of the database)
ORDERDATE → ORDERSTATUS	1	Medium (few thousands)
ORDERSTATUS → SHIPPRIORITY	1	Low (few tens)

of rules by using the synthetic order TPC-H table, when varying the cardinality of the dataset from 10 to 10000, for the three considered dependencies.

We performed a set of experiments to compare the update time per tuple of the proposed incremental approach with respect to the non-incremental approach by varying the cardinality of the initial database. Given a functional or a quasi-functional dependency and a new tuple, the update time per tuple is defined as the time needed to update the dependency degree value of the input dependency and the values of support and confidence of the association rules that involve the same attributes. We performed the experiments by using the synthetic order TPC-H table and by varying the cardinality of the initial database from 10 to 100000.

Figure 9 reports the update time per tuple of incremental and non-incremental algorithm when varying the cardinality of the database for the three dependencies (for sake of readability we only reported detailed results for the range from 10 to 10000 tuples).

The results show that the incremental approach is significantly faster than the non-incremental approach. Different execution times have been obtained for each dependency. Such differences are due to the different number of rules associated to each dependency (i.e., the number of rules involving the attributes of the dependency).

The execution time of the incremental approach and the number of rules are characterized by a similar trend (the execution time grows almost linearly with respect to the number of rules). This is given by the fact that the proposed incremental algorithm, for each new insertion/deletion operation, scans the whole rule set to update confidence and support of rules and then updates the dependency degree value of the dependency of interest. The update time per tuple is exclusively related to the number of rules to be considered by the incremental approach and to the number of tuples for the non-incremental approach. Since there is no relationship between the dependency degree value of a dependency and the number of mined rules associated to the considered dependency,

Figure 8. Number of mined association rules when varying the cardinality of the database for each considered dependency.

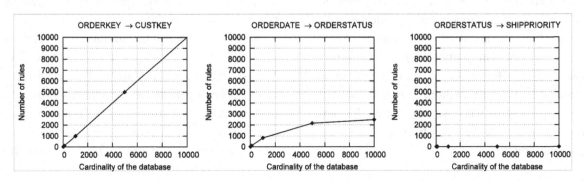

Figure 9. Update time per tuple of incremental and non-incremental algorithm when varying the cardinality of the database for each considered dependency.

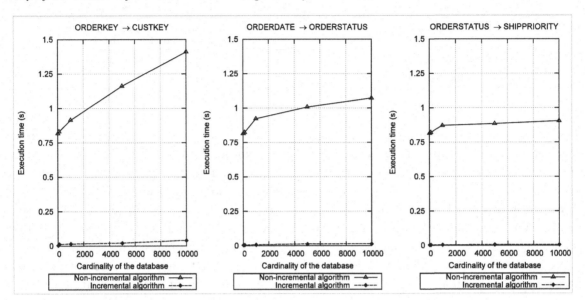

if follows that the dependency degree value of a dependency does not affect the update time per tuple.

Update Time per Set of Tuples

The reported results show that the incremental approach is better than the non-incremental approach when the dependency degree value of the functional or quasi-functional dependency under observation (and hence the associated rules) is to be updated after each tuple insertion/deletion operation (i.e., real time applications).

However, in not real time applications, in order to not overload the system during working hours, the dependency degree value of the dependencies and the values of support and confidence of the association rules are usually updated periodically and not immediately after each tuple insertion (or deletion). Hence, the update is performed on demand (e.g., every night at a predefined time) and processes the whole set of N tuples that have been inserted (or deleted) from the last value computation.

In this case, we can apply two different approaches: (i) mine the dependency degree value of the dependency of interest by applying the non-incremental algorithm to the whole database (the initial tuples joined with the N tuples added (removed) to the database), or (ii) apply N times the incremental algorithm by adding (removing) new tuples one at a time.

We performed a set of experiments on the TPC-H database to analyze which of the two approaches is more efficient by using an initial order tables with 10000 tuples, and by varying the number of new tuples (N) from 10 to 10000 tuples. Figure 10 shows the obtained results for the three dependencies reported in Table 9 (for sake of clarity we only reported detailed results for N varying from 10 to 2500 tuples).

As expected, when the number of association rules is low (see the dependency ORDERSTA-TUS → SHIPPRIORITY in the third graph), the incremental algorithm always outperforms the non-incremental approach because the number of rules does not increase with the number of new data. On the contrary, depending on the

Figure 10. Total time needed to process a set of new data when varying the number of new data for each considered dependency.

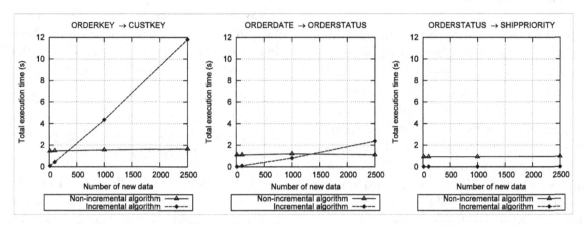

considered functional or quasi-functional dependency, and hence on the number of rules to scan, the incremental approach is better then the non-incremental approach only when the number of new tuples is respectively lower than about 400 for the ORDERKEY→CUSTKEY dependency, and lower than about 1450 for the ORDERDATE→ORDERSTATUS dependency. Hence, when the number of association rules to analyze is lower than a specific threshold, which depends on the considered dependency, the incremental version of the algorithm is faster then the non-incremental approach. Since the incremental approach works better than the non-incremental one when the number of new update is lower than a specific threshold, while it works worst for higher values, the two approaches could be combined to improve the global performance. In particular, by considering the number of new data to be analyzed the system could automatically, and easily, select the most efficient approach for each situation.

Table 10. Execution time of the incremental and the non-incremental approaches on the UCI data sets.

Dataset	Dependency	Number of rules	P	Update time per tuple	
				Incremental approach	Non-incremental approach
Census	age→workclass	53	0.7	0.008	1.105
Flare	code-class→ code-largest-spot- size	27	0.6	0.005	0.905
Mushroom	cap-shape→cap-surface	18	0.4	0.005	0.919
Nursery	parents→has-nurs	15	0.2	0.005	0.996
Tic-tac-toe	top-left-square→ top-middle-square	12	0.4	0.005	0.897
Voting	class→immigration	9	0.5	0.005	0.848
Zoo	hair→feathers	3	0.8	0.004	0.852

Update Time per Tuple on Real Datasets

Finally, we performed a set of experiments on real datasets to analyze the performance of our approach on real data. For each data set, we randomly selected only one quasi-functional dependency and we applied the incremental outlier detection approach on the selected quasi-functional dependency. Table 10 reports the obtained update time per tuple for the used datasets. The obtained results are comparable to those obtained by using the TPC-H dataset and highlight the efficiency of the proposed approach on real context.

CONCLUSION AND FUTURE WORK

Since databases are not static repositories, but they can be continuously updated over time, a procedure to maintain up-to-date the information previously extracted from them is useful, in order to perform the discovery of new knowledge not from the beginning, but from the current instance of the dataset. In this chapter, we have proposed a method to incrementally update rare association rules and functional and quasi-functional dependencies previously found, in the context of anomaly detection. Hence, we reduced the execution time, as reported in the experimental section.

As an ongoing work, we plan to further extend our incremental algorithm by combining it with an application of the extraction procedure on the new data sets, with the aim of merging the new rules with the ones previously extracted, and update more efficiently the set of rare association rules and quasi-functional dependencies to detect new anomalies.

REFERENCES

Agrawal, R., & Srikant, R. (1994). Fast algorithms for mining association rules in large data-bases. In *International Conference on Very Large Data Bases* (pp. 478-499). Morgan Kaufmann.

Angiulli, F., Greco, G., & Palopoli, L. (2007). Outlier Detection by Logic Programming. *ACM Transactions on Computational Logic, 9*(1). doi:10.1145/1297658.1297665

Angiulli, F., & Pizzuti, C. (2005). Outlier mining in large high dimensional datasets. *IEEE Transactions on Knowledge and Data Engineering, 17*(2). doi:10.1109/TKDE.2005.31

Apiletti, D., Bruno, G., Ficarra, E., & Baralis, E. (2006). Data Cleaning and Semantic Improvement in Biological Databases. *Journal of Integrative Bioinformatics, 3*(2).

Arenas, M., & Libkin, L. (2004). A Normal Form for XML Documents. *ACM Transactions on Database Systems, 29*(1), 195–232. doi:10.1145/974750.974757

Baralis, E., Garza, P., Quintarelli, E., & Tanca, L. (2004). Answering Queries on XML Data by means of Association Rules. *Current Trends in Database Technology, 3268.* Springer-Verlag.

Bohannon, P., Fan, W., Geerts, F., Jia, X., & Kementsietsidis, A. (2007, April 15-20) Conditional functional dependencies for data cleaning. In *ICDE '07: IEEE 23rd International Conference on Data Engineering,* (pp.746-755).

Bruno, G., Garza, P., Quintarelli, E., & Rossato, R. (2007a). Anomaly Detection Through Quasi Functional Dependency Analysis. *Journal of Digital Information Management, 5*(4).

Bruno, G., Garza, P., Quintarelli, E., & Rossato, R. (2007b, September 3-7). Anomaly Detection in XML databases by means of Association Rules. *Second International Workshop on Flexible Database and Information Systems Technology,* (pp. 387-391).

Ceri, S., Di Guinta, F., & Lanzi, P. (2007). Mining Constraint Violations. *ACM Transactions on Database Systems*, *32*(1). doi:10.1145/1206049.1206055

Elmasri, R., & Navathe, S. B. (2005). *Fundamentals of Database Systems*. Pearson, Addison Wesley.

Hodge, V. J., & Austin, J. (2004). A Survey of Outlier Detection Methodologies. *Artificial Intelligence Review*, *22*(2), 85–126.

Huhtala, Y., Krkkinen, Y., Porkka, P., & Toivonen, H. (1999). TANE: An Efficient Algorithm for Discovering Functional and Approximate Dependencies. *The Computer Journal*, *42*(2), 100–111. doi:10.1093/comjnl/42.2.100

Jensen, C. S., Dyreson, C. E., Bohlen, M. H., et al. (1998). The consensus glossary of temporal database concepts - february 1998 version. In *Temporal Databases: Research and Practice. (the book grow out of a Dagstuhl Seminar, June 23-27, 1997), volume 1399 of Lecture Notes in Computer Science* (pp. 367-405). Springer.

Kivinen, J., & Mannila, H. (1992). Approximate inference of functional dependencies from relations. *Theoretical Computer Science*, *149*(1), 129–149. doi:10.1016/0304-3975(95)00028-U

Newman, D. J., Hettich, S., Blake, C. L., & Merz, C. J. (1998). UCI Repository of machine learning databases, Irvine, CA: University of California, Department of Information and Computer Science, retrieved August 2008 from http://www.ics.uci.edu/~mlearn/MLRepository.html.

NIST/SEMATECH e-Handbook of Statistical Methodsn (2007), retrieved August 2008 from http://www.itl.nist.gov/div898/handbook/.

Rizzolo, F., & Vaisman, A. (2008). Temporal XML: modelling, indexing, and query processing. *The VLDB Journal*, *17*, 1179–1212. doi:10.1007/s00778-007-0058-x

TPC benchmark H. Transaction Processing Performance Council, retrieved August 2008 from http://www.tpc.org/tpch/default.asp

XML. Extensible Markup Language 1.0 (1998), retrieved August 2008 from http://www.w3C.org/TR/REC-xml/.

XQuery. An XML Query Language (2002), retrieved August 2008 from http://www.w3C.org/TR/REC-xml/.

Chapter 10
Mining Unexpected Sequential Patterns and Implication Rules

Dong (Haoyuan) Li
LGI2P, École des Mines d'Alès, France

Anne Laurent
LIRMM, Université Montpellier II, France

Pascal Poncelet
LIRMM, Université Montpellier II, France

ABSTRACT

As common criteria in data mining methods, the frequency-based interestingness measures provide a statistical view of the correlation in the data, such as sequential patterns. However, when the authors consider domain knowledge within the mining process, the unexpected information that contradicts existing knowledge on the data has never less importance than the regularly frequent information. For this purpose, the authors present the approach USER for mining unexpected sequential rules in sequence databases. They propose a belief-driven formalization of the unexpectedness contained in sequential data, with which we propose 3 forms of unexpected sequences. They further propose the notion of unexpected sequential patterns and implication rules for determining the structures and implications of the unexpectedness. The experimental results on various types of data sets show the usefulness and effectiveness of our approach.

INTRODUCTION

Most real world applications process the data stored in sequence format, where the elements in data are sequentially ordered with temporal or spatial relation. For instances, in a customer retail database, a sequence can be all purchases of a customer ordered by the time of transaction; in a Web access log file, a sequence can be all of those resources accessed during a user session ordered by the time of request; in a telecommunication network monitoring database, a sequence can be all events during a period ordered by the time of occurrence; in a DNA segment, a sequence is a succession of nucleotide subunits with spatial order, etc. In order to discover the knowledge hidden in such sequential data, sequence data mining techniques (Dong & Pei, 2007; Han & Kamber, 2006) have been highly

DOI: 10.4018/978-1-60566-754-6.ch010

developed and widely applied in many application domains.

As one of the most important models of sequence data mining, the sequential pattern proposed by Agrawal and Srikant (1995) provides a statistical frequency based view of the correlations between the elements in sequential data. The problem of mining sequential patterns can be formally described as follows.

Given a set of binary-valued attributes $R = \{i_1, i_2, ..., i_n\}$, an attribute is an *item*. An *itemset*, denoted as $I = (i_1 i_2 ... i_m)$, is an unordered collection of items. A *sequence* is an ordered list of itemsets, denoted as $s = \langle I_1 I_2 ... I_k \rangle$. A *sequence database*, denoted as D, is a large set of sequences. Given two sequences $s = \langle I_1 I_2 ... I_m \rangle$ and $s' = \langle I'_1 I'_2 ... I'_n \rangle$, if there exist integers $1 \leq i_1 \leq i_2 \leq ... \leq i_m \leq n$ such that $I_1 \subseteq I'_{i1}, I_2 \subseteq I'_{i2}, ..., I_m \subseteq I'_{im}$, then the sequence s is a *subsequence* of the sequence s' and the sequence s' is a *super sequence* of the sequence s, denoted as $s \sqsubseteq s'$, and we say that the sequence s *is included in* the sequence s', or the sequence s' *supports* the sequence s. If a sequence s is not included in any other sequences, then the sequence s is a *maximal sequence*. The *support* (or the *frequency*) of a sequence s in a sequence database D, denoted as $\sigma(s, D)$, is the fraction of the total number of sequences in the database D that support s. Given a minimal frequency threshold *minimum support* specified by user, denoted as σ_{min}, a sequence s is *frequent* if $\sigma(s, D) \geq \sigma_{min}$. A *sequential pattern* is a frequent maximal sequence, so that the problem of *mining sequential patterns* is to find all frequent maximal sequences in a sequence database.

Example 1. Let D be a customer retail database, with the minimum support σmin = 0.5, we may find the sequential pattern s = ⟨(Sci-Fi-Novel) (Action-Film Sci-Fi-Film)(Rock-Music)⟩ where σ (s, D) = 0.6, which can be interpreted as "60% of customers purchase a Sci-Fi novel, then purchase action and Sci-Fi films later, and then purchase a rock music CD". +

Example 2. Let D be a Web access log database, with the minimum support $\sigma_{min} = 0.5$, we may find the sequential pattern $s = \langle (login)$ (*msglist*)(*msgread*)(*msgread*)(*logout*)⟩ where σ $(s, D) = 0.8$, which can then be interpreted as *"80% of users visit the login page, then visit the message list page, then read messages, and at last logout"*. +

Up to now, a great deal of research work focuses on effectively mining sequential patterns (Ayres et al, 2002; Li et al, 2007; Masseglia et al, 1998; Pei et al, 2004; Srikant & Agrawal, 1996; Zaki, 2001) and the variances (Garofalakis et al, 1999; Lo et al, 2007; Mannila et al, 1997; Wang & Han, 2004; Yan et al, 2003). With sequential pattern mining, we can extract the sequences that reflect the most general behaviors within the context of sequential data, which can be further interpreted as domain knowledge for different purposes. However, although sequential patterns are essential for behavior recognition, when we consider domain knowledge within the mining process, the unexpected sequences that contradict existing knowledge on the data have never less importance than the frequent sequences. On the other hand, such unexpected sequences do not mean that they cannot be frequent, so that there exist following problems in discovering the unexpectedness in data with the frequency-based interestingness measures.

First, the redundancy problem of frequency-based data mining methods undermines many real world applications where the exponential pattern or sequence sets generated by mining processes make the post analysis extremely hard. Hence, the identification of unexpected information might be impossible when the support of such unexpected sequences, within the context of sequence data mining, is very low such that the unexpectedness may be hidden in millions of sequential patterns.

Example 3. Let us consider the instance illustrated in Example 1. Assume that in the database D, there exist 6% of customers who purchase a Sci-Fi novel then action and Sci-Fi films, purchase a classical music CD instead of a rock music CD. This behavior is unexpected to the frequent behavior described in Example 1 and can be interesting for product promotion. In fact, with sequential pattern mining, we are able to find such a behavior only if the minimum support threshold is no greater than 0.06. However, with $\sigma_{min} = 0.06$, the result sequence set of all sequential patterns s such that $\sigma(s, D) \geq 0.06$ might be very large and that makes it impossible to identify the above behavior. +

Secondly, if an unexpected sequence is "incomplete" in comparison with an expected sequence, it is impossible to determine the former with classical sequential pattern mining: according to the definition of sequential pattern, the former is included in the latter so that the former will not appear in the result sequence set while the latter is frequent. The following example illustrates this issue (notice that we do not strictly indicate the difference between *sequence* and *sequential pattern*, however, we use the term *sequence* for a full sequence contained in the database, and the term *sequential pattern* for a potentially frequent part of a full sequence contained in the database).

Example 4. Considering again the Web access log database D illustrated in Example 2, let the sequential pattern $s_0 = \langle(login)(msglist)(logout)\rangle$ be an expected access sequence with respect to the workflow of the service, where we do not require the access of the resource "*msgread*" in the workflow since there can be no new unread messages for a user. Assume that the sequence $s = \langle(login)(logout)\rangle$ is unexpected to the workflow s_0 and it is caused by failing to list all messages of a user. Let $s_1 = \langle(login)(msglist)(msgread)(msgread)(logout)\rangle$ and $s_2 = \langle(login)(option)(password)(logout)\rangle$ be two sequential patterns (in order to simplify the example, s_1 and s_2 are not included in a same sequence), then we have $\sigma(s, D) \geq \sigma(s_0, D) \geq \sigma(s_1, D)$ and $\sigma(s, D) \geq \sigma(s_2, D)$. Assume that s_1 and s_2 are the only sequential patterns other than s_0 that

include s, then we can conclude the existence of the unexpected sequence s if and only if $\sigma(s, D) > \sigma(s_1, D) + \sigma(s_2, D)$. Nevertheless, if s is unknown, then we have to examine the support values of all possible combinations of subsequences of s_0, s_1 and s_2 for seeking the unexpected information, and the computation and identification tasks will become extremely hard. +

The complex constraint based approaches like SPIRIT proposed by Garofalakis et al (1999) can find the unexpected sequences, however the premise is that we must know the composition of an unexpected sequence before the extraction, and an important drawback is that we cannot find all sequences representing the behavior. The closed sequential pattern mining (Yan et al, 2003) may tell the existence of the unexpected one by computing the difference of the support values of all sequences that include the unexpected sequence, however, only if we have already known what the unexpected sequences are, we have to seek the unexpectedness in the result set of all possible combinations of candidate unexpected sequences.

In this chapter, we propose a novel approach USER (Mining unexpected sequential rules) for finding unexpected sequential rules in large sequence databases. Furthermore, when we consider the unexpectedness in sequential data, we are interested not only in the internal structures, but also in the premises and consequences represented as rules on the discovered unexpected sequences. Such rules are important to a lot of real world applications, especially to the early prediction of critical events or behaviors in the domains such as telecommunication network monitoring, credit card fraud detection, financial risk investigation, DNA segment analysis, and so on. Notice that our goal is not to find infrequent rules from sequence databases, but to find the rules disclosing the information that contradicts existing knowledge.

The rest of this chapter is organized as follows. Section 2 the related work on unexpected pattern and sequence mining. Section 3 presents the discovery of unexpected sequences and sequential implication rules for determining the unexpectedness in sequence databases. Section 4 shows the results of the experimental evaluation of our approach on real data and synthetic data for testing the effectiveness and the scalability. Finally, we discuss our further research direction and we conclude in Section 5.

RELATED WORK

In this chapter, we propose a subjective measure for sequence data mining. McGarry (2005) systematically investigated the interestingness measures for data mining, which are classified into two categories: the objective measures based on the statistical frequency or properties of discovered patterns, and the subjective measures based on the domain knowledge or the class of users. Silberschatz and Tuzhilin (1995) studied the subjective measures, in particular the unexpectedness and actionability. The term *unexpectedness* stands for the newly discovered (sequential) patterns that are surprising to users. For example, if most of the customers who purchase Sci-Fi movies purchase rock music, then the customers who purchase Sci-Fi movies but purchase classical music are unexpected. The term *actionability* stands for reacting to the discovered (sequential) patterns to user's advantage. For example, for the customers who purchase Sci-Fi movies without purchasing any kind of music, it is actionable to improve the promotion of rock music, even though it is unexpected. Therefore, in many cases, the unexpectedness and actionability exist at the same time, however, clearly, some actionable (sequential) patterns can be expected and some unexpected (sequential) patterns can also be non-actionable (Silberschatz & Tuzhilin, 1995).

Silberschatz and Tuzhilin (1995) further introduced two types of beliefs, *hard belief* and *soft belief*, for addressing unexpectedness. According

to authors' proposition, the hard belief is a belief that cannot be changed by new evidences in data, and any contradiction of such a belief implies data error. For example, in the Web access log analysis, the error "404 Not Found" can be considered as a contradiction of a head belief: "the resources visited by users must be available"; however, the soft belief corresponds to the constraints on data that are measured by a degree, which can be modified with new evidences in data that contradict such a belief and interestingness of new evidences is measured by the change of the degree. For example, when more and more users visit the Web site at night, the degree of the belief "users access the Web site at day time" will be changed. The computation of the degree can be handled by various methods, such as the Bayesian approach and the conditional probability.

With the unexpectedness measure, Padmanabhan and Tuzhilin (1998) propose a belief-driven approach for finding unexpected association rules. In that approach, a belief is given from association rule, and the unexpectedness is stated by semantic contradictions of patterns. Given a belief $X \rightarrow Y$, a rule $A \rightarrow B$ is unexpected if: (1) the patterns B and Y semantically contradict each other; (2) the support and confidence of the rule $A \cup X \rightarrow B$ hold in the data; (3) the support and confidence of the rule $A \cup X \rightarrow Y$ do not hold in the data. The discovery process is performed within the framework of the *a priori* algorithm.

Spiliopoulou (1999) proposed an approach for mining unexpectedness with sequence rules transformed from frequent sequences. The sequence rule is built by dividing a sequence into two adjacent parts, which are determined by the *support*, *confidence* and *improvement* from association rule mining. A belief on sequences is constrained by the frequency of the two parts of a rule, so that if a sequence respects a sequence rule but the frequency constraints are broken, then this sequence is unexpected. Although this work considers the unexpected sequences and rules, it is however very different to our problem in the measure and the notion of unexpectedness contained in data.

The outlier mining focuses on finding infrequent patterns in data with objective measures of interestingness, which are mostly distance-based (Angiulli & Pizzuti, 2002, 2005; Jin et al, 2001; Knorr & Ng, 1998; Ramaswamy et al, 2000). The study of outlier mining in sequential data is very limited. To the best of our knowledge, the approach proposed by Sun et al (2006) is currently the unique one. In our approach, the unexpectedness is stated by the semantics and temporal occurrences, instead of the statistical frequency or distance. Moreover, we concentrate on finding sequential implication rules of unexpectedness, which is not covered by outlier mining. For these meanings, we consider the unexpectedness within the context of domain knowledge and the aspect "*valid*" within the contact of the classical notions of support and confidence.

Mining Implication Rules in Unexpected Sequences

Let $s_\alpha \rightarrow s_\beta$ be a *sequential rule* of sequences, where s_α, s_β are two sequences. Let τ be the constraint on the number of itemsets, or the *occurrence distance*, between the sequences s_α and s_β. Let η be the constraint on the semantics of sequences that $s_\beta \neq_{sem} s_\gamma$, where s_γ is a sequence that semantically opposite to the sequence s_β. A *belief* is considered as a sequential rule and the constraints τ and η on the rule. A sequence s is *unexpected* if s contradicts a belief.

We concentrate on finding the premises that possess the unexpectedness in sequences and the consequences engendered in the sequential data. In this section, we present the discovery of unexpected sequences and sequential implication rules for determining the unexpectedness in sequence databases.

Belief Base

In order to construct the belief base for mining unexpected sequences, let us first introduce some additional notions on sequential data.

The *length* of a sequence s is the number of itemsets contained in the sequence, denoted as $|s|$. An *empty sequence* is denoted as φ, where $|\varphi| = 0$. The *concatenation* of sequences is denoted as the form $s_1 \cdot s_2$, so that we have $|s_1 \cdot s_2| = |s_1| + |s_2|$. We denote $[s$ the first itemset of the sequence s, and $s]$ the last itemset of the sequence s. For two sequences s and s' such that $s \hat{o} s'$, we note $s \hat{o}^{[}s'$ if we have $[s \subseteq [s'$, note $s \hat{o}^{]}s'$ if we have $s] \subseteq s']$, and note $s \hat{o}^{[\cdot]}s'$ if we have $[s \subseteq [s'$ and $s] \subseteq s']$. We denote $s \hat{o}_c s'$ that the sequence s is a *consecutive subsequence* of the sequence s'. For example, we have $\langle(a)(b)(c)\rangle \hat{o}_c \langle(b)(\underline{a})(a\underline{b})(\underline{c})(d)\rangle$, but $\langle(a)(b)(c)\rangle \not\sqsubseteq_c \langle(\underline{a})(\underline{b})(ab)(\underline{c})(d)\rangle$.

Given sequences s, s_1 and s_2 such that $s_1 \cdot s_2$ $\hat{o}$ s, the *occurrence relation*, denoted as a^r, is a relation r between the occurrences of s_1 and s_2 in s, where $\tau = [min..max]$ ($min, max \in ¥$ and $min \leq max$) is the constraint on the occurrence distance between s_1 and s_2. Let $|s| \vDash [min..max]$ (or $|s| \vDash \tau$) denote that the length of the sequence s satisfies the constraint $[min..max]$, that is, $min \leq |s| \leq max$, then the relation $s_1 a^\tau s_2$ represents

$$s_1 \cdot s_2 \sqsubseteq s' \Rightarrow \left(s_1 \cdot s \cdot s_2 \sqsubseteq_c s'\right) \wedge \left(|s| \vDash \tau\right).$$

When *max* is not specified (or cannot be specified, like $max = \infty$), we note *max* as *, that is, $\tau = [min..*]$. In the particular cases, for $min = max = 0$, we note $s_1 a^{[0..0]}s_2$ as $s_1 a s_2$; for $min = 0$ and $max = *$, we note $s_1 a^{[0..*]}s_2$ as $s_1 a^* s_2$. Given a sequence s and an occurrence relation r, we note $s \vDash r$ if the sequence s satisfies the relation r.

Example 5. Given an occurrence relation $r = \langle(a)\rangle a^{[1..2]} \langle(c)\rangle$, we have $\langle(a)(c)\rangle \longrightarrow r$, $\langle(a)(b)(c)\rangle \vDash r$, $\langle(a)(b)(b)(c)\rangle \vDash r$, $\langle(a)(be)(b)(c)\rangle \vDash r$, and $\langle(a)(\underline{b})(\underline{b})(\underline{b})(c)\rangle \longrightarrow r$. +

Given a sequential rule $s_\alpha \rightarrow s_\beta$, the semantic constraint $s_\beta \neq_{sem} s_\gamma$ requires that the occurrence of the sequence s_β should not be replaced by the occurrence of the sequence s_γ, since s_β and s_γ are semantically opposite to each other. That is, with this meaning, since the rule $s_\alpha \rightarrow s_\beta$ can be interpreted as the implication $s_\alpha \hat{o} s \Rightarrow s_\alpha \cdot s_\beta \hat{o} s$, according to $s_\beta \neq_{sem} s_\gamma$ we have the implication $s_\alpha \hat{o} s \Rightarrow s_\alpha \cdot s_\gamma \not\sqsubseteq s$. Moreover, considering the semantic constraint η together with the occurrence constraint τ, we have the following relation:

$$s_\alpha \sqsubseteq s \Rightarrow \left(s_\alpha \cdot s' \cdot s_\beta \sqsubseteq_c s\right) \wedge \left(s_\alpha \cdot s' \cdot s_\gamma \not\sqsubseteq_c s\right) \wedge \left(|s'| \models \tau\right)$$

From these constraints, we define the belief on user behaviors as follows.

Definition 1. A *belief* on sequences consists of a sequential rule $s_\alpha \rightarrow s_\beta$, an occurrence constraint $\tau = [min..max]$ (min, $max \in \yen$ and $min \leq max$), and a semantic constraint $\eta : s_\beta \neq_{sem} s_\gamma$ on the rule, denoted as $b = [s_\alpha ; s_\beta ; s_\gamma ; min..max]$, such that for any sequence s satisfies the belief b, denoted as s ' b, we have that $s_\alpha \hat{o} s$ implies $s_\alpha \cdot s' \cdot s_\beta \hat{o}_c s$ and $s_\alpha \cdot s' \cdot s_\gamma \not\sqsubseteq_c s$, where $|s'|$ ' τ. +

Beliefs can be generated from existing domain knowledge on common behaviors of the data, or from the predefined workflows. Let us examine the Example 3 and 4 for illustrating how beliefs work.

Example 6. Let us consider Example 3. According to customer purchase behaviors, we first create the sequential rule $\langle(Sci\text{-}Fi\text{-}Novel)(Action\text{-}Film\ Sci\text{-}Fi\text{-}Film)\rangle \rightarrow \langle(Rock\text{-}Music)\rangle$, which indicates that the purchases of a Sci-Fi novel then action and Sci-Fi films later imply the purchase of a rock music CD. If we just expect that a purchase of rock music CD should be performed after the precedent purchases, then the following belief can be established for describing this requirement:

$[\langle(Sci\text{-}Fi\text{-}Novel)(Action\text{-}Film\ Sci\text{-}Fi\text{-}Film)\rangle;$
$\langle(Rock\text{-}Music)\rangle; \varphi; 0..*],$

where the position of the sequence s_γ is empty since at this moment we are not yet taking the semantic opposition into account.

Now we consider the classical music to be semantically opposite to the rock music, then we have the semantic constraint as $\langle(Rock\text{-}Music)\rangle \neq_{sem} \langle(Classical\text{-}Music)\rangle$, then the above belief can be rewritten as follows:

$[\langle(Sci\text{-}Fi\text{-}Novel)(Action\text{-}Film\ Sci\text{-}Fi\text{-}Film)\rangle;$
$\langle(Rock\text{-}Music)\rangle; \langle(Classical\text{-}Music)\rangle; 0..*].$

Moreover, if the customer transaction records show that most of customers purchase a rock music CD in a short delay after purchasing a Sci-Fi novel then action and Sci-Fi films, for example in the next 3 to 5 purchases, then the second belief can be further rewritten as:

$[\langle(Sci\text{-}Fi\text{-}Novel)(Action\text{-}Film\ Sci\text{-}Fi\text{-}Film)\rangle;$
$\langle(Rock\text{-}Music)\rangle; \langle(Classical\text{-}Music)\rangle; 3..5].$ +

Example 7. Considering Example 4, the user access sequence $\langle(login)(msglist)(logout)\rangle$ is expected to be frequent. According to the workflow of the Web site, the following rules can be generated: $\langle(login)(msglist)\rangle \rightarrow \langle(logout)\rangle$ and $\langle(login)\rangle \rightarrow \langle(logout)\rangle$, respectively with the occurrence constraints $[0..*]$ and $[1..*]$, since the access of *logout* should not just be after the access of *login*. Hence, we have the following beliefs without semantic constraint:

$[\langle(login)(msglist)\rangle; \langle(logout)\rangle; \varphi; 0..*]$ and
$[\langle(login)\rangle; \langle(logout)\rangle; \varphi; 1..*].$

In order to constrain the relation between *login* and *logout*, the above two beliefs can be rewritten as:

$[\langle(login)\rangle; \langle(msglist)\rangle; \langle(logout)\rangle; 0..0],$

where *logout* is semantically opposite to *msglist* according to the access of *login*. Other user behaviors can also be represented by beliefs. The following belief,

$$[\langle(login)(msglist)\rangle; \langle(msgread)\rangle; \langle(logout)\rangle; 0..5]$$

depicts that we expect that users will not logout to the system too early, for example, after at least 5 visits of other resources. +

In our approach, we consider the *consistent belief* in the semantics, that is, for any belief $b = [s_\alpha ; s_\beta ; s_\gamma ; min..max]$, we have $s_\gamma \not\sqsubseteq s_\beta$. For example, considering a belief $b = [\langle(a)\rangle; \langle(b)(c)\rangle; \langle(c)\rangle; 0..3]$, although we cannot assert that the sequence $\langle(b)(c)\rangle$ is not semantically opposite to the sequence $\langle(c)\rangle$ (such as (b) stands for "*not*" and (c) stands for "*good*" within the context of text mining), such a belief is rather ambiguous in the semantics: since $\langle(c)\rangle$ ô $\langle(b)(c)\rangle$, we can say that $\langle(c)\rangle$ is more general than $\langle(b)(c)\rangle$, which means that *the unexpectedness is more general than the expectedness* in a sequence. In this case, any unexpected sequence is always expected. Notice that our goal is to find the unexpectedness, but not the expectedness, so that the inverse, that *the expectedness is more general than the unexpectedness*, is allowed in a sequence. Obviously, as to be consistent, the semantics of two beliefs in the same belief base must not contradict each other. For instance, the beliefs $[s_1 ; s_2 ; s_3 ; min..max]$ and $[s_1 ; s_3 ; s_2 ; min..max]$ semantically contradict each other, and must be take into account during the construction of a belief base.

A *belief base*, denoted as B, is a set of consistent beliefs, which are stored in a prefix represented *belief tree*, denoted as T, defined below.

1. The belief tree T consists of one root node and three groups of sub-trees (α-*tree*, β-*trees* and γ-*trees*) as the children of the root, where

each group respectively represents the s_α, s_β, and s_γ parts of each belief $b \in B$.

2. Only one α-*tree* is contained in a belief base, which consists of two kinds of nodes: *i-node* and *τ-node*, where *i-node* constitutes the prefix-tree representation of a s_α sequence and *τ-node* consists of two fields for holding the *min* and *max* values. The prefix tree representation of sequences is detailed in the approach PSP proposed by Masseglia et al (1998).

3. Each *i-node* is connected by a *set-edge* or a *seq-edge* for representing sequences.

4. A *β-tree* is a prefix tree representation of sequences, and is connected with a *τ-node* in the *α-tree* by the *τ-link*, a special edge inter-sub-trees.

5. A *γ-tree* consists of *i-nodes* for storing sequences and *u-nodes* identifying unique unexpectedness IDs, and is connected with a leaf of a *β-tree* by the *η-link*, another special edge inter-sub-trees.

6. Each *η-link* has a copy connected to its parent *τ-node* for the needs of skipping s_β.

For instance, all beliefs concentrated in Example 6 and 7 are shown in Figure 1 as a belief tree.

Based on the above definition and the semantic consistence of a belief, we propose the following belief tree construction algorithm.

Algorithm 1 (*Belief tree construction*).

Input: A belief tree T and a belief $b = [s_\alpha ; s_\beta ; s_\gamma ; min..max]$.

Output: The belief tree T with the belief b appended.

1. If the belief tree T is empty, then initialize the global belief base information (e.g., number of nodes, number of beliefs, etc.) and create the root node for the belief tree.

2. Verify the input belief b. If s_γ ô s_β, $min > max$, or $min < 0$, then reject b and exit the construction procedure.

Figure 1. The belief tree for Example 6 and 7.

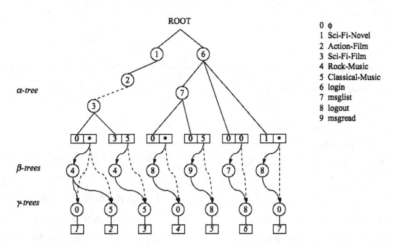

3. Append s_α as prefix tree to the root node of the belief tree, where each item is an *i-node*. Any two items inter-itemsets are connected by a *seq-edge* and any two items within an itemset are connected by a *set-edge*. Append a *τ-node* with *min* and *max* to the last *i-node* of s_α.

4. Transform s_β to prefix tree representation and connect it to the newly created *τ-node* by *τ-link*.

5. Transform s_γ to prefix tree representation and connect it to the newly created leaf of the *β-tree* by *η-link* and copy this link to the parent *τ-node*, and then label the belief *b* by a unique identification.

6. Update the global belief base information and exit the construction procedure.

Given a belief tree *T* constructed from a belief base *B*, a sequence *s* can be verified in at most |*B*| traverses of the belief tree *T* with respect to each belief *b* in the belief base *B*.

Unexpected Sequences and Features

Given a belief *b* and a sequence *s*, if *s* satisfies the belief *b*, then *s* is an *expected sequence* with respect to the belief *b*, denoted as *s* ' *b*, and *s* — *b* denotes that *s* does not verify the belief *b*; if *s* contradicts the belief *b*, then *s* is an *unexpected sequence*, denoted as *s* ™ *b*. We denote the *un-*

expectedness that "contradicting the belief *b*" as {™*b*}. According to the occurrence constraint and the semantic constraint, we propose three forms of unexpected sequences: *α-unexpected*, *β-unexpected* and *γ-unexpected*.

Definition 2. Given a belief $b = [s_\alpha ; s_\beta ; s_\gamma ; 0..*]$ and a sequence *s*, if $s_\alpha \hat{o} s$ and there does not exist s_β, s_γ such that $s_\alpha \cdot s_\beta \hat{o} s$ or $s_\alpha \cdot s_\gamma \hat{o} s$, then the sequence *s* is an *α-unexpected sequence* stated by the belief *b*, denoted as $s ™_\alpha b$. The *α-unexpectedness* stated by the belief *b* is denoted as $\{™_\alpha b\}$. +

A belief with the occurrence constraint $\tau = [0..*]$ states that s_β should occur after the occurrence of s_α in a sequence *s*. Hence, the sequence *s* contradicts the constraint $\tau = [0..*]$ if and only if $s_\alpha \sqsubseteq s$ and $s_\alpha \cdot s_\beta \not\sqsubseteq s$. Notice that for not confusing the unexpected sequences caused by the occurrence constraint or the semantic constraint, s_γ should not occur after the occurrence of s_α in an *α*-unexpected sequence.

Example 8. Let us consider the beliefs listed in Example 6, where the two beliefs

$b_1 = [\langle(Sci\text{-}Fi\text{-}Novel)(Action\text{-}Film\ Sci\text{-}Fi\text{-}Film)\rangle; \langle(Rock\text{-}Music)\rangle; \varphi; 0..*]$

and

$b_2 = [\langle(\textit{Sci-Fi-Novel})(\textit{Action-Film Sci-Fi-Film})\rangle; \langle(\textit{Rock-Music})\rangle; \langle(\textit{Classical-Music})\rangle; 0..*]$

determine α-unexpected sequences. The belief b_1 depicts that a purchase of rock music CD is expected after the purchases of a Sci-Fi novel then action and Sci-Fi films later. The belief b_2 further requires that the purchase of a classical music CD should not occur. Therefore, given the sequence

$s = \langle(\textit{Sci-Fi-Novel})(\textit{Printer})(\textit{Action-Film Sci-Fi-Film})(\textit{Classical-Music})(\textit{PS3-Station})\rangle$,

we have $s \,^{TM}_{\ \alpha}\, b_1$ but $s - b_2$, that is, s is not an α-unexpected sequence with respect to the belief b_2. +

Now let us consider the recognition of α-unexpected sequences with respect to a belief base, i.e., a set of beliefs. For instance, given a belief base consists of 3 beliefs

$b_1 = [\langle(a)\rangle; \langle(b)\rangle; \varphi; 0..*]$,

$b_2 = [\langle(a)\rangle; \langle(c)\rangle; \varphi; 0..*]$,

$b_3 = [\langle(a)\rangle; \langle(d)\rangle; \varphi; 0..*]$,

and a set of sequences

$s_1 = \langle(a)(b)\rangle$,

$s_2 = \langle(a)(c)\rangle$,

$s_3 = \langle(a)(d)\rangle$,

$s_4 = \langle(a)(e)\rangle$,

we have the following relations:

$s_1 \,^{TM}_{\ \alpha}\, b_2, s_1 \,^{TM}_{\ \alpha}\, b_3;$

$s_2 \,^{TM}_{\ \alpha}\, b_1, s_2 \,^{TM}_{\ \alpha}\, b_3;$

$s_3 \,^{TM}_{\ \alpha}\, b_1, s_3 \,^{TM}_{\ \alpha}\, b_2;$

and

$s_4 \,^{TM}_{\ \alpha}\, b_1, s_4 \,^{TM}_{\ \alpha}\, b_2, s_4 \,^{TM}_{\ \alpha}\, b_3.$

Clearly, the beliefs $b_1, b_2,$ and b_3 depicts that $\langle(b)\rangle, \langle(c)\rangle,$ or $\langle(d)\rangle$ should occur after the occurrence of $\langle(a)\rangle$, thus, in this meaning, only the sequence s_4 is unexpected. However, according to Definition 2, all of the 4 sequences are α-unexpected. In order to avoid this redundancy problem, we further define the notion of α-unexpected sequence within the context of belief base as below.

Definition 3. Given a belief $b = [s_\alpha; s_\beta; s_\gamma; 0..*]$ and a sequence s, let B be the belief base such that $b \in B$. Let B_α be a subset of B such that for each $b' \in B$, where $b' = [s'_\alpha; s'_\beta; s'_\gamma; 0..*]$, we have $s'_\alpha = s_\alpha$ implies $b' \in B_\alpha$. If $s_\alpha \,\hat{o}\, s$ and there does not exist $b' \in B$, where $b' = [s'_\alpha; s'_\beta; s'_\gamma; 0..*]$, such that $s_\alpha \cdot s'_\beta \,\hat{o}\, s$ or $s_\alpha \cdot s'_\gamma \,\hat{o}\, s$, then the sequence s is an *α-unexpected sequence* stated by the belief b of the belief base B, denoted as $s \,^{TM}_{\ \alpha}\, b_{(B)}$. Respectively, the *$\alpha$-unexpectedness* stated by the belief b of the belief base B is denoted as $\{^{TM}_{\ \alpha}\, b_{(B)}\}$. +

In fact, an α-unexpected sequence stated by a belief b of a belief base B is an unexpected sequence determined by all sub-trees of a same τ-*node* where $min = 0$ and $max = *$. In the rest of the paper, without special notice, the notation $s \,^{TM}_{\ \alpha}\, b$ and $\{^{TM}_{\ \alpha}\, b\}$ denote the α-unexpected sequence and α-unexpectedness stated by a belief b within the context of a given belief base B.

Definition 4. Given a belief $b = [s_\alpha; s_\beta; s_\gamma; min..max]$ ($min \neq 0$ or $max \neq *$) and a sequence s, if $s_\alpha \cdot s_\beta \,\hat{o}\, s$ and there does not exist a sequence s' such that $|s'| ' [min..max]$ and $s_\alpha \cdot s' \cdot s_\beta \,\hat{o}_c\, s$, then the sequence s is a *β-unexpected sequence* stated by the

Figure 2. Determining α-unexpected sequences in a belief base

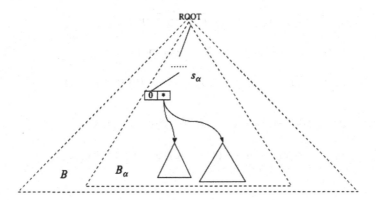

belief b, denoted as s ™$_\beta$ b. The *β-unexpectedness* stated by the belief b is denoted as $\{$™$_\beta$ $b\}$. +

A *β-unexpected* sequence reflects that the occurrence constraint $\tau = [min..max]$ $(\tau \neq [0..*])$ on the sequential rule $s_\alpha \rightarrow s_\beta$ is broken because the occurrence of s_β in the sequence s contradicts the constraint τ.

Example 9. Let us consider the below belief proposed in Example 6:

$[\langle(Sci\text{-}Fi\text{-}Novel)(Action\text{-}Film\ Sci\text{-}Fi\text{-}Film)\rangle;$
$\langle(Rock\text{-}Music)\rangle; \langle(Classical\text{-}Music)\rangle; 3..5].$

The purchase of a rock music CD is expected within the next 3 to 5 purchases after the purchases of a Sci-Fi novel then action and Sci-Fi films later. In this case, the customers who purchase a rock music CD just in the next purchase or after many purchases of other products are unexpected to this belief and might be valuable to make new promotion strategies on related products. Notice that $\langle(Classical\text{-}Music)\rangle$ in this belief is not considered within the context of *β-unexpected* sequences. +

Definition 5. Given a belief $b = [s_\alpha ; s_\beta ; s_\gamma ; min..max]$ and a sequence s, if $s_\alpha \cdot s_\gamma \sqsubseteq s$ and there exists a sequence s' such that $|s'| \notin [min..max]$ and $s_\alpha \cdot s' \cdot s_\gamma \, \hat{o}_c \, s$, then the sequence s is a *γ-unexpected sequence* stated by the belief b, denoted as s ™$_\gamma$ b. The *γ-unexpectedness* stated by the belief b is

denoted as $\{$™$_\gamma$ $b\}$. +

A *γ-unexpected* sequence is concentrated on the semantics: the occurrence of s_β is replaced by its semantic opposition s_γ within the occurrence constraint $\tau = [min..max]$.

Example 10. Let us consider again the belief studied in Example 9:

$[\langle(Sci\text{-}Fi\text{-}Novel)(Action\text{-}Film\ Sci\text{-}Fi\text{-}Film)\rangle;$
$\langle(Rock\text{-}Music)\rangle; \langle(Classical\text{-}Music)\rangle; 3..5].$

The rock music can be considered as being opposite to the classical music. Therefore, the purchase of a rock music CD cannot be replaced by the purchase of a classical music CD. In this example, since the purchase of a rock music CD is expected within the next 3 to 5 purchases after the purchases of a Sci-Fi novel then action and Sci-Fi films later, the purchase of a classical music CD is not expected within the interval of the next 3 to 5 purchases. Of course, in this case, the purchase of a classical music CD is allowed within the next 3 purchases or after the next 5 purchases according the purpose of this belief. +

A feature is the unexpected part of an unexpected sequence, which informs the internal structure of the unexpectedness.

Definition 6. Given a belief $b = [s_\alpha ; s_\beta ; s_\gamma ; min..max]$ and an unexpected sequence s such that s ™ b, the *feature* of the unexpected sequence s

Figure 3. Features of unexpected sequences

(c) (f) (ab) (e) (f) (a) (a) (a) (a) (d) (bc) (a) (f)

(d) (b) (ab) (e) (f) (a) (a) (b) (a) (d) (bc) (g) (e)

(a) (x) (ab) (e) (f) (a) (e) (a) (e) (a) (e) (d) (bc) (x) (y)

(a) (c) (a) (b) (e) (f) (b) (b) (b) (c) (b) (ab) (c) (x)

(x) (a) (c) (y) (e) (b) (f) (b) (b) (c) (a) (ab) (d) (e) (y)

is the maximum consecutive subsequence u of the sequence s such that: (1) if s ™$_\alpha$ b, we have $s_a \cdot u = s$, where s_a is a sequence such that $|s_a| \geq 0$; (2) if s ™$_\beta$ b, we have $s_a \cdot u \cdot s_c = s$, where s_a and s_c are two sequences such that $|s_a| \geq 0$, $|s_c| \geq 0$, $s_a \not\sqsubseteq s_a$, $s_a \sqsubseteq [u$, and $s_\beta \sqsubseteq]u$ (i.e., $s_a \cdot s_\beta$ $\hat{o}^{[\cdot]}u$); (3) if s ™$_\gamma$ b, we have $s_a \cdot u \cdot s_c = s$, where s_a and s_c are two sequences such that $|s_a| \geq 0$, $|s_c| \geq 0$, $s_a \not\sqsubseteq s_a$, $s_a \sqsubseteq [u$, and $s_\gamma \sqsubseteq]u$ (i.e., $s_a \cdot s_\gamma \sqsubseteq^{[\cdot]}u$). The feature of an unexpected sequence s with respect to a belief b is denoted as u ' $(s$ ™ $b)$. +

Example 11. Let us consider a belief $b = [\langle(e)(f)\rangle; \langle(d)\rangle; \langle(c)\rangle; 0..3]$, Figure 3 shows the features of a set of β-unexpected or γ-unexpected sequences. +

Based on the definitions of unexpected sequences and the structure of belief tree, we have the following algorithm for mining unexpected sequences.

Algorithm 2 (*USE: Mining unexpected sequences*).

Input: A sequence database D, a belief base B stored as a belief tree T.

Output: All unexpected sequences with respect to each belief $b \in B$.

1. Read a sequence s from the sequence database D. If all sequences in D have been processed, exit the procedure.

2. Use depth-first method for traversing the α-tree of the belief tree T, till to reach a τ-node. If no τ-node can be reached, reject current sequence and back to step 1 for restarting with next

sequence.

3. If current τ-node consists of [0..*], then use depth-first method for traversing all β-trees by following each τ-link. If no leaf-node of any β-tree and of any γ-tree can be reached, mark current sequence s as α-unexpected. If any leaf-node of any γ-tree can be reached, mark current sequence s as γ-unexpected. If the sequence s is unexpected, output the sequence s, the feature u, the antecedent and consequent sequences with belief identification. Continue step 2.

4. If current τ-node does not consist of [0..*], then use depth-first method for traversing all nodes of all β-trees by following each τ-link. If any leaf-node of any β-tree can be reached and the path can be verified with respect to the complement of [*min..max*] contained in current τ-node, mark current sequence s as β-unexpected. Use depth-first method for traversing all γ-trees by following each η-link from current leaf-node of current β-tree. If any leaf-node of any γ-tree can be reached, mark current sequence s as γ-unexpected. If the sequence s is unexpected, output the sequence s, the feature u, the antecedent and consequent sequences with belief identification. Continue step 2.

Unexpected Sequential Patterns and Implication Rules

According to Definition 6, given an unexpected sequence s stated by a belief b, the feature u is the part of the sequence s that causes the unexpectedness $\{™b\}$. With features, we can study the internal structure of the unexpectedness via the notion of unexpected sequential patterns.

Definition 7. Given a belief b and a sequence database D, let $D_{\{™b\}}$ be a subset of the sequence database D consisting of all sequences $s \in D$ such that $s ™ b$, and let $U_{\{™b\}}$ be the feature set of $u\ '\ (s ™ b)$ of each unexpected sequence $s \in D_{\{™b\}}$. Given a user specified minimum support threshold σ_{min}, an *unexpected sequential pattern* is a maximal sequence p in the feature set $U_{\{™b\}}$ such that $\sigma (p, U_{\{™b\}}) \geq \sigma_{min}$. +

Notice that in the feature set $U_{\{™b\}}$, the support value of the unexpected part (i.e., s_α in α-unexpected sequences, $s_\alpha \cdot s_\beta$ in β-unexpected sequences, and $s_\alpha \cdot s_\gamma$ in γ-unexpected sequences) is 100% with perforce. For example, for the β-unexpectedness, the support of the sequence $s_\alpha \cdot s_\beta$ in the feature set $U_{\{™b\}}$ is 100%, since for each feature $u \in U_{\{™b\}}$, we have the same structure $u = s_\alpha \cdot s\ ' \cdot s_\beta$. Therefore, for extracting unexpected sequential patterns, we do not consider the subsequences s_α , s_β and (or) s_γ in the feature set $U_{\{™b\}}$. Since any existing sequential pattern mining algorithms can extract the unexpected sequential patterns, we do not repeat such a process in this chapter.

Example 12. For the sequence database shown in Figure 3, in the feature set of β-unexpected sequences, we find that the sequence $\langle (a)(a)(a) \rangle$ is an unexpected sequential pattern that its presence gives the β-unexpectedness; in the feature set of γ-unexpected sequences, we find that the presence of the sequential pattern $\langle (b)(b)(b) \rangle$ indicates β-unexpectedness. +

Given an unexpected sequence s and its feature u, the sequence s can be represented as $s = s_a \cdot u \cdot s_c$, where $|s_a|, |s_c| \geq 0$ (we have $|s_c| \equiv 0$ for an α-unexpected sequence). The sequences s_a and s_c are called the *antecedent sequence* and the *consequent sequence* of an unexpected sequence.

Definition 8. Given a belief b and a sequence database D, let $D^A_{\{™b\}}$ be the subset of the database D that consists of the antecedent sequences s_a of each sequence $s \in D$ such that $s ™ b$. An

antecedent rule of the unexpectedness $\{™b\}$ is a rule $a \rightarrow \{™b\}$ where a is a frequent sequence in the sequence set $D^A_{\{™b\}}$. +

Antecedent rules reflect the causes of the unexpectedness contradicting a given belief b. With respect to a belief b, the support of an antecedent rule in a sequence database D, denoted as $\sigma\,(a \rightarrow \{™b\}, D)$, is the fraction of the total number of the sequences in the sequence set $D^A_{\{™b\}}$ that support the sequence a on the sequence database D, that is,

$$\sigma(a \rightarrow \{\nvDash b\}, D) = \frac{\left|\left\{ s \,\middle|\, (a \sqsubseteq s) \wedge \left(s \in D^A_{\{\nvDash b\}} \right) \right\}\right|}{|D|}$$

The confidence of an antecedent rule in the sequence database D, denoted as $\delta\,(a \rightarrow \{™b\}, D)$, is the fraction of the total number of the sequences in the sequence database D that support the sequence a, that is,

$$\delta(a \rightarrow \{\nvDash b\}, D) = \frac{\left|\left\{ s \,\middle|\, (a \sqsubseteq s) \wedge \left(s \in D^A_{\{\nvDash b\}} \right) \right\}\right|}{\left|\left\{ s \,\middle|\, (a \sqsubseteq s) \wedge (s \in D) \right\}\right|} \cdot$$

Example 13. Considering the sequence database shown in Figure 3, according to the belief $b = [\langle (e)(f) \rangle; \langle (d) \rangle; \langle (c) \rangle; 0..3]$, given a minimum support 50% and a minimum confidence 50%, we have the rule $\langle (ab) \rangle \rightarrow \{™_\beta b\}$, whose support is 60% and confidence is 100%. +

Definition 9. Given a belief b and a sequence database D, let $D^C_{\{™b\}}$ be the subset of the database D that consists of the consequent sequences s_c of each sequence $s \in D$ such that $s ™ b$. An *antecedent rule* of the unexpectedness $\{™b\}$ is a rule $\{™b\} \rightarrow c$ where c is a frequent sequence in the sequence set $D^C_{\{™b\}}$. +

Consequent rules reflect the causes of the unexpectedness contradicting a given belief b. With respect to a belief b, the support of a consequent rule in a sequence database D, denoted as $\sigma(\{™b\} \rightarrow c, D)$, is the total number of sequences in the sequence set $D^C_{\{\text{TM}b\}}$ that support the sequence c on the sequence database D, that is,

$$\sigma(\{\not\models b\} \to c, D) = \frac{\left|\left\{s \middle| (c \sqsubseteq s) \wedge \left(c \in D^C_{\{\not\models b\}}\right)\right\}\right|}{|D|}.$$

The confidence of a consequent rule in the sequence database D, denoted as $\delta(\{\text{TM}b\} \to c, D)$, is the fraction of the total number of the sequences in the sequence set $D^C_{\{\text{TM}b\}}$ that support the sequence c, that is,

$$\delta(\{\not\models b\} \to c, D) = \frac{\left|\left\{s \middle| (c \sqsubseteq s) \wedge \left(c \in D^C_{\{\not\models b\}}\right)\right\}\right|}{\left|D^C_{\{\not\models b\}}\right|}.$$

Example 14. Considering again the sequence database shown in Figure 3, according to the belief $b = [\langle (e)(f) \rangle; \langle (d) \rangle; \langle (c) \rangle; 0..3]$, given a minimum support 50% and a minimum confidence 50%, we have the rule $\{^{\text{TM}}_\beta b\} \to \langle (bc) \rangle$, whose support is 60% and confidence is 100%. +

For globally illustrating the purpose of mining unexpected sequential rules including the antecedent rules and the consequent rules, let us study the following example.

Example 15. Considering a WebMail system, assume a log file containing 10,000 user sessions of (*Time, IP, Request*) where *Time* identifies the time range of the session, *IP* identifies the range of remote IP addresses, and *Request* identifies the resources requested such that *Request* $\in$ {*Begin-Session, End-Session, Help, Login, Logout, Mailbox, Reset-Password, ...*}, where *Help, Login, Logout, Reset-Password*, etc. note Web pages. In such a log file, each user session is a sequence. A valid user login process (the access of *Login*) should redirect the user session to the mailbox page (the access of *Mailbox*), so that a belief on such a behavior can be $b = [\langle (Login) \rangle; (Mailbox) \rangle; \langle (Logout) \rangle; 0..0]$. Suppose that we found 100 β-unexpected sequences.

Assume that we found that 100 sequences in the whole log file with 80 β-unexpected sequences support the antecedent sequence $\langle (T1, IP1, Begin-Session) \rangle$; 9,000 sequences in the whole log file with 20 β-unexpected sequences support the antecedent sequence $\langle (IP2, Begin-Session) \rangle$; 90 β-sequences support the consequent sequence $\langle (T1, IP1, End-Session) \rangle$; 15 β-unexpected sequences support the consequent sequence $\langle (IP2, Reset-Password)(IP2, End-Session) \rangle$; 10 β-unexpected sequences support the frequent consequent sequence $\langle (IP2, Help)(IP2, End-Session) \rangle$.

According to the above assumes, we have: the antecedent rule $\langle (T1, IP1, Begin-Session) \rangle \to \{^{\text{TM}}_\beta b\}$ with support $80/10,000 = 0.8\%$ and confidence $80/100 = 80\%$; the antecedent rule $\langle (IP2, Begin-Session) \rangle \to \{^{\text{TM}}_\beta b\}$ with support $10/10,000 = 0.1\%$ and confidence $10/9,000 \cong 0.1\%$; the consequent rule $\{^{\text{TM}}_\beta b\} \to \langle (T1, IP1, End-Session) \rangle$ with support $90/10,000 = 0.09\%$ and confidence $90/100 = 90\%$; the consequent rule $\{^{\text{TM}}_\beta b\} \to \langle (IP2, Reset-Password)(IP2, End-Session) \rangle$ with support $15/10,000 = 0.15\%$ and confidence $15/100 = 15\%$; the consequent rule $\{^{\text{TM}}_\beta b\} \to \langle (IP2, Help)(IP2, End-Session) \rangle$ with support $10/10,000 = 0.1\%$ and confidence $10/100 = 10\%$.

Obviously, we can interpret the antecedent rule $\langle (T1, IP1, Begin-Session) \rangle \to \{^{\text{TM}}_\beta b\}$ and the consequent rule $\{^{\text{TM}}_\beta b\} \to \langle (T1, IP1, End-Session) \rangle$ as that the connections from IP range 1 at time range 1 can be considered as critical event since the confidences of these two rules are strong, however, the antecedent rule $\langle (IP2, Begin-Session) \rangle \to \{^{\text{TM}}_\beta b\}$ can be safely ignored not only because the very low confidence, but also the consequent rules $\{^{\text{TM}}_\beta b\} \to \langle (IP2, Reset-Password)(IP2, End-Session) \rangle$ and $\{^{\text{TM}}_\beta b\} \to \langle (IP2, Help)(IP2, End-Session) \rangle$ show that the connections from IP2 do not contain strong behaviors that can be interpreted as critical events. +

Based on the above propositions, Algorithm 3 shows the procedure of mining unexpected antecedent and consequent rules in a sequence database, with user defined minimum support and confidence threshold values.

Algorithm 3 (*USR: Mining unexpected sequential rules*).

Input: A sequence database D, a belief base B stored as a belief tree T, minimum support σ_{min}, minimum confidence δ_{min}.

Output: All antecedent and consequent rules stated by each belief $b \in B$, with respect to the minimum support σ_{min} and minimum confidence δ_{min}.

1. Call the procedure *USE* for extract the antecedent sequence set $D^A_{\{TMb\}}$ and the consequent set $D^C_{\{TMb\}}$ stated by each belief $b \in B$.

2. For each antecedent sequence s_a in the antecedent sequence set $D^A_{\{TMb\}}$, find all sequential patterns $a \in D^A_{\{TMb\}}$ such that the support $\sigma(a, D) \geq \sigma_{min}$. If the fraction of $\sigma(a, D^A_{\{TMb\}})/\sigma(a, D) \geq \delta_{min}$, output the rule $a \rightarrow \{TMb\}$.

3. For each consequent sequence s_c in the consequent sequence set $D^C_{\{TMb\}}$, find all sequential patterns $c \in D^C_{\{TMb\}}$ such that the support $\sigma(c, D) \geq \sigma_{min}$. If the support $\sigma(c, D^C_{\{TMb\}}) \geq \delta_{min}$, output the rule $\{TMb\} \rightarrow c$.

Notice that we separate the process of mining unexpected sequential implication rules into two standalone sub-routines: we first compute the support value of the premise a or the consequence c, then we compute the confidence of the rules, in order to obtain the best performance and flexibility.

Experimental Evaluation

To evaluate the effectiveness and scalability of our approach, we have performed two groups of experiments. The first group of experiments is performed on large log files of two real Web servers, with the belief base defined by domain experts. The second group of experiments is performed on various dense synthetic data files generated by the IBM Quest Synthetic Data Generator[1], where we use a set of random generated beliefs as the belief bases. All experiments have been performed on a Sun Fire V880 system with 8 1.2GHz UltraSPARC

III processors and 32GB main memory running Solaris 10 operating system.

Experiments on Web Access Logs

We performed a group of experiments on two large log files containing the access records of two Web servers during a period of 3 months. The first log file, labeled as LOGBBS, corresponds to a PHP based discussion forum Web site of an online game provider; the second log file, labeled as LOGWWW, corresponds to a Web site that hosts personal home pages of researchers and teaching staffs. We split each log file into three 1-month period files, i.e., LOGBBS-{1,2,3} and LOGWWW-{1,2,3}. Table 1 details the number of sequences, distinct items, and the average length of the sequences contained in the Web access logs.

In order to compare our approach with the sequential pattern mining, we first apply the sequential pattern mining algorithm to find the frequent behaviors from LOGBBS-{1,2,3} and LOGWWW-{1,2,3} with different minimum support thresholds, shown in Figure 4 (a) and (b); Figure 4 (c) and (d) show the number of unexpected sequential implication rules discovered by *USER*. Post analysis of the experimental results shows the effectiveness of our approach.

The result set of our approach is much less than the extremely large sequence set generated by sequential pattern mining, where the many

Table 1. Web access logs in experiments

Access Log	Sessions	Distinct Items	Average Length
LOGBBS-1	27,294	38,678	12.8934
LOGBBS-2	47,868	42,052	20.3905
LOGBBS-3	28,146	33,890	8.5762
LOGWWW-1	6,534	8,436	6.3276
LOGWWW-2	11,304	49,242	7.3905
LOGWWW-3	28,400	50,312	9.5762

discovered frequent sequences are similar in the data sets LOGBBS-{1,2,3}. One important reason is that the accesses of the Web server of LOGBBS-{1,2,3} are very regular and the most frequent behaviors are similar. Moreover, with the minimum confidence 20%, totally 15 antecedent rules and 2 consequent rules are finally recognized as representing new navigation behaviors of users, however, such behaviors have low support values (< 1%) and cannot be discovered by frequency based approaches in our experiments, since according to Figure 4 (a), with the minimum support 2%, more than 1000 frequent sequences are extracted.

The experiments on the data sets LOG-WWW-{1,2,3} show that the comparison of the result size is similar to the experiments data sets LOGBBS-{1,2,3}. An important note is that the antecedent rules discovered by *USER* with the minimum confidence 10%, totally 12 rules show the relevant information of Web security problems. However, in the data sets LOGWWW-{1,2,3}, only 1 consequent rule shows a weak connection of Web security.

Experiments on Synthetic Data

The scalability of the *USER* approach has been tested first with a fixed belief number of 20 by increasing the size of sequence database from 10,000 sequences to 500,000 sequences, and then with a fixed sequence database size of 100,000

Figure 4. (a) Sequential patterns in data sets LOGBBS-{1,2,3}. (b) Unexpected sequential implication rules in data sets LOGBBS-{1,2,3}. (c) Sequential patterns in data sets LOGWWW-{1,2,3}. (b) Unexpected sequential implication rules in data sets LOGWWW-{1,2,3}.

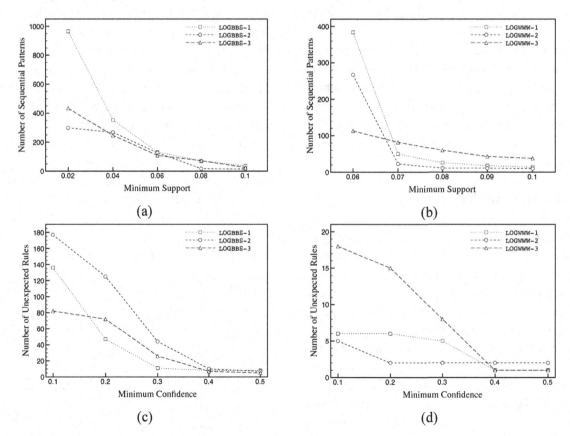

Figure 5. (a) Number of all unexpected sequences stated by 20 beliefs. (b) Run time for extracting all unexpected sequences stated by 20 beliefs. (c) Number of all unexpected sequences in 100,000 sequences. (d) Run time for extracting all unexpected sequences from 100,000 sequences.

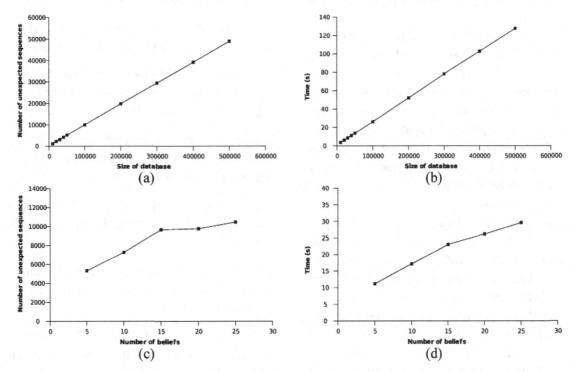

sequences by increasing the number of beliefs from 5 to 25.

Figure 5(a) shows that, when the belief number is fixed, the number of all unexpected sequences increases linearly with the increasing of the size of sequence database. Because the data sets generated by the IBM Quest Synthetic Data Generator contain repeated blocks, the unexpected sequences with respect to the same 20 beliefs are repeated. Therefore, Figure 5(b) shows that, when the belief number is fixed to 20, the run time of the extraction of all unexpected sequences increases linearly with the increasing of the size of sequence database.

Figure 5(c) shows that, when the size of sequence database is fixed, the number of all unexpected sequences extracted increases, but not linearly, when the number of beliefs increases. This is a previewed result since the number of unexpected sequences depends on the structure of

beliefs. In this test the last 10 beliefs address much less unexpected sequences than others. Figure 5(d) shows the increment of run time of the extraction of all unexpected sequences illustrated in Figure 5(c), and from which we can find that the increasing rate of extracting time depends on the number of unexpected sequences. In our implementation of the USER approach, to predict and process a non-matched sequence is much faster than to predict and process a matched sequence.

CONCLUSION

In this chapter, we introduce a belief-driven approach *USER* for mining unexpected sequential patterns and implication rules in sequence databases. We first formalize the belief base and propose 3 forms of unexpected of sequences, and then we propose the notions and discoveries of the unexpected sequential patterns and implication rules, including antecedent rules and consequent rules for measuring the unexpected behaviors in sequence data.

The approach *USER* is evaluated with different types of Web access logs and synthetic data. Our experimental results show that: (1) our approach permits to extract unexpected sequential patterns and implication rules with low support value; (2) our approach is capable to find unexpected sequences that are included in expected sequences; (3) the unexpected sequences depend on the belief base and the characteristics of the sequence database.

Our approach can be extended with an application of soft beliefs. For example, in a data set, we know that 90% of customers purchase a Sci-Fi novel and then action and Sci-Fi films later, so it is possible to create a soft belief like "the purchase of a Sci-Fi novel implies the purchase of action and Sci-Fi films", and its degree can be defined by a soft measure function μ (0.9). If in another data set, there are only 10% of customers who confirm this belief, then the change of degree can be computed by the a soft measure function ψ (0.9, 0.1). We are also interested in mining unexpected sequences and sequential rules with the notion of hierarchies and soft hierarchies.

REFERENCES

Agrawal, R., & Srikant, R. (1995). Mining sequential patterns. In *ICDE* (pp. 3-14).

Angiulli, F., & Pizzuti, C. (2002). Fast outlier detection in high dimensional spaces. In *PKDD* (pp. 15-26).

Angiulli, F., & Pizzuti, C. (2005). Outlier mining in large high-dimensional data sets. *IEEE Transactions on Knowledge and Data Engineering, 17*(2), 203–215. doi:10.1109/TKDE.2005.31

Ayres, J., Flannick, J., Gehrke, J., & Yiu, T. (2002). Sequential PAttern Mining using a bitmap representation. In *KDD* (pp. 429-435).

Dong, G., & Pei, J. (2007). *Sequence Data Mining (Advances in Database Systems)*. Springer.

Garofalakis, M. N., Rastogi, R., & Shim, K. (1999). SPIRIT: Sequential pattern mining with regular expression constraints. In *VLDB* (pp. 223-234).

Han, J., & Kamber, M. (2006). *Data Mining: Concepts and Techniques* (2nd ed.). Morgan Kaufmann Publishers.

Jin, W., Tung, A. K. H., & Han, J. (2001). Mining top-n local outliers in large databases. In *KDD* (pp. 293-298).

Knorr, E. M., & Ng, R. T. (1998). Algorithms for mining distance-based outliers in large datasets. In *VLDB* (pp. 392-403).

Li, D. H., Laurent, A., & Teisseire, M. (2007). On transversal hypergraph enumeration in mining sequential patterns. In *IDEAS* (pp. 303-307).

Lo, D., Khoo, S.-C., & Liu, C. (2007). Efficient mining of iterative patterns for software specification discovery. In *KDD* (pp. 460-469).

Mannila, H., Toivonen, H., & Verkamo, A. I. (1997). Discovery of frequent episodes in event sequences. *Data Mining and Knowledge Discovery, 1*(3), 259–289. doi:10.1023/A:1009748302351

Masseglia, F., Cathala, F., & Poncelet, P. (1998). The PSP approach for mining sequential patterns. In *PKDD* (pp. 176-184).

McGarry, K. (2005). A survey of interestingness measures for knowledge discovery. *The Knowledge Engineering Review, 20*(1), 39–61. doi:10.1017/S0269888905000408

Padmanabhan, B., & Tuzhilin, A. (1998). A belief-driven method for discovering unexpected patterns. In *KDD* (pp. 94-100).

Pei, J., Han, J., Mortazavi-Asl, B., Wang, J., Pinto, H., & Chen, Q. (2004). Mining sequential patterns by pattern-growth: the PrefixSpan approach. *IEEE Transactions on Knowledge and Data Engineering, 16*(11), 1424–1440. doi:10.1109/TKDE.2004.77

Ramaswamy, S., Rastogi, R., & Shim, K. (2000). Efficient Algorithms for Mining Outliers from Large Data Sets. In *SIGMOD* (pp. 427-438).

Spiliopoulou, M. (1999). Managing interesting rules in sequence mining. In *PKDD* (pp. 554-560).

Srikant, R., & Agrawal, R. (1996). Mining sequential patterns: generalizations and performance improvements. In *EDBT* (pp. 3-17).

Sun, P., Chawla, S., & Arunasalam, B. (2006). Mining for Outliers in Sequential Databases. In *SDM* (pp. 94-105).

Wang, J., & Han, J. (2004). BIDE: Efficient mining of frequent closed sequences. In *ICDE* (pp. 79-90).

Yan, X., Han, J., & Afshar, R. (2003). CloSpan: Mining closed sequential patterns in large databases. In *SDM* (pp. 166-177).

Zaki, M. J. (2001). SPADE: An efficient algorithm for mining frequent sequences. *Machine Learning, 42*(1-2).

ENDNOTE

[1]   http://www.almaden.ibm.com/cs/quest/

Chapter 11
Mining Hidden Association Rules from Real-Life Data

Marco-Antonio Balderas Cepeda
Universidad de Granada, Spain

ABSTRACT

Association rule mining has been a highly active research field over the past decade. Extraction of frequency-related patterns has been applied to several domains. However, the way association rules are defined has limited people's ability to obtain all the patterns of interest. In this chapter, the authors present an alternative approach that allows us to obtain new kinds of association rules that represent deviations from common behaviors. These new rules are called anomalous rules. To obtain such rules requires that we extract all the most frequent patterns together with certain extension patterns that may occur very infrequently. An approach that relies on anomalous rules has possible application in the areas of counterterrorism, fraud detection, pharmaceutical data analysis and network intrusion detection. They provide an adaption of measures of interest to our anomalous rule sets, and we propose an algorithm that can extract anomalous rules as well. Their experiments with benchmark and real-life datasets suggest that the set of anomalous rules is smaller than the set of association rules. Their work also provides evidence that our proposed approach can discover hidden patterns with good reliability.

INTRODUCTION

Traditionally, association rule (AR) mining is based on the definition of "frequent item-sets," a concept that was originally derived using transactional data (Agrawal, Imielinski, & Swami, 1993). A significant drawback of the traditional approach to association

DOI: 10.4018/978-1-60566-754-6.ch011

rules is the large number of rules that are generated and processed. Even a small database often generates several thousand rules. In addition, potentially interesting "infrequent item-sets" are discarded a priori by the very definition of the association rules. These drawbacks have led to an increasing number of studies concerning interest measures (Geng & Hamilton, 2006; Tan, Kumar, & Srivastava, 2004), and they have prompted research into the connections between association rules and so-called "rare item-sets."

The connection between association rules and rarities or anomalies is especially helpful in several specific knowledge domains in which the presence of unusual recorded data can prompt a decision to protect, counter-attack or to investigate further. Detection of anomalies is a specific case in the broader supercategory of hidden pattern detection. Anomalies are traditionally defined as deviations from a normal behavior (Denning, 1987). In network communications, this concept is particularly useful since it can be used to detect intrusions and to alert administrators to novel types of network attacks. In counter-terrorism, the detection of anomalies can help identify abnormal emails (or email content), unusual activities, etc. (Thuraisingham, 2004). However, a limitation of existing anomaly detection systems is the rate of false positives.

In this chapter, we propose a new set of anomalous association rules (AARs) that can reliably identify several kinds of hidden patterns, including those that may occur infrequently. A pattern that represents a common behavior consistent with the association rules, together with the anomalous patterns that are derived by association, can include non-frequent itemsets and can lead to reliable inferences about the data. Applications of anomalous rules extend from the areas previously highlighted to medical or agricultural domains, and also to general applications in which identifying rare patterns is considered important.

This chapter is organized as follows: we first offer a brief background on how to model deviations from a given common behavior, and we subsequently provide definitions of the anomalous rules and associated metrics that we used for our research. We also explore the effects of using various discretization methods. We present our algorithm for generating anomalous rules, and we illustrate the anomalous rule data mining process with simulated data.

Finally, we summarize the results of our experiments using real-world data. Our findings demonstrate the effectiveness of our chosen metrics and provide evidence that anomalous rules can be used to identify hidden patterns that may potentially reveal interesting associations.

BACKGROUND

Association rules (Agrawal et al., 1993) is a term that refers to patterns that relate sets of items. For a given set of *k* items, known as a *k-itemset*, an association rule has two components: an antecedent and a consequent, both of which may themselves involve k-itemsets. The association rule can be evaluated by two measures; support and confidence. Support quantifies the statistical significance of the pattern, and it is defined as the probability of a certain k-itemset being part of the dataset. The confidence, defined as the conditional probability between the pattern and the antecedent of the association rule, provides evidence of the relevance of a certain rule. An association rule is confirmed if its support and confidence values are greater than or equal to certain thresholds specified by the user.

Unlike the traditional frequent itemset framework that is used to obtain association rules, research into the detection of rare and hidden patterns must consider the specific definitions that pertain to each case. Several recent publications have explored the modeling of patterns that reflect deviations from a common behavior.

Exception rules (ERs) (Suzuki, 2002) represent changes in the consequent of an AR that are caused by the presence of a specific item. These changes are reinforced by a so-called reference rule, which treats both the item causing the exception and the new consequent. The reference rule states that the item causing the exception is not associated with the exception that it causes. In this context, the anomalous rules do not require the presence of items that cause exceptions. However, the AARs also use negative itemsets in the definitions to find uncommon patterns. Our proposal differs from the ERs since the AARs are defined in such a way as to identify deviations from a common behavior, i.e., excluding the dominant effect of the consequent of ARs. The ERs are defined in such a way as to find behavior changes, i.e., adding items to the antecedent of ARs. Therefore, in some cases, ERs are found, and AARs are not and vice versa (Berzal, Cubero, Marín, & Gámez, 2004b). Exception rules have been widely studied in conjunction with application areas of relevance (Suzuki, Watanabe, Yokoi, & Takabayashi, 2003; Suzuki & Zytkow, 2005).

Negative AR mining is an effort to obtain all of the rules that negate some k-itemset of a certain AR. Consider that for a given association rule, e.g., Sky Cloudy $\Rightarrow$ Rain, the negative rules are Sky Cloudy $\Rightarrow$ Not Rain, Not Sky Cloudy $\Rightarrow$ Rain, and Not Sky Cloudy $\Rightarrow$ Not Rain. Recent research (Wu, Zhang, & Zhang, 2004) showed that some constraints must be implemented in order to prune the search space and then obtain negative rules. The study also showed that the rules of a form similar to Sky Cloudy $\Rightarrow$ Not Rain can be important in the decision making process.

The work of Cornelis, Yan, Zhang, and Chen (2006) demonstrated the use of an algorithm to find all of the positive and negative ARs, and clearly showed the differences relating to how to consider the negation of items in the database transactions and the impact over the theoretical number of positive and negative ARs. The AARs are proposed to obtain positive rules. Although AARs have some relation to the negative ARs field, the AARs are constrained by the obtained ARs, and the AARs are defined to identify specific items.

The research by Yun, Ha, Hwang, and Ryu (2003) showed patterns of items that appear rarely together. These patterns are evaluated with an additional measure of support, which is called relative support. This measure is in fact the maximum value of the confidence measure among the possible association rules in a k-itemset. Therefore, the rules that are obtained are the most confident and can contain rare data.

Work on sporadic rules (Koh, Rountree, & O'Keefe, 2008) demonstrated patterns of items that occur together but have a low support value. The sporadic rules that are mined are more restrictive than those of the work of Yun et al. (2003); an imperfect sporadic rule must contain frequent k-itemsets in the antecedent and infrequent itemsets in the consequent. Fisher's exact test is used to evaluate the correlation of k-itemsets, and an additional constraint tests the reverse of the rule, i.e., $(X \Rightarrow Y)$ or $(Y \Rightarrow X)$, to avoid very frequent consequents. As compared to the AARs proposal, both works can involve infrequent items. However, the aims of the work are significantly different; the AARs are defined in such a way as to identify confident deviations within a strong and confident pattern, while the sporadic rules are defined in such a way as to identify confident rules with a low support value. Therefore, the semantics and the ruleset that is discovered from a given dataset are different.

Research on dissociation rules (Morzy, 2006) presents patterns in which some k-itemsets rarely occur together $(X \cup Y)$ and then forms a pattern notated by X *do not imply* Y. This pattern is evaluated with a modified support measure. The dissociation rules present a negative relation between items, while the AARs proposal represents specific positive relations between items.

Research into conditional anomaly detection (Song, Wu, Jermaine, & Ranka, 2007) has aimed to identify ambience and indicator attributes. Anomalies can be detected in the context of ambience attributes, and most research to date has been oriented towards the detection of outliers.

Peculiarity rules (Zhong, Yao, & Ohshima, 2003) aim to identify peculiar (i.e., rare) data using distance measures. Such rules can detect oddities in the data and can be tuned by modifying the calculations that are used to measure distance (Ohshima, Zhong, Yao, & Murata, 2004;

Zhong, et al., 2004). Recently, work on peculiarity rules has been extended (Ohshima, Zhong, Yao, & Liu, 2007) to work at record-level in the relational databases context. The distance functions used to obtain peculiar data and rules orients this research near to our proposal in terms of the discovery of uncommon patterns but maintains a clear methodological difference. The obtained peculiar ruleset is potentially different from the rule set obtained with AARs.

DEFINITIONS OF ANOMALOUS RULES

Anomalous rules (Balderas, Cubero, Berzal, Marin, & Einsman, 2005; Berzal, Cubero, Marín, & Gámez, 2004a) are deviations from a common behavior that is modeled by association rules. The original definition was arrived at using transactional data, but it is equally possible to use relational data instead. Let A, B, C denote arbitrary k-itemsets in a dataset R. We define four minimum thresholds: the support threshold ($MinSupp$, ε), the confidence threshold ($MinConf$, θ), the domain threshold for relational data ($MinDom$, β) and the absolute minimum threshold ($AbsMinSupp$, ω). An anomalous rule is obtained if the following conditions exist; an association rule $B \Rightarrow C$ exists where:

$$sprt(B \Rightarrow C) = \hat{\Pr}(BC) \geq MinSupp$$

$$conf(B \Rightarrow C) = \hat{\Pr}(C \mid B) \geq MinConf$$

$$conf(B\neg C \Rightarrow A) = \hat{\Pr}(A \mid B\neg C) \geq MinConf$$

$$conf(BC \Rightarrow \neg A) = \hat{\Pr}(\neg A \mid BC) \geq MinConf$$

$$ams(B\neg C \Rightarrow A) = \hat{\Pr}(AB\neg C) \geq AbsMinSupp$$

Where $B \cap C = \varnothing$ and $B \cap A = \varnothing$, and A represents a specific k-itemset. The *MinDom* threshold is used only in the case of relational data. In this context, the attribute domain of an anomalous item must be greater than or equal to the *MinDom* threshold:

$$A = \left\{ a_1 : v_i, a_2 : v_j, ..., a_n : v_k \mid D(a_n) \geq \beta \right\}$$

Canonical Anomalous Rules

To present anomalous rules in a compact structure, we define the following syntax that references both a traditional association rule and an anomalous rule:

$$B \xrightarrow{\;anom\;} A \;/\; C$$

Anomalous rules can be decomposed into three elements; the antecedent (B), the consequent (C) and the anomalous consequent (A). Each one of these elements is a k-itemset. The interpretation of the above syntax can be read as follows: B anomalously implies A, but (B) commonly implies C. In the medical domain, an anomalous rule may look like the following example:

diagnostic = renal tumor THEN treatment = radical nephrectomy / treatment = chemo-therapy

A canonical anomalous rule is a rule whose anomalous consequent comprises only one item (1-itemset). In such a case, the following definition applies:

$$B \xrightarrow{\;anom\;} A \;/\; C, \mid A \mid = 1$$

The following property of an anomalous rule rationalizes the use of canonical anomalous rules to search for the hidden associations in the general case:

$$B \xrightarrow{anom} AE \ / \ C, implies; B \xrightarrow{anom} A \ / \ C$$

$$because, \hat{\mathrm{Pr}}(AE \mid B\neg C) \leq \hat{\mathrm{Pr}}(A \mid B\neg C)$$

This property (monotonicity of consequent contraction) indicates that, in the case of anomalous rules whose anomalous consequent has two or more items, there also exists an anomalous rule whose anomalous consequent has fewer items. In this chapter, we search for canonical anomalous rules in order to find the most general hidden associations.

Calculating Support and Confidence

To calculate k-itemset support and determine rule confidence, the frequency count of the k-itemset must be derived from the employed dataset. We define the support of a k-itemset as being equal to its probability in the chosen dataset:

$$sprt(B) = \hat{\mathrm{Pr}}(B)$$

To calculate a confidence level for anomalous rules, we calculate the conditional probability in the following manner:

$$conf(B \Rightarrow C) = \frac{sprt(BC)}{sprt(B)}$$

$$conf(B\neg C \Rightarrow A) = \frac{sprt(AB) - sprt(ABC)}{sprt(B) - sprt(BC)}$$

$$conf(BC \Rightarrow \neg A) = \frac{sprt(BC) - sprt(ABC)}{sprt(BC)}$$

Mining Anomalous Association Rules

In the literature concerning Knowledge Discovery in Data (KDD), it is well known that the data pre-processing stage is important for increasing the quality of mined results (Dasu & Johnson,

2003) and for increasing the efficiency of the algorithms (Dunkel & Soparkar, 1999). One analogy is a photographer who first measures light levels in a scene, before moving the subject and the background in order to achieve a perfect composition. Ultimately, once the photographer has done his work, anyone can press the camera button to take the picture.

Mining anomalous rules requires a deep understanding of the data to be analyzed. Scrambled data must be organized or separated if possible. For example, in a dataset that records medical surgeries, we found that textual diagnostics and related surgery notes were recorded in a single relational data entry field. Textual diagnostics first had to be homogenized because the entries "Radical Treatment with Dissection" and "RT with Dissection" have the same meaning at a semantic level but are not understood this way by a computer algorithm.

Anomalous rules must be defined in the context of the type of categorical data that are being analyzed. To work with numerical data, a discretization method is needed. However, the results of discretization must be carefully monitored. The following subsection provides examples of various suitable discretization methods.

Discretization

All the discretization methods proposed in the literature necessarily feature a certain bias. This bias must be interpreted in order to better understand the dataset. In Figures 1 and 2, we present the "age" attribute of a dataset referenced as "Adult" (Asuncion & Newman, 2007), discretized using two methods; the equal-width method and the equal-frequency method. Both of these unsupervised methods were applied in order to generate five sorting bins.

The equal-width discretization method first finds the extreme values of the numerical attribute, and it then separates the resulting range into the user-specified number of bins. Each value is

Figure 1. Histogram and discretization results using five bins to sort the "age" attribute of the dataset known as "Adult."

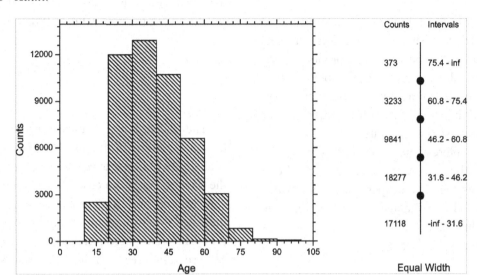

subsequently assigned to the appropriate bin. In the case of the equal-width method, anomalous rules will identify the exact same intervals because data distribution is preserved. To better preserve the distribution of the original data, the number of bins must be increased. In Figure 1, the histogram shows that the "Adult" dataset contains few people aged over 75. The equal-width algorithm illustrates that the data distribution is preserved, with the last two intervals (60.8 - 75.4, 75.4 - infinite) containing only 3233 and 373 elements respectively, consistent with the histogram.

The equal-frequency method first determines the extreme values, then sorts the values and attempts to assign the same number of elements to each one of the user-specified number of bins. The equal-frequency method from figure 2 illustrates

the adjustment of the data intervals. The anomalous rules obtained from this (discretized) attribute do not correspond to the original data distribution. Increasing the number of bins will reduce the number of elements in each bin, thereby destroying the original data distribution. Consequently, the way in which an anomalous rule is interpreted must take into account which methods are applied to pre-process the datasets.

Interest Measures

The interest measures (IM) metric helps provide evidence of statistical independence within rules. It can also help to identify spurious rules (Webb & Zhang, 2002). Interest measures operate in two main directions, pruning or ranking the resulting

Figure 2. The "age" attribute of the Adult dataset, discretized using the equal-frequency method with five bins.

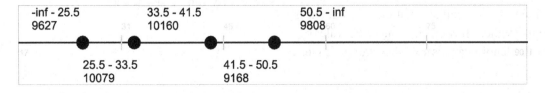

rules according to the following definitions:

- In the case of pruning, if a threshold is defined consistent with the interest metric, then the ruleset can be pruned immediately, thereby reducing the total number of rules. It is important to note that the selected threshold is a control parameter, not a critical statistical value.
- If the interest metric is used to rank the rules, the rules identified as the "best" can be presented to an expert for further evaluation. The advantage of this approach is that the expert is able to access all the rules at once if required.

An interest metric allows quantitative evaluation, but its interpretability may not be straightforward in all cases (Lallich, Teytaud, & Prudhomme, 2007). Research by Geng and Hamilton (2006), and by Tan et al. (2004), illustrates more than ten interest metrics and concludes that a metric that is appropriate for one dataset may not be meaningful for all possible real-life datasets. Therefore, the adoption of appropriate interest metrics can increase the effectiveness of discovering hidden patterns.

In the following definitions, we present an adaption of the *Lift* and *Jaccard* interest metrics to the anomalous rules scenario. Lift is used to evaluate rule reliability because it indicates the presence of a very frequently occurring k-itemset, in the consequent of a rule.

$$lift(B \xrightarrow{anom} A \:/\: C) = \frac{sprt(AB\neg C)}{sprt(B\neg C) \times sprt(A)}$$

Lift represents the ratio between rule confidence and the probability that the consequent is present. Higher lift values indicate better rules because the denominator is low when the consequent

probability is low. In the case of a consequent with high probability, the denominator will be greater, in which case the Lift value will be low.

$$Jaccard(B \xrightarrow{anom} A \:/\: C) = \frac{sprt(AB\neg C)}{sprt(B\neg C) + sprt(A) - sprt(AB\neg C)}$$

The Jaccard measure represents the ratio between pattern probability (support) and the probability of occurrence for all the items across the dataset. As in the case of Lift, a higher Jaccard value is preferred, and a low Jaccard value indicates a very frequently occurring consequent. A key difference between these metrics is that the Jaccard value treats all the items that occur in a certain pattern.

A Posteriori Pruning of the Anomalous Ruleset

Once the set of anomalous rules has been derived, it is convenient to reduce the results to the most general possible set of rules. Thereafter, an expert can analyze a succinct and generalized version of the discovered associations. Accordingly, we define the following filter that can be used to generate the most general anomalous rules. It requires pruning each anomalous rule that is an expansion of the rule antecedent. Let an anomalous rule be defined by

$$X \xrightarrow{anom} A \:/\: C$$

Then, prune each anomalous rule as follows:

$$XH \xrightarrow{anom} A \:/\: C$$

The monotonicity of the antecedent contraction property can be defined as:

Figure 3.

```
main {
        store.Initiatilize(MinSupp,absMinSupp,MinDom)
        itemsets = store.Supported(1)
        k = 2
        while(k ≤ columns && itemsets ≥ k){
                itemsets = store.Supported(k)
                store.Extensions(k)
                if(itemsets < 0)
                        stop
                k++
        }
        store.LastExtensions()
        AssociationRulesGenerator(store,MinConf)
        save.AnomalousRuleGenerator(store,MinConf)
}
```

$$XQ \xrightarrow{anom} A \ / \ C \text{ not implies}$$
$$X \xrightarrow{anom} A \ / \ C$$

The above expression indicates the existence of anomalous rules with antecedent expansions, but not all the anomalous rules whose antecedent itemset contains two or more items can be pruned. The pruned anomalous rules can then be distinguished if we wish to review the specialized rules.

The Extraction Algorithm for Anomalous Rules

In this section, we present a new algorithm called the In-Memory Anomalous Association Miner (IMAAM). This algorithm uses a traditional (Agrawal et al., 1993) two-step decomposition to generate associations. The first stage generates k-itemset support while the second stage generates the association rules and anomalous rules. To obtain k-itemset support and the necessary extension support, the IMAAM algorithm retains the k-itemsets whose support values are above the absMinSupp. The following pseudo-code presents the IMAAM main algorithm: (See Figure 3)

The *Initialize* procedure generates support values for the 1-itemsets and at the same time prunes the results. The relevant 1-itemsets are stored, and those that are above the *absMinSupp* threshold are stored as well, since they are anomalous candidate items. Then, the algorithm verifies that the number of columns (known as "attributes" in relational terminology) is less than the desired itemset length (k) and that the itemsets required to generate the next itemset level are available.

In Table 1, we present an artificial dataset that was used to illustrate the extraction process for anomalous rules. The *L1* level references the *Initialize* method call, while the *Pruned* level contains items that were discarded. The values of the thresholds that we used are: *MinConf=65%, MinSupp=30%, absMinSupp=20% and MinDom=3.*

This algorithm iteratively constructs a tree of itemsets in computer memory, in which each branch represents an itemset. The *Supported(k)* procedure adds items to the itemset of the lowest tree level, consistent with TBAR (Berzal, Cubero, Marin, & Serrano, 2001). For each item at the low-

Table 1. Simulated data to illustrate the anomalous rules and the IMAAM algorithm. On the right hand side, each itemset is shown alongside its frequency

Raw data					Itemsets		
					Relevant	Extensions	Pruned
A	B	C1	D1				
A	B	C2	D2	L1	A=6, B=8, C=8, D=6		A1, A2, A3, A4,
A	B	C	D				B1, B2, C1, C2,
A	B	C	D				D1, D2, D3, D4
A	B1	C	D	L2	AB=4, AC=4, AD=4,		
A	B2	C	D		BC=6, BD=4,		
A2	B	C	D		CD=6		
A1	B	C	D	L3	BCD=4	ABC=2,	
A3	B	C	D3			ABD=2	
A4	B	C	D4	L4		ABCD=2	

est tree level, the algorithm copies the items on the rightmost side, under the working item. Obtaining itemset support occurs immediately as a result of logical operations because the item locations (transaction identifiers) are stored in memory as sets of bits. The following pseudo-code presents the remaining algorithm: (See Figure 4)

In Table 1, levels *L2* and *L3* contain the results of the *Supported(k)* method call. The 3-itemsets ABC, ABD, ACD and BCD are organized, following evaluation with the support metric. The itemsets ABC and ABD are stored in the tree as shown in Figure 5 with a dashed rectangle; these itemsets are candidates for being classed as anomalies.

Within the *LastExtensions* procedure, the *IMAAM* algorithm generates support values for the remaining extensions. This step is necessary for the following reason: the k-itemsets must be associated with extensions in order to identify anomalous rules. Without this procedure, the itemset tree is incomplete. As is shown in Figure 5, if the itemset ABC is non-relevant, then the itemset ABCD does not exist. However, in the event that the itemset BCD were relevant, then a candidate anomaly would be the "A" item. Therefore, the ABCD support value must be generated. On the other hand, if the BCD 3-itemset were non-relevant, there would be no need to obtain

the support value for ABCD. Therefore this final evaluation is performed simply to complete the itemset tree at the desired extension level. A hash-encoded table helps to identify the k-itemsets in the tree; consequently, no k-itemset support ever gets generated twice.

The *association rule generation* process commences operation on the 2-itemset while the remaining k-itemsets are still available. In each iteration, the powerset of a k-itemset is obtained, and then the association rule is evaluated using each element of the powerset as the antecedent and the difference between this element and the k-itemset as the consequent. The support value for the antecedent is obtained by localizing the k-itemset through the encoded table of the itemset tree. Finally, the association rules are finalized if the related confidence value is greater than or equal to the *MinConf* threshold.

According to the *anomalous rule generator* procedure, the algorithm first begins to search for anomalous rules within each association rule. To evaluate the confidence associated with each of the anomalous rules, the algorithm finds each extension of the k-itemset of the association rule (antecedent and consequent) and the extension of the k-itemset of the antecedent of the association rule. For example, in Figure 5 the association

Figure 4.

```
store.LastExtensions(){
        for each leaf in tree do{
                anomalousCandidates = simDiff (leafItemset,1-itemsets)
                for each anomalousCandidate
                        store.anomalousCandidates = leafItemset + 1-itemset
        }
        store.getCandidatesSprt()
}

AssociationRulesGenerator (store,MinConf){
K = 2
while (store.Supported(k).hasNext()){
        X = itemsets.next()
        for each Iᵢ Є powerset(X)
        if (sprt(X) ≥ MinConf * sprt(Iᵢ)
                store.associations Iᵢ → (X-Iᵢ), confidence = sprt(X)/sprt(Iᵢ)
        } k++
}
AnomalousRulesGenerator (store, MinConf){
while (store.associations.hasNext()){
        rule = store.getNextRule()
        for each A = (k+n)-itemset – k-itemset of the rule.kitemset {
        if (conf(A|B¬C) ≥ MinConf &&
                conf(¬A|BC) ≥ MinConf)
                return rule.antecedent → A / rule.consequent
        }
}
```

rule $B \Rightarrow C$ has a confidence rating of 6/8, the k value is two, and the n value is one. Therefore the k-itemsets ABC and BCD are localized through the itemset tree. Subsequently, the candidates for being anomalies are obtained from ABC - BC = A, and BCD - BC = D. Finally, to calculate the

Figure 5. Itemset tree generated by the IMAAM algorithm, using the simulated data from Table 1.

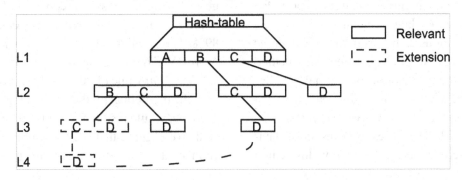

Table 2. Six datasets used in the experiments and their relevant characteristics in terms of number of attributes, number of data rows and number of distinct items.

Dataset	Dimensions	Items	Dataset	Dimensions	Items
post-operative	9x90	27	adult	15x48842	134
wb-cancer	10x699	50	cornHV1	7x80	35
german-credit	21x1000	85	cancer-sugeries	13x2992	434

confidence associated with these anomalous rules, the k-itemsets AB and BD are used, consistent with the definitions shown in the previous subsection titled *Calculation of support and confidence*. In our example, we generate the anomalous rule B $\Rightarrow$ A/C with a confidence level of 2/2, and the reference rule BC $\Rightarrow$ ¬A with confidence 4/6.

RESULTS AND DISCUSSION

The experiments were performed using a Pentium 4 PC equipped with 2GB of RAM and running the Scientific Linux v5.1 operating system. The algorithm was implemented in the Java programming language.

Table 2 summarizes four benchmark datasets from the machine learning repository of the University of California, Irvine (UCI) (Asuncion & Newman, 2007). The "post-operative" and "wb-cancer" (Wisconsin breast cancer) datasets are from the medical domain, while the "german-credit" and adult datasets are financial data from individuals. The "cornHV1" dataset comes from scientific agricultural studies in Mexico and was provided by Manuel Aguirre Bortoni, Ph.D. The (human) "cancer-surgeries" dataset was provided by a hospital in Andalusia, Spain.

The continuous values from the UCI datasets were discretized using the equal-frequency method to illustrate the behavior of the anomalous rules without the bias imposed by the distribution of such continuous values. Five bins were specified.

The "cornHV1" and "cancer-surgeries" datasets were discretized using the equal-width method to generate anomalous rules that were consistent with the original data distribution. The specified number of bins was five in this case as well. The "cornHV1" dataset contains information about corn plant characteristics: length, plant size, diameter and weight. This dataset contains information about five geographic locations in which a corn variety was planted. The "cancer-surgeries" dataset contains patient records regarding cancer diagnostics and surgery. Other relevant variables are also recorded, namely, if blood transfusions were necessary during the surgery, the number of the operating room, and whether the patient has an artificial organ.

The results illustrated in this section were generated with the following thresholds: *MinConf = 75% and 90%, MinSupp = 10%, MinDom = 4 and absMinSupp=3*. The pattern length was set to 4-itemset, and the results are ordered by the number of items in the antecedent of each rule.

Figure 6 illustrates a quantitative comparison between association rules and anomalous rules. The anomalous ruleset is smaller than the association ruleset, and, therefore, it is clear that only a small subset of the association ruleset generates anomalous rules. In the case of the "cancer-surgeries" dataset, we saw a reduction of 79%, and in the case of "german-credit," the reduction was 89%. The smaller datasets "post-operative" and "cornHV1" did not generate any anomalous rules at a *MinConf* value of 90%, and this is consistent with the theoretical prediction that high values of *MinConf* would result in fewer rules being generated. We observe that the anomalous rules were connected with certain non-relevant k-itemsets.

Figure 6. Association rules (left side) and anomalous rules (right side) from six datasets, with minimum confidence thresholds of 75% and 90%, and minimum support thresholds of 10%.

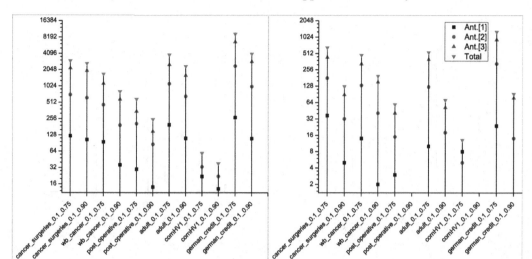

Consequently, it is clear that the anomalous ruleset does contain rules that are connected to items that the association rules do not reveal.

Through this section, we focused on discussing the quantitative aspects of the rules as compared with the ARs. Because AARs, sporadic rules, peculiar rules, and ERs utilize different semantics and different proposed methods, we do not compare them explicitly. As previously mentioned in the background section, all of these proposals are able to detect rare patterns. However, the main differences are as follows: the AARs are generated considering the ARs, and the AARs identify anomalies that in some cases can be infrequent.

The results of using the *Lift* metric are illustrated in Figure 7. First, the association rules were pruned using the Lift metric. Second, the anomalous rules that had been generated from the unpruned association rules were then pruned with the Lift metric. The pruned association rules approximated the unpruned anomalous rules, but when compared with the pruned anomalous rules, the reduction percentages were substantial. In the case of the "cancer-surgeries" dataset, the value was about 93%, while in the case of "german-credit," the value was about 98%.

The control parameter used for the Lift metric requires that 1/4 of the consequent support values connected with each rule must support the rule. Anomalous rules with very frequent consequents are pruned, so that the obtained patterns may be better supported. This result provides evidence for the effectiveness of the Lift metric to control the significance of the rules. This is because very frequent consequents get pruned, and as a result the anomalous ruleset is compact.

Very frequently occurring consequents connected with k-itemsets are undesirable because those very frequent k-itemsets can be present in many rules, leading to many k-itemsets having to be linked with the same consequent k-itemset. This causes confusion, diminishes total rule significance and leads to unnecessary complexity in the associative model. Consider the following anomalous rule: IF treatment X THEN outcome A / Where Not Outcome B. If A is a very frequently occurring consequent, this means that A is not a relevant anomaly, but a member of a group of anomalous rules that shares this anomaly, perhaps one that is also associated with other treatments.

When we generate anomalous rules from the

Figure 7. Association rules (left side) and anomalous rules (right side), both of which are pruned using the Lift metric.

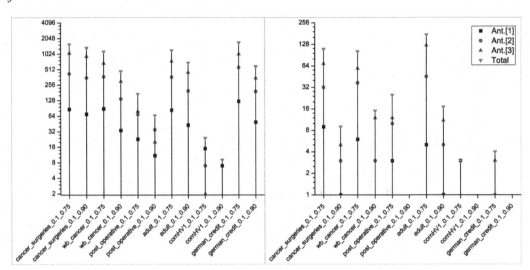

set of association rules that have been pruned with Lift, we observe that the resulting patterns are more diverse. This can be empirically explained by the increased reliability and robustness of the association rules.

Table 3 shows the total number of rules obtained using the Lift metric and the a posteriori filter. The A.Rs column represents the unpruned association rules, the A.Rs Lift column represents the pruned association rules, the Anom. Rs Lift represents the pruned anomalous rules generated from the pruned association rules, and the Anom. Rs CS represents the anomalous rules created from a posteriori filtering of the pruned anomalous rules. These results show that the anomalous rules optionally require the a posteriori filter, presented in the last column, to provide the most general AARs, and that, after filtering, all the rules are pruned if they are of the form:

$$BH \xrightarrow{\ anom\ } A \ / \ C$$

We observe that the selected metrics and filters are effective in controlling the number of anomalous rules and in generating a significant ruleset. The anomalous rules generated by these datasets

can be readily processed by humans.

To work with the anomalous rules, we developed an application that organizes the AARs into a tree, in which each node carries the consequents of the anomalous rule. Figure 8 shows a screenshot of this application: each node is numbered and shows the anomalous consequent adjacent to the association rule consequent. Each node also contains a count of the rules that share these consequents. The antecedents of the AARs are listed inside each corresponding node.

The following anomalous rules from the "corn-HV1" dataset provide an example of the kind of knowledge that anomalous rules can provide, and what items are involved.

land location = native-corn THEN cob height = 64.08–96.05 / plant-height = 2.26–inf

The interpretation of this anomalous rule can be understood as stating that the geographic location where native corn is planted is associated with a plant height within the interval 2.26-infinite, but if the plant height is not in this interval, then cob height within the range 64.08-96.05 is associated (anomalously) with native corn. This is the first

Table 3. Rule sets pruned with the following filters: Lift on association rules, Lift on anomalous rules and the "a-posteriori" pruning criteria on anomalous rules. Threshold values: MinConf = 75% and 90%, MinSupp = 10%, MinDom = 4, absMinSupp = 3.

Dataset	A.Rs	A.Rs Lift	Anom. Rs Lift	Anom. *Rs CS*
ca_surgeries_0.1_0.75	3014	1571	94	19
ca_surgeries_0.1_0.90	2673	1343	8	2
wb_cancer_0.1_0.75	1693	1140	91	20
wb_cancer_0.1_0.90	810	473	15	8
post_operative_0.1_0.75	588	170	24	3
post_operative_0.1_0.90	250	66	0	0
adult_0.1_0.75	3893	1197	128	6
adult_0.1_0.90	2378	691	17	3
cornHV1_0.1_0.75	59	24	3	3
cornHV1_0.1_0.90	38	9	0	0
german_credit_0.1_0.75	9393	1714	3	1
german_credit_0.1_0.90	4026	588	0	0

anomalous rule, consistent with the Jaccard metric. The relevance of this statement is that the item *cob height* has a support of 3/80, which falls beneath the *MinSupp* threshold, but what is more interesting is that this anomalous rule has support equal to three. Therefore, the anomalous rule reveals a hidden pattern with high confidence that states, within this data, that all cobs with height between 64.08 and 96.05 were of the native corn type and

were planted in a specific geographic location.

From the "cancer-surgeries" dataset, we can identify the following anomalous rule;

blood:n, sex:2 THEN diagnostic: v. cancer / anesthesia:2

The interpretation of this anomalous rule is as follows: commonly, surgeries involving women

Figure 8. Presentation of anomalous rules organized as a tree. The anomalous rules are loaded through Java object serialization methods, and the windowing application was also developed in Java.

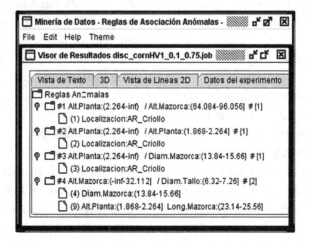

and that do not require a blood transfusion are treated with anesthesia type two; however, in cases where another type of anesthesia was used, the diagnosis was of the rare disease of v. cancer. What is interesting here is that some patients were treated for v. cancer without a blood transfusion, and these patients represent three out of nine cases. An association rule that can involve this type of cancer is impossible because this type of cancer represents just nine cases of 2,992 instances. Accordingly, the derived AAR provides insights about this rare disease, and it is able to detect patterns involving itemsets with low support.

FUTURE TRENDS

The detection of rare and hidden patterns certainly can increase our insight about a chosen data set. Therefore, research and rarities in decision support systems is an interesting field. Other emerging trends include distributed anomalous pattern research and the development of suitable measures of rarity. Future work on the discovery of hidden patterns may involve the adoption of specific interest metrics, experimentation with large-scale databases, and applications to real-world problems.

As outlined in the following subsections, we present the research directions in a general sense, but at the same time, we hope to ensure that future research will increase our understanding of the relationships within stored data.

Suitable Measures of Rarity

Although some interest measures can be applied to the rare association rule mining problem, suitable measures of rarity can enhance the research. If they are model independent, they can accelerate the development of the rarities detection technology. For example, by definition a rare event in recorded data is infrequent and is therefore potentially associated with any frequent pattern.

Consider as well that a pattern is rare within its neighborhood context and that such a pattern must be incorporated within other systems. Therefore, some research must be pursued in order to provide the right set of rare metrics.

Distributed Anomalous Pattern Mining

In the today's world of inter-communications and emerging interactions on the Internet, the distributed processing and searching for patterns are a natural way to research for rarities. For example, in the hypothetical case of an Internet social-network of foreign students who take aviation courses, everything on this social-network often seems common (e.g., no method is employed to track if you like to fly often or if some people have a tendency towards pursuing disastrous objectives). A distributed approach is needed in order to consider a wider context and then to be able to determine what is rare and to what degree.

Decision Support Systems (DSS)

This trend aims towards the development of production-ready applications for rare association rule mining and the integration of the discovery of rarities in data within systems and robots.

For example, consider an automated system (e.g., a robot) in charge of a hothouse. In the case of a shortage of water, the rare chemical compound A with a specified amount of water can help the plants. Such a robot must be able to discover rare patterns and take advantage of the mined knowledge to accomplish his goals.

CONCLUSION

This chapter has focused on anomalous association rules, a kind of hidden pattern that has high confidence but which may have a low associated support value and may involve non-relevant itemsets. These new rules use the minimum thresholds specified for data mining of association rules. The semantic interpretation is straightforward, and as with association rules, the anomalous rules are written in an IF-THEN format.

We presented the IMAAM algorithm, which is suitable for generating anomalous rules, and we suggested several methods to modify association rule algorithms. In the context of the anomalous rule definition, we provided two adapted interest measures, and we suggested certain filtering criteria to prune the generated anomalous ruleset. Finally, through experiments using benchmark test data, we demonstrated the effectiveness of the interest metrics. Through experiments using private real-world data, we showcased the discovery of potentially interesting hidden patterns.

ACKNOWLEDGMENT

To the University Hospital of Andalusia and Prof. Manuel Aguirre Bortoni for sharing data on cancer patients and on corn-related agriculture, respectively. Marco-Antonio Balderas was supported by the Mexican SEP-PROMEP under grant 103.5/04/2112.

REFERENCES

Agrawal, R., Imielinski, T., & Swami, A. (1993). Mining association rules between sets of items in large databases. *SIGMOD Record, 22*(2), 207–216. doi:10.1145/170036.170072

Asuncion, A., & Newman, D. J. (2007). *UCI Machine Learning Repository.* Retrieved March 2008, from http://www.ics.uci.edu/~mlearn/mlrepository.html

Balderas, M.-A., Cubero, J.-C., Berzal, F., Marin, N., & Einsman, E. (2005). *Discovering Hidden Association Rules.* Paper presented at the SIGKDD Knowledge Discovery and Data Mining, Workshop for Anomaly Detection, Chicago, USA.

Berzal, F., Cubero, J.-C., Marin, J., & Serrano, J. (2001). An efficient method for association rule mining in relational databases. *Data & Knowledge Engineering,* (37): 47–84. doi:10.1016/S0169-023X(00)00055-0

Berzal, F., Cubero, J.-C., Marín, N., & Gámez, M. (2004a). *Anomalous Association Rules.* Paper presented at the Workshop on Alternative Techniques for Data Mining and Knowledge Discovery in the IEEE International Conference on Data Mining. From http://elvex.ugr.es/icdm2004/program.html

Berzal, F., Cubero, J.-C., Marín, N., & Gámez, M. (2004b). Finding anomalies in databases. In R. Giráldez, J. Riquelme & J. Aguilar-Ruiz (Eds.), *Tendencias de la Minería de Datos en España* (p. 14), Seville, Spain: Red Española de Minería de Datos y Aprendizaje.

Cornelis, C., Yan, P., Zhang, X., & Chen, G. (2006). *Mining Positive and Negative Association Rules from Large Databases.* Paper presented at the 2006 IEEE Conference on Cybernetics and Intelligent Systems.

Dasu, T., & Johnson, T. (2003). *Exploratory Data Mining and Data Cleaning.* Hoboken, New Jersey: Wiley-Interscience.

Denning, D. E. (1987). An Intrusion-Detection Model. *IEEE Transactions on Software Engineering, 13*(2), 10.

Dunkel, B., & Soparkar, N. (1999). *Data organization and access for efficient data mining.* Paper presented at the 15th International conference on data engineering.

Geng, L., & Hamilton, H. J. (2006). Interestingness measures for data mining: A survey. [CSUR]. *ACM Computing Surveys, 38*(3). doi:10.1145/1132960.1132963

Koh, Y. S., Rountree, N., & O'Keefe, R. A. (2008). Mining interesting imperfectly sporadic rules. *Knowledge and Information Systems, 14*(2), 17. doi:10.1007/s10115-007-0074-6

Lallich, S., Teytaud, O., & Prudhomme, E. (2007). Association rule Interestingness: Measure and statistical validation. In F. Guillet & J. H. Howard (Eds.), *Quality Measures in Data Mining* (pp. 251-275): Springer.

Morzy, M. (2006). *Efficient Mining of Dissociation Rules.* Paper presented at the 8th Conference on Data Warehousing and Knowledge Discovery, Krakow, Poland.

Ohshima, M., Zhong, N., Yao, Y. Y. Y., & Liu, C. (2007). Relational peculiarity-oriented mining. *Data Mining and Knowledge Discovery, 15*(2), 249–273. doi:10.1007/s10618-006-0046-6

Ohshima, M., Zhong, N., Yao, Y. Y. Y., & Murata, S. (2004). Peculiarity Oriented Analysis in Multipeople Tracking Images *Advances in Knowledge Discovery and Data Mining* (pp. 508-518). Springer.

Song, X., Wu, M., Jermaine, C., & Ranka, S. (2007). Conditional Anomaly Detection. *IEEE Transactions on Knowledge and Data Engineering, 19*(5), 631–645. doi:10.1109/TKDE.2007.1009

Suzuki, E. (2002). Undirected Discovery of Interesting Exception Rules. *International Journal of Pattern Recognition and Artificial Intelligence, 16*(8), 1065–1086. doi:10.1142/S0218001402002155

Suzuki, E., Watanabe, T., Yokoi, H., & Takabayashi, K. (2003). *Detecting Interesting Exceptions from Medical Test Data with Visual Summarization.* Paper presented at the Proceedings of the Third IEEE International Conference on Data Mining.

Suzuki, E., & Zytkow, J. M. (2005). Unified algorithm for undirected discovery of exception rules. *International Journal of Intelligent Systems, 20*(6), 673–691. doi:10.1002/int.20090

Tan, P.-N., Kumar, V., & Srivastava, J. (2004). Selecting the Right Objective Measure for Association Analysis. *Information Systems,* (29): 293–313. doi:10.1016/S0306-4379(03)00072-3

Thuraisingham, B. (2004). Data Mining for Counter-terrorism. In H. Kargupta, A. Joshi, K. Sivakumar & Y. Yesha (Eds.), *In Data Mining: Next Generation Challenges and Future Directions* (pp. 157-). MIT Press.

Webb, G., & Zhang, S. (2002). *Removing Trivial Associations in Association Rule Discovery.* Paper presented at the First International NAISO Congress on Autonomous Intelligent Systems.

Wu, X., Zhang, C., & Zhang, S. (2004). Efficient mining of both positive and negative association rules. *ACM Transactions on Information Systems, 22*(3), 381–405. doi:10.1145/1010614.1010616

Yun, H., Ha, D., Hwang, B., & Ryu, K. H. (2003). Mining association rules on significant rare data using relative support. *Journal of Systems and Software, 67*(3), 181–191. doi:10.1016/S0164-1212(02)00128-0

Zhong, N., Liu, C., Yao, Y. Y. Y., Ohshima, M., Huang, M., & Huang, J. (2004). *Relational peculiarity oriented data mining.* Paper presented at the Fourth IEEE International Conference on Data Mining.

Zhong, N., Yao, Y. Y. Y., & Ohshima, M. (2003). Peculiarity Oriented Multidatabase Mining. *IEEE Transactions on Knowledge and Data Engineering, 15*(4), 952–960. doi:10.1109/TKDE.2003.1209011

Chapter 12
Strong Symmetric Association Rules and Interestingness Measures

Agathe Merceron
University of Applied Sciences TFH Berlin, Germany

ABSTRACT

Strong symmetric association rules are defined as follows. Strong means that the association rule has a strong support and a strong confidence, well above the minimum thresholds. Symmetric means that X→Y and Y→X are both association rules. Common objective interestingness measures such as lift, correlation, conviction or Chi-square tend to rate this kind of rule poorly. By contrast, cosine is high for such rules. However, depending on the application domain, these rules may be interesting regarding criteria such as unexpectedness or actionability. In this chapter, the authors investigate why the above-mentioned measures, except cosine, rate strong symmetric association rules poorly, and show that the underlying data might take a quite special shape. This kind of rule can be qualified as rare, as they would be pruned by many objective interestingness measures. Then the authors present lift and cosine in depth, giving their intuitive meaning, their definition and typical values. Because lift has its roots in probability and cosine in geometry, these two interestingness measures give different information on the rules they rate. Furthermore they are fairly easy to interpret by domain experts, who are not necessarily data mining experts. They round off our investigation with a discussion on contrast rules and show that strong symmetric association rules give a hint to mine further rare rules, rare in the sense of a low support but a high confidence. Finally they present case studies from the field of education and discuss challenges.

INTRODUCTION

Association rules are very useful and used in Educational Data Mining, which is a particular ap-plication domain: data used to extract association rules come from learning systems. Examples in this application domain include Merceron & Yacef (2004) in which association rules are used to find mistakes often made together while students solve

DOI: 10.4018/978-1-60566-754-6.ch012

exercises in propositional logic. Wang (2006) and Wang & Shao (2004) used association rules, combined with other methods, to personalize students' recommendation while browsing the web. Minaei-Bidgoli et al. (2003) used them to find various associations of student's behavior in their Web-based educational system LON-CAPA. Lu (2004) used fuzzy rules in a personalized e-learning material recommender system to discover associations between students' requirements and learning materials. Romero et al. (2002) combined them with genetic programming to discover relations between knowledge levels, times and scores that help teachers modify the course's original structure and content. A more extensive overview is given in Romero & Ventura (2007).

We extracted association rules from the data stored by the Logic-ITA, an intelligent tutoring system for formal proof in propositional logic Merceron & Yacef (2003). Our aim was to know whether there were mistakes that often occurred together while students are training. This information could be used to act on the course or on the tutoring system itself. The results gave strong symmetric associations between three mistakes. Strong means that all associations had a strong support and a strong confidence. Symmetric means that $X{\rightarrow}Y$ and $Y{\rightarrow}X$ were both extracted association rules.

It is well known that even rules with a strong support and confidence may in fact be uninteresting (Han & Kamber, 2006). This is why, once the association rule $X{\rightarrow}Y$ has been extracted, it is wise to double-check how much X and Y are related. About 20 objective measures have been proposed in the literature to do so. We explore in this paper a few measures in the context of our data. We have observed that common objective interestingness measures such as lift, correlation, conviction or Chi-square tend to rate our strong symmetric association rules poorly. By contrast, cosine is high. However, the extracted rules are actionable in the sense that the information they give can be used to act on the course and on the

tutoring system. Thus this kind of rule can be qualified as rare as they are actionable but would be pruned by a number of objective interestingness measures.

In this chapter, we investigate various interestingness measures for the strong symmetric association rules we have obtained and show that the underlying data have a quite special shape. Further, we look for restricting the number of interestingness measures a teacher, who is not necessarily a data mining expert, has to consider while picking out meaningful rules from all the extracted rules. Therefore we focus on two measures, lift and cosine, and investigate them in more depth. The reason to focus on these two measures is twofold. First, because lift has its roots in probability and cosine in geometry, these two interestingness measures give different information on the rules they rate. Second, they are fairly easy to interpret by domain experts, who are not necessarily data mining experts. We round off our investigation of strong symmetric association rules with a section on contrast rules. We investigate whether strong symmetric association rules can give a hint to mine other rare association rules, rare having the more classical meaning of rules with a low support but a strong confidence. This is indeed the case, however lift and cosine rate these rare rules poorly. Finally we present case studies that use cosine and lift to prune the extracted association rules, the case study of the Logic-ITA already mentioned and a case study with the Learning Management System Moodle. This chapter merges and deepens results presented in Merceron & Yacef (2007) and Merceron & Yacef (2008).

BACKGROUND

As has been said above, it is well known that, once association rules have been extracted, a prune step is necessary. This step involves using further interestingness measures to double check how much X and Y are related. Unfortunately, no objective measure is better than all the others in all situations, though measures tend to agree when support is high (Tan et al., 2002). Therefore it is not easy to select the right interestingness measure to prune association rules and, as a consequence, it is important to keep the application domain in mind.

Educational data mining differs from knowledge discovery in other domains in several ways. In some domains it is possible to try several sets of measures or parameters and experiment for what works best. Such an experimentation phase is difficult in the educational field because the data is very dynamic, can vary a lot between samples and teachers just cannot afford the time and access to the expertise to do these tests on each sample, especially in real time. Therefore, as argued in Beck (2007), one should care about the intuition of the measures, parameters or methods used in educational data mining. Another difference between educational data mining and other application domains is the size of the data: while tremendous amounts of data are collected about students' work, the size of the data on one sample is usually small (Garcia et al., 2007). Therefore one has to question whether the chosen measures, parameters and methods are compatible with the sample size. Further, in educational data mining it is intended that teachers will do the mining. Teachers are not necessarily data mining experts. Therefore one has to offer them means to interpret easily the results they get and turn them into information.

STRONG SYMMETRIC ASSOCIATION RULES AND MEASURING INTERESTINGNESS

Strong Symmetric Association Rules

Association rules come from basket analysis (Agrawal & Srikant, 1994) and capture information such as if customers buy beer, they also buy diapers, written as beer→diapers. Two measures are used to extract association rules: support and confidence. We introduce these concepts now. We refer to Han & Kamber (2006) for algorithms to extract rules using these two measures.

Let $I = \{I_1, I_2, ...,I_m\}$ be a set of m items and $T = \{t_1, t_2, ...,t_n\}$ be a set of n transactions, with each t_i being a subset of I. An *association rule* is a rule of the form $X \rightarrow Y$, where X and Y are disjoint subsets of I having a support and a confidence above a minimum threshold. X and Y are also called itemsets.

Let us denote by $|X|$ the number of transactions that contain X, by $|Y|$ the number of transactions that contain Y and by $|X, Y|$ the number of transactions that contain both X and Y.

Support: $sup(X \rightarrow Y) = |X, Y|/n$. In other words, the support of a rule $X \rightarrow Y$ is the proportion of transactions that contain both X and Y. This is also called $P(X, Y)$, the probability that a transaction contains both X and Y. Note that support is symmetric: $sup(X \rightarrow Y) = sup(Y \rightarrow X)$.

Confidence: $conf(X \rightarrow Y) = |X, Y|/|X|$. In other words, the confidence of a rule $X \rightarrow Y$ is the proportion of transactions that contain both X and Y among those that contain X. An equivalent definition is: $conf(X \rightarrow Y) = P(X, Y) / P(X)$, with $P(X) = |X|/n$, or equivalently, $P(X | Y)$, the probability that a transaction contains Y knowing that it contains X already. Usually $conf(X \rightarrow Y)$ is different from $conf(Y \rightarrow X)$ and gives its direction to a rule.

Support makes sure that only items occurring often enough in the data will be taken into account to establish the association rules. Confidence is the proportion of transactions containing both X and Y among all transactions containing X. If X occurs a lot naturally, then almost any subset Y could be associated with it. In that case $P(X)$ will be high and, as a consequence, $conf(X \rightarrow Y)$ will be lower.

Symmetric association rules: We call a rule $X \rightarrow Y$ a symmetric association rule if $sup(X \rightarrow Y)$ is above a given minimum threshold and both $conf(X \rightarrow Y)$ and $conf(Y \rightarrow X)$ are above a given minimum threshold.

Strong symmetric association rules are rules such that all three values: $sup(X{\rightarrow}Y)$, $conf(X{\rightarrow}Y)$ and $conf(Y{\rightarrow}X)$ are strong. This is the kind of association rules we obtained with the educational system Logic-ITA, see case study 1 below.

Once rules are extracted, the next step consists in picking out meaningful rules and discarding others. To see that this prune step is necessary, consider a set of 5000 transactions and three different probabilities for X, Y and X,Y:

1. $|X, Y| = 1000$, $|X| = 1000$ and $|Y| = 2500$. We obtain $sup(X{\rightarrow}Y) = 20\%$ and $conf(X{\rightarrow}Y) = 100\%$.
2. $|X, Y| = 1000$, $|X| = 1000$ and $|Y| = 5000$. We obtain $sup(X{\rightarrow}Y) = 20\%$ and $conf(X{\rightarrow}Y) = 100\%$.
3. $|X, Y| = 4800$, $|X| = 4800$ and $|Y| = 5000$. We obtain $sup(X{\rightarrow}Y) = 96\%$ and $conf(X{\rightarrow}Y) = 100\%$.

One notices that support and confidence give exactly the same results in the first two cases, though probability of Y changes dramatically. Support and confidence do not allow distinguishing between these two cases. This shows that support and confidence alone do not capture how well X and Y are related. In the third case $conf(Y{\rightarrow}X) = 96\%$, $X{\rightarrow}Y$ is a strong symmetric rule.

Some Interestingness Measures

Several measures, besides confidence, have been proposed to better measure how well X and Y are related (Aggarwal & Yu, 1998; Tan et al., 2002; Brijs et al., 2003; Omiecinski, 2003). We explore here a few measures in the context of our data, namely lift, correlation, conviction, Chi-square testing and cosine.

$Lift(X{\rightarrow}Y) = conf(X \rightarrow Y) / P(Y)$. An equivalent definition is: $P(X, Y) / P(X)P(Y)$. Lift is a symmetric measure. A lift well above 1 indicates a strong correlation between X and Y while a lift below 1 means that X prevents Y to occur. A lift around 1 says that $P(X, Y) = P(X)P(Y)$. In terms of probability, this means that the occurrence of X and the occurrence of Y in the same transaction are independent events, hence X and Y not correlated. Notice that $lift(X{\rightarrow}Y)$ simplifies to: $n |X, Y| / |X| |Y|$, n being the total number of transactions.

$Correlation(X{\rightarrow}Y) = P(X, Y) - P(X)P(Y) / sqrt(P(X)P(Y)(1-P(X))(1-P(Y)))$, where $sqrt$ means square root. Correlation is a symmetric measure. A correlation around 0 indicates that X and Y are not correlated, a negative figure indicates that X and Y are negatively correlated and a positive figure that they a positively correlated. Note that the denominator of the division is positive and smaller than 1. Thus the absolute value $|correlation(X{\rightarrow}Y)|$ is greater than $|P(X, Y)-P(X)P(Y)|$. In other words, if the lift is around 1, correlation can still be significantly different from 0.

$Conviction(X{\rightarrow}Y) = (1 - P(Y)) / (1 - conf(X{\rightarrow}Y))$. Conviction is not a symmetric measure. A conviction around 1 says that X and Y are independent, while conviction is infinite as $conf(X{\rightarrow}Y)$ is tending to 1. Note that if $P(Y)$ is high, $1 - P(Y)$ is small. In that case, even if $conf(X, Y)$ is strong, $conviction(X{\rightarrow}Y)$ may be small.

To perform the *Chi-square test*, a table of expected frequencies is first calculated using $P(X)$ and $P(Y)$ from the contingency table. The expected frequency for (X and Y) is given by the product $P(X)P(Y)$. Performing a grand total over observed frequencies versus expected frequencies gives a number which we denote by *Chi*. Consider the contingency table shown in Table 1. $P(X) = P(Y) = 550/2000$. Therefore the expected frequency (Xe and Ye) is $550 \times 550 / 2000 = 151.25$ as shown in Table 2. We calculate the other frequencies similarly. The grand total for Chi is therefore:

$Chi = (500-151.25)^2 / 151.25 + (50-398.75)^2 / 398.75 + (50-398.75)^2 / 398.75 + (1400-1051.25)^2 / 1051.25 = 1529.87$. The obtained number *Chi* is compared with a cut-off value read from a Chi-square table. For the probability value of 0.05 with

Table 1. A contingency table

	X	Not X	Total
Y	500	50	550
not Y	50	1400	1450
Total	550	1450	2000

Table 2. Expected frequencies for low support and strong confidence

	Xe	not Xe	Total
Ye	151.25	398.75	550
not Ye	398.75	1051.25	1450
Total	550	1450	2000

one degree of freedom, the cut-off value is *3.84*. If *Chi* is greater than *3.84*, *X* and *Y* are regarded as correlated with a *95%* confidence level. Otherwise they are regarded as non-correlated also with a *95%* confidence level. Therefore in the example above, *X* and *Y* are highly correlated.

$Cosine(X{\rightarrow}Y) = P(X, Y) / sqrt(P(X)P(Y))$, where again $sqrt(P(X)P(Y))$ means the square root of the product $P(X)P(Y)$. Equivalently: $Cosine(X{\rightarrow}Y) = |X, Y| / sqrt(|X| |Y|)$. Cosine is a number between *0* and *1*. This is due to the fact that $P(X, Y)$ is smaller than or equal to both $P(X)$ and $P(Y)$. A value close to *1* indicates a good correlation between *X* and *Y*. Contrasting with the previous measures, the total number of transactions *n* is not taken into account by the cosine measure as shown by the last formula. The number of transactions containing both *X* and *Y*, the number of transactions containing *X*, and the number of transactions containing *Y* are used to calculate the cosine measure. This fact is known as the null-invariant property. Therefore cosine is more appropriate when the items contained in *X* or *Y* are non-symmetric in the following sense: it is more important to be aware of the occurrence of these items than of their non-occurrence.

Comparing Interestingness Measures

Measures for interestingness as given in the previous section differ not only in their definition but also in their result. They do not rate the same sets the same way. Tan et al. (2002) have done some extensive work in exploring those measures and how well they capture the dependencies between

variables across various datasets. They considered 10 sets and 19 interestingness measures and, for each measure, gave a ranking for the 10 sets. Out of these 10 sets, the first 3 sets (for convenience let us call them E1, E2 and E3 as they did in their article) lead to strong symmetric rules. However there is still a substantial difference between these 3 sets and our sets from the Logic-ITA. In Tan et al.'s (2002) datasets E1, E2 and E3, the values for *P(X, Y)*, *P(X)* and *P(Y)* are very similar, meaning that *X* and *Y* do not occur often one without the other. In contrast, in the sets from the Logic-ITA, *P(X)* and *P(Y)* are significantly bigger than *P(X, Y)*. As we will see this fact has consequences both for correlation and conviction.

Since the datasets from Tan et al. (2002) were different in character from our datasets, we also explored the interestingness measures under different variants of other datasets. In the following we take various examples of contingency tables giving symmetric association rules for a minimum confidence threshold of 80% and we look at the various interestingness results that we get. These contingency tables are presented in Table 3. The set S3 and S4 are the ones that match best our data from the Logic-ITA. To complete the picture, we included symmetric rules with a relatively low support of 25%, though we are interested in strong rules with a minimum support of 60%. Table 3 is to be interpreted as follows. 2000 solutions to exercises have been submitted by about 230 students. Thus a transaction is interpreted as a submitted solution to an exercise. The item set *I* is the set of mistakes that students can make while solving an exercise. To make explanations easier, in the fol-

Table 3. Contingency tables giving symmetric rules with strong confidence

	X, Y	*X*, not *Y*	not *X, Y*	not *X*, not *Y*.
S1	500 (25%)	50 (2.5%)	50 (2.5%)	1400 (70%)
S2	1340 (67%)	300 (15%)	300 (15%)	60 (3%)
S3	1340 (67%)	270 (13.5%)	330 (16.5%)	60 (3%)
S4	1340 (67%)	200 (10%)	400 (20%)	60 (3%)
S5	1340 (67%)	0 (0%)	0 (0%)	660 (33%)
S6	2000 (100%)	0 (0%)	0 (0%)	0 (0%)
S7	13400 (67%)	3000 (15%)	3000 (15%)	600 (3%)
S8	13400 (67%)	2700 (13.5%)	3300 (16.5%)	600 (3%)
S9	13400 (67%)	2000 (10%)	4000 (20%)	600 (3%)

lowing we consider that X or Y contains only one mistake and speak of mistake X and of mistake Y. However nothing fundamental is changed when X or Y are itemsets, that means they contain several mistakes. (X, Y) gives the number of solutions in which both mistakes X and Y were made followed by the probability between brackets, $(X,$ not $Y)$ the number of exercises in which the mistake X was made but not the mistake Y, and so on. For the set S3 for example, 1340 attempted solutions contain both mistake X and mistake Y which means 67% of the submitted solutions contains both mistake X and mistake Y, 270 contain mistake X but not mistake Y, 330 contain mistake Y but not mistake X and 60 attempted solutions contain neither mistake X nor mistake Y. The last 3 lines, S7 to S9, are the same as S2 to S4 with a multiplying factor of 10.

For each of these datasets, we calculated the various measures of interestingness we discussed earlier. Results are shown in Table 4. Expected frequencies are calculated assuming the independence of X and Y. Note that expected frequencies coincide with observed frequencies for S6, though Chi cannot be calculated. We have put in bold the results that indicate a positive dependency between X and Y. We also highlighted the lines for S3 and S4, representing our data from the Logic-ITA and, in a lighter shade, S8 and S9, which have the same characteristics but with a multiplying factor of 10.

We now discuss the results. First, let us consider the lift. One notices that, when the number X and Y increase and consequently $P(X)$ and $P(Y)$ increase, mechanically the lift decreases. As an illustration of this phenomenon, let us consider that a person is characterized by things she does everyday. Suppose X is 'seeing the Eiffel tower' and Y is 'taking the subway'. If association rules are mined considering the Parisians, then the lift of $X \rightarrow Y$ is likely to be low because a high proportion of Parisians both see the Eiffel tower everyday and take the subway everyday. However if association rules are mined taking the whole French population, the lift is likely to be high because only 20% of the French are Parisians, hence both $P(X)$ and $P(Y)$ cannot be greater then 0.20. The ranking for the lift given in Tan et al. (2002) is rather poor for their sets E1, E2 and E3, that give strong symmetric association rules.

Let us now consider the correlation. Note that $P(X)$ and $P(Y)$ are positive numbers smaller than 1, hence their product is smaller than $P(X)$ and smaller than $P(Y)$. If $P(X, Y)$ is significantly smaller than $P(X)$ and significantly smaller than $P(Y)$, the difference between the product $P(X)P(Y)$ and $P(X, Y)$ is very small, and, as a result, correlation is around 0. This is exactly what happens with our data, and this fact leads to a strong difference with the E1, E2 and E3 sets by Tan et al. (2002), where the correlation was highly ranked: except for S1

Table 4. Measures for all contingency tables

	sup	conf XY conf YX	lift	corr	conv XY conv YX	Chi	Cos
S1	0.25	0.90	**3.31**	**0.87**	**7.98** **7.98**	1522.88	**0.91**
S2	0.67	0.82 0.82	1.00	-0.02	0.98 0.98	0.53	**0.82**
S3	0.67	0.83 0.82	1.00	-0.01	0.98 0.99	0.44	**0.82**
S4	0.67	0.87 0.77	1.00	0	1.00 1.00	0,00	**0.82**
S5	0.67	1.00 1.00	1.49	1	- -	2000	1
S6	1.00	1.00 1.00	1.00	-	- -	-	1
S7	0.67	0.82 0.82	1.00	-0.02	0.98 0.98	**5.29**	**0.82**
S8	0.67	0.83 0.80	1.00	-0.01	0.98 0.99	**4.37**	**0.82**
S9	0.67	0.87 0.77	1.00	0	1.00 1.00	0.01	**0.82**

and S5, our correlation results are around 0 for our sets with strong association rules.

Another feature of our data is that *1-P(X), 1-P(Y)* and *1-conf(X→Y)* are similar, hence conviction values remain around 1.

It is well known (see S7 to S9) that Chi-square is not invariant under the row-column scaling property, as opposed to all the other measures which yielded the same results as for S2 to S4. Chi-square rate *X* and *Y* as independent for S2 and S3, but rate them as dependent in S7 and S8. As the numbers increases, Chi-square finds increasing dependency between the variables.

Finally cosine is the only measure that always rate *X* and *Y* as correlated. This is due to the fact that cosine calculation is independent of *n*, the size of the population, and considers only the number of transactions where *X* or *Y* occur, leaving out transactions where neither *X* nor *Y* occur.

Intuitive Interpretation of Cosine and Lift

Cosine

Cosine has its roots in geometry. Let x and y be two vectors of length n: $x = (x_1, x_2, ..., x_n)$, $y = (y_1, y_2, ..., y_n)$. $Cosine(x, y) = (x \cdot y) / (|x| |y|)$, where $(x \cdot y)$ indicates the vector dot product of vectors x and y and $|x|$ is the length of vector x.

In geometry, cosine is a measure of the angle θ formed by the two vectors x and y. Two vectors are the most similar when their coordinates are the same or positively proportional. In that case, the angle they form is 0° and *cosine(x, y) = 1*. Two vectors are the most dissimilar when they are orthogonal to each other. In that case, the angle they formed is 90° and *cosine(x, y) = 0*.

Borrowing that idea it is easy to associate two vectors x and y to the rule $X→Y$. Let us interpret x_k as being *1* if transaction t_k contains X and *0* otherwise, and similarly for y_k and Y. Then it is immediate that the equation for cosine can be rewritten as $cosine(x, y) = P(X, Y) / sqrt(P(X)P(Y))$ $= cosine(X \rightarrow Y)$, the usual form that is given for cosine of an association rule $X \rightarrow Y$. As already mentioned, notice that $cosine(X \rightarrow Y)$ simplifies to $|X, Y| / sqrt(|X| |Y|)$. X and Y are the most related when any transaction containing X does also contain Y and vice versa. In that case $cosine(X \rightarrow Y) = 1$. X and Y are the least related when any transaction containing X does not contain Y, and vice versa. In that case $cosine(X \rightarrow Y) = 0$. Transactions containing neither X nor Y do not impact on the result. This fact is known as the null-invariant property, which is desirable when the information conveyed by the presence X, or Y, is more important that the information conveyed by its absence.

Lift

Lift has its roots in probability. Consider first *Added Value* of the rule $X \rightarrow Y$, denoted by *AV* $(X \rightarrow Y)$, which measures whether the proportion of transactions containing Y among the transactions containing X is greater than the proportion of transactions containing Y among all transactions. Thus $AV (X \rightarrow Y) = P(Y/X) - P(Y)$. Similarly $AV (Y \rightarrow X)$ $= P(X/Y) - P(X)$. Equivalently $AV (X \rightarrow Y) = |X,$ $Y|/|X| - |Y|/n$ and $AV (Y \rightarrow X) = |X, Y|/|Y| - |X|/n$. Thus Added Value is not a symmetric measure. However notice that $AV (X \rightarrow Y) = 0$ exactly when $AV (Y \rightarrow X) = 0$, that $AV (X \rightarrow Y) > 0$ exactly when $AV (Y \rightarrow X) > 0$ and that $AV (Y \rightarrow X) < 0$, exactly when $AV (Y \rightarrow X) < 0$.

Remember that $lift(X \rightarrow Y) = lift(Y \rightarrow X)$ and simplifies to $n |X, Y| / |X| |Y|$. It is easy to show that the lift is *1* exactly when added value is *0*, the lift is greater than *1* exactly when added value is positive and the lift is below *1* exactly when added value is negative. This holds regardless of the direction $X \rightarrow Y$ or $Y \rightarrow X$ because of the relation between $AV (X \rightarrow Y)$ and $AV (Y \rightarrow X)$. Further $AV(X \rightarrow Y)$ or $AV(Y \rightarrow X)$ tends towards *1* when $lift(X \rightarrow Y)$ tends towards infinity, and $AV(X \rightarrow Y)$ or $AV(Y \rightarrow X)$ tends towards *-1* when $lift(X \rightarrow Y)$ tends towards 0, and vice versa. Thus a lift bigger than

1 says that the probability of Y occurring with X is higher than the mere probability of Y and also that the probability of X occurring with Y is higher than the mere probability of X. One can see lift as a compact measure to summarize Added Value. One notices that n, the total number of transactions, impacts on the result of lift.

Typical Values

To fix ideas let us look at typical values for cosine, Added Value and lift. Though, as we have just seen, lift is enough to decide whether X and Y are positively related or not, we add results on Added Value here for completeness. Suppose that among n transactions, m contain either X or Y or both, with $m \leq n$, and that $n - m$ transactions contain neither X nor Y.

First consider the case where all m transactions contain both X and Y. Then: $cosine(X \rightarrow Y) = 1$. Conversely, it is easy to show that $cosine(X \rightarrow Y) = 1$ implies that all m transactions contain both X and Y. Consider now lift. $lift(X \rightarrow Y) = m n / m m$. So if $m = n$, $lift(X \rightarrow Y) = 1$. If $m = \frac{1}{2} n$, $lift(X \rightarrow Y) = 2$ and so on. As for Added Value $AV(X \rightarrow Y) = AV(Y \rightarrow X)$ $= m/m - m/n = 1 - m/n$. So if $m = n$, $AV(X \rightarrow Y) = 0$. If $m = \frac{1}{2} n$, $AV(X \rightarrow Y) = 1/2$ and so on.

Consider now the case where 90% of the m transactions contain both X and Y, and 10% of the rest contain X but not Y. Then: $cosine(X \rightarrow Y) = m$ $0.9 / sqrt(m m 0.9) = 0.949$. $lift(X \rightarrow Y) = (0.9 m n)$ $/ (0.9 m m) = n/m$. $AV(X \rightarrow Y) = (0.9 m / m) - (0.9$ $m / n) = 0.9 (1 - m/n)$ and $AV(Y \rightarrow X) = (0.9 m /$ $0.9 m) - (m / n) = 1 - m/n$.

Now consider again the case where *90%* of the m transactions contain both X and Y, but *5%* of the rest contain X and not Y, and the other *5%* contain Y and not X. In other words X and Y are evenly spread among the transactions containing either X or Y but not both. Then: $cosine(X \rightarrow Y) =$ $0.9 m / sqrt(0.95 m 0.95 m) = 0.9/0.95 = 0.947$. $lift(X \rightarrow Y) = (0.9 m n) / (0.95 m 0.95 m) = 0.99$ n/m. $AV(X \rightarrow Y) = AV(Y \rightarrow X) = (0.9 m / 0.95 m) -$ $(0.95 m / n)$ which is almost $0.95(1 - m/n)$.

Table 5. Typical values for cosine and lift, where the 3 figures of the first column show the percentage of transactions containing X and Y, X, Y

% transactions (X and Y, X, Y)	cosine(X→Y)	lift(X→Y)	AV(X→Y)	AV(Y→X)
(100, 100, 100)	1	n/m	1 - m/n	1 - m/n
(90, 100, 90)	0.949	n/m	0.9(1 - m/n)	1 - m/n
(90, 95, 95)	0.947	0.997 (n/m)	0.948 − 0.95m/n	0.948 − 0.95m/n
(75, 100, 75)	0.87	n/m	0.75(1 - m/n)	1 - m/n
(75, 87.5, 87.5)	0.86	0.98 (n/m)	0.86 − 0.875m/n	0.86 − 0.875m/n
(60, 100, 60)	0.77	n/m	0.60(1 - m/n)	1 - m/n
(60, 80, 80)	0.75	0.94 (n/m)	0.75 − 0.80m/n	0.75 − 0.80m/n
(50, 100, 50)	0.707	n/m	0.50(1 - m/n)	1 - m/n
(50, 75, 75)	0.66	0.88 (n/m)	0.66 − 0.75m/n	0.66 − 0.75m/n
(40, 100, 40)	0.63	n/m	0.40(1 - m/n)	1 - m/n
(40, 70, 70)	0.57	0.82 (n/m)	0.57 − 0.70m/n	0.57 − 0.70m/n
(30, 100, 30)	0.55	n/m	0.30(1 - m/n)	1 - m/n
(30, 65, 65)	0.46	0.71 (n/m)	0.46 − 0.65m/n	0.46 − 0.65m/n

Table 5 summarizes further results. Lines should be read as follows: (a,b,c) means that a% of the m transactions contain both X and Y, b% contain X and c% contain Y. Therefore (75, 100, 75) means that 75% of the m transactions contain both X and Y and that the remaining 25% contain X but not Y (X is present in 100% of the transactions and Y in 75% of them), while (75, 87.5, 87.5) means that X or Y are evenly spread among the 25% of the remaining transactions.

As can be read from Table 5 an association rule with a cosine value around or below 0.65 is rated as uninteresting as 0.66 corresponds to the lowest threshold with 50% of common values (50, 75, 75). Notice that if $sup(X→Y) >= 60\%$, $P(X) ≤ 90\%$ and $P(Y) ≤ 90\%$, then $cosine(X→Y) >= 0.65$. Thus, generally, strong symmetric association rules are rated as interesting by cosine.

Consider again the set of 5000 transactions we had earlier with the three different probabilities for X, Y and X,Y. The two measures cosine and lift agree in the second case that the rule is not interesting, and give contradictory results in the two other cases:

1. $|X, Y| = 1000$, $|X| = 1000$ and $|Y| = 2500$. We obtain $cosine(X→Y) = 0.63$ and $lift(X→Y) = 2$.

2. $|X, Y| = 1000$, $|X| = 1000$ and $|Y| = 5000$. We obtain $cosine(X→Y) = 0.45$ and $lift(X→Y) = 1$.

3. $|X, Y| = 4800$, $|X| = 4800$ and $|Y| = 5000$. We obtain $cosine(X→Y) = 0.98$ and $lift(X→Y) = 1$.

Contrast Rules

In Minaei-Bidgoli et al. (2004), contrast rules have been put forward to discover interesting rules that do not have necessarily a strong support. One aspect of contrast rules is to define a neighbourhood to which the base rule is compared. Contrast rules are generally formulated as follows. The set of all possible associations that can be extracted from a contingency table is denoted by Ω. Thus Ω contains 8 associations and is the set {$X → Y$, $not X → Y$, $X → not Y$, $not X → not Y$, $Y → X$, $not Y → X$, $Y → not X$, $not Y → not X$}.

Table 6. Contrast rules for $X \rightarrow Y$

	$X \rightarrow Y$	$not\ X \rightarrow Y$	$X \rightarrow not\ Y$	$not\ X \rightarrow not\ Y$
support	0.67	0.17	0.14	0.03
confidence	0.83	0.85	0.21	0.15
cosine	0.82	0.41	0.37	0.17
lift	1.00	1.01	1.02	0.93

A contrast rule *cr* is a 4-tuple *<br, v(br), M, Δ>* where:

- *br* is a subset of Ω,
- *v(br)* is also a subset of Ω and is called the neighbourhood to which the base rule *br* is compared,
- $M=<m_{br}, m_{neighbor}>$ is an ordered pair of measures to measure the rules in *br* and the rules in *v(br)*,
- $\Delta(m_{br}(br), m_{neighbor}(v(br)))$ is a comparison function between $m_{br}(br)$ and $m_{neighbor}(v(br))$.

A contrast rule, *cr*, is interesting if and only if $\Delta(m_{br}(br), m_{neighbor}(v(br)))$ is above a user defined threshold σ which implies that there is a large difference between *br* and its neighbourhood with respect to *M*.

We investigate this idea and consider as a base rule $X \rightarrow Y$ and the neighbourhood *{not X → Y, X → not Y, not X → not Y}* assuming that $X \rightarrow Y$ is a strong symmetric rule. For *M* we consider in turn *<sup, sup>*, *<conf, conf>*, *<cos, cos>* and *<lift, lift>*.The results obtained with the contingency table given by S3 in Table 4 are given in Table 6 and gives a fair idea of the general pattern.

Taking the base rule $Y \rightarrow X$ and the neighbourhood *{not Y → X, Y → not X, not Y → not X}*, we obtain similar results shown if Figure 7.

Generally, observe if a strong symmetric rule $X \rightarrow Y$ is extracted, all other rules except Y → X of course in Ω have a weak support. Assume that $P(X) = |X| / n >= 80\%$ and $P(Y) = |Y| / n >= 80\%$. Then $P(not\ X) \leq 20\%$ and $P(not\ Y) \leq 20\%$.

Due to the anti-monotonicity property of support, $P(not\ X, Y)$, $P(X, not\ Y)$ and $P(not\ X, not\ Y) \leq 20\%$. This means that if the support is high enough, in case of strong symmetric rules, only $X \rightarrow Y$ and get $Y \rightarrow X$ extracted.

Further, $X \rightarrow not\ Y$ and $Y \rightarrow not\ X$ have a poor confidence. With the same assumptions as before for $P(X)$ and $P(Y)$, we have: $conf\ (X \rightarrow not\ Y) \leq 0.2\ /\ 0.8 \leq 0.25$ and similarly for $conf\ (Y \rightarrow not\ X)$. However because support of *not X* and of *not Y* are small both $conf\ (not\ X \rightarrow Y)$ and $conf\ (not\ Y \rightarrow X)$ are likely to be high. Thus discovering strong symmetric association rules gives a good hint for discovering further associations with a low support but a strong confidence.

Nonetheless, if the prune step is applied with lift or cosine, then the rules will be rejected. In the case of cosine the strong support of both *X* and *Y* makes that the numbers obtained will be too small. In the case of lift the numbers obtained will be around *1* since the strong support of *X* or *Y* tends to cancel out with the total number of transactions.

Case Studies

Our case studies are in the Education domain. In the first case study association rules have been extracted using students' data stored by Logic-ITA, an intelligent tutoring system (Merceron & Yacef, 2004; Yacef, 2005). The obtained association rules are all strong and symmetric. They are well rated by cosine and poorly rated by lift. In the second case study, association rules have been extracted using students' data stored by the Learning Management

System Moodle. Few of the extracted rules are strong and symmetric. Cosine and lift agree on most of the extracted rules. The intuition behind the rules is used to choose whether to keep or to discard the rule when cosine and lift disagree on rules that are not strong symmetric.

Case Study 1

Our motivation was to analyse student interaction data with an intelligent tutoring system in order to better understand students' learning difficulties and progress. Detecting associations between mistakes made by students while solving an exercise is very useful to understand which underlying topic is ill-understood. This case study presents the association rules extracted with students' data stored by the Logic-ITA, an intelligent tutoring system to train students in logical proof. The study spans over 4 years and the rules were used as one instrument to improve teaching over 4 years, leading to a significant improvement in the learning outcomes. The extracted association rules are strong and symmetric. We have shown that cosine rates those rules very strongly.

The Logic-ITA was used at Sydney University from 2001 to 2004 in a course formerly taught by the authors. Over the four years, around 860 students attended the course and used the tool. An exercise consists of a set of formulas (called premises) and another formula (called the conclusion). The aim is to prove that the conclusion can validly be derived from the premises. For this, the student has to construct new formulas, step by step, using logic rules and formulas previously established in the proof, until the conclusion is derived. There is no unique solution and any valid path is acceptable. Steps are checked on the fly and, if incorrect, an error message and possibly a tip are displayed.

All steps, whether correct or not, are stored for each user and each attempted exercise. In case of incorrect steps, the error message is also stored. A very interesting task was to analyse these mistakes and try to detect associations within them. This is why we used association rules. We defined the set of items I as the set of possible mistakes or error messages. We defined a transaction as the set of mistakes made by one student on one exercise. Therefore we obtain as many transactions as exercises attempted with the Logic-ITA during the semester, which is about 2000.

We used association rules to find mistakes often occurring together while solving exercises. The purpose of looking for these associations was for the teacher to ponder and, maybe, to review the course material or emphasize subtleties while explaining concepts to students. Thus, it made sense to have a support that is not too low. The strongest rules for 2004 are shown in Table 8. The first association rule says that if students make mistake "Rule can be applied, but deduction incorrect" while solving an exercise, then they also make the mistake "Wrong number of line references given while solving the same exercise." As we can see in the small subset of 3 pairs of rules shown in this table, the rules are symmetric and display comparable support and confidence. Findings were quite similar across the years (2001 to 2004). As pointed out in the paragraph on contrast rules,

Table 7. Contrast rules for $Y \rightarrow X$

	$Y \rightarrow X$	*not Y→X*	*Y→not X*	*not Y→not X*
support	0.67	0.14	0.17	0.03
confidence	0.82	0.82	0.20	0.18
cosine	0.82	0.37	0.41	0.17
lift	1.00	1.02	1.01	0.93

Table 8. Some association rules for Year 2004

M11 Þ M12 [sup: 77%, conf: 89%]	M10: Premise set incorrect
M12 Þ M11 [sup: 77%, conf: 87%]	M11: Rule can be applied, but deduction incorrect
M11 Þ M10 [sup: 74%, conf: 86%]	M12: Wrong number of line reference given
M10 Þ M11 [sup: 78%, conf: 93%]	
M12 Þ M10 [sup: 78%, conf: 89%]	
M10 Þ M12 [sup: 74%, conf: 88%]	

these 6 rules induce 6 further rules with a low support but a strong confidence. As an example, the association induced by the first rule says that if students do not make the mistake "Rule can be applied, but deduction incorrect while solving an exercise", then they make the mistake "Wrong number of line references given while solving the same exercise."

Actionability

We have shown in earlier papers how the information gained from the extracted patterns led to actions for improving teaching (Merceron & Yacef, 2003; Merceron & Yacef, 2004; Merceron & Yacef, 2005). Note that since our goal was to improve the course as much as possible, our experiment did not test the sole impact of using the association rules but the impact of all other patterns found in the data. After we first extracted association rules from 2002 and 2001 data, we used these rules to redesign the course and provide more adaptive teaching. One finding was that mistakes related to the structure of the formal proof (as opposed to, for instance, the use and applicability of a logic rule) were associated together. This led us to realise that the very concept of formal proofs was causing problems and that some concepts such as the difference between the two types of logical rules, the deduction rules and the equivalence rules, might not be clear enough. In 2003, that portion of the course was redesigned to take this problem into account and the role of each part of the proof was emphasized. After the end of the semester, mining for mistakes associations was conducted again. Surprisingly, results did not

change much (a slight decrease in support and confidence levels in 2003 followed by a slight increase in 2004). However, marks in the final exam questions related to formal proofs continued increasing. We concluded that making mistakes, especially while using a training tool, is simply part of the learning process and this interpretation was supported by the fact that the number of completed exercises per student increased in 2003 and 2004 (Merceron & Yacef, 2005).

Case Study 2

The present case study describes a standard use of a Learning Management System (LMS) for providing additional resources to students in a face-to-face teaching context. Teachers want to figure out whether and how students use these resources and possibly whether their use has any (positive) impact on marks.

The LMS Moodle (Dougiamas, 1999) was used in the context of the course *Formal Basics of Computer Science* for first semester students enrolled in the degree "Computer Science and Media" at the University of Applied Sciences TFH Berlin during Winter Semester 2007/08. The cohort of 84 students enrolled in that course is divided into two groups. Students had a 3-hour weekly lecture. It includes formal teaching where concepts are explained, paper/pencil exercises to apply these concepts, and exercises discussed on the spot. To pass this course students take two exams. The first one takes place about 8 weeks after the beginning of the semester and the second one at the end of the semester. The present case study uses data gathered till the first exam.

Table 9. Exploring exercises among all students

Exercise	Ex1	Ex2	Ex3	Ex4	Ex5	Ex6	Ex7
No attempt	46	53	63	65	70	70	71
Success	21	19	11	8	6	9	8
Fail	14	9	7	8	5	2	2

Table 10. Viewing resources

TrEx01	TrEx01S	TrEx02	TrEx02S	JFlap	DP	Book	AtLeast1Ex
59	52	53	47	39	36	23	38

Moodle is used for posting lecture slides and accessing the following extra resources:

Book: a link to the homepage of the text book "Introduction to Automata Theory, Languages and Computation" used for this course (Hopcroft et al., 2006). From this homepage students can access a set of exercises with solutions.

DP: extra reading "Design Patterns for finite automata" (Merceron, 2008).

Jflap (Rodger, 1996), a software to practice automata construction.

Ex1, Ex2 ... Ex7: a set of seven extra self-evaluation exercises. One exercise is published in Moodle each week right after the lecture. The last exercise *Ex7* was put 2 weeks before the exam.

TrEx01 and *TrEx02*: two sample exams, published 3 weeks before the exam.

TrEx01S and *TrEx02S*, the solutions to the sample exams, published 10 days before the exam.

The use of Moodle, its additional resources and its self-evaluation exercises were not compulsory though strongly encouraged. Therefore for the teacher it is quite important to know: what do students do with those extra resources? What do they view? Is there any relationship between their use of these resources and their result in the exam? To answer these questions we have used solely the log data available in Moodle. Log data gives, for each resource and each student login, when the resource was accessed. It also gives, for each exercise and each student login, whether the exercise has been attempted, and whether the first trial was a success or not.

Exploring Data

From the 84 students enrolled in the course, 81 were enrolled in Moodle. The case study considers only those 81 students. From them, 52 passed the exam, 8 failed and 21 did not come. From the 60 who took the exam, statistics on their marks is given in the first line "General" of Table 11.

Did students do the exercises? Table 7 summarizes the figures. Lines should be read as follows. For example column 2 means that 46 students did not attempt exercise 1, 21 students gave a correct answer on their first trial and 14 gave a wrong answer on their first trial. One notices that as time goes there is always less students attempting exercises.

Did they access other resources? Table 8 summarizes the figures. The first column says that 59 students have viewed the first sample exam, the second column says that 52 students have viewed the solution of the first sample exam, and so on. One extra column has been added. AtLeast1Ex says that 38 students have attempted at least 1 exercise.

Table 11. Viewing resources and marks in the exam

Resource	minimum	maximum	Average	s.deviation
General	11	50	36.45	10.85
TrEx01	14	50	36.86	10.57
TrEx01S	14	50	36.61	10.71
TrEx02	14	50	37.12	10.59
TrEx02S	14	50	36.73	10.79
JFlap	14	50	37.90	10.52
DP	14	50	44.08	8.83
Book	14	50	40.22	9.37
NoEx	11	50	33	10.91
AtLeast1Ex	14	50	39.09	10.18

What are the results in the exam for each group of Table 8? Table 11 summarizes the results. Two extra lines have been added. NoEx shows the results for students who have never attempted any exercise. AtLeast1Ex shows the results for the students who have attempted at least 1 exercise. Table 7 and Table 8 suggest that the standard preparation for the exam is to look at sample exams and/or their solutions. Students who invest some more time with extra material tend to have better marks. The biggest positive impact on the marks is given by DP.

Table 8 and 9 confirm the expected outcome. Table 8 also shows something that was not known before: students tend to access a sample exam more that its solution.

This first exploration gives also directions for more investigation: If students attempt exercise 2, do they also attempt exercise 1? If they look at the solution of a sample exam, do they also look at the sample exam itself? This kind of questions can be investigated with association rules.

Association Rules

We begin with association rules tackling sample exams. The following rules again confirm the expected finding. If students look at the solution of a sample exam, they look also at the sample

exam itself. Further, if they view the second exam, then they also view the first one. The other way round does also hold, but with a slightly lower confidence.

Results are similar when rules are mined restricting the population to the students who came to the exam as shown for the first sample exam in the lines in italic of Table 12. Notice however that the lift diminishes as the rules become stronger.

Table 7 gives a direction for further rules to investigate: Is there any association between attempting exercise i and exercise j? One expects that many students enthusiastically have begun with exercise 1 at the beginning of the semester and then slowly have stopped doing them, till exercise 4 where a bunch of students just keep doing them. The rules we have obtained confirm this interpretation.

We have mined these rules restricting the data to students who have attempted at least 1 exercise, which means 38 transactions. Rules with a high confidence relate attempting exercise 2 and exercise 3, exercises 4 to 7, as well as exercise 1, and not attempting exercises 2 to 3, or not attempting exercises 4 to 7. Table 13 presents a sample of the extracted associations. Note that !Ex2 means that exercise 2 has not been attempted. So the first line says if students don't attempt exercise 2, then they don't attempt exercise 3.

Table 12. Association rules for sample exams

rule	sup.	conf.	cos.	lift
TrEx01S → TrEx01	0.59	0.92	0.87	1.27
TrEx01 → TrEx01S	0.59	0.81	0.87	1.27
TrEx02S → TrEx02	0.56	0.96	0.90	1.46
TrEx02 → TrEx02S	0.56	0.85	0.90	1.46
TrEx01S → TrEx01	*0.72*	*0.96*	*0.90*	*1.11*
TrEx01 → TrEx01S	*0.72*	*0.84*	*0.90*	*1.11*
TrEx02 → TrEx01	0.64	0.98	0.93	1.35
TrEx01 → TrEx02	0.64	0.88	0.93	1.35

For all these rules, except the last one, cosine and lift rate associations the same way. The drop between attempting exercises 1 to 3 and attempting the others has led us to investigate the marks of this population. Surprisingly, their average mark is smaller than for all students who have attempted at least 1 exercise, see Table 14.

As for the other resources, were they consulted by the same students? We have looked at associations between DP, Jflap, Book and AtLeast1Ex considering the full population and show two rules found in Table 15. Here lift does not confirm the non-interesting rating given by cosine. As before, !DP means that the resource DP has not been viewed.

Keeping in mind the meaning of measures can help deciding what to do with an association.

Let us consider the last rule of Table 13. Cosine indicates that, among the students who have not done Ex5 nor Ex6, over 60% had done Ex1 (consult the typical figures in Table 1), while lift indicates that the proportion of students who have not done Ex5 and Ex6 is not larger in students who did Ex1 (which represented 43% of the students, according to table 2) than in all students. However, from a pedagogical point of view, the case of students who did not attempt Ex1 is not relevant for this analysis. Therefore the teacher would probably find it useful to keep this rule, hence following cosine, though lift gives here some interesting complementary information.

Let us now consider the second rule of Table 15. Cosine gives us the following information: among the students who consulted the Book web site, the extra material on Design Patterns (DP) and done at least one exercise, less than 40% used Jflap (refer to the typical values in Table 1). The lift gives us the following information: the proportion

Table 13. Association rules for attempted exercises

Rule	sup.	conf.	cos.	lift
!Ex2 → !Ex3	0.26	1	0.71	1.9
Ex3 → Ex2	0.47	1	0.80	1.36
!Ex4, !Ex5 → !Ex6	0.56	1	0.93	1.41
!Ex6, !Ex7 → !Ex5	0.63	0.96	0.92	1.35
Ex1, !Ex4 → !Ex5, !Ex6	0.55	1	0.90	1.46
Ex1, Ex7 → Ex5, Ex6	0.21	1	0.89	3.8
!Ex5, !Ex6 → Ex1	0.63	1	0.80	1.0

Table 14. Attempting exercises 4 to 7 and marks in the exam

Resource	minimum	maximum	Average	s.deviation
Ex 4 to 7	16	50	38.76	10.35

Table 15. Association rules for the other resources

rule	sup.	conf.	cos.	Lift
!DP, !AtLeast1Ex → !Book	0.32	0.92	0.62	1.29
Book, DP, AtLeast1Ex → Jflap	0.12	1	0.51	2.08

of students who looked at Jflap is higher among the students who looked at the Book web site, the DP material and done at least one exercise than in the whole student population. Given the very small number of students (as we can see from the support, there are 10 students who satisfied these three criteria on the left hand side of the rule), it is prudent to follow cosine and reject the rule. It is interesting to note though that if the cosine and lift had given similar values, but with a higher number of students, it would then have been advisable to follow the lift and retain the rule.

CONCLUSION

In this chapter we have introduced the concept of strong symmetric association rules. We have shown that many objective measures of interestingness rate these rules as not interesting, therefore these rules can be qualified as rare because many objective measures would prune them. Cosine is one particular objective interestingness measure that rates strong symmetric association rules highly. An essential feature that distinguishes cosine from many other objective interestingness measures is that the value of cosine does not depend on n, the total number of transactions while most of other measures do. This feature is known

as the null-invariant property.

This distinguishing feature has led us to investigate deeper the intuition behind cosine and lift, a very popular interestingness measure. Cosine has its roots in geometry. Its value tells us about the number of transactions in which X and Y co-occur, when considering only transactions that contain X or Y and dismissing transactions that do not contain neither X nor Y, which is to consider when the information conveyed by the presence X, or Y, is more important that the information conveyed by its absence. Lift has its root in probability. Its value tells us whether it is more probable to find Y among the transactions containing X than among all transactions. Because these two measures have an easy intuitive meaning, we think that they are well suited for application in the education field.

We have investigated the question of whether the discovering of strong symmetric association rules could lead to discover further rare rules, rare having the more classical meaning of rules with a low support but a strong confidence. For this investigation we have used the concept of contrast rules introduced in Minaei-Bidgoli et al. (2004). The answer is positive though not completely convincing. Indeed strong symmetric association rules $X{\rightarrow}Y$ and $Y{\rightarrow}X$ generally will imply that *not $X{\rightarrow}Y$* and *not $Y{\rightarrow}X$* have a low support but a strong confidence. However both lift and cosine are likely to rate these rules poorly.

The two studies reported in this paper come from the field of education. In the first case study data stored by an intelligent tutoring system, the Logic-ITA, has been mined. Logic-ITA has been used as a training tool to support a course in face to face teaching at the University of Sydney. All obtained association rules are strong and symmetric. Therefore they are rated as interesting by cosine and as not interesting by lift. They are actionable. The information conveyed has been used to adapt the course and to adapt the tool as well. In the second case study, log data stored by the LMS Moodle has been mined. Few obtained rules were strong and symmetric. Cosine and lift did agree on most of the obtained rules. For the few non-strong symmetric rules they disagree upon, the intuition behind these two measures help to understand and interpret the obtained values, and therefore to decide whether to keep or to drop the rules.

FUTURE WORK

In this chapter we have focused on objective interestingness measures. They are essential to obtain a sensible set of association rules. In the author's view, education is an application domain for which the intuition behind the measures plays a vital role to understand and interpret the results. We aim at selecting a subset of interestingness measures that are appropriate for educational data mining. Our work needs to be pursued in two directions.

Our study of objective interestingness measures regarding their ease of interpretation is not complete. It would be worthwhile to systematically investigate all objective measures proposed so far. Work along these lines has already begun and show that other objective measures such as all-confidence or Jaccard having like cosine the null-invariant property do rate strong symmetric association rules as interesting. Other concepts like entropy (Pavlov et al., 2003) should be explored to be sure that considering only cosine and lift is not too restrictive.

The second direction concerns pruning with subjective measures. In the first case study the obtained rules were actionable; they lead to two actions: adapting the course and adapting the tool. In the second case study most of the obtained rules confirmed what was expected from data exploration. Considering subjective criteria such as actionability or expectedness, these rules are interesting and therefore were not pruned further. An open question in the education application domain is whether and which subjective measures can be used to prune further the set of association rules.

REFERENCES

Aggarwal, C. C., & Yu, P. S. (1998). A new framework for itemset generation. In *Proceedings of the 1998 ACM Symposium Prinicples of Database Systems (PODS'98)* (pp. 18-24), Seattle, WA, USA.

Agrawal, R., & Srikant, R. (1994). Fast Algorithms for Mining Association Rules. In J. B. Bocca, M. Jarke, & C. Zaniolo (Eds.), *Proceedings of International Conference on Very Large Data Base VLDB 94*. Santiago, Chile, Morgan Kaufmann.

Beck, J. (2007, July). Difficulties in inferring student knowledge from observations (and why you shouldcare). In *Proceedings of the Educational Data Mining workshop, in conjunction with 13th International Conference of Artificial Intelligence in Education* (pp. 21-30). Marina del Rey, CA. USA. IOS Press.

Brijs, T., Vanhoof, K., & Wets, G. (2003). Defining interestingness for association rules. In *International journal of information theories and applications, 10*(4), 370-376.

Dougiamas, M. (1999). *Moodle*. Retrieved August 01, 2008, from http://moodle.org/

Garcia, J., Romero, C., Ventura, S., & Calders, T. (2007). Drawbacks and solutions of applying association rules mining in learning management systems. In *Proceedings of the International Workshop on Applying Data Mining in e-learning (ADML'07)*, (pp. 13-22). Crete, Greece. Retrieved August 01, 2008, from http://ftp.informatik.rwth-aachen.de/Publications/CEUR-WS/Vol-305/

Geng, L. Q., & Howard, J. H. (2006). Interestingness Measures for Data Mining: A Survey. *ACM Computing Surveys, 38*(3), 9. doi:10.1145/1132960.1132963

Han, J., & Kamber, M. (2006). *Concepts and Techniques.* Morgan Kaufmann Publishers.

Hopcroft, J. E., Motwani, R., & Ullman, J. D. (2006*). Introduction to Automata Theory, Languages, and Computation.* Retrieved August 01, 2008, from http://infolab.stanford.edu/~ullman/ialc.html

Lu, J. (2004). Personalized e-learning material recommender system. In Proceedings of the *International conference on information technology for application (ICITA'04)* (pp. 374-379). China.

Merceron, A. (2008). Unterstützung des Erlernens von endlichen Automaten mit Hilfe von Mustern. In J. Desel & M. Gliz (Eds.) *Proceedings Wokshop für Modellierung in Lehre und Weiterbildung,* (pp. 27-36). Modellierung 2008, Berlin, Germany. Retrieved August 01, 2008, from http://www.ifi.uzh.ch/techreports/TR_2008.html See also http://public.tfh-berlin.de/~merceron/pub/DP-DFA_eng.pdf

Merceron, A., & Yacef, K. (2003). A Web-based Tutoring Tool with Mining Facilities to Improve Learning and Teaching. In *Proceedings of the 11th International Conference on Artificial Intelligence in Education,* (pp. 201-208). Sydney: IOS Press.

Merceron, A., & Yacef, K. (2004). Mining Student Data Captured from a Web-Based Tutoring Tool: Initial Exploration and Results. [JILR]. *Journal of Interactive Learning Research, 15*(4), 319–346.

Merceron, A., & Yacef, K. (2005). Educational Data Mining: a Case Study. In *Proceedings of the International Conference on Artificial Intelligence in Education (AIED2005)* (pp. 467-475). Amsterdam, The Netherlands. IOS Press.

Merceron, A., & Yacef, K. (2007). Revisiting interestingness of strong symmetric association rules in educational data. In *Proceedings of the International Workshop on Applying Data Mining in elearning (ADML'07)* (pp. 3-12). Crete, Greece 2007. Retrieved August 01, 2008, from http://ftp.informatik.rwth-aachen.de/Publications/CEUR-WS/Vol-305/

Merceron, A., & Yacef, K. (2008). Interestingness Measures for Association Rules in Educational Data. In R. de Baker, T. Barnes & J.E. Beck (Eds.), *Proceedings of the first International Conference on Educational Data Mining (EDM'08)* (pp. 57-66). Montreal, Canada. Retrieved August 01, 2008, from http://www.educationaldatamining.org/EDM2008/uploads/proc/full proceedings.pdf

Minaei-Bidgoli, B., Kashy, D. A., Kortemeyer, G., & Punch, W. F. (2003). Predicting student performance: an application of data mining methods with the educational web-based system LON-CAPA. *33rd ASEE/IEEE Frontiers in Education Conference*. Boulder, Colorado.

Minaei-Bidgoli, B., Tan, P. N., & Punch, W. F. (2004). Mining Interesting Contrast Rules for a Web-based Educational System. In *Proceedings of the International Conference on Machine Learning Applications (ICMLA 2004),* Louisville, KY, USA, CSREA Press.

Omiecinski, E. R. (2003). Alternative Interest Measures for Mining Associations in Databases. *IEEE Transactions on Knowledge and Data Engineering, 15*(1), 57–69. doi:10.1109/TKDE.2003.1161582

Pavlov, D., Mannila, H., & Smyth, P. (2003). Beyond independence: Probabilistic models for query approximation on binary transaction data. *IEEE Transactions on Knowledge and Data Engineering, 5*(6), 1409–1421. doi:10.1109/TKDE.2003.1245281

Rodger, S. (1996). *JFLAP*. Retrieved August 01, 2008, from http://www.jflap.org/

Romero, C., & Ventura, S. (2007). Educational Data Mining: A Survey from 1995 to 2005. *Expert Systems with Applications, 33*(1), 135–146. doi:10.1016/j.eswa.2006.04.005

Romero, C., Ventura, S., de Castro, C., Hall, W., & Ng, M. H. (2002). Using Genetic Algorithms for Data Mining in Web-based Educational Hypermedia Systems. In P. M. de Bra, P. Bruzilovsky, R. Conejo (Eds.), *Adaptive Hypermedia and Adaptive Web-Based Systems (Ah02)*. Lecture Notes in Computer Science 2347. New York: Springer Verlag.

Tan, P. N., Kumar, V., & Srivastava, J. (2002). *Selecting the Right Interestingness Measure for Association Patterns*. In *Proceedings of the 8th ACM SIGKDD International Conference on Knowledge Discovery and Data Mining* (pp. 67-76). San Francisco, USA. ACM Publisher.

Wang, F. (2006). On using Data Mining for browsing log analysis in learning environments. In C. Romero & S. Ventura (Ed.), *Data Mining in E-Learning. Series: Advances in Management Information* (pp. 57-75). WIT press.

Wang, F.-H., & Shao, H.-M. (2004). Effective personalized recommendation based on time-framed navigation clustering and association mining. *Expert Systems with Applications, 27*(3), 365–377. doi:10.1016/j.eswa.2004.05.005

Xin, D., Cheng, H., Yan, X., & Han, J. (2006) Extracting redundancy-aware top-k patterns. In *Proceedings of the 2006 ACM SIGKDD International Conference on Knowledge Discovery and Data Mining (KDD'06)*, Philadelphia, Pennsylvania, USA.

Yacef, K. (2005). The Logic-ITA in the classroom: a medium scale experiment. *International Journal of Artificial Intelligence in Education, 15*, 41–60.

Section 4
Critical Event Detection and Applications

Chapter 13
He Wasn't There Again Today

Richard A. O'Keefe
University of Otago, New Zealand

Nathan Rountree
University of Otago, New Zealand

ABSTRACT

In this chapter, the authors discuss the characteristics of data collected by the New Zealand Centre for Adverse Drug Reaction Monitoring (CARM) over a five-year period. The authors begin by noting the ways in which adverse reaction data are similar to market basket data, and the ways in which they are different. They go on to develop a model for estimating the amount of missing data in the dataset, and another to decide whether a drug is rare simply because it was only available for a short time. They also discuss the notion of "rarity" with respect to drugs, and with respect to reactions. Although the discussion is confined to the CARM data, the models and techniques presented here are useful to anyone who is about to embark on an association mining project, or who needs to interpret association rules in the context of a particular database.

INTRODUCTION

Having collected data on medical conditions and their treatments, it seems to make sense to derive association rules as pioneered by Agrawal et al. (1993). It would be nice to be able to report such things as "when conditions A and B are present with treatment C, then we have an unacceptably high confidence of seeing adverse reaction X." Before we embark on such an analysis, it is wise to consider the characteristics of the database: does the support/confidence framework make sense here? Are we going to be affected by rare cases and missing data? And to what extent? It should be remembered that association mining was developed in the context of market basket analysis; in what way is our data like or unlike a set of market baskets?

These questions became pertinent to us as we began to analyse data from New Zealand's Centre for Adverse Reaction Monitoring (CARM). CARM "...collects and evaluates spontaneous reports of adverse reactions to medicines, vaccines, herbal

DOI: 10.4018/978-1-60566-754-6.ch013

products and dietary supplements from health professionals in New Zealand. Currently the CARM database holds over 50 000 reports and provides New Zealand-specific information on adverse reactions to these products, and serves to support clinical decision making when unusual symptoms are thought to be therapy related." (http://carm. otago.ac.nz/index.asp?link=carm) CARM is believed to produce the highest reporting rate of adverse drug reactions in the world, relative to both number of doctors and size of population (Zolezzi & Parsotam, 2005).

MARKET BASKETS VS. ADVERSE REACTIONS

Let's start by considering how we get our cases in market basket analysis.

1. A shopper decides to buy some items on
2. a shopping list and makes
3. a shopping trip to get them. During this trip,
4. s/he enters a shop,
5. selects some items,
6. is unable to locate others,
7. and chooses others on impulse.
8. S/he pays at the cash register and leaves.
9. The register record is later analysed.

There are demographic facts about the shopper like age, sex, and home district that are normally missing from the cash register record. It is not that such data are not available in principle, it is that they are not measured or recorded. Loyalty cards may permit such information to be gathered. Researchers might still not have access to it for privacy reasons.

Market basket analysis is sometimes presented as giving us information about shoppers. Without loyalty card or banking information to link one shopping episode to another, what we actually have is information about trips, not people. If someone habitually shops for food on Mondays and cleaning products on Wednesdays, we will never learn about associations between food products and cleaning products for that shopper.

We do not learn about people who wish to buy goods we have for sale but who never enter the shop, or who enter and leave without making any purchase. Perhaps they do not like the lighting, or the scents of the cleaning products make them feel sick. (Such scents are often unpleasantly strong.)

We do not learn about the things people wanted to buy but could not find. The free market does not work very well when there are too many intermediaries: manufacturers cannot set prices to suit customers who are never allowed to see those products by supermarkets. If someone wants to buy brand X guacamole whenever he buys mashed potato flakes, but only brand Y, a sort of watery slime, is on offer, market basket analysis will never discover the association that wasn't allowed to occur. In particular, we may fail to discover an association between two products because the two are not offered at the same time.

We cannot easily tell which purchases were intentional and which were the result of manipulation ("impulse purchases"). To some extent that can be discovered by experimental manipulation.

There is important information about customer response to prices that could be mined from cash register records, but in market basket association mining that information is ignored.

There are three characteristics of the market basket setup:

1. Every purchase is recorded and available for analysis.
2. Purchase numbers are generally high.
3. The aim of analysis is to increase these numbers, and other people are continually working to increase them anyway.

Now let's think about adverse reaction monitoring, the area that we are interested in.

1. A patient develops some disorder.
2. This disorder is reported to a doctor,
3. who diagnoses it, and
4. prescribes one or more treatments.
5. The patient develops an adverse reaction.
6. This reaction is reported to a doctor,
7. who categorises it,
8. may validate it experimentally,
9. and reports it to the Centre for Adverse Reaction Monitoring.

Demographic data such as age, sex, smoking status, other conditions, other drugs, and location are recorded.

Mild disorders might not be reported to a doctor. Mild cases that are reported to a doctor might not be treated (it'll get better by itself). Those that are treated will probably be treated differently from severe cases.

We know with certainty what products a shopper purchased. Unfortunately, medical diagnoses are not so certain. It took one author a year and three different doctors to get a diagnosis for knee pain that was confirmed, not disconfirmed, by a test. The other two were very confident of their diagnoses.

Some "disorders," such as "need for contraception" or "need for vaccination against meningitis" are expressions of the patient's or society's wishes rather than characterizations of the patient's physical state. Those we can have high confidence in. Some, particularly mental diagnoses, are much fuzzier.

In order to be reported as an adverse reaction, a doctor first has to *believe* that it is an adverse reaction. This requires the doctor to admit that s/he has done something that made the patient sicker. This is understandably very hard. One author suffered with a cough for 18 months before a doctor at another practice pointed out that his blood pressure medicine was probably causing it. So it proved. Doctors at the practice where he was normally treated had thought of almost everything except "oops, we did it."

There is a recognised procedure for checking that an adverse situation is a result of medication (Spitzer, 1986). Change the medication ("dechallenge"). See if the problem gets better. Change it back ("rechallenge"). See if the problem comes back. This is necessarily time consuming, and if a change of medication makes the patient better, doctors would generally rather not try the rechallenge. It's one thing to make a patient sick unintentionally, quite another to deliberately risk it just for diagnostic precision. Of course, if the patient died, which sometimes happens, you cannot do such experimental checking. So the link between treatment and reaction has stronger support in some cases than others.

Finally, it has been observed that doctors often don't bother reporting a reaction unless it is unusual or severe. After all, if a reaction is common, the Centre must know about it already, so why bother telling them? And if a reaction is mild, is it really worth the effort?

The result is that the Ministry of Health estimate that 95% of the adverse reaction cases are missing.

There are three characteristics of the adverse reaction setup:

1. Most adverse reactions are not reported.
2. Reaction numbers are generally low.
3. The aim of analysis is to decrease these numbers, and other people are continually working to reduce them anyway.

Within the cases that are present, many of the fields are missing. For example, for each drug, there is a "dose" field and a "unit" field. Out of 28392 drug/dose/unit triples in the data we're working with, 33 are missing either dose or unit, and 7670 (27+%) are missing both. To the doctors writing the reports, the correct values for these fields are so obvious that there's no need to bother writing them. In some cases (intra-uterine device => dose = 1, unit = standard dose) it's obvious to anyone.

Statistics Doesn't Help Much

Statisticians have been concerned about missing data for a long time. Little & Rubin (1987) is a good beginning. Unfortunately, the adverse reaction cases are "missing not at random." They are systematically missing. A statistical approach to the problem would require modelling the missingness. Given information on the number of cases with certain diagnoses and/or the number of times the various treatments were prescribed, it would be possible to do this. Such data does exist. It even exists at our University. However, we have been unable to gain access to it.

There is a further issue, which is that both market basket data and adverse reaction data are really time series data. Products enter and leave the market: a product cannot be purchased when it is not on the market. Drugs are approved and have their approval taken away: a drug cannot be prescribed before it is approved (which is how we know that the Pill could not possibly have been responsible for the end of the baby boom) and will not be prescribed once it is deregistered.

Estimating Reporting Rate

Our data set is all the available adverse reaction reports for about five years. The data include demographic data, diagnoses, treatments, and reactions. One measurement that we were specifically advised to ignore is the date that a report reached the Centre. Examining this date illuminates the reporting process, and lets us gain some idea of the scale of the missing data problem. The techniques used may be relevant to other application areas.

First, we simply plot the number of reports per month. (The data do not permit any finer grain of analysis.)

We would expect that most treatment/reaction problems would either be seasonal (hay fever) or campaign related (meningitis vaccination) or fairly steady throughout the year. If cases arise at the rate of n per month and are reported at random with probability p, we would expect the number of reports per month to have a Binomial(n,p) distribution, or at least not to be too far from that. Instead, the data are dramatically "bursty." (See Figure 1(a))

The data are of two kinds. There are four "intensive monitoring programmes," for Intra-Uterine Devices (IUD), vaccinations (VAC), migraine medication (MIG), and Salbutamol (SAL). For these treatments, doctors have been asked to report *every* adverse reaction, no matter how minor it appears, or even whether they believe in the association or not. We ought to have good data for these treatments. The other (OTH) treatments are "report at will." There are

4393 IUD reports (24%)
4782 VAC reports (26%)
1241 MIG reports (7%)
576 SAL reports (3%)
7326 OTH reports (40%)

Intra-uterine device and vaccinations are not especially dangerous; they are especially *suspect* and watched more carefully.

Having found that the data are bursty, the obvious question is whether this burstiness comes from the other treatments, or whether the rates are highly variable for the intensive monitoring programmes as well. With more than half the data coming from the intensive monitoring programmes, perhaps it is not surprising that they are bursty too.

We see at once that the largest peaks are all due to IUDs (Figure 1 (b)); a broad peak at the right is due to vaccinations (Figure 1 (c)), and other peaks can clearly be traced (Figure 1 (d-f)).

We have another label that gives us an advantage in this dataset: reactions are labeled if they are *serious* (i.e., life-threatening). If we plot the proportion of serious reports against the total number of reports in each month (see Figure 2 (a)), we see that a reasonable first approximation is that at high reporting levels the proportion of serious reports is roughly constant, while at low reporting levels the proportion of serious reports is much higher. This is consistent with a model where when there

Figure 1. Plots of report totals by month received in the CARM dataset

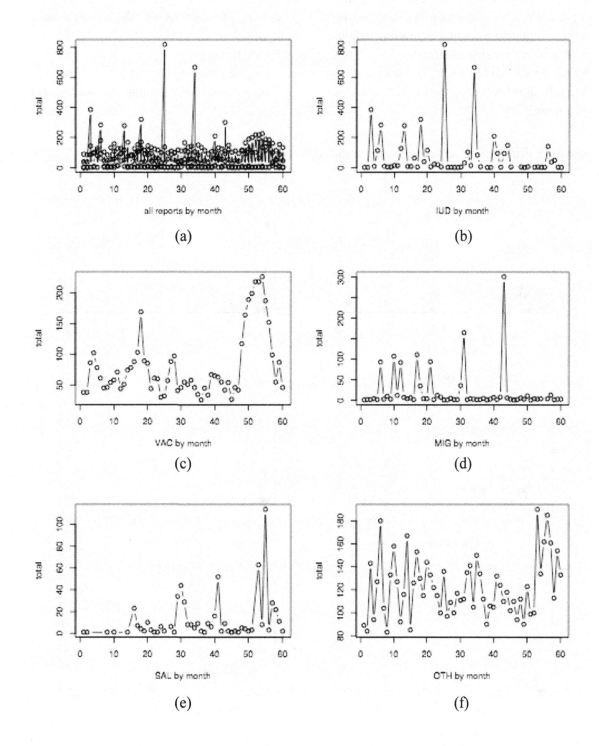

(a)

(b)

(c)

(d)

(e)

(f)

is a burst of serious cases, doctors start reporting all cases, whereas in more humdrum times they report fewer of the mild cases. We can use this model to estimate the amount of missing data in the intensive monitoring programme:

let n_{obs} be the observed total in each month.

let s_{obs} be the observed number of serious cases in each month.

let s' be the average proportion of serious cases

among the 8 months with the highest number of reports.

let tot_s be sum(s_{obs})

let n_{est} be pmax(n_{obs}, s_{obs} / s')

Then the estimated amount of missing data is

Figure 2. Probabilities of seeing serious adverse reactions by month in the CARM dataset

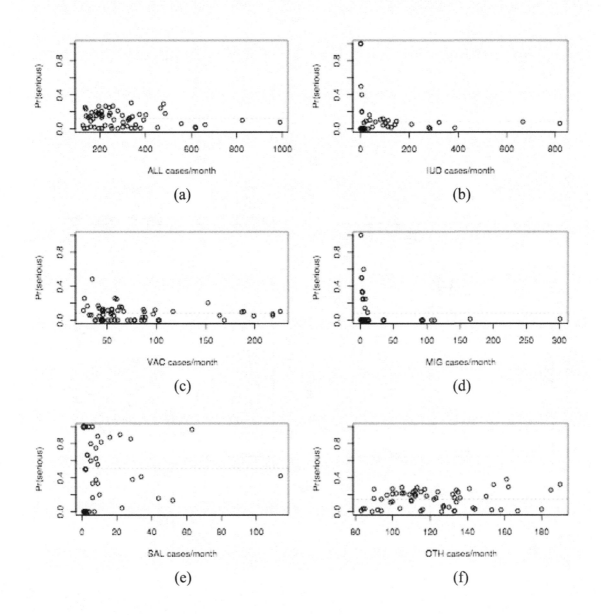

$$100*(1-\text{sum}(n_{obs})/\text{sum}(n_{est}))\%$$

This estimate suggests that about three quarters of the migraine data may be missing and about one quarter of the other intensively monitored treatment data may be missing.

If this much "intensively monitored" data may be missing, how much more so the rest? Overall, considering the crudity of this estimate, it is consistent with the Ministry of Health conclusion that up to 95% of the data is missing.

So far we have concluded that

- about 20% of the intensively monitored cases are missing
- most of the rest is missing
- the serious reports come in bursts
- high reporting levels seem to be reasonably thorough, but low reporting levels omit many less serious cases.

How can we explain this? One model is that doctors report bad cases most of the time, but get habituated to mild reactions. From time to time they are reminded of the importance of reporting reactions to some treatment, perhaps through the NZ Medical Journal, and for a while they report more cases. This is not unrealistic. One of the first associations I found was a strong link between reactions to X-ray dyes and a particular locality. The Centre told me, "we know about that: we gave a talk there and they sent us a whole lot of old records." This is a clear example of reporting influenced by attitude rather than real-world rate.

There are two notions of "badness" associated with reactions in this data set. A reaction is SERIOUS if it is life-threatening; SEVERE if it is bad of its kind. A severe nosebleed is better to have than a non-serious cancer. Under our "reminder" model of reporting, we expect that the more reports there are in a month, the lower the proportion of serious ones, because the serious ones are being reported anyway. This is indeed what we find (see Figures 2 and 3 – dashed lines are means).

For IUD, VAC, MIG, and SAL we see a general tendency for there to be a spike of months with few reports but many of them serious down at the left, tailing off to a fairly steady state as the number of cases in a month rises. (This is spoiled for SAL by an outlier.) The simplest way to account for these results is to assume that most of the serious cases are getting through all the time, while less serious cases often are not. This pattern is not seen in the OTH graph because it is a mix of many different kinds of problems. Readers are reminded always to consider Simpson's paradox when examining data merged from several distinct categories.

The graphs of the probabilities of seeing a severe reaction (of its type) against the number of cases in a month show a similar pattern. For IUD and MIG we see exactly the same pattern as for the serious cases. For OTH we again see no pattern. For ALL we see that all the high-severity months have fewer than 500 cases. Curiously, and to remind us not to jump to conclusions, the VAC graph shows a rise. Looking back at the graphs of total reports by month, we see that vaccination reports peak at intervals of 10 to 14 months. Amongst other things, there are pulses of vaccination against each year's influenza variant. This needs to be investigated further: possibly a case of Simpson's paradox again.

Examining Rarity

To what extent *should* we suppose that, in any given dataset, we shall have to deal with issues of rarity? We are beginning to see a reasonable number of ways of dealing with rare associations when we expect them (see, for instance, Bayardo et al., (2000), Koh et al., (2005 and 20082008), Li et al., (1999), Liu et al., (1999), Szathmary et al., (2007)), but when should we expect to have to deal with rare associations? There are several possible explanations for rarity of observations within a dataset, and different ways you might choose to detect or deal with each.

Figure 3. Probabilities of seeing severe adverse reactions by month in the CARM dataset

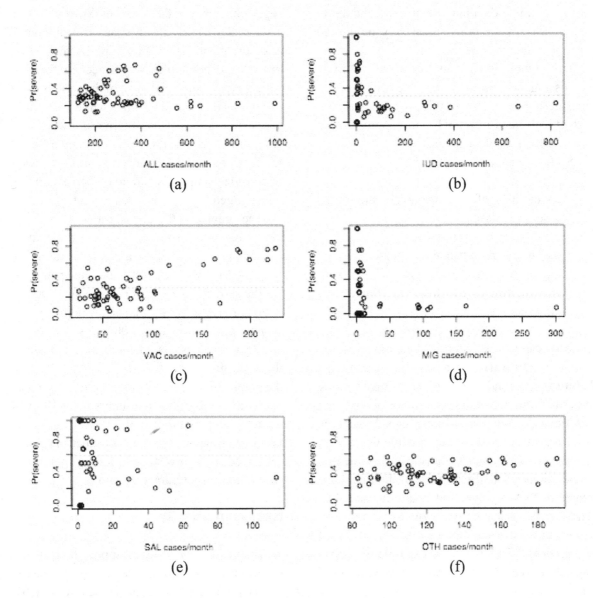

(a)   (b)

(c)   (d)

(e)   (f)

First, cases may be uncontrolled, and items just plain unlikely. For example, suppose you wish to study supernovae from general astronomical observations – there just aren't that many of them. The two usual remedies in cases like these are to get more data (i.e. to increase the absolute frequency of the items of interest) or to select a subpopulation (i.e. to increase the relative frequency). The

first may be costly, and the second runs the risk of introducing artifacts into the signal.

Second, cases may be uncontrolled, and cases of interest not at all unlikely, but remain unrecognized. For instance, associations between peptic ulcers and H. Pylori seemed rare, even though they weren't, because it wasn't considered necessary to detect or record the presence of the bacteria, only the presence of stress and other lifestyle factors. There is a chicken-and-egg problem here: researchers need a reason to record a relevant detail, and you can't record everything.

Third, and relevant to the CARM dataset, is that data are partly controlled, and items are rare because there is a) great effort to keep them rare, and b) some disincentive to record them when they happen (such as concerns of malpractice or liability). Remedies involve trying to increase reporting rates (which can introduce "bursts" of data as with the X-ray dye cases mentioned earlier) or simply waiting for more data (which can run the risk of allowing avoidable suffering).

It is entirely possible that some drugs or some reactions are rare because they were only available or only happened (or were only recorded) over a small window of time. It is possible to detect these cases by creating an estimated window size on a per-observation-type basis. The trick is to recognize that, as the period of time *outside* a window of occurrence in which you *don't* see the item increases, the *more* likely it is that the item *only* occurs in that window (i.e. has now *stopped* occurring). We can therefore determine a confidence interval for the size the window should be before we can reasonably conclude that we won't see any more of them.

Begin with a Series of Observations 1..N

Each of them may be what we are looking for ($x[i] = 1$) or not ($x[i] = 0$). (See Table 1)

The adjusted value p' is always very close to the raw value p_0. The adjusted value w' is never smaller than the raw window w_0; on the CARM data, it stretches the observed windows by an average of 5 months, which in a span of 60 months seems a reasonable level of caution. This technique successfully finds several drugs which came into or out of service during the 5 years.

Rare Data in the CARM Dataset are Really Rare

There are 28,391 drug administrations in the data, corresponding to 987 distinct drugs. The distribution is quite Zipfian:

286 drugs occur once.

125 drugs occur twice.

76 drugs occur thrice.

...

1 drug (a migraine treatment) occurs 1166 times.

1 drug (a vaccine) occurs 1282 times.

1 drug (a copper IUD) occurs 4070 times.

Just because something is rare does not mean it is unimportant.

A drug may be rare in the data because

Table 1.

let *first* = min { i | x[i] }	**First case**
let *last* = max { i | x[i] }	**Last case**
$w_0 = last - first + 1$	**Maximum likelihood window**
tally = # {i | x[i] }	**Number of cases**
$p_0 = (tally - 1)/(w_0 - 1)$	**Initial probability estimate**
delta = round($0.839/p_0 - 0.981$)	**Numbers determined by Monte Carlo simulation on the data-**
last' = min(*last* + *delta*, N)	**set to get a 95% confidence interval**
first' = max(*first* - 2*delta + (*last'* - *last*), 1)	**Where we take the window to end**
$w' = last' - first' + 1$	**Where we take the window to start**
$p' = tally/w'$	**Fitted window width**
	Fitted probability within window

213

Table 2.

number of drugs	proportion of cases of disease
17	1/1
14	1/2
8	1/3
7	1/4
7	1/5
5	1/6
...	
107	< 1/10
106	can't tell, disease not recorded

1. the condition for which it is prescribed is rare
2. the drug has largely been superseded by other drugs
3. and is mainly used by people for whom the others are unsuitable
4. the drug has been withdrawn from use as too dangerous and
5. the cases in our data are among the last few uses
6. the drug is new and our cases are among the first few uses
7. the drug is actually very safe.

Information on the number of people diagnosed with various conditions does exist, but has not been made available to us. In order to check possibility 1, we could look at whether the condition a rare drug was prescribed for occurs elsewhere in our data. In 18% of cases, alas, we don't know what a drug was prescribed for, because the report doesn't say. This also limits our ability to check whether some reactions might actually be responses to the disease. Let's see: of the 286 drugs that occur only once, (See Table 2)

The 74 drugs that account for 10% or more of the reports for the condition they were prescribed for may well belong to the "rare condition" category.

As for reactions: there are 27,604 adverse reactions in the data, corresponding to 1094 distinct reactions. The distribution is also quite Zipfian:

332 reactions occur once.

151 reactions occur twice.

89 reactions occur thrice.

...

1 reaction (rash) occurs 671 times.

1 reaction (menorrhagia) occurs 825 times.

1 reaction (inflammation at injection site) occurs 1385 times.

The link between inflammation at injection site and vaccinations will surprise no-one, nor will the link between menorrhagia and IUDs. If anyone were to predict a reaction among the t op three, "rash" would be it.

Just because something is rare does not mean it is unimportant. Rare reactions include death. A reaction may be rare in the data because

1. the circumstances that provoke it are rare
2. it is not recognised as a reaction to treatment
3. it used to be common but the cause has been recognised and eliminated
4. it's becoming common but the cause is new
5. people die of something else first

One of the main reasons for monitoring adverse reactions is to catch reason 2. This is why the intensive monitoring programs exist, so that anything that *might* be a reaction should be reported even if each individual reporter thinks it isn't. Foetal Alcohol Syndrome is now recognised as a reaction to the over-the-counter medication called ethanol. For a long time it was not.

Categories 3 and 4 here correspond to categories 3 and 4 for drugs. At first glance, it seems silly to consider the possibility of a reaction being confined to a "window" of the data; surely human physiology doesn't change that much. But checking for the possibility might reveal a reaction to an environmental cause.

CONCLUSION

There are three lessons demonstrated by the CARM data.

1. Don't treat a data field as unimportant just because you're told it's unimportant. It may tell you more than you (or anyone else) might believe.
2. Sometimes things are rare because we try to make them rare. Our modelling needs to take this into account.
3. Having labels on instances (such as "severe" or "serious") is not just useful for the purpose of classification or for deriving classification models.

And we should not ever forget John Tukey's advice: "There is no excuse for failing to plot and look." (Tukey, 1977).

REFERENCES

Agrawal, R., Imielinski, T., & Swami, A. (1993). Mining association rules between sets of items in large databases. In P. Buneman & S. Jajodia (Eds.), *Proceedings of the 1993 ACM SIGMOD international conference on management of data* (pp. 207–216). New York, NY: ACM Press.

Bayardo, R. J., Agrawal, R., & Gunopulos, D. (2000). Constraint-based rule mining in large, dense databases. *Data Mining and Knowledge Discovery*, *4*(2/3), 217–240. doi:10.1023/A:1009895914772

Koh, Y. S., & Rountree, N. (2005). Finding sporadic rules using Apriori-Inverse. *Advances in Knowledge Discovery and Data Mining, 9th Pacific-Asia Conference on Knowledge Discovery and Data Mining 2005* (pp. 97–106). Berlin / Heidelberg: Springer.

Koh, Y. S., Rountree, N., & O'Keefe, R. A. (2008). Mining interesting imperfectly sporadic rules. *Knowledge and Information Systems*, *14*(2), 179–196. doi:10.1007/s10115-007-0074-6

Li, J., Zhang, X., Dong, G., Ramamohanarao, K., & Sun, Q. (1999). Efficient mining of high confidence association rules without support threshold In *Proceedings of the 3rd European Conference on Principle and Practice of Knowledge Discovery in Databases, PKDD '99* (pp. 406–411).

Little, R. J. A., & Rubin, D. B. (1987). Statistical analysis with missing data. New York: Wiley.

Liu, B., Hsu, W., & Ma, Y. (1999). Mining association rules with multiple minimum supports. In *Proceedings of the 5th ACM SIGKDD International Conference on Knowledge Discovery and Data Mining* (pp. 337–341). New York, NY: ACM Press.

Spitzer, W. (1986). Importance of valid measurements of benefit and risk. *Medical Toxicology*, *1*(1), 74–78.

Szathmary, L., Napoli, A., & Valtchev, P. (2007, October 29-31). Towards Rare Itemset Mining. In *Proceedings of the 19th IEEE international Conference on Tools with Artificial intelligence - Vol.1 (ICTAI 2007) - Volume 01 ICTAI* (pp. 305-312). Washington, DC: IEEE Computer Society.

Tukey, J. (1977). *Exploratory Data Analysis*, Addison-Wesley.

Zolezzi, M., & Parsotam, N. (2005). Adverse drug reaction reporting in New Zealand: implications for pharmacists. *Theraputics and Clinical Risk Management*, *1*(3), 181–188.

Chapter 14
Filtering Association Rules by Their Semantics and Structures

Rangsipan Marukatat
Mahidol University, Thailand

ABSTRACT

Association rule mining produces a large number of rules but many of them are usually redundant ones. When a data set contains infrequent items, the authors need to set the minimum support criterion very low; otherwise, these items will not be discovered. The downside is that it leads to even more redundancy. To deal with this dilemma, some proposed more efficient, and perhaps more complicated, rule generation methods. The others suggested using simple rule generation methods and rather focused on the post-pruning of the rules. This chapter follows the latter approach. The classic Apriori is employed for the rule generation. Their goal is to gain as much insight as possible about the domain. Therefore, the discovered rules are filtered by their semantics and structures. An individual rule is classified by its own semantic, or by how clear its domain description is. It can be labelled as one of the following: strongly meaningless, weakly meaningless, partially meaningful, and meaningful. In addition, multiple rules are compared. Rules with repetitive patterns are removed, while those conveying the most complete information are retained. They demonstrate an application of our techniques to a real case study, an analysis of traffic accidents in Nakorn Pathom, Thailand.

INTRODUCTION

Association rules describe relationship between items in a transactional database. Intuitively, a rule $X \rightarrow Y$ implies that when X occurs in a transaction, Y is likely to occur as well. *Apriori* is the most well-

known method to extract association rules from a data set (Agrawal et al., 1993; Agrawal & Srikant, 1994). It works in two major steps. First, frequent itemsets, or sets of items whose support is greater than a minimum support threshold (*minsup*), are discovered. Then, association rules whose confidence is greater than a minimum confidence threshold (*minconf*) are generated from these frequent item-

DOI: 10.4018/978-1-60566-754-6.ch014

sets. Rules that describe frequent patterns can be exploited in many real-world applications. For example, in retailing, products which are highly associated can be sold together as a special offer package (Svetina & Zupancic, 2005).

Some applications focus on rare or infrequent patterns only. An example is a surveillance of nosocomial infection, or infection that patients acquire during their hospital stay (Ma et al., 2003). Patients' microbiological transactions were sampled over the period of three months, and three sets of association rules were generated, one for each month. Ma and his colleagues focused on rules with low support (less than 1%) and low confidence (less than 30%) because these rules may capture irregularity in patients' antibiotic resistance. They identified potential outbreaks of the infection by comparing similar patterns across three months, and noticing sudden changes in their confidence measures.

When a database contains a huge number of transactions and some items rarely occur, we usually set the *minsup* criterion very low, in order to not miss useful association rules. A downside of this strategy is that such rules would be overwhelmed by redundant, spurious ones. There are two ways to tackle this problem. First, rule generation methods equipped with filters or pruning mechanisms are employed instead of Apriori. MSApriori (Liu et al., 1999b), RSAA (Yun et al. 2003), and Apriori-Inverse (Ko & Rountree, 2005) used alternative support criteria so that rules with low support but high confidence are generated. These rules are called sporadic or exceptional rules. Daly and Taniar (2004) proposed another method to find exceptional rules by combining the ideas of infrequent and negative patterns. They introduced an exceptionality measure. By their definition, if a rule $X \rightarrow Y$ has high support and high confidence, then $\sim X \rightarrow Y$ or $X \rightarrow \sim Y$ is an exceptional rule if it has low support but high exceptionality measure. Zhou and Yau (2007) proposed two algorithms for mining infrequent patterns, which are matrix-based and hash-based.

These algorithms required few database accesses and were able to discover rules from a minimum search space.

Unlike the classic Apriori, the above methods have not yet been available in mainstream data mining software. It is quite common in applied research (including this work) that standard, widely-acknowledged tools are applied to certain problems or domains. It allows us to focus on the domains and not worry about developing the tools. Hence, the second way to tackle the rare item problem is to employ Apriori for the rule generation, and use some criteria to select or prune the discovered rules afterwards. The second approach is the main focus of our chapter.

Negative patterns are also useful in many applications. A negative association rule has one of the following forms: $\sim X \rightarrow Y$, $X \rightarrow \sim Y$, or $\sim X \rightarrow \sim Y$. In marketing research, it helps identify a pair of replacement items in case that one of them is in short supply. In some data mining software such as Weka (University of Waikato, n.d.), Apriori can be set to enable or disable the generation of negative association rules. Suppose that each item is represented by a binary attribute, where 0 means "absent" and 1 means "present". The binary attribute can be treated as an asymmetric or a symmetric one. In the asymmetric treatment, absentees are considered missing values; therefore, an item is counted only when its value is 1. This approach disallows negative rule generation. On the other hand, the symmetric treatment treats 0 and 1 as two distinct categories, allowing negative rules to also be generated. These rules are harder to interpret than positive rules and plenty of them are redundant. Techniques that generate negative rules more efficiently have been proposed, such as Antonie and Zaiane (2004), Wu et al. (2004), and Yuan et al. (2002).

Several techniques have been proposed to select or prune the discovered rules. For instance, entropy-based pruning was proposed by Jaroszewicz and Simovici (2002), and statistic-based pruning by Ableson and Glasgow (2003). Liu et al. (1999a) and Toivonen et al. (1995) both attempted to select a few general rules from the entire set of rules. These general rules gave an overall picture about the domain. The remaining ones were discarded (according to Toivonen et al.), or kept for further analysis (according to Liu et al.). The rules can also be filtered by the semantics or knowledge they convey. Klemettinen et al. (1994) and Ma et al. (2003) selected rules that matched user-defined templates. Silberschatz and Tuzhilin (1996) and Liu et al. (1997) selected surprising rules or rules that did not follow users' existing knowledge. These techniques will be described in details later.

As stated earlier, this chapter focuses on the post-mining of association rules. Using Apriori for the rule generation, we acknowledge its lack of effective pruning mechanisms. We assume that the algorithm might be executed several times, with different combinations of *minsup* and *minconf* parameters. In some executions, *minsup* may be set very low. The algorithm is also set to generate negative rules. Once a large number of rules are generated, we apply semantic and structure analyses to filter out redundant rules. The semantic analysis considers how clearly an individual rule describes certain aspects of the domain. It classifies rules into four groups: strongly meaningless, weakly meaningless, partially meaningful, and meaningful. The structure analysis compares rules that carry the same piece of information but are in slightly different forms, and chooses only one with the highest significance score. The central idea of this chapter is the selection of association rules based on the information they convey. Hence, specific rules are preferable to general ones.

The rest of this chapter is organized as follows. In the second section (Background and Literature Survey), we briefly review the fundamentals of association rule mining. Then, we survey related works on the filtering and the semantic consideration of association rules. The third section (Alternative Filtering Methods: Semantic and Structure Analyses) introduces the filtering of

association rules by their patterns and degrees of semantic redundancy. The next section (A Case Study) presents an example of applying the proposed techniques to a real case study. We use traffic accident data which were collected from local police stations in Nakorn Pathom, Thailand. In the final section, we conclude this chapter and suggest future research directions.

BACKGROUND AND LITERATURE SURVEY

Association Rule Mining Fundamentals

Let $D = \{T_1, T_2, ..., T_n\}$ be a transactional database. Each transaction T is a subset of I, where $I = \{i_1, i_2, ..., i_m\}$ is a set of distinct items. An association rule can be expressed as $X \rightarrow Y$ where $X \subset I$ is the set of antecedent items, $Y \subset I$ is the set of consequence items, and $X \cap Y = \emptyset$. The support of this rule is the fraction of database that contain both X and Y, i.e. $support(X \rightarrow Y) = P(X \cap Y)$. The confidence of this rule is the fraction of database that also contain Y when they contain X, i.e. $confidence(X \rightarrow Y) = P(Y|X) = P(X \cap Y) / P(X)$. The lift or interest of this rule measures the dependency between X and Y, i.e. $lift(X \rightarrow Y) = P(X \cap Y) / (P(X) \times P(Y))$. Three conclusions can be drawn from the lift measure. First, if it equals 1.0, then X and Y are completely independent of one another. Second, if it is less than 1.0, then X and Y are negatively associated or one is less likely to occur if the other has occurred. Third, if it is greater than 1.0, then X and Y are positively associated or they are likely to occur together.

Apriori (Agrawal et al., 1993; Agrawal & Srikant, 1994) is composed of two main tasks:

1. Frequent itemset generation generates itemsets that pass *minsup* threshold.
2. Rule generation generates association rules that pass *minconf* threshold.

Figure 1. Algorithm Apriori

```
Input:          minsup, lower_minsup, delta, criterion, minscore, numrules
Output:         ruleset
Method:
    1.      ruleset = ∅, N = 0
    2.      do {
    3.          // (1) Frequent itemset generation
    4.          for k = 1 to numitems {
    5.              Find frequent k-itemset, Sₖ, that satisfies the condition:
    6.              lower_minsup ≤ support(Sₖ) ≤ minsup
    7.          }
    8.          // (2) Rule generation
    9.          for each frequent itemset S {
   10.              for each subset SS of S {
   11.                  Rule R = SS → (S − SS)
   12.                  Compute confidence(R) and lift(R)
   13.                  if (criterion == "lift") then score = lift(R) else score = confidence(R)
   14.                  if (score ≥ minscore) then {
   15.                      Add R to ruleset
   16.                      N = N + 1
   17.                  }
   18.              }
   19.          }
   20.          minsup = minsup − delta
   21.      } until (minsup ≤ lower_minsup) or (N == numrules)
   22.      Sort ruleset by criterion
```

Choosing the right thresholds is not easy because rules with high support tend to have low confidence, and vice versa. Moreover, if *minsup* is too high, some important rules may not be discovered. But if it is too low, over-abundant rules may be generated. This work used Weka's Apriori which wraps the itemset generation and rule generation in a loop (University of Waikato, n.d.). Either confidence or lift can be used as the criterion (*minscore*) for the rule generation. The *minsup* threshold is gradually decreased at the end of loop iteration, allowing rules with different combinations of support, confidence, and lift measures to be generated. Our rule filtering methods were built upon Weka. (See Figure 1)

Suppose that there are three items {*a, b, c*} in a transactional database. Each item has two possible values: 0, if it is absent from a transaction; and 1, if it is present in a transaction. If the items are treated as asymmetric attributes, the itemset generation will consider only three items: $a = 1$, $b = 1$, and $c = 1$. If they are treated as symmetric attributes, then items $a = 0$, $b = 0$, and $c = 0$ are also considered during the itemset generation.

The Filtering of Association Rules

In this section, we survey related techniques to select, prune, or filter association rules. Some of them selected a small set of general rules that summarize the whole findings. According to Toivonen et al. (1995), rule R_1 covers R_2 if they have exactly the same consequence and R_1's antecedent is a subset of R_2's. Following this definition, {*a, b*} → {*d*} covers {*a, b, c*} → {*d*} and is consequently the more general one. The specific rule, i.e. {*a, b, c*} → {*d*}, is pruned out. Similar ideas were suggested by the others, but some of them did not remove all specific rules. For example, Webb and Zhang (2002) kept a specific rule if its measures surpassed the measures of the more general one. Bayardo et al. (1999) added that the improvement in the rule's measures (confidence, in their work) must exceed a minimum improvement threshold.

Liu et al. (1999a) used chi-square correlation between the rule's antecedent and consequence as another selection criterion. The correlation measure implies the rule's direction, which may be positive, negative, or zero (independence). They used the terms direction setting (DS) rules instead of general rules. A rule is a DS rule if it has positive direction but its subrules do not. For instance, $\{a, b\} \rightarrow \{d\}$ has two subrules: $\{a\} \rightarrow \{d\}$ and $\{b\} \rightarrow \{d\}$. If neither of them has positive direction, then the positive direction of $\{a, b\} \rightarrow \{d\}$ is considered unexpected and this rule is labelled a DS rule. Non-DS rules follow the directions of DS rules since they are combinations of multiple DS rules. Rules that are neither DS nor non-DS are discarded. This concept was adopted in DS-WEB (Ma et al., 2000), a visualization system that allows users to navigate from each DS rule to related non-DS ones.

Li et al. (2001) selected informative association rules based on their confidence or predictive power. Their method compares rules which have either the same consequence or the same antecedent. For example, suppose that two groups of rules are discovered:

- Rules having the same consequence: $\{a\} \rightarrow \{d\}$, $\{b\} \rightarrow \{d\}$, and $\{a, b\} \rightarrow \{d\}$
- Rules having the same antecedent: $\{d\} \rightarrow \{a\}$, $\{d\} \rightarrow \{b\}$, and $\{d\} \rightarrow \{a, b\}$

In each group, the last rule will be pruned if it has lower confidence than its subrules (the first and the second rules). Li and his colleagues proposed an efficient algorithm that generated fewer itemsets than Apriori. But their concept is

also applicable to the post-mining of discovered rules.

Other criteria to filter association rules are, for example, maximum entropy (Jaroszewicz & Simovici, 2002) and statistical significance score (Ableson & Glasgow, 2003).

Semantic Consideration of the Rules

There have also been techniques that take semantics or knowledge carried in the rules into account. Klemettinen et al. (1994) filtered rules by user-specified templates. They allowed users to construct two types of templates: inclusive and exclusive (or restrictive) ones. A rule is selected if it matches at least one inclusive template and does not match any exclusive template. Detecting the outbreak of nosocomial infection, Ma et al. (2003) used templates to select rules consisting of related items such as organism species and organism's susceptibility test. Their work has been mentioned in the introduction.

According to Silberschatz and Tuzhilin (1996), there are two subjective criteria to determine whether a rule is interesting: (1) it is surprising or unexpected; and (2) it is actionable. Their work focused on the former criterion. They considered a rule unexpected if it contradicts user-specified belief. There are a few methods to specify the user's belief, as also reviewed in their paper, but these methods are quite difficult to execute in practice. Liu et al. (1997) proposed an alternative model called general impression (GI). They used fuzzy linguistic to express user's general impressions, i.e. some vague or imprecise ideas, about the domain. A rule is compared against a set of GIs and classified as one of the following:

1. Conforming rule, or a rule whose both condition (antecedent) and class (consequence) match a GI's condition and class.
2. Unexpected conclusion rule, or a rule whose only condition matches a GI's condition. Thus, its class or conclusion is

unexpected.

3.   Unexpected condition rule. It is a rule whose condition leading to its class is not found in any GI, or whose only class matches a GI's class. Thus, its condition is unexpected.

In another work by Liu et al. (1996), these concepts were applied to the finding of actionable rules. Instead of supplying general impressions, the users specified situations under which they would take some actions. These situations needed not be precise, and could be either expected or unexpected by the users.

Other techniques employed concept hierarchies or taxonomy trees for the semantic analysis. Li and Sweeney (2005) used concept hierarchy to group rules that carried the same piece of information, and construct a robust rule that expressed this information more thoroughly. They suggested that a rule's antecedent implied a hypothesis that should cover a large number of cases. In contrast, a rule's consequence implied knowledge description that should be exact. Therefore, from a group of related rules, the most general expression is selected as the robust rule's antecedent while the most specific expression is selected as the robust rule's consequence. Furthermore, Li and Sweeney proposed a semantic measure called knowledge rating which indicated a robust rule's degree of insightfulness.

Making association rules easily understandable to human sometimes does not require precise semantics. For example, given a rule describing a traffic accident, saying that the time of this accident is in "the afternoon" is preferable to stating the exact time "14.00 or 2pm". Delgado et al. (2001), suggested a fuzzy model for association rules which substituted casual, imprecise expressions for precise ones. They also incorporated the concepts of certainty factor and very strong rules, which had been introduced in their previous works. The former measures the degree of change in user's belief. It can be used along with the support measure to select very strong association rules.

By their definition, if both $X \rightarrow Y$ and $\sim Y \rightarrow \sim X$ have high certainty factor and high support, then $X \rightarrow Y$ is said to be a very strong rule.

Alternative Filtering Method: Semantic and Structure Analyses

In this section, we introduce alternative methods to filter association rules by using semantic and structure analyses. First of all, we give the following assumptions:

- Our data sets contain attributes which can be binary or categorical ones. For a binary attribute, 0 usually means false/absent and 1 usually means true/present. For a categorical attribute, there is usually one value such as 0, -1, or 99 that represents category outside the scope of interest. It is common in surveying practice that this value refers to the answer "unknown", "others", etc. In this chapter, we use *nil* for absent item (in case of a binary attribute) or unknown category (in case of a categorical attribute).

- A traditional rule generation method, Apriori, is used to generate rules. We employ the one available in Weka, an opensource data mining software (University of Waikato, n.d.). Negative rules are allowed – the setup will be explained in the next section, when we present a case study. We assume that the *minsup* threshold might be set very low, in order to not miss rules that carry useful information but have low support.

- From the set of discovered rules, we would like to select ones that help us understand the domain as much as possible. Some of them may surprise us. The others may only confirm what we already knew. There are methods to evaluate or further select rules against users' prior knowledge, as reviewed in the previous section. However, this issue is left to our future work.

We consider a domain as being composed of several perspectives. For example, in traffic accident domain, we may be interested in following perspectives: vehicles involved, causes of accident, time of accident, district area, scene of accident, and human losses. Positive rules surely describe what occur in a data set, but plenty of them may offer similar information. We apply structure analysis to select ones that carry the most information. In negative rules, some items are absent or do not occur in the data set. Consider the following negative rules:

- Rule 1: {*motorcycle = nil, truck = nil*} → {*bus = nil*}
- Rule 2: {*motorcycle = 1, truck = nil*} → {*bus = 1*}
- Rule 3: {*motorcycle = nil, speeding = nil*} → {*human death = nil*}

The first rule seems to not help us obtain any insight about vehicles involved in an accident, whereas the second rule offers some (incomplete) insight about this subject. The third rule gives some vague impression about vehicles involved, causes of accident, and human losses; but it needs to be analyzed in conjunction with some other rules. We apply semantic analysis to determine whether a rule offers any insight about the domain.

Semantic Analysis

We learn about a domain by analyzing rules extracted from a data set. First of all, variables are grouped into *subjects*, which correspond to the domain's perspectives. For instance, in a traffic accident data set, variables are grouped into six subjects, as shown in Table 1. This data set will be used as our case study afterwards.

Refined on our previous work (Marukatat, 2007), formal definitions for the semantic analysis are as follows. Let $\{S_1, S_2, ..., S_n\}$ be subjects; $\{V_{a1}, V_{a2}, ..., V_{ap}\}$ be a rule's antecedent variables; and $\{V_{c1}, V_{c2}, ..., V_{cq}\}$ be a rule's consequence

variables. A rule can be semantically classified into one of the following classes:

1. *Strongly meaningless rule.* It is a rule in which all the variables have *nil* values, and these variables are members of the same subject. A rule can be written as

$$\{V_{ai} = nil \mid V_{ai} \in S, i = 1 \text{ to } p\} \rightarrow \{V_{ck} = nil \mid V_{ck} \in S, k = 1 \text{ to } q\} . \quad (1)$$

An example of strongly meaningless rules is $\{V1 = nil, V5 = nil\} \rightarrow \{V3 = nil\}$, implying that an accident not involving motorcycle and truck is likely to not involve bus. It only tells that these vehicles are absent from the accident. But since there are several types of vehicles in the domain, we cannot infer how the remaining ones are involved. That is, the rule does not help us understand the vehicle subject any better.

2. *Weakly meaningless rule.* It is a rule in which all the variables have *nil* values, but these variables are members of more than one subjects. A rule can be written as

$$\{V_{ai} = nil \mid V_{ai} \in S_t, i = 1 \text{ to } p, t = 1 \text{ to } n\} \rightarrow$$

$$\{V_{ck} = nil \mid V_{ck} \in S_t, k = 1 \text{ to } q, t = 1 \text{ to } n\} . \quad (2)$$

An example of weakly meaningless rules is $\{V5 = nil, C5 = nil\} \rightarrow \{H1 = nil\}$, implying that an accident not involving truck and not being caused by swerving in close distance is likely to not result in human death. It does not offer insight about each individual subject, but there is some vague impression as multiple subjects are tied up. Nonetheless, the rule is not much worthy on its own, unless it is used in conjunction with meaningful ones.

3. *Partially meaningful rule.* It is a rule in which some, but not all, variables have *nil*

Table 1. Subjects of variables in a traffic accident data set (types "bin" and "cat" are shorthands for "binary" and "categorical", respectively)

Subject	Variable	Type	Description
Vehicles involved	V0	bin	bicycle or tricycle
	V1	bin	motorcycle
	V2	bin	sedan
	V3	bin	van or bus
	V4	bin	pick-up
	V5	bin	truck or trailer
	V6	bin	pedestrian
Causes of accident	C0	bin	vehicle overloaded or malfunctioned
	C1	bin	speeding
	C2	bin	violating traffic signs
	C3	bin	illegal blocking
	C4	bin	illegal overtaking
	C5	bin	swerving in close distance
	C6	bin	driving in the wrong lane or direction
	C7	bin	failing to signal
	C8	bin	careless driving
	C9	bin	following in close distance
Time of accident	T1	cat	quarter of day
	T2	cat	day of week
	T3	cat	quarter of year
District area	D1	cat	Nakorn Pathom's district area
Scene of accident	S1	cat	type of road (highway, local road, etc.)
	S2	cat	road feature (straight, curve, etc.)
	S3	cat	road material (concrete, laterite, etc.)
	S4	cat	traffic direction (one-way, two-way)
Human losses	H1	bin	dead
	H2	bin	seriously injured
	H3	bin	slightly injured

values. A rule can be written as

$$\{V_{ah} \neq nil, V_{ai} = nil \mid h, i = 1 \text{ to } p; h \neq i\} \rightarrow \{V_{cj} \neq nil, V_{ck} = nil \mid j, k = 1 \text{ to } q; j \neq k\} . \quad (3)$$

An example of partially meaningful rules is $\{V2 = 1, V4 = 1\} \rightarrow \{C5 = nil\}$, implying that an accident involving sedan and pick-up is likely to not being caused by swerving in close distance.

4. *Meaningful rule.* It is a rule that does not fall into any of the above categories.

Comparison to Other Works

Our definitions can be linked to the concept of positive/negative association rules as follows.

*   Meaningful rules are comparable to

positive rules, $X \rightarrow Y$.

- Partially meaningful rules are comparable to negative rules in $\sim X \rightarrow Y$ or $X \rightarrow \sim Y$ forms.
- Meaningless rules are comparable to negative rules in $\sim X \rightarrow \sim Y$ forms.

A few works suggested the use of negative rules $\sim X \rightarrow Y$ or $X \rightarrow \sim Y$ to identify competing or replacement items (Antonie & Zaiane, 2004; Wu et al., 2004; Yuan et al., 2002). They also mentioned the negative rule in $\sim X \rightarrow \sim Y$ form, but none gave an example of how to exploit it. Only Yuan et al. briefly suggested that $\sim X \rightarrow \sim Y$ was equivalent to $Y \rightarrow X$. That is, when X is absent, so is Y; therefore, the presence of Y implies that X is also present. However, since we allow an association rule to be composed of multiple antecedent and consequence items, it is hard to draw such inference. In this work, we would not suggest that $\{V5 = nil, C5 = nil\} \rightarrow \{H1 = nil\}$ is equivalent to any of its inverse forms, $\{H1 = 1\} \rightarrow \{V5 = 1, C5 = 1\}$ or $\{V5 = 1, C5 = 1\} \rightarrow \{H1 = 1\}$. We use weakly meaningless rules only as a confirmation of what is learned from meaningful ones. In future work, we will try to exploit them more effectively.

Structure Analysis

Recall that Apriori generates rule by permuting items in a frequent itemset, and choosing ones that satisfy the user's minimum confidence (or minimum lift) threshold. As a result, repetitive or redundant patterns tend to exist. In the semantic analysis, we filter rules by their individual contents but do not compare between them. Here, we compare rules against one another and select ones that carry the most information.

Let S_1 be a set of items in rule R_1. This set simply includes every item in the rule, as the effect of each item being in the antecedent or consequence is already captured by the rule's measures. For example, the confidence of $\{V2 = $

$1, V4 = 1\} \rightarrow \{C5 = nil\}$ equals $P(V2 = 1 \cap V4 = 1 \cap C5 = nil) / P(V2 = 1 \cap V4 = 1)$, whereas the confidence of $\{V2 = 1\} \rightarrow \{V4 = 1, C5 = nil\}$ equals $P(V2 = 1 \cap V4 = 1 \cap C5 = nil) / P(V2 = 1)$. Likewise, S_2 is a set of all the items in rule R_2. When R_1 and R_2 are compared, their relationship is determined as follows.

1. If S_1 equals S_2, then R_1 is equivalent to R_2.

Therefore, rules $\{V2 = 1, V4 = 1\} \rightarrow \{C5 = nil\}$ and $\{V2 = 1\} \rightarrow \{V4 = 1, C5 = nil\}$ are equivalent. Once a set of equivalent rules are identified, only the most significant one is selected. The rule's significance is determined according to user's criteria. Simple ones are confidence and lift measures. The other rule's measures, such as those mentioned in the literature survey, can also be used.

2. If S_1 includes all items in S_2 and at least one item in S_1 does not exist in S_2 (i.e. $S_2 \subset S_1$ and $| S_1 | > | S_2 |$), then R_1 covers R_2 or R_2 is covered by R_1.

Therefore, rule $\{V2 = 1, V4 = 1\} \rightarrow \{C5 = nil\}$ is said to cover $\{V2 = 1\} \rightarrow \{C5 = nil\}$. The former is selected while the latter is pruned out.

Comparison to Other Works

Our definition is in the opposite direction of what was proposed by Toivonen et al. (1995). In their work, the aim is to get an overview of the entire domain. A general rule is chosen over a specific one because it covers a larger portion of the domain's population. In contrast, we aim at getting as much information as possible about the domain. A specific rule is chosen over a general one because it covers a larger piece of information.

As mentioned in the literature survey, Bayardo et al. (1999) and Webb and Zhang (2002) picked specific rules only if their measures surpassed the measures of the more general ones. From our point of view, both were generated because their measures had surpassed the user's accepted criteria. Hence, they both deserve attention from the user, depending on the purpose of the analysis. Suppose that the following rules are generated:

- Rule 1: $\{a, b\} \rightarrow \{d\}$ with support = s1, confidence = c1
- Rule 2: $\{a, b, c\} \rightarrow \{d\}$ with support = s2, confidence = c2; s1 > s2 and c1 > c2

The first rule sufficiently summarizes the domain without the need for the second rule. But for in-depth analysis, knowing that a specific case $\{a, b, c\} \rightarrow \{d\}$ happened, while others such as $\{a, b, x\} \rightarrow \{d\}$ did not, would also be useful. This idea is similar to Liu et al. (1999a). In their work, once the user gets an overall picture from direction setting (DS) rules, he/she can proceed to investigate non-DS rules for further details. Moreover, Li and Sweeney (2005) constructed robust rules which presented the most complete knowledge by also picking the most specific expressions as their robust rules' consequence.

A CASE STUDY

In this section, we demonstrate an application of our rule filtering methods to an analysis of traffic accident in Nakorn Pathom. Nakorn Pathom is a province located 56 kilometers west of Bangkok, the capital of Thailand. It is known as a gateway to the western and the southern parts of the country. Traffic accident data, dated between January 1st, 2003 and March 31st, 2006, were collected from local police stations in Nakorn Pathom. The data set contains a total of 1103 records, 20 binary variables, and 8 categorical variables. The variables were grouped into six subjects, as summarized in Table 1.

Uing Weka's Apriori to discover association rules, the data set can be prepared as follows. To disable the negative rule generation, the *nil* value

is replaced by Weka's missing value symbol "?". Otherwise, *nil* can be any user-defined value that represents a *nil* category. In this case study, we prepared our data set as the latter. As presented in the background section, there are six key parameters in Weka's Apriori. They were set as follows.

- *minsup* = 0.4, 0.5, …, 0.9
- *lower_minsup* = 0.1
- *delta* = 0.05
- *criterion* = lift
- *minscore* (minimum lift) = 1.5, 2, 3, 4
- *numrules* (maximum rules) = 500

We used six values for *minsup* and four values for *minscore*, so that items with low support were not missed out. However, some combinations did not produce any rules – only 12 of them did, as summarized in Table 2. There were 4368 rules in total. Their contents varied from 2 to 9 items. Few rules (2.2% of total) had all *nil* values. They were classified as meaningless, while the remaining 32% and 65.8% were classified as meaningful and partially meaningful, respectively.

Next, we performed structure analysis to remove redundant patterns and retain rules that carried the most information. About 5.3% of the meaningful rules were retained. Similarly, about 5.4% of the partially meaningful rules were retained. The results are summarized in Table 3.

Some of the meaningful and partially meaningful rules that were retained are displayed in Table 4. To make the rules more understandable, we substituted each item with its category's description. Hence, an item *S1 = 1* would become *highway*.

Getting a good insight about traffic accidents in Nakorn Pathom requires some background knowledge about the domain. For example, we knew that trucks and trailers normally travel through Nakorn Pathom during the night and the early morning, delivering goods between the western/southern and the other parts of Thailand. Rule 5 seems like one of Nakorn Pathom's typical

Table 2. Summary of association rules discovered by Apriori

Apriori's Parameters		Discovered Rules		
minscore (lift)	minsup	Max Lift	Max Confidence	No. of Rules
0.4	0.8	4.43	0.77	24
0.3	0.8	4.43	0.95	210
0.2	0.8	2.99	0.91	500
0.2	0.7	4.37	0.91	500
0.2	0.6	4.37	0.95	500
0.2	0.5	4.37	0.95	500
0.2	0.4	3.42	0.95	38
1.5	0.8	1.65	0.90	500
1.5	0.7	2.15	0.97	500
1.5	0.6	2.32	0.91	500
1.5	0.5	3.73	0.94	500
1.5	0.4	3.42	0.95	96
Total				4368

traffic accident patterns. On the other hand, rule 3 is a little unexpected as it implies, with 69% confidence, a deadly accident that happens in the afternoon and involves truck.

From the table, there are two rules describing accident patterns at intersections. Rule 2 implies that an accident involving bus and being caused by swerving in close distance tends to occur at the intersection. Rule 6 implies that an accident occurring at the intersection of local roads, in the afternoon, tends to be caused by illegal blocking. This might indicate the inadequacy of traffic lights around the intersection areas. Another related issue is the enforcement of traffic law and regulation which has been a major problem in many parts of the country. It also exists in Nakorn Pathom, as implied by rules 9 and 10. The information extracted from rule 9 is not surprising because it

is quite common to see pedestrians crossing the roads wherever they like and vehicles seldom stopping for them, although we initially expected higher confidence.

Partially meaningful rules offer additional insight about traffic accidents. For example, rule 15 implies that when truck and highway are associated, the accident does not involve sedan and is not caused by speeding or swerving in close distance. With this information, it is possible to infer that an accident described by rule 4 (the one occurring between midnight and the early morning, on highway, and being caused by speeding) involves vehicles other than truck. Rule 13 is a complement to rule 7. We learn from the latter that an accident which occurs in the evening until midnight, and involves pedestrian, tends to be caused by speeding and result in human death.

Table 3. Result after semantic classification and structure analysis

	No. of Rules			
	Meaningful	Partially Meaningful	Meaningless	Total
Before pruning redundant patterns	1398 (32% of total)	2874 (65.8% of total)	96 (2.2% of total)	4368
After pruning redundant patterns	74 (5.3% retained)	155 (5.4% retained)	-	229

Table 4. Examples of meaningful and partially meaningful rules

	Meaningful	Confidence
1	Swerving in close distance → bicycle	0.77
2	Bus, swerving in close distance → intersection	0.71
3	12.01-18.00, straight, dead → truck	0.67
4	00.01-06.00, highway, straight → speeding	0.62
5	00.01-06.00, truck → dead	0.59
6	12.01-18.00, local road, intersection → illegal blocking	0.48
7	18.01-24.00, pedestrian → speeding, dead	0.46
8	Local road, illegal overtaking → curve	0.29
9	Violating traffic signs → pedestrian	0.18
10	Violating traffic signs → 06.01-12.00, community area	0.16
	Partially Meaningful	
11	Local road, slightly injured → two-way, asphalt surface, *no sedan, not speeding*	0.64
12	Bicycle, truck → straight, *no pick-up, no slightly injured*	0.47
13	18.01-24.00, pedestrian → *no motorcycle*, dead	0.46
14	*No motorcycle*, dead → highway, speeding	0.43
15	Truck → highway, *no sedan, not speeding, not swerving in close distance*	0.38

The former adds that this accident is likely to not involve motorcycle.

Limitation

We have demonstrated the filtering of discovered rules by their semantics and structures. We have also presented a few examples of using selected rules to obtain a better understanding about the domain. From the case study, we could observe a few limitations of our proposed methods. First, in the semantic analysis, we group variables into subjects which correspond to the domain's perspectives. In some subjects, it is common that multiple items may co-exist. For instance, every type of vehicles ($V0$-$V6$) may be involved in a single pile-up accident. But in the other subjects, one or at most a couple of items may co-exist. For instance, it is unlikely (but still remotely possible) that an accident would be caused by all the ten reasons ($C0$-$C9$). Suppose that we have the following rules:

- Rule 1: $\{V3 = 1, C5 = 1\} \rightarrow \{S2 = 2, V1 = 1, V2 = nil, V4 = nil, V5 = nil, V6 = 1\}$
- Rule 2: $\{V3 = 1, C5 = 1\} \rightarrow \{S2 = 2, C1 = nil, C3 = nil, C4 = nil, C8 = nil\}$

They both say that an accident involving bus and being caused by swerving in close distance tends to occur at an intersection. Extra information carried in the first rule is useful because it indicates other vehicles that are also involved and not involved. But extra information carried in the second rule, indicating that there is no other cause of accident, is rather redundant.

In our structure analysis, the comparison is not restricted to rules with the same consequence or the same antecedent. Given the following rules:

- Rule 1: $\{V2 = 1\} \rightarrow \{S1 = 1, H2 = 1\}$
- Rule 2: $\{V2 = 1\} \rightarrow \{C1 = nil, V1 = 1\}$
- Rule 3: $\{V1 = 1, C1 = nil\} \rightarrow \{V2 = 1\}$

The second and the third rules carry the same piece of information, but are in different forms.

Our method selects the more significant one, or the one with the higher confidence. Suppose that the first rule has already been selected. The second rule can be linked or merged with the first rule instantly, delivering more complete information about an accident involving sedan. In this case, we wish to retain the second rule even if it is less significant than the third one. Unfortunately, this idea has not yet been incorporated in our structure analysis.

CONCLUSION

Association rule mining is a powerful technique to extract patterns from a data set. However, the lack of pruning mechanisms in classical methods like Apriori causes abundant rules to be generated. Added to that, when the data set contains infrequent items, Apriori's minimum support threshold will be set very low, in order to not miss potentially useful associations. As a result, we are usually left to deal with an overwhelming amount of rules afterwards. This chapter presents methods to filter association rules based on their semantics and structures. The semantic analysis considers how clearly an association rule describes certain aspects of the domain. It classifies rules into four groups: strongly meaningless, weakly meaningless, partially meaningful, and meaningful. Meaningful rules describe something which are known to exist (in the data set), while meaningless rules are the opposite. Partially meaningful rules are somewhere in the middle. The structure analysis compares multiple rules and selects ones that carry the most information. Among equivalent rules, the most significant one will be selected. A rule's significance is determined by its confidence and lift measures. Since the analyses are performed independently of the rule generation, they can be used in conjunction with the other methods besides Apriori as well.

From our case study, we observe that while some of the selected rules present unexpected information, the others merely describe what we already knew. Further refinement can be made to the semantic analysis, so that user's prior knowledge and unexpectedness measure are taken into account. This can be done by using templates (Klemettinen et al., 1994) or other complex models (Liu et al., 1997; Silberschatz & Tuzhilin, 1996). Moreover, the notion of subjects or domain's perspectives can be extended to cover conditions on which multiple items may or may not co-exist. This would help filter out even more redundant rules.

The structure analysis helps remove repetitive patterns and retain the most specific ones. In some works, specific rules are considered trivial because they have much lower support and confidence than general rules (Bayardo et al., 1999; Toivonen et al., 1995; Webb & Zhang, 2002). We recapitulate our goal to extract as much information as possible about the domain. If the rules' measures are found to be too low, then the thresholds for the rule generation should have been raised. Otherwise, discovered rules with too low measures can be pruned out before we apply the structure analysis. Finally, as demonstrated in the previous section, the selected rules are not always easily organized and interpreted. Other criteria for choosing between equivalent rules may be added. In addition, visualization systems would help users navigate through the set of rules (Ma et al., 2000) or view the rules in more comprehensible formats (Blanchard et al., 2003; Techapichetvanich & Datta, 2005).

REFERENCES

Ableson, A., & Glasgow, J. (2003). Efficient statistical pruning of association rules. In N. Lavrac et al. (Eds.), *PKDD 2003, Lecture Notes in Computer Science, Vol. 2838* (pp. 23-34). Springer.

Agrawal, R., Imielinski, T., & Swami, A. (1993, May). Mining association rules between sets of items in large databases. *Proceedings of the ACM SIGMOD International Conference on Management of Data* (pp. 207-216), Washington, DC.

Agrawal, R., & Srikant, R. (1994, September). Fast algorithms for mining association rules. *Proceedings of the 20th International Conference on Very Large Databases (VLDB)* (pp. 487-499), Santiago, Chile. Morgan Kaufmann.

Antonie, M.-L., & Zaiane, O. R. (2004). Mining positive and negative association rules: An approach for confined rules. In J. F. Boulicaut, et al. (Eds.), *PKDD 2004, Lecture Notes in Computer Science, Vol. 3202* (pp. 27-38). Springer.

Bayardo, R. J., Agrawal, R., & Gunopulos, D. (1999, March). Constraint-based rule mining in large, dense databases. *Proceedings of the 15th International Conference on Data Engineering (ICDE)* (pp. 188-197), Sydney, Australia. IEEE Computer Society.

Blanchard, J., Guillet, F., & Briand, H. (2003, August). *Exploratory visualization for association rule rummaging.* Paper presented at the 4th International Workshop on Multimedia Data Mining (MDM/KDD), Washington, DC.

Daly, O., & Taniar, D. (2004). Exception rule mining based on negative association rules. In A. Lagana et al. (Eds.), *ICCSA 2004, Lecture Notes in Computer Science, Vol. 3046* (pp. 543-552). Springer.

Delgado, M., Sanchez, D., Martin-Bautista, M. J., & Vila, M.-A. (2001). Mining association rule with improved semantics in medical databases. *Artificial Intelligence in Medicine, 21*(1-3), 241–245. doi:10.1016/S0933-3657(00)00092-0

Jaroszewicz, S., & Simovici, D. A. (2002). Pruning redundant association rules using maximum entropy principle. In M.-S. Cheng et al. (Eds.), *PAKDD 2002, Lecture Notes n Computer Science, Vol. 2336* (pp. 135-147). Springer.

Klemettinen, M., Mannila, H., Ronkainen, P., Toivonen, H., & Verkamo, A. I. (1994, November). Finding interesting rules from large sets of discovered association rules. *Proceedings of the 3rd International Conference on Information and Knowledge Management (ICKM)* (pp. 401-407), Gaithersburg, MD.

Ko, Y. S., & Rountree, N. (2005). Finding sporadic rules using Apriori-Inverse. In T. B. Ho, et al. (Eds.), *PAKDD 2005, Lecture Notes in Computer Science, Vol. 3518* (pp. 97-106). Springer.

Li, J., Shen, H., & Topor, R. (2001, November). Mining the smallest association rule set for predictions. *Proceedings of the IEEE International Conference on Data Mining (ICDM)* (pp. 361-368), San Jose, CA. IEEE Computer Society.

Li, Y., & Sweeney, L. (2005). *Adding semantics and rigor to association rule learning: the GenTree approach* (Technical Report CMU ISRI 05-101). Pittsburgh, PA: Carnegie Mellon University, School of Computer Science, Institute for Software Research International.

Liu, B., Hsu, W., & Chen, S. (1997, August). Using general impressions to analyze discovered classification rules. *Proceedings of the 3rd International Conference on Knowledge Discovery and Data Mining (KDD)* (pp. 31-36), Newport Beach, CA. AAAI Press.

Liu, B., Hsu, W., & Ma, Y. (1999a, August). Pruning and summarizing the discovered association. *Proceedings of the 5th ACM SIGKDD International Conference on Knowledge Discovery and Data Mining* (pp. 125-134), San Diego, CA.

Liu, B., Hsu, W., & Ma, Y. (1999b, August). Mining association rules with multiple minimum supports. *Proceedings of the 5th ACM SIGKDD International Conference on Knowledge Discovery and Data Mining* (pp. 337-341), San Diego, CA.

Liu, B., Hsu, W., Mun, L.-F., & Lee, H.-Y. (1996). *Finding interesting patterns using user expectations* (Technical Report TRA 7/96). Singapore: National University of Singapore, Department of Information Systems and Computer Science.

Ma, L., Tsui, F.-C., Hogan, W. R., Wagner, M. M., & Ma, H. (2003). A framework for infection control surveillance using association rules. *AMIA Annual Symposium Proceedings* (pp. 410-414). American Medical Informatics Association.

Ma, Y., Liu, B., & Wong, C. K. (2000). Web for data mining: Organizing and interpreting the discovered rules using the web. *SIGKDD Explorations, 2*(1), 16–23. doi:10.1145/360402.360408

Marukatat, R. (2007). Structure-based rule selection framework for association rule mining of traffic accident data. In Y. Wang, et al. (Eds.), *CIS 2006, Lecture Notes in Computer Science, Vol. 4456* (pp. 231-239). Springer.

Silberschatz, A., & Tuzhilin, A. (1996). What makes patterns interesting in knowledge discovery systems. *IEEE Transactions on Knowledge and Data Engineering, 8*(6), 970–974. doi:10.1109/69.553165

Svetina, M., & Zupancic, Joze. (2005). How to increase sales in retail with market basket analysis. *Systems Integration,* 418-428.

Techapichetvanich, K., & Datta, A. (2005). VisAr: A new technique for visualizing mined association rules. In X. Li, et al. (Eds.), *ADMA 2005, Lecture Notes in Computer Science, Vol. 3584* (pp. 88-95). Springer.

Toivonen, H., Klemettinen, M., Ronkainen, P., Hatonen, K., & Mannila, H. (1995). Pruning and grouping of discovered association rules. *Workshop Notes of the ECML 95 Workshop in Statistics, Machine Learning, and Knowledge Discovery in Databases* (pp. 47-52), Greece. University of Waikato (n.d.). Weka 3 – data mining software in Java (version 3.4.12) [software]. Available from http://www.cs.waikato.ac.nz/ml/weka/.

Webb, G. I., & Zhang, S. (2002). Removing trivial association in association rule discovery. *Proceedings of the 1st International NAISO Congress on Autonomous Intelligent Systems (ICAIS)*, Geelong, Australia. NAISO Academic Press.

Wu, X., Zhang, C., & Zhang, S. (2004). Efficient mining of both positive and negative association rules. *ACM Transactions on Information Systems, 22*(3), 381–405. doi:10.1145/1010614.1010616

Yuan, X., Buckles, B. P., Yuan, Z., & Zhang, J. (2002, July). Mining negative association rules. *Proceedings of the 7th IEEE International Symposium on Computers and Communications (ISCC)* (pp. 623-628), Taormina, Italy. IEEE Computer Society.

Yun, H., Ha, D., Hwang, B., & Ryu, K. H. (2003). Mining association rules on significant rare data using relative support. *Journal of Systems and Software, 67*(3), 181–191. doi:10.1016/S0164-1212(02)00128-0

Zhou, L., & Yau, S. (2007). Efficient association rule mining among both frequent and infrequent items. *Computers & Mathematics with Applications (Oxford, England), 54*, 737–749. doi:10.1016/j.camwa.2007.02.010

Chapter 15
Creating Risk–Scores in Very Imbalanced Datasets:
Predicting Extremely Violent Crime among Criminal Offenders Following Release from Prison

Markus Breitenbach
Northpointe Institute for Public Management, USA

William Dieterich
Northpointe Institute for Public Management, USA

Tim Brennan
Northpointe Institute for Public Management, USA

Adrian Fan
University of Colorado at Boulder, USA

ABSTRACT

In this chapter, the authors explore Area under Curve (AUC) as an error-metric suitable for imbalanced data, as well as survey methods of optimizing this metric directly. We also address the issue of cut-point thresholds for practical decision-making. The techniques will be illustrated by a study that examines predictive rule development and validation procedures for establishing risk levels for violent felony crimes committed when criminal offenders are released from prison in the USA. The "violent felony" category was selected as the key outcome since these crimes are a major public safety concern, have a low base-rate (around 7%), and represent the most extreme forms of violence. The authors compare the performance of different algorithms on the dataset and validate using survival analysis whether the risk scores produced by these techniques are computing reasonable estimates of the true risk.

DOI: 10.4018/978-1-60566-754-6.ch015

INTRODUCTION AND BACKGROUND

In this chapter, we will discuss the many benefits of the Area under the Curve metric (AUC), not only as a performance measure, but also as a tool for optimizing models on very imbalanced datasets. We first introduce the measure formally and then discuss a few modeling techniques that can be used specifically for imbalanced datasets. Then we will include techniques that optimize the AUC directly. We will discuss how to choose suitable cut-points on an AUC optimized score and present a case study on predicting violent felony offenses (VFO) on a parole population.

Background

The use of predictive modeling has become pervasive as a decision support tool in criminal justice organizations in the USA. Even before the current shift to technical methods, prediction and classification tasks were central in criminal justice decision-making. Until the late 1970's, most risk estimations regarding criminal offenders were made in an informal manner largely relying on the subjective or "expert" judgment of judges, clinical psychologists, parole boards etc. These decision-makers usually had access to substantial data on criminal histories and other relevant social and psychological data; however, they generally produced their decisions intuitively without the aid of any predictive model.

The last two decades have seen a dramatic shift by most national and state criminal justice agencies to incorporate more reliable, objective, data-driven, and formal predictive models. The motivation for this shift included: the desire for higher predictive accuracy, for more reliable and defensible procedures that could be justified and replicated, and, at the policy level, a desire to appropriately balance public safety with the competing goals of equity and protecting the rights of prisoners (Gottfredson, 1987; Brennan, 1987). A further motivation was the consistent finding

in research studies that statistical and numerical models could systematically outperform the accuracy of human "expert" decision-makers, e.g. judges, prosecutors, trained prison classification officers, and so on (Quinsey, Harris, Rice, & Cormier, 1998b; Grove & Meehl, 1996).

The focus on criminal violence is critical since public safety is among the major goals of correctional agencies. Additionally, the scope of the task of estimating the risk of criminal violence is enormous. In recent years, state prisons in the USA admitted over 600,000 new inmates each year, and almost the same number were released each year from secure facilities. Thus, approximately 1,600 released prisoners each day were arriving back to communities across the country (Petersilia, 2001). Making estimations of the risk of criminal and violent behavior is thus a continual challenge for correctional/forensic professional staff. Risk estimations are also needed at several decision points that may involve different decision-makers across criminal justice. For example, probation officers must estimate the risk of future violence when preparing pre-sentence reports for judges. Judges, in turn, face similar predictive questions in struggling with sentencing decisions, i.e., is the expected risk so high that an offender should be locked up as an incapacitative or public safety strategy. Thus, the sheer number and the demand for timely decisions can overwhelm parole boards that must make and then justify such decisions. The performance and efficiency of numerical decision support risk estimations is thus of considerable value and importance to criminal justice agencies.

The Changing Array of Methods

In the beginning of the shift to numerical and statistical risk assessment, the most widely used methods in criminal justice were simple unweighted additive scales (Dawes, 1979). These methods were followed by regression models, including ordinary least squares (OLS), logistic regression, and survival analysis. More recently, several methods emerging from computer science, machine learning, and data mining have been used in criminal justice risk assessments. Modern data mining methods include: regression trees (CART), Random Forests(Breiman, 2001), Support Vector Machines (SVM)(Schölkopf & Smola, 2002; Vapnik, 1998), Artificial Neural Networks, Ensemble and Mixed Method models, and so forth (Zeng, 1999; Caulkins, Cohen, Gorr, & Wei, 1996; Monahan, Steadman, Silver, Appelbaum, Robbins, & Mulvey, 2001; Silver & Miller, 2002; Brennan, Breitenbach, & Dieterich, 2008a; Berk, Kriegler, & Baek, 2006). While this changing array of methods has aimed at improving predictive accuracy, there have been very few comparative studies of the relative predictive accuracies of these methods - particularly for predicting violent offenses (Caulkins et al., 1996; Berk, 2008).

What Measure of Predictive Performance Should be Used?

Much attention in violence prediction research has focused on how best to evaluate the performance of predictive methods. A good comparative measure must be clearly independent of the base-rates and selection ratios across diverse studies. Prior evaluative work on the comparative accuracy of risk assessment methods is now seen as being dubious in value and often misleading because the coefficients used were not independent of base-rates and selection ratios across studies (Rice & Harris, 1995; Smith, 1996). The field of criminal justice requires direct and uncontaminated comparisons across predictive factors and overall predictive models.

A consensus has emerged that the receiver operating characteristic (ROC) procedure from signal detection theory (Swets, 1988) and its performance coefficient the Area under the Curve (AUC) is the most useful measure for comparing predictive accuracy of different predictive models

and factors. This is especially true for datasets with low base-rates as they are common in criminology. The ROC procedure is now used extensively in designing actuarial devices to predict violence.

MEASURING PERFORMANCE IN IMBALANCED DATASETS

The most commonly used metric for assessing a model's performance for binary classification is the error rate on a hold-out dataset. In the case of unbalanced datasets, the error rate can be fairly misleading, because without knowing the base-rate of the majority class the number is meaningless. If the smaller class is only three percent of the dataset, a simple classifier predicting the majority class all the time will still result in a 97% correct prediction - a number that would be fairly good if the classes were evenly distributed.

Imbalanced classes are commonly addressed by either re-sampling (over-sampling of the rare class) or by assigning a high cost for misclassifying cases of the rare class. Re-sampling can skew the prediction too much in favor of the rare class while assigning costs requires either experimentation or knowing those application dependant costs of misclassification beforehand and is not supported by every classification algorithm. In these situations, the user often has to make a decision as to where to set the threshold for classifying an item into one class or the other.

Receiver Operator Characteristic (ROC)

However, a better way of measuring performance in imbalanced datasets is the receiver operating characteristic (or simply ROC curve). The ROC is a graphical plot of the true versus false positives (TPR vs. FPR, or True Positive Rate versus False Positive Rate) for a binary (two class) classification system as its discrimination threshold is varied. It was originally used in signal detection theory.

As an example, consider a two-class prediction problem (binary classification), in which the outcomes are labeled either as positive or negative class. There are four possible outcomes for a two class prediction problem. If the outcome from a prediction and the actual value are both positive, then it is called a true positive (TP). A true negative (TN) has occurred when both the prediction outcome and the actual value are negative. However, if the actual value is negative while being predicted as positive, then it is said to be a false positive (FP). Likewise a false negative (FN) is when the prediction outcome is negative while the actual value is positive.

To plot a ROC curve the True Positive Rate (*TPR=TP/(TP+FN)*) and False Positive Rate (*FPR=FP/(FP+TN)*) are required. The True Positive Rate shows the performance of classifying positive instances correctly among all known positive samples available during the test. The False Positive Rate shows how many incorrect positive results occur among all known negative samples available during the test. By plotting FPR and TPR as *x* and *y* axes in a line-plot one can illustrate the relative trade-offs between the fractions of true positives (benefits) and false positives (costs or false alarms).

The best possible prediction method would yield a point in the upper left corner of the ROC plot, representing the fact that all true positives were found with no false positives and the line going into the upper right corner indicating perfect classification for all discrimination thresholds. A completely random guess would give a point along a diagonal line (the so-called line of no-discrimination) from the left bottom to the top right corners.

In practice, the ROC is used to determine thresholds for the classification; that is, the user can choose a cut-point somewhere on the curve for cases to be classified as positive or negative. This choice can also be made with respect to the costs of misclassification in the application at hand.

Area under Curve

The ROC is a more suitable way to determine the cut-points for thresholds than doing so using error rates. However, comparing plots of different models to each other is still difficult. In order to summarize the performance expressed in this 2D-plot in a single number, the Area under Curve (AUC) is often reported as a summary of the performance. A perfect classifier would have an AUC of 1, and a random guess would have an AUC of 0.5. For risk scores that have a reasonable performance for practical applications, the AUC is usually above 0.7 (Quinsey et al., 1998b).

The AUC is a non-parametric statistic (free of distributional assumptions) and is equal to the probability that the classifier at hand will rank a randomly chosen positive instance higher than a randomly chosen negative one (Fawcett, 2006). It can be shown that the AUC is mathematically equivalent to the Mann-Whitney statistic, which determines the median difference between scores obtained in the two classes scored on a continuous scale. Let n^+ and n^- denote the number of positive and negative examples respectively and let $f()$ be a function computing the risk score, then

$$AUC(f) = \frac{\sum_{i=1}^{n+}\sum_{j=1}^{n-}1f(x_i^+) > f(x_j^-)}{n^+n^-} \tag{1}$$

where **1** is the indicator function. This does imply that the score is independent of thresholds, i.e. $f(x)>f(x')\Rightarrow f(x)+c>f(x')+c, \forall c$

An important property is that ROC graphs measure the ability of producing good relative instance scores. This means an algorithm does not have to produce accurate confidence probability estimates for its prediction that are close to the probability of a correct prediction for the instance at hand. The AUC encourages the classifier to separate the two classes with a relative accurate score; i.e., the probability that the scores for true positives are larger than true negatives increases and measures the general ability to discriminate between classes. This is especially useful if the classifier produces a continuous score instead of a discrete class assignment as it is the case for risk-scores.

Performance measured by the AUC can sometimes lead to confusion, because it is not always completely intuitive. For example, a classifier can have an imperfect accuracy of less than 100 percent, yet still have a high AUC score. This can happen if the classifier ranks all the true positives over the true negatives (closer to perfect ranking implies an AUC closer to one), but the threshold is set such that some cases are not assigned to the correct class (e.g., to avoid false negatives). It is important to keep in mind that the AUC is independent of thresholds.

This independence of the threshold leads to an insensitivity to class skew. Thus, for example, this makes performance results easier to interpret as the base-rate must not be known. Classifiers that optimize the AUC directly are independent of the *a priori* distribution of the classes and hence it is unnecessary to assign penalty costs to encourage a classifier to learn non-trivial models.

Evaluating Risk Scores

Risk scores that originate from binary classification are harder to evaluate since they express a risk of failing, not necessarily the complete certainty. For example, we expect on average people with higher risk scores to fail earlier and more often than people with lower risk scores. In order to evaluate risk scores, one can use survival models to estimate three measures that are useful for evaluating the predictive value of the risk scales: failure probabilities, hazard ratios, and the concordance index - the later being the area under the receiver operating characteristic curve (AUC) for survival models.

- *Failure Probability.* In typical survival data without competing events, the Kaplan-Meier statistic is used as an estimate of survival or failure probability (1 - KM) at different time points. However, in the context of competing risks, 1 - KM is neither proper nor interpretable as a measure of failure probabilities. Hence the cumulative incidence functions are calculated for this purpose. We use a specialized proportional hazards survival model for competing risks (Fine and Gray, 1999) to estimate and plot failure probabilities (cumulative incidence curves) for each type of failure within the levels of the risk scores. The goal is to compare the **probability of the event of interest** (e.g. arrest) within different levels of the risk scores. The generality of the results from competing risk models are limited to populations with similar characteristics and similar patterns of competing events (Pintilie, 2007).

- *Hazard Ratio.* We use the Cox survival model to model the effect of the respective risk scores on the cause-specific hazard for the outcome. In this type of model, failures due to competing events are censored. The cause-specific hazards reflect the risk of the event of interest (e.g. arrest) as if the competing events did not exist. The goal is to compare the **hazard rates for the event of interest** within different levels of the risk scores. The results are valid for any population with similar characteristics regardless of the pattern of competing events (Pintilie, 2007).

- *Concordance Index.* The concordance index is defined as the probability that the predictor values and survival times for a pair of randomly selected cases are concordant. A pair is concordant if the case with the higher predictor value has a shorter survival time. For survival models, the concordance index is equivalent to the AUC.

The calculation is based on the number of all possible pairs of non-missing observations for which survival time can be ordered and the proportion of relevant pairs for which the predictor and survival time are concordant (Harrell, Califf, Pryor, Lee, & Rosati, 1982).

Optimizing the AUC directly has a couple of benefits such as being intuitive, making performance results easier to interpret, and being independent of the *a priori* distribution of the classes. Even if the two classes are not completely separable, optimizing for the AUC will "encourage" the algorithm to find a solution that separates the cases as well as possible. Optimizing the AUC directly is also beneficial if no cost ratio for misclassifications is known *a priori*. Note that optimizing for the AUC still leaves the choice of the cut-point up to the user. We will describe a simple method to determine the cut-point by minimizing the probability of misclassification in Section 4. The AUC is a good method for evaluating prognostic models because the estimate is not influenced by the base-rate (proportion of the sample that fails). This characteristic makes it easier to compare results across studies.

However, the base-rate can affect the precision of the AUC. The AUC ranges from .50 to 1.00. An AUC of .50 indicates no relationship between the risk scale and the outcome. An AUC of 1.00 indicates that the risk scale predicts the outcome perfectly. The vast majority of published studies for predicting criminal behavior in which the validity of instruments such as the COMPAS Reentry (Brennan and Dieterich, 2008) have been tested report AUCs in the range of .65 to .75. Criminal justice researchers have suggested an AUC between .60 and .70 indicates moderate predictive utility, and an AUC of .70 and above indicates strong predictive utility (Quinsey et al., 1998b). The performance of any instrument will vary depending on the population (e.g., prison releases or probation cases), measurement error in the scale or outcome, and type of outcome (e.g., arrests versus violations or returns).

ALGORITHMS

A risk score is often represented as a weighted sum of independents, i.e. $f(x) = \sum_i w_i x_i = \langle w, x \rangle$. Note that this effectively describes a hyperplane through the origin that the new data is mapped onto. Unlike decision tree or association rule based learning, the hyperplanes are not necessarily parallel to one of the axis. This property makes the rules more difficult to interpret, but often provides more accurate models in practice. Expressing a model as a linearly weighted sum, however, can give insights into the importance of variables. In general, the larger the absolute value of a weight is, the more influence the variable has on the classification. While this does not allow for clear-cut rules such as "IF A AND B THEN C", it gives strong indications for major factors of recidivism. For some types of models, algorithms have been developed that extract readable rules (Thrun, Tesauro, Touretzky, & Leen, 1995). As we will show in our case-study, many of the factors in our equations are well established associations of violent crime (e.g. prior violent crime, young age, poverty, low education, anti-social personality, etc). The weights for each factor in the formula represent the strength of association with violent crime and are easily interpretable. They can give additional insights into possible preventive measures by suggesting intervention programs that can reduce the risk factors with the most weight.

In this section, we will discuss three algorithms that optimize the AUC directly and can be used to create a risk score from a labeled dataset (supervised learning). The first algorithm is a variation of the Support Vector Machine (SVM) family of algorithms. This family of learning algorithms has attracted attention for its robustness and good performance. Furthermore, the algorithms are easily generalized to others domains such as string matching for text classification or gene expressions for bio-informatics applications by the use of kernel functions.

The second algorithm is a simple gradient descent method that approximates the AUC step-function. Furthermore, the authors introduce a way to perform the gradient descent by a single linear scan over the data allowing this method to be applied to datasets that exceed the computer's available RAM.

The third method is a neural network using the Broyden-Fletcher-Goldfarb-Shanno (BFGS) methodology for training. This algorithm has a history of effective use in telecom churn analysis which contains highly imbalanced and often incomplete data. In general, neural networks are well known for their robustness amongst noisy inputs with variants of the BFGS methodology scaling well in both runtime and memory usage.

AUC Optimizing Support Vector Machines

Support vector machines (SVMs) are a family of related supervised learning methods used for binary classification and regression. They belong to a family of generalized classifiers learning models of the form $f(x) = \sum_i a_i K(x, v_i) + b$ where $K()$ is a kernel function, α are learned weights and v_i are the "support vectors" (SV). Kernel-functions behave like dot-products, but can be non-linear mappings and are used as "generalization devices" to build non-linear models (e.g. the non-linear Gaussian kernel). Sometimes they are represented with a mapping φ, which does not need to be explicitly known, that maps x to a higher-dimensional vector-space where the data becomes separable, i.e. $K(x,y)=\langle\varphi(x),\varphi(y)\rangle$. The sign of the output of $f(x)$ indicates to which class the new case is believed to belong. The set of support vectors are a subset of the training cases and is usually much smaller than the entire training set, i.e. a small number of examples is used to form the learned function (sparsity). A special property of SVMs is that they simultaneously minimize the empirical classification error and maximize the geometric margin; hence they are also known as maximum margin classifiers. Viewing the input data as two sets of vectors in a d-dimensional space, an SVM will construct a separating hyperplane, one which maximizes the "margin" between the two datasets. This hyperplane is represented by the weights α_i and some examples from the training set. As an alternative representation, one can represent the function as $f(x) = w^T x = b$ where w is d-dimensional vector of weights. This solution can be obtained from the dual of the optimization problem.

Support vector machines can be formulated as a quadratic programming problem (QP) for n training examples as follows:

$$minimize \frac{1}{2} \| w \|^2 + C\sum_i \xi_i, s.t. c_i K(w, x_i)$$
$$-b \geq 1 - \xi_i, 1 \leq i \leq n$$

(2)

The slack-variables ξ_i become larger than zero if the problem is not completely separable (e.g. mislabeled examples). The parameter C specifies the tradeoff between growing slack-variables and a more complicated model and has to be determined by the user.

Support vector machines optimize for the empirical classification error and hence are very sensitive to very imbalanced classes. The "vanilla" SVM does not explicitly optimize the Area under Curve. For a more detailed overview over Support vector machines, see (Burges, 1998).

Brefeld and Scheffer (2005) introduce a support vector machine that optimizes a bound for the area under curve, i.e. by improving a lower bound the AUC is implicitly increased. The key idea is the observation that the AUC performance depends on the number of example pairs (x_i^+, x_j^-) for all $i \in 1...n^+, j \in 1...n^-$ that satisfy $f(x_i^+) > f(x_j^-)$. This can be expressed equivalently as $\left\langle w, \varphi\binom{+}{x_i} \right\rangle - \left\langle w, \varphi\binom{-}{x_j} \right\rangle > 0$ for a mapping φ (kernel) and a weight-vector *w*.

This QP problem can be turned into a convex "soft-margin" optimization problem. For *C*>0 and $r \in \{1,2\}$ one can solve the following quadratic programming problem:

$$\min imize \frac{1}{2} \| w \|^2 + \frac{C}{r} \sum_i \xi_{ij}^r, s.t. \langle w, \phi(x_j^-) \rangle \geq 1 - \xi_{ij}$$

(3)

One problem is that the execution time of this algorithm is prohibitive for larger datasets, because the number of constraints is quadratic in the number of examples. Given that solving a QP optimization problem is quadratic in the number of the constraints, we are looking at run-time of order $O(n^4)$. One way of speeding up the computation is to reduce the n^+n^- number of constraints to n^++n^- constraints by clustering the examples with k-Means. The pre-processing by clustering and QP-Solving are both quadratic in run-time, and reduce the overall run-time to $O(n^2)$ with a small loss in classification performance.

Joachims (2005) introduces a variation to a Quadratic Programming solver that limits the number of constraints being created. The method first reformulates the problem by treating it as an n-dimensional multi-output problem, i.e. each example is mapped to a binary output. This reformulation allows for measuring a sample-based loss (e.g. AUC) instead of an example-based loss (e.g. error rate). The reformulation results in only a single training example as a collection of all input-vectors with labels mapped to them. Since there is only one training example, there is only one slack-variable which directly bounds the AUC. Again, instead of optimizing AUC directly a bound on the AUC is improved with each step. This is the key difference with the previously discussed approach: instead of an example based approach which results in a quadratically increasing number of constraints the sample based approach learns a mapping for a multi-variate output and generally results in exponentially many constraints.

The exponentially many constraints seem like a bad trade-off, but allows for the use of sparse approximations. A variation of a quadratic programming solver is used which in each iteration introduces only the most violated constraint of the exponentially large set of all constraints. The run-time of finding the constraint is dominated by a sort operation to order examples by their current rank, i.e. $O(n \log n)$. It turns out that only relatively few constraints need to be added before convergence of the convex problems is reached. In practice, this is often limited (depending on the dataset) to under 100 constraints in our experience and is probably the fastest support vector based method for optimizing AUC directly.

Gradient Descent

A more interesting approach would be to directly optimize the Area under Curve instead of improving upon a lower bound as the techniques in the previous section do. However, since equation (1) is not differentiable due to containing a step-function, it cannot be optimized for directly. A commonly used trick for approximating step-functions is to use a sigmoidal function that is fully differentiable (parameterized by β determining the steepness of the slope) to approximate the function:

$$SoftAUG_\beta(f) = \frac{\sum_{i=j}^{n+} \sum_{j=1}^{n-} \frac{1}{1 + e - \beta(f(f_i^+) - f(x_j^-))}}{n^+ n^-}$$

(4)

However, this approximation still requires full scans each time the weight-vector of a linear classifier is updated.

Calders and Jaroszewicz (2007) propose an approximation for both equations (1) and (4) by approximating the step-function $H()$ by a polynomial of degree d of the form $\sum_{k=0}^{d} c_k x^k$ as follows:

$$H(f(x_i^+) - f(x_j^-)) \approx \sum_{k=0}^{d} c_k (f(x_i^+) - f(x_j^-))^k \quad (5)$$

using the Binomial theorem this results in

$$= \sum_{k=0}^{d} \sum_{l=0}^{k} c_k \binom{k}{l} (-1)^{k-l} f(x_i^+)^{k-l} f(x_j^-)^l \quad (6)$$

which can be used in equation (1):

$$AUC(f) \approx \frac{\sum_{k=0}^{d} \sum_{l=0}^{k} \binom{k}{l}(-1)^{k-l}(\sum_i f(x_i^+))^{k-l}(\sum_j f(x_j^-))^l}{n^+ n^-}$$

$$(7)$$

Note that these sums can be computed in one scan and independently. The gradient can be similarly approximated by computing the partial derivatives for the polynomial approximations.

With both these approximations we can now update a weight-vector w iteratively, i.e. $w \leftarrow w + \gamma g$ for a learning rate γ determining the size of each step in the direction indicated by the derivative. One other outstanding feature of this algorithm is the ability to determine the learning rate automatically by computing the resulting AUC directly for various values of γ without having to rescan the data. This can be done because the AUC only depends on the direction of the weight-vector, but not on the length. This allows for arbitrary re-scaling of the weight-vector w since re-scaling only affects the magnitude of the scores. This property also makes it easier to find the ideal angle between the old weight vector and the new direction indicated by the gradient instead of finding the right learning rate. After

the gradient has been computed, one scan over the database is needed to compute the output of the approximated step-functions. Further updates to the weight-vector in this iteration can be done without a re-scan of the data.

BFGS Neural Networks

Neural networks are a class of algorithms that, despite being discovered more than 30 years ago, still produce excellent results in classification tasks due to their robustness to noise within real world datasets (Haykin, 1998).

In a neural network model, simple nodes consisting of a summation and transform function, are connected together to form a network. These in turn propagate a signal forward and adapt to a target through altering the strength of weights within nodes. Neural network models can be used to infer a function, including classification functions, by adapting to a given target and propagating error throughout the network. The most common technique is to retrace the flow of the network and propagate the error backwards from the expected target, altering weights in each node in a manner similar to gradient descent. This method is known as the back-propagation approach to neural network training.

Neural networks are a class of algorithms which also optimize Area under Curve through the use of a sigmoidal instead of a step function. First, we set the binary classification target in the range of 0 and 1. Given an error in the final node of a network $error = (y_i - g(x))^2$ where $g(x) = \dfrac{1}{1 + exp(\sum_i x_{ij} w_j)}$ in any node, we perform gradient descent in order to optimize our sigmoidal output with respect to the AUC.

The performance of neural networks can be greatly augmented by pre-processing the data. For preparation of the data, many setup tricks such as standardization of inputs, using logarithms of inputs, and weighting examples are used to optimize our search space. Standardization and outlier removal are common sanitization procedures. Adding in the logarithms of inputs affords us an interaction between variables which can be learned through training. The logarithm equalities $log(a) - log(b) = log(\frac{a}{b})$ can be used to compute ratios of inputs. For example, given two factors a and b within our input array, we find that during our calculation of $\sum_{i} x_{ij} x_{j}$ we, in fact, have the terms

$$log(a)w_{log(a)} - log(b)w_{log(b)} \qquad (8)$$

or $log\left(\dfrac{a^{w_{log(a)}}}{b^{w_{log(b)}}}\right)$ where $w_{log(a)}$ indicates the weight associated with this input.

The weighting of examples in the gradient descent rule is due to our earlier concern regarding imbalanced datasets. Underrepresented classes receive variable higher weights to tailor our model in regards to a specific classification. For example, if class A consists of 98% of the population and class B consists of 2% of the population, we may weight class B to contribute 10 times what class A contributes during neural network learning in order to prevent a classifier that assumes everything is class A, for a 2% error rate.

Modifying the Broyden-Fletcher-Goldfarb-Shanno (BFGS) method (Fletcher, 1970, Broyden, 1970, Goldfarb, 1970, Shanno, 1970), we solve a binary classification task with competitive results. The BFGS method is a derivative of Newton's method in optimization literature. The main advantages of this flavor of neural network are mostly logistical as the BFGS method has a low memory footprint and fast runtime, while maintaining a convergence very similar to Quasi-Newton methods.

FINDING CUT-POINTS ON AUC OPTMIZED RISK SCORES

Where to set the threshold for classifying a case into one class or another is often dependent on the application and the costs associated with either of the two error types.

Picking the threshold can be done by training another classifier that optimizes for accuracy with respect to misclassification-costs on the scores produced by the AUC optimized classifier. For example, the C4.5 decision tree could be built on the score and the first split of the tree could be used as the threshold (Quinlan, 1986).

Another method would be to use deciles to group cases of a normative sample into bins. The score of new cases can then be assigned to a decile group and this organization allows for a much more fine-grained approach to managing risks than a strict yes/no decision. This approach is particularly popular in the criminal justice context as varying levels of supervision are available.

Minimizing the Probability of Misclassification

In the following, we will describe an approach that simply minimizes the probability of misclassification. This criterion has been successfully used for building optimization based classifiers. Minimizing the probability of misclassification has led to the family of the minimax probability machine classifiers with competitive results in practice (Lanckriet, Ghaoui, Bhattacharyya, and Jordan, 2002, Strohmann, Belitski, Grudic, and DeCoste, 2004). By choosing a cut-point that minimizes misclassification probability, we obtain a classifier that is optimal in maximizing the AUC and minimizing the probability of misclassification. The method is free of any distributional assumptions and *a priori* information of the initial class distribution.

Let $F(w), w \in \mathbf{R}^d$, be the original hypothesis learned by an ROC-optimized classifier. Let μ_x and μ_y be the mean of the scores produced by F for the two classes X, Y. Let σ_x and σ_y be the standard deviation of the score for the two classes $\{x, y\}$. To find an optimal cut that minimizes the probability of misclassification for a decision hyperplane $aF(W) = b$, one computes

$$a = \frac{1}{\mu_x - \mu_y} \tag{9}$$

$$\kappa = \frac{1}{\sqrt{a^2\sigma_x^2} + \sqrt{a^2\sigma_y^2}} = \frac{1}{a(\sigma_x^2 + \sigma_y^2)} \tag{10}$$

$$b = a\mu - \kappa\sqrt{a^2\sigma_x^2} = a\mu_x - \kappa a \sigma_x = a\mu_x - \frac{\sigma_x}{\sigma_x + \sigma_y} \tag{11}$$

$$\alpha = 1 - \frac{\kappa^2}{1 + \kappa^2} \tag{12}$$

The classifier is then $sign(aF(w) - b)$. This minimizes the probability of misclassification α for this hyper-plane classifier. Note that the quality of the solution depends on the estimates of the mean and variance for both of the classes. This can be a problem when one is dealing with imbalanced problems with both extremely few cases, as well as a large variance in one of the classes. The variable α gives an upper bound on the misclassification probability.

CONTEXTUAL ISSUES IN CRIMINAL JUSTICE REGARDING VIOLENT CRIME PREDICTION

In our work to develop risk estimation models for serious violent offenders, several contextual issues emerged that increased the difficulty of both implementing quantitative decision support procedures and in achieving higher levels of accuracy:

Outcome Measures: Diversity and Definitions of Violent Crimes

The first issue is that predictive modeling that addresses violent crime forces researchers to carefully define the outcome variable. A key issue is the specificity or generality of how the violent outcome criterion is defined and measured. For example, a very broad range of violent crimes is included in the USA Uniform Crime Code definitions, e.g. murder, voluntary manslaughter, forcible rape, robbery, aggravated assault, simple assault, burglary (of an occupied dwelling with a weapon), possession of dangerous weapons, sex offenses, extortion, arson, and kidnap. Choices must often be made in aggregating or separating these offenses. Secondly, violent offences have ranges of seriousness, i.e. less serious misdemeanors and or serious felonies. Clearly, a broad or more inclusive definition - that may aggregate all of the above - will obviously be a composite of several forms of violence. Such broader variables are useful in increasing the base-rate for predictive modeling. However, the potential cost is that unrelated kinds of violence are mixed within a single common class. This may be hazardous if different causal processes with differing predictor variables are mixed in the class, e.g. felony drug violence may have a quite different causal process from domestic violence homicide.

Given that even within the felony classes crimes can vary in degree of seriousness, the use of a crude binary variable (i.e. violent/non-violent) may in some situations seriously oversimplify the dependent variable. Binary measures are especially problematic in cases where the degree of violence is of key importance (e.g. sexual offenses). Another problem with the outcome variable is that local criminal justice practices may introduce noise into its measure. For example, police may arrest a person on several charges, but court prosecutors then "plea-bargain" with defense lawyers and charge the offender only with one of the lesser crimes. This will erode the reliability and validity of the criterion variable (violent offending) and may weaken the ability to identify valid predictors and establish overall predictive accuracy.

The Base-Rate Problem

Many prediction situations in criminal justice, particularly of serious violence, confront the complicated issue of low base-rates in the outcome behavior. In predictive modeling this increases the difficulty of finding levels of accuracy that are sufficiently high for practical use. In reviewing criminal justice prediction studies, Quinsey, Harris, Rice, and Cormier (1998a) concluded that for the outcome follow-up periods usually used in violence studies, the base-rates for the crimes of concern were usually fewer than 20% and often much lower. Also, for very serious violent crimes (murder, armed robbery, etc.) the base-rates are typically lower; i.e., prevalence of violent crime is inversely related to its seriousness. Prevalence will also be larger with longer follow-up periods. For example, when longer follow-up periods are used (e.g., 10 years) with specific high-risk samples (e.g., violent sex offenders) the base-rates can approach or exceed the 50% level (Quinsey et al., 1998a). Thus, a simple strategy to achieve higher base-rates is to use the broader category of "any person offense" which as noted earlier has the hazard of mixing different forms of violence with possibly different underlying causal processes.

Do our Model Assumptions Match the Complexity of the Violent Behaviors being Modeled?

It is possible that criminal populations are heterogeneous in the causal processes generating their criminal violence (Lykken, 1995, Brennan, Breitenbach, and Dieterich, 2008b). This possibility will be a challenge to any "global" model (e.g., regression, classification tree, survival model) as to whether it appropriately matches this heteroge-

neity. For example, Lykken argues for a structural heterogeneity among diverse kinds of offenders and proposes several distinct pathways to crime, each with its own explanatory variables (Lykken, 1995). An implication is that any risk estimation study may require a preliminary dis-aggregation of the overall population of criminally violent offenders into homogeneous sub-populations and then appropriate models can be applied for each sub-population.

A related critique is that any global numerical model will be suspect if it ignores the individuality of specific offenders or selected groups. This challenge - often from defendants, defense lawyers and psychological counselors - is when a specific offender or specific offender category (e.g., women) does not "fit" the global model. Again, it is asserted that the violent behavior of a selected person or group is driven by different factors than those used in the model and that more specific models are required for these groups (Daly, 1992, Owen, 1998). This complex issue is not yet resolved. There are advocates on both sides, and recent research is addressing the issue of gender and racial differences in predictive models (Blanchette and Brown, 2006, Brennan et al., 2008b).

Limited Technical Knowledge of Criminal Justice Decision-Makers

A widespread problem when implementing technical decision support procedures is that many criminal justice decision-makers have very limited training in the technical issues related to risk estimation methods. They are, however, often comfortable with traditional "subjective" decision-making and may resent, mistrust, or feel threatened by technical approaches. They naturally prefer their subjective judgments since these represent their own personal "experiences", hunches, assumptions, and personal biases (Hastie and Dawes, 2001). Unfortunately, these assumptions, hunches, and implicit mental models are mostly untested and often wrong. In addition, these decision makers, including judges, often cannot articulate the logic or rational basis for their decisions (Tata, 2002). Thus, a major challenge in successful implementation of decision support technologies is to achieve trust and cooperation among the users (Walton, 1989, Brennan, 1999).

Ethical Issues and Predictive Technologies

A final contextual issue in criminal justice violence prediction is that although predictive methods come from the world of technology they will typically be used in people-processing justice organizations embedded in a world of values and politics. Thus technology, policy, and ethics become intertwined. This is particularly so in decisions involving the loss of freedom for offenders. The limitations of predictive methods, particularly in low base-rate events such as serious violence may result in ethical conflicts and challenging lawsuits against correctional agencies for apparent "errors" of prediction. Social and political pressures largely focus on two broad consequences of error: 1) the threat to public safety from false negative errors and 2) the loss of fairness and equity from false positive errors. A policy of applying longer sentences to offenders who have higher risk probabilities of future violence may raise ethical considerations and, in some cases, legal challenge. The political balance between false positives and false negatives typically requires intensive policy debate so that acceptable decision thresholds are implicit in policies. Increasingly, the different "costs" or "stakes" of false positive and false negative errors are now factored into the final balancing of these two errors (Quinsey et al., 1998a).

CASE STUDY

In the following, we will conduct a case study using criminal justice data of parolees, as well as build and evaluate a risk score predicting violent felony offenses (VFO). We will evaluate the methods we have introduced in Section 3 and compare against a few established machine learning methods as baseline that have shown overall good performance in empirical comparisons (Caruana and Niculescu-Mizil, 2006), but do not optimize the AUC directly. Furthermore, we will show using survival analysis that the risk score actually sufficiently differentiates between high, medium, and low risk groups.

Methods and Data

The data for this study were collected through COMPAS Reentry (Northpointe, 2006) assessments conducted by parole staff with 874 soon-to-be-released inmates at 25 correctional facilities in an eastern state. The assessments were conducted between December 2005 and July 2006. The COMPAS Reentry assessment tool covers several risk- and need domains relevant for parole decision-making with inmates preparing for the transition from prison to community (see table 2).

We developed new risk models to predict violent felony offenses. To develop the models, we started with a set of candidate variables that included 13 COMPAS Reentry scales plus age, age at first arrest, and gender. We regard this approach of working with the established scales as conservative because there is less opportunity to capitalize on chance, as opposed to data mining at the item level.

Sample

A stratified cluster sampling methodology was used to select the study sample. The sampling frame consisted of soon-to-be-released inmates who had been incarcerated in prison for at least 12 months, clustered in prisons, stratified by parole cluster, security level (minimum, medium, maximum) and gender (male, female). At the first stage, we randomly selected facilities from each stratum of the sampling frame. This resulted in 24 prisons selected - four from each of the six parole clusters. In the second stage, field parole officers periodically visited the selected prisons and assessed soon-to-be-released inmates with the COMPAS Reentry. The parole officers who conducted the assessments attended a short training in data collection prior to the start of the pilot study. Selected inmates were actively consented. Approximately 10% of selected inmates declined to participate.

The estimation sample used in the outcomes analyses consists of the original pilot sample with completed assessments (n=866) plus 30 randomly selected cases from a sample of 200 assessments conducted at a short-term holding and training facility for parole violators. These data were originally collected for a supplemental study. A small subset is incorporated into our main sample. From the combined sample of 896 cases, 22 cases were excluded because they were not released onto parole within 180 days of the COMPAS Reentry assessment. The mean time from COMPAS Reentry assessment date to parole release date is 15 days (median = 4 days). An additional 67 cases were excluded due to missing data on either the General Recidivism Risk scale or the Violent Recidivism Risk scale. There are 800 cases remaining in the estimation sample.

The sample is 78.4% male. Note that women represent only 7% of the parolee population in the research jurisdiction; they were oversampled for the pilot study. The average age is 35.2 years (SD = 9.9) and ranges from 17.9 years to 83.3 years. The median age is 34.9. The median age in the parole population is 34 years. The ethnicity breakdown in the sample is 29.1% Caucasian, 53.7% African American, 15.9% Latino/a, and 1.3% other ethnic group. In the parolee population the breakdown is 20% Caucasian, 52% African American, 26%

Latino/a, and 2% other ethnic group. The mean age-at-first-arrest in the sample is 19.9 years (SD = 6.7); the mean number of prior arrests is 8.9 (SD =13.6); and the mean number of felony convictions is 1.5 (SD = 1.8). Table 1 shows the types of original conviction offenses for the individuals in the sample. Two types of conviction offense predominate, legislative violent felony offenses [VFO] (33.2%) and drug offenses (35.9%). In the parolee population in the study jurisdiction, 36% are VFO and 39% are drug offenses. For 74% of the individuals in the sample, this is their first release onto parole for the current sentence.

Outcomes Measures

We developed a model to predict violent felony arrests (VFO). For the binary models, the criterion is defined as the first occurrence of an arrest for a violent felony offense within 600 days of release from prison. The follow-up time is adjusted for competing events (parole discharge, death, and return to prison) as described in Section 6.5.

Predictive Modeling Strategy

To develop the model predicting VFOs, we started with a set of candidate variables that included 13 COMPAS Reentry scales plus age, age-at-first-arrest, gender, and a re-parole indicator. The re-parole indicator is coded 1 if the current release onto parole is a re-release on the same sentence

Table 1. Original conviction offense

Original Conviction Offense	Frequency	Percent
A1 Violent	7	0.9
Legislative VFO	263	32.9
Other Coercive	58	7.2
Drug Offenses	286	35.8
Major Property	108	13.5
Other Felony	59	7.4
YO/JO	19	2.4

Table 2. Candidate variables used in model development

Variable	Items	Alpha
Early Onset	4	0.73
Criminal Involvement	4	0.81
Violence History	6	0.69
Prison Misconduct	7	0.52
Substance Abuse	7	0.75
Housing Problems	4	0.64
Financial Problems	6	0.67
Vocational/Educational Assets	9	0.70
Family Support	5	0.77
Social Isolation	5	0.64
Purpose/Direction	7	0.61
Criminal Personality	20	0.84
Self-Efficacy	15	0.82
Re-paroled	1	0.00
Gender	1	0.00
Age-at-Assessment	1	0.00
Age-at-first-Arrest	1	0.00

after a return to prison for a parole violation or 0 if it is the first release onto parole on the current sentence. Table 2 shows the candidate variables along with their respective number of items and alpha reliability coefficients in the pilot data.

A step-wise selection approach with cross-validation was used to identify a subset of variables listed in table 6. It is well-known that variable selection procedures capitalize on chance and are prone to problems with over-fitting. We feel that problems with over-fitting are not as serious in our case because we limited the candidate pool to only a small number of variables, the majority of which are previously established scales. Additionally, we adjusted the AUC estimates to account for shrinkage in new data. Finally, we found similar results using several different approaches to variable selection and penalized estimation, including bootstrapped backward stepwise variable selection and the lasso method for variable selection in survival models.

ROC Analysis

The tables below show AUCs for a variety of outcomes, including VFOs. Table 3 shows the Area under Curve based on the survival model estimates for each risk score and outcome. Eight out of thirteen evaluations had AUCs at 0.70 or above. Table 4 shows the results of using the risk scores calculated from the survival model estimates as predictors in logistic regression models. Twelve out of thirteen studies using logistic regression had AUCs above 0.70. These results were particularly encouraging.

In Table 5, we compare different algorithm capabilities in modeling our VFO data. The data was randomly split into training and test sets (90/10), a model was built on the training set, and then the ROC was measured on the test set. The random split was done on the entire dataset and not per class, i.e., some of the splits might by chance have far less of the VFO examples in it allowing for a more conservative estimate. Using a corrected two-tailed test the results of 100 test-iterations were averaged and found to be significant. We used the implementations of a few classical classification algorithms in WEKA (software version 3.5.7) (Garner, 1995). We will also compare the results to the algorithms described in Section 3. Algorithms were run with the default parameters from Weka, and no tweaking of parameters or settings was performed. The neural network in Weka performs an automated discovery of the

Table 3. Survival model estimates of the area under the receiver operating characteristic curve for each risk scale model and different outcomes.

Outcome Risk Score	AUC
Arrest Risk Score	.72
VFO Risk Score	.77
Abscond Risk	.72
Noncompliance	.68
Prison Return	.68

Table 4. Logistic regression estimates of the area under the receiver operating characteristic curve for each risk scale model and different outcomes.

Outcome Risk Score	AUC All
Arrest Risk Score	.72
VFO Risk Score	.77
Abscond Risk Score	.72
Noncompliance	.75
Prison Return	.70

number of neurons in the hidden layer, though. We set the tradeoff parameter C in SVMperf to one (default).

We first try all the scales we have introduced earlier and note that, as expected, the classical algorithms are outperformed by the AUC optimizing algorithms. Some of the classical algorithms do not perform better than chance. To our surprise Random Forests (Breiman, 2001) performs fairly well selecting features in this task and outperforms even the AUC optimizing techniques.

Once we select a subset of the scales, the performance generally increases. ADTrees (Freund & Mason, 1999) also demonstrated a fairly good performance in both cases. We can see that many classical algorithms do not perform better than chance in this imbalanced setting, while the AUC optimizing algorithms all result in the best

performance we were able to obtain on these data. One surprise was that logistic regression and multilayer perceptron perform almost as well as the AUC optimizing methods.

VFO Risk Score

In this section, we present results of validity tests for the VFO risk score for predicting the first occurrence of a VFO arrest during the follow-up.

The components entering into the VFO Risk Score are shown in Table 6. None of the input variables were transformed. Only mean-centering was applied. The risk score requires 33 Reentry scale items.

Survival Models

We fit survival models to assess the effects of the COMPAS risk scales on parole outcomes. Survival models are appropriate for this data because we are interested in both the occurrence and timing of the parole outcomes. Our analysis focuses on VFO arrests as well as any arrest, absconding, noncompliance, and return to prison. We model return to prison and discharge from parole as competing events (see below). Survival time begins on the release from prison date. The risk set at this point contains all inmates in the estimation sample (valid $N = 800$). Survival time is measured

Table 5. Comparison of different algorithms on the VFO data.

Algorithm	AUC all features	AUC feature subset
J48	0.50	0.52
SVM (SMO)	0.50	0.50
Random Forest	0.70	0.58
ADTree	0.60	0.65
Neural Network	0.58	0.74
Logistic	0.63	0.74
AUCOpt	0.66	0.76
Neural Network (BFGS)	0.63	0.74
SVMperf	0.60	0.72

Table 6. VFO Risk Score Items.

Items	Description of VFO Risk Score Inputs
miscon.c	Misconduct
hxviol.c	History of Violence
crimpers.c	Criminal Personality
age.c	Age at assessment
gender	Gender

in days from release date to the point of the first failure of interest, first competing event, or end of the follow-up, whichever occurs first. The failure point is determined by the warrant date associated with the failure of interest. For returns to prison the most proximate warrant date prior to the return date is used as the failure time point. Cases that do not fail by the failure of interest date or a competing event date during the follow-up are censored at the end of the study (December 31, 2007). Cases remain in the risk set and contribute information to the analysis until the point of failure of interest, occurrence of a competing event, or the end of follow-up, whichever occurs first.

Cases can fail by an event of interest, such as a new arrest, as well as the competing events return to prison or discharge from parole. These competing events alter the probability of observing the event of interest. For example, if a parolee is revoked and returned to prison, they cannot fail by the event of interest (e.g., new arrest), at least not while in prison for the competing reason. Even though a parolee could reoffend after discharge or after return and expiration of their time allocation,

we only tracked cases while they were on parole. Thus, within our survival models discharge and return are terminal competing events.

Parole jail time is controlled for during the follow-up by removing cases from the risk set during these periods. The models only account for jail time that is associated with parole warrants where the jail begin- and end dates are known.

Description of Events of Interest During the Follow-Up

Table 7 shows the number of events observed in each failure-specific survival model. The number failed gives the number of first failures. Some cases had multiple arrests and warrants, so the actual total number of arrests and abscond warrants observed in the sample over the follow-up was much higher. Table 8 shows the reasons for removal from parole for the cases in the estimation sample.

Figure 1 shows a plot of the cumulative crude incidence function for return to prison in the presence of parole discharge. The jumps in the discharge curve reflect groups of inmates being discharged at one year and two years. Here parole discharge alters the probability of return to prison. Both discharge and return to prison compete with the other study outcomes any arrest, VFO, absconding, and noncompliance.

Table 7. Distribution of Events for Each Failure-Specific Model.

Event	Censored	Failed	All
Abscond	600	200	800
Arrest	496	304	800
Return	539	261	800
VFO	743	57	800
Noncompliance	358	440	798

Table 8. Distribution of reasons for removal from parole supervision.

Reason	Woman	Men	All
Maximum Expiration	40	81	121
Board Action	0	10	10
Revoked-PV	48	213	261
Death	3	4	7
Merit Termination	9	13	22
Mandatory Termination	2	4	6
CDME	1	6	7
Revoked-PVNT	2	6	8
New Felony Conviction	4	26	30
Sum	109	363	472

Failure Probability

Table 9 shows the distribution of cases across the deciles of the VFO risk score, including the proportion of cases that fail and the crude cumulative incidence of failure. The crude cumulative incidence of VFO arrest in the first, fifth, and tenth deciles of the VFO risk score are 0.01, 0.03, and 0.16,

Figure 1. Estimates of the probability of return to prison in the presence of parole discharge, based on cumulative incidence functions.

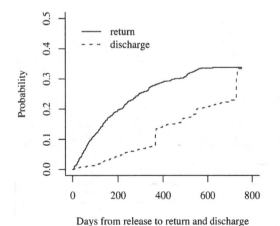

Days from release to return and discharge

respectively. With the cuts at deciles D5 and D9, there are 156 (20%) inmates classified as high-risk on this scale. There is a consistent trend of increasing probability of a VFO arrest across the deciles. With the cuts at D5 and D9, there is a sevenfold difference in the failure probability between the high-risk (.14) and low-risk (.02) levels.

Figure 2 shows a plot of the fitted failure probabilities for the levels of the VFO risk score from the competing risks model for VFO arrest. The plot indicates good separation of the fitted probability curves across the low, medium, and high levels of the scale. There is about a sevenfold increase in the failure probability of the high-risk group compared to the low-risk group.

Hazard Ratios

Table 10 shows the results from the Cox proportional hazards regression on the cause-specific hazards. The point estimate for the hazard ratio of the high-risk category relative to the low-risk category is 13.27, which indicates inmates classified as high-risk on the VFO risk score have a hazard for VFO arrest that is 13 times higher than the hazard for inmates classified as low-risk. The p-value is less than .001, indicating the effect is significantly different than zero. The confidence interval suggests the hazard ratio could be as low

Figure 2. Predicted cumulative incidence of first VFO arrest within the levels of the VFO risk score.

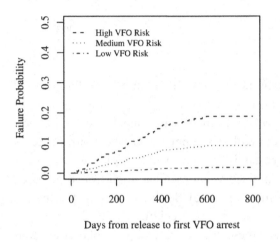

Days from release to first VFO arrest

Table 9. Distribution of VFO risk score deciles and crude cumulative incidence of a VFO within each decile.

Decile	Cases in Level	Failing	Incidence
D1	79	1	0.01
D2	79	3	0.04
D3	79	0	0.00
D4	78	1	0.01
D5	79	2	0.03
D6	79	8	0.10
D7	78	3	0.04
D8	79	10	0.13
D9	79	17	0.22
D10	77	12	0.16

as 5.8 or as high as 30.35. The hazard for the medium category relative to the low category is 5.45 (*p*-value <.001). This indicates that inmates classified as medium-risk have a failure hazard that is 5 times higher than the hazard for inmates classified as low-risk.

We also set up contrast comparisons with the medium-risk group as the reference category to test if the hazard for the high-risk category was different than the hazard for the medium-risk category. The results indicate that the hazard for inmates classified as high-risk is 2.44 times higher relative to the hazard for inmates classified as medium-risk (*p*-value <.002). This result is consistent with the plot of the fitted failure probabilities above.

Comparison to other Instruments

The AUCs of the other main instruments often used for offender risk prediction may help to contextualize the findings in our study. Perhaps the best known instruments are the Violence Risk Appraisal Guide [VRAG] (Quinsey et al., 1998b); the Level of Services Inventory-Revised [LSI-R] (Andrews and Bonta, 1995); and the Psychopathy Checklist-Revised [PCL-R] (Hare, 1991). The AUC values for these instruments in recent studies are quite varied according to the specific populations, outcome periods, and dependent variables used in specific studies.

- *VRAG*: Quinsey et al. (1998b) found an AUC of 0.76 in a large scale, multiyear recidivism study. Barbaree, Seto, Langton, and Peacock (2001) reported AUCs of 0.69 in predicting serious re-offending and 0.77 when predicting any re-offense for sex offenders. Kroner, Stadtland, Eidt, and Nedopil (2007) obtained an AUC of 0.703 in a study of re-offending among mentally ill offenders.
- *LSI-R*: The recent review by Andrews, Bonta, and Wormith (2006) did not provide AUCs for the LSI-R. However, Barnoski and Aos (2003) found AUCs of 0.64-0.66 for the LSI-R in predicting felony and violent recidivism among Washington State prisoners. Flores, Lowenkamp, Smith, and Latessa (2006) found an AUC of 0.689

Table 10. Cox proportional hazards model regressing the hazard for VFO arrest on the levels of the VFO risk score: Estimated cause-specific coefficients, standard errors, p-values, and hazard ratios with 95% confidence intervals. Note: The reference category for the test of medium- and high-risk categories is the low-risk category.

Risk Level	Coeff.	SE	p-value	Hazard Ratio	95% CI
Medium	1.695	0.436	0	5.45	[2.32,12.82]
High	2.586	0.422	0	13.27	[5.80,30.35]

using the LSI-R to predict reincarceration among federal probationers. Dahle (2006) reported an AUC of 0.65 using the LSI-R to predict violent recidivism. Barnoski (2006) reported an AUC of 0.65 using the LSI-R to predict felony sex recidivism.

- *PCL-R*: AUC levels again varied across studies. For example, in a Swedish study of mentally ill violent offenders, Grann, Belfrage, and Tengstrom (2000) found AUC levels of 0.64-0.75 based on various follow-up timeframes. Barbaree et al. (2001) reported AUCs of 0.61, 0.65, and 0.71 for the PCL-R in predicting various recidivism outcomes among sex offenders. The above findings clearly do not exhaust the full range of studies in this area. As more studies report AUCs for specific instruments, varying populations, outcome variables, and timeframes, it may become possible to identify which instruments perform well in these varying conditions.

CONCLUSION

In this chapter, we explored AUC as an error-metric suitable for imbalanced data, argued for its effectiveness, and surveyed methods of optimizing this metric directly. We introduced three techniques that scale to large datasets and are based on different paradigms of machine learning: support vector machines, neural networks, and a simple gradient descent-based method. We also address

the issue of cutting-point thresholds for practical decision-making.

We performed a case study that examines predictive rule development and validation procedures for establishing risk levels for violent felony crimes committed when criminal offenders are released from prison in the USA. We were estimating the risk of "violent felony" recidivism as the key outcome since these crimes are a major public safety concern, have a low base-rate (around 7 percent), and represent the most extreme forms of violence.

We compared the performance of different algorithms on the dataset, including classical methods like decision trees and found that the AUC-based methods perform much better in the presence of more (potentially irrelevant) features than other methods. Random Forests, to our surprise, outperformed every algorithm in this category. Once we selected a more relevant subset of features, we obtained a better result with the algorithms, but also noticed that some classical techniques like logistic regression performed almost equally well to the AUC optimizing techniques.

By using survival analysis we showed that the risk scores produced by these techniques are computing estimates that are consistent with the recidivism observed in the different low-, medium-, and high-risk groups.

REFERENCES

Andrews, D. A., & Bonta, J. (1995). *LSI-R: The Level of Service Inventory–Revised.* Toronto, Canada: Multi–Health Systems.

Andrews, D. A., Bonta, J., & Wormith, J. S. (2006). The recent past and near future of risk and/or needs assessment. *Crime and Delinquency, 52*(1), 7–27. doi:10.1177/0011128705281756

Barbaree, H. E., Seto, M., Langton, C. M., & Peacock, E. J. (2001). Evaluating the predictive accuracy of six risk assessment instruments for adult sex offenders. *Criminal Justice and Behavior, 28*(4), 490–521. doi:10.1177/009385480102800406

Barnoski, R. (2006). *Sex offender sentencing in Washington State: Predicting recidivism based on the LSI-R.* Technical report, Washington State Institute for Public Policy, Olympia, WA.

Barnoski, R., & Aos, S. (2003). *Washington's offender accountability act: An analysis of the Department of Corrections' risk assessment* (document no. 03-12-1202). Technical report, Washington State Institute for Public Policy, Olympia, WA.

Berk, R. (2008). *Statistical Learning from a Regression Perspective.* Springer-Verlag, New York.

Berk, R., Kriegler, B., & Baek, J. (2006). Forecasting dangerous inmate misconduct: An application of ensemble statistical procedures. *Journal of Quantitative Criminology, 22*(2), 131–145. doi:10.1007/s10940-006-9005-z

Blanchette, K., & Brown, S. (2006). *The assessment and treatment of women offenders: An integrative perspective.* West Sussex, England: John Wiley and Sons.

Brefeld, U., & Scheffer, T. (2005). Auc maximizing support vector learning. In *Proceedings of the ICML Workshop on ROC Analysis in Machine Learning.*

Breiman, L. (2001). Random forests. *Machine Learning, 1*(45), 5–32. doi:10.1023/A:1010933404324

Brennan, T. (1987). Classification: An overview of selected methodological issues. In D. M. Gottfredson & M. Tonry (Eds.), *Prediction and Classification: Criminal Justice Decision Making* (pp. 201–248). Chicago: University of Chicago Press.

Brennan, T. (1999). Implementing organizational change in criminal justice: Some lessons from jail classification systems. *Corrections Management Quarterly, 3*(2), 11–27.

Brennan, T., Breitenbach, M., & Dieterich, W. (2008a). Towards an explanatory taxonomy of adolescent delinquents: Identifying several social-psychological profiles. *Journal of Quantitative Criminology, 24*(2), 179–203. doi:10.1007/s10940-008-9045-7

Brennan, T., Breitenbach, M., & Dieterich, W. (2008b). Towards an explanatory taxonomy of adolescent delinquents: Identifying several social-psychological profiles. *Journal of Quantitative Criminology, 24*(2), 179–203. doi:10.1007/s10940-008-9045-7

Brennan, T., & Dieterich, W. (2008). *New York State Division of Parole COMPAS Reentry Pilot Study: Two-Year Follow-Up.* Traverse City, MI: Northpointe Institute Inc.

Broyden, C. G. (1970). The convergence of a class of double-rank minimization algorithms. *Journal of the Institute of Mathematics and Its Applications, 6,* 76–90.

Burges, C. (1998). A tutorial on support vector machines for pattern recognition. *Data Mining and Knowledge Discovery, 2,* 121–168. doi:10.1023/A:1009715923555

Calders, T., & Jaroszewicz, S. (2007). Efficient auc optimization for classification. In *In 11th European Conference on Principles and Practice of Knowledge Discovery in Databases (PKDD 2007)*.

Caruana, R., & Niculescu-Mizil, A. (2006). An empirical comparison of supervised learning algorithms. In *ICML '06: Proceedings of the 23rd international conference on Machine learning* (pp. 161–168). ACM: New York, NY, USA.

Caulkins, J., Cohen, J., Gorr, W., & Wei, J. (1996). Predicting criminal recidivism: A comparison of neural network models with statistical methods. *Journal of Criminal Justice, 24*(3), 227–240. doi:10.1016/0047-2352(96)00012-8

Dahle, K. P. (2006). Strengths and limitations of actuarial prediction of criminal re-offence in a German prison sample: A comparative study of LSI-R, HCR-20 and PCL-R. *International Journal of Law and Psychiatry, 29*(5), 431–442. doi:10.1016/j.ijlp.2006.03.001

Daly, K. (1992). Women's pathway to felony court: Feminist theories of lawbreaking and problems of representation. *Review of Law and Women's Studies, 2*, 11–52.

Dawes, R. (1979). The robust beauty of improper linear models in decision models. *The American Psychologist, 34*, 571–582. doi:10.1037/0003-066X.34.7.571

Fawcett, T. (2006). An introduction to ROC analysis. *Pattern Recognition Letters, 27*, 861–874. doi:10.1016/j.patrec.2005.10.010

Fine, J. P., & Gray, R. J. (1999). A proportional hazards model for the subdistribution of a competing risk. *Journal of the American Statistical Association, 94*(446), 496–509. doi:10.2307/2670170

Fletcher, R. (1970). A new approach to variable metric algorithms. *The Computer Journal, 13*, 317–322. doi:10.1093/comjnl/13.3.317

Flores, A. W., Lowenkamp, C. T., Smith, P., & Latessa, E. J. (2006). Validating the Level of Service Inventory-Revised on a sample of federal probationers. *Federal Probation, 70*(2), 44–78.

Freund, Y., & Mason, L. (1999). The alternating decision tree learning algorithm. In *Proceeding of the Sixteenth International Conference on Machine Learning* (pp. 124–133). Bled, Slovenia

Garner, S. R. (1995). Weka: The Waikato environment for knowledge analysis. In *Proc. of the New Zealand Computer Science Research Students Conference* (pp. 57–64).

Goldfarb, D. (1970). A family of variable metric updates derived by variational means. *Mathematics of Computation, 24*, 23–26. doi:10.2307/2004873

Gottfredson, M. (1987). Prediction: An Overview of Selected Issues. *Prediction and Classification: Criminal Justice Decision Making*. Chicago: University of Chicago Press.

Grann, M., Belfrage, H., & Tengstrom, A. (2000). Actuarial assessment of risk for violence: Predictive validity of the VRAG and the historical part of the HCR-20. *Criminal Justice and Behavior, 27*, 97–114. doi:10.1177/0093854800027001006

Grove, W., & Meehl, P. (1996). Comparative efficiency of informal (subjective, impressionistic) and formal (mechanical, algorithmic) prediction procedures: The clinical-statistical controversy. *Psychology, Public Policy, and Law, 2*, 293–323. doi:10.1037/1076-8971.2.2.293

Hare, R. D. (1991). *Manual for the Hare Psychopathy Checklist-Revised*. Toronto, Canada: Multi-Health Systems.

Harrell, F., Califf, R., Pryor, D., Lee, K., & Rosati, R. (1982). Evaluating the yield of medical tests. *Journal of the American Medical Association, 247*, 2543–2546. doi:10.1001/jama.247.18.2543

Hastie, R., & Dawes, R. (2001). *Rational Choice in an Uncertain World: The Psychology of Judgment and Decision Making*. Thousand Oaks, CA: Sage Publications.

Haykin, S. (1998). *Neural networks: a comprehensive foundation*. 2nd Edition. Prentice Hall.

Joachims, T. (2005). A support vector method for multivariate performance measures. In *Proceedings of the ICML 2005*.

Kroner, C., Stadtland, C., Eidt, M., & Nedopil, N. (2007). The validity of the violence risk appraisal guide (VRAG) in predicting criminal recidivism. *Criminal Behaviour and Mental Health*, *17*(2), 89–100. doi:10.1002/cbm.644

Lanckriet, G. R. G., Ghaoui, L. E., Bhattacharyya, C., & Jordan, M. I. (2002). Minimax probability machine. In *Advances in Neural Information Processing Systems, 14*. MIT Press.

Lykken, D. (1995). *The Antisocial Personalities*. Lawrence Erlbaum: Hillsdale, N.J.

Monahan, J., Steadman, H., Silver, E., Appelbaum, P., Robbins, P., & Mulvey, E. (2001). *Rethinking risk assessment: The MacArthur study of mental disorder and violence*. New York: Oxford University Press.

Northpointe (2006). Compas reentry [computer software].

Owen, B. (1998). *In the Mix: Struggle and Survival in a Woman's Prison*. Albany, N.Y: State University of New York Press.

Petersilia, J. (2001). Prisoner reentry: Public safety and reintegration challenges. *The Prison Journal*, *81*(3), 360–375. doi:10.1177/0032885501081003004

Pintilie, M. (2007). Analysing and interpreting competing risk data. *Statistics in Medicine*, *26*, 1360–1367. doi:10.1002/sim.2655

Quinlan, J. R. (1986). Induction of decision trees. *Journal of Machine Learning*, *1*(1), 81–106.

Quinsey, V., Harris, G., Rice, M., & Cormier, C. (1998a). Violent recidivism of mentally disordered offenders: The development of a statistical prediction instrument. In *American Psychological Association*.

Quinsey, V. L., Harris, G. T., Rice, M. E., & Cormier, C. A. (1998b). *Violent Offenders: Appraising and Managing Risk*, Washington, DC: American Psychological Association.

Rice, M. E., & Harris, G. T. (1995). Methodological development, violent recidivism: Assessing predictive validity. *Journal of Consulting and Clinical Psychology*, *63*, 737–748. doi:10.1037/0022-006X.63.5.737

Schölkopf, B., & Smola, A. (2002). *Learning with Kernels*. Cambridge, MA: MIT Press.

Shanno, D. (1970). Conditioning of quasi-newton methods for function minimization. *Mathematics of Computation*, *24*, 647–656. doi:10.2307/2004840

Silver, E., & Miller, L. (2002). A cautionary note on the use of actuarial risk assessment tools for social control. *Crime and Delinquency*, *48*, 138–161. doi:10.1177/0011128702048001006

Smith, W. (1996). The effects of base rate and cutoff point choice on commonly used measures of association and accuracy in recidivism research. *Journal of Quantitative Criminology*, *12*, 83–111. doi:10.1007/BF02354472

Strohmann, T., Belitski, A., Grudic, G., & DeCoste, D. (2004). Sparse greedy minimax probability machine classification. In S. Thrun, L. Saul, and B. Schölkopf (Eds.), *Advances in Neural Information Processing Systems, 16*. Cambridge, MA: MIT Press.

Swets, J. (1988). Measuring the accuracy of diagnostic systems. *Science, 240*(4857), 1285–1293. doi:10.1126/science.3287615

Tata, C. (2002). The quest for coherence in the sentencing decision process: Noble dream or chimera? In *Sentencing and Society: Second International Conference.* Glasgow, Scotland.

Thrun, S., Tesauro, G., Touretzky, D., & Leen, T. (1995). Extracting rules from artificial neural networks with distributed representations. [MIT Press.]. *Advances in Neural Information Processing Systems, 7*, 505–512.

Vapnik, V. (1998). *The Nature of Statistical Learning Theory.* Wiley, NY.

Walton, R. (1989). *Up and Running.* Boston: Harvard Business School Press.

Zeng, L. (1999). Prediction and classification with neural network models. *Sociological Methods & Research, 27*(4), 499–524. doi:10.1177/0049124199027004002

Chapter 16
Boosting Prediction Accuracy of Bad Payments in Financial Credit Applications

Russel Pears
Auckland University of Technology, New Zealand

Raymond Oetama
Auckland University of Technology, New Zealand

ABSTRACT

Credit scoring is a tool commonly employed by lenders in credit risk management. However credit scoring methods are prone to error. Failures from credit scoring result in granting loans to high risk customers, thus significantly increasing the incidence of overdue payments, or in the worst case, customers defaulting on the loan altogether. In this research the authors use a machine learning approach to improve the identification of such customers. However, identifying such bad customers is not a trivial task as they form the minority of customers and standard machine learning algorithms have difficulty in learning accurate models on such imbalanced datasets. They propose a novel approach based on a data segmentation strategy that progressively partitions the original data set into segments where bad customers form the majority. These segments, known as Majority Bad Payment Segments (MBPS) are then used to train machine learning classifiers such as Logistic Regression, C4.5, and Bayesian Network to identify high risk customers in advance. The authors compare their approach to the traditional approach of under sampling the majority class of good customers using a variety of metrics such as Hit Rate, Coverage and the Area under the Curve (AUC) metrics which have been designed to evaluate classification performance on imbalanced data sets. The results of our experimentation showed that the MBPS generally outperformed the under sampling method on all of these measures. Although MBPS has been used in this research in the context of a financial credit application, the technique is a generic one and can be used in any application domain that involves imbalanced data.

DOI: 10.4018/978-1-60566-754-6.ch016

INTRODUCTION

In today's market place customers typically utilize credit to purchase a variety of consumer goods and automobiles. While credit terms and repayment periods vary the basic mechanism of evaluating the credit worthiness of customers follows a well-defined framework. Such a framework helps to assess the probability that the loan will be repaid in full by the customer at a future point in time.

Credit worthiness is usually assessed by five different categories of criteria, the first of which assesses customer *characteristics*. This is used to get a general idea of customer demographics. The second category is customer *capacity* to repay the loan. Customer capacities typically refer to the monthly surplus once all expenses have been met. The third category is *collateral*, which are valuable assets that can be pledged as security. The next category is customer *capital*, which includes individual investments, insurances, etc. The last category is *condition*, which covers other related situational facts such as market condition, social condition, etc.

Data on the above criteria is captured in an application form and may be assessed by a human credit analyst. However, due to rapid business expansion of credit products such as consumer credits, property mortgages, etc, the manual approval process tends to overwhelm credit analysts with too many credit applications (Abdou, Masry, & Pointon, 2007). Crook et al. (2006) shows that between 1970 and 2005, consumer credit outstanding balance in the US grew by 231% with a dramatic growth of 705% on property mortgages. As a result of the massive volumes involved, the manual credit analysis process is enhanced through the use of statistical methods (Servigny & Renault, 2004). A typical statistical approval method is credit scoring. Credit Scoring is defined as a set of tools that help to determine prospects for loan approval (Johnson, 2006).

After the credit application has been approved, lenders inform customers that their credit applica-

tions have been granted. This will generally lead to a customer signing a contract. On the contract, a payment schedule informs the customer of the amount and due date of payments on which the customer must repay the lender.

The majority of customers make their payments on schedule, but some customers do make late payments. Payments that are paid after the due date are called overdue payments. Collecting overdue payments may not be easy, depending on the willingness of customers to pay. If customers still want to pay their overdue payments, lenders may devise special schemes to facilitate loan repayment for such customers. In other cases, customers simply refuse to make their payments. As a result, such customers create collection problems. Overdue payments occur because credit scoring fails to filter all of the bad customers. We identify two related problems that will be addressed in this research. Firstly, the credit scoring process is imperfect causing overdue payments. Secondly, overdue payments directly give rise to payment collection problems.

The objective of this research is to provide solutions to both credit scoring and collection problems. The proposed solution is essentially a payment prediction of overdue payments at the next payment round in a bid to find potential overdue payments in advance. As a result, proactive action can be taken to pre-empt overdue payment. Payment prediction models built by classifiers show combinations of credit scoring parameters that characterize overdue payments. Such information can also be utilized to improve the current credit scoring method used.

We utilize classifiers based on machine learning approaches such as Logistic Regression, C4.5 and the Bayesian Network to classify customers into two categories, good customers who are predicted to make their payments on time and bad customers who either default on the loan or make late payments. The overdue payment prediction process is complicated by the fact that bad customers form a small but significant minority thus challenging standard machine learning classifiers that tend to perform poorly on such imbalanced data (Weiss, 2004; Chawla, 2002).

The most popular techniques for dealing with imbalanced data are to re-balance such data by either under sampling the majority class or over sampling the minority class. Both sampling methods have been shown to improve accuracy in certain situations, but each method has been criticized on different grounds. The over sampling technique replicates minority class instances at random and is therefore vulnerable to the problem of over fitting as its models tend to be too reliant on the artificial distribution that is created, resulting in poor generalization to new, unseen data that arrives in the future Chawla et al. (2002).

The under sampling technique on the other hand, randomly removes instances from the majority class and the models that are built can suffer from the loss of information resulting from the removal of these instances (Maloof, 2003). The drawback of this method is that it removes potentially useful information which could be important in differentiating majority instances from minority instances.

We take a different approach to address the problem of class imbalance. We believe that a single model that gives good precision on both majority and minority instances is hard to achieve in general. Our method builds a model on data segments where instances from the minority class inherently dominate majority instances. A segment consists of a cluster of instances that share the same combination of credit scoring parameter values and payment histories. Clusters are only created for parameter combinations where the minority class dominates. This means that segments are not formed by blindly removing instances of the majority class. In contrast, majority instances are excluded from a segment only if they do not belong to any cluster within a segment.

Essentially, a segment reflects signatures of minority instances that naturally dominate over majority instances in feature space, thus creating

an environment that facilitates easier learning of the characteristics of the minority class. Standard classification algorithms can now be trained with a high degree of accuracy to recognize instances from the bad customer class. Our empirical analysis show that models built on such data segments are far superior to those built with conventional data re-balancing methods.

The rest of this chapter is organized as follows. The next section reviews past work done in the area of credit scoring and learning from imbalanced data sets. Thereafter, we present the Majority Bad Payment Segmentation (MBPS) data scheme. Our empirical results follow next. We conclude by summarising the main contributions of this research and discuss some directions for future research.

Current Payment Prediction Methods

Credit has had a long and rich history. Credit scoring comes in many forms and we will first briefly catalogue these different formulations before discussing algorithms and methods for prediction of bad customers. In general, credit scoring models comprise of credit scoring parameters and mathematical functions that project customer credit worthiness. Finlay (2006) gives examples of credit scoring parameters used for personal loans such as applicant gross income, time in employment, car ownership, etc. Payment prediction consists of adopting a suitable model for credit scoring that defines the states that a payment can exist. Thereafter, suitable methods to address the class imbalance are required in order to provide accurate predictions on payment status. We review each of these themes separately.

Credit Scoring

Credit scoring or credit worthiness comes in many different forms, depending on the application domain. A large body of researchers focuses on behavioral scoring. The Behavioral scoring problem is to predict the odds of a customer being in default of payment (Thomas, Ho, & Scherer, 2001; Lee, Chiu, Lu, & Chen, 2002). Another credit scoring research objective is bankruptcy scoring, where the study objectives are mainly to predict the likelihood of an individual customer declaring himself or herself bankrupt (Sun & Senoy, 2006). A further form is profit scoring (Crook et al., 2006), whereby lenders calculate the profitability of customers to the lender instead of calculating his or her credit risk. Finally, we find that other researchers pay more attention to predicting financial status such as outstanding balance, called loan projection scoring in this research. Financial state classification may differ amongst lenders. Avery et al. (1996) divide their financial state classification into periods covering 1-30, 31-60, 61-90, and 91-120 overdue days. However, Smith et al apply a different form that comprises of five states: current (payment on schedule), 30 to 89 overdue days, more than 90 overdue days, defaulted, and paid off (Smith, Sanchez, & Lawrence, 1996). Boyes et al. (1989) simplify their classifications as repaid or defaulted. Of all the different forms of credit scoring that exist, loan projection scoring is the form most relevant to the research that we conducted. We adopt Boyes binary classification scheme for tracking loan payment status.

Although credit scoring enables lenders to accelerate the credit approval process, it is far from being perfect. A credit scoring model from Tsaih et al's study shows an error rate of 20% (Tsaih, Liu, Liu, & Lien, 2004). A proposed credit scoring model from Li et al. (2004) shows better performance from their current scoring model, but still shows an error rate of 7.3%. Some researchers apply credit scoring to mobile phone users. They report 9.75% of trusted customer's bills are not paid whilst only 11.38% of non trusted customers pay on time (Li, Xu, & Xu, 2004). Another study result shows a good applicant hit rate is 76.3% with a bad applicant hit rate of 84.6% (Zekic-Susac, Sarlija, & Bensic, 2004), but such figures are relatively far from an ideal hit rate of 100%.

Failures from credit scoring will significantly impact the next process, which is payment collection from bad customers. Bad customers are those who fail to make their payments on schedule. In 1991, overdue payments in real estate products of Manufacturers Hanover were US$3.5 billions (West, 2000). If lenders are unable to recover their money from those bad customers, lenders incur huge losses, impacting on the economic performance of the companies involved. West highlights that this company lost US$385 million in the same year. A relationship between failures of credit scoring and overdue payments is found in the Avery et al. (1996) study. Generally, a higher credit score will reflect a higher creditworthiness of a customer. Those customers who are scored higher are expected to pay their payments on schedule than lower scored customers. However, Avery et al find some surprising results. They find that the largest portion of overdue payments comes from the higher end of the credit score range. By using mortgage data covering October 1993 to June 1994, Avery et al show that from a total of 109,433 customers, 417 have payments overdue by at least 30 days. Most of those overdue payments (60.9%) are from the high end of the credit score range, 21.8% from middle range, and the rest, comprising 17.3%, from the low range.

Most previous researchers overlook overdue payments since their work is focused on the improvement of credit scoring performance. Moreover, there is no proactive action from lenders to pre-empt such overdue payments. Typically lenders can find overdue payments when they generate overdue payment reports. By using such overdue reports, lenders will know which customers fail to make their payments on time. Thereafter, lenders generally take steps to collect overdue payments from such customers. However, identifying such overdue payments in advance will enable the company involved to be more pro-active in terms of negotiating with the customer prior to the payment date.

Algorithmic Methods for Addressing Class Imbalance

In general, there are a number of different methods to mining imbalanced datasets. These include, sampling methods to re-balance the dataset, cost-sensitive learning, minority class learning and data segmentation. Each of these methods has their own strengths and drawbacks. Weiss (2004) provides an excellent overview of the issues involved in using these different methods.

With respect to sampling, the commonly used solutions are under-sampling and over-sampling. In under-sampling, some instances of the majority class are excluded so that the ratio between majority and minority class is more balanced with respect to each other. In contrast, over-sampling works by adding instances to the minority class. A popular variant on simple over-sampling method for numerical data called SMOTE (Synthetic Minority Oversampling Technique) uses a random generator to create new instances of minority class that lie on the boundary between majority class instances and minority class instances (Chawla, Bowyer, Hall, & Kegelmeyer, 2002). As noted earlier, the key issues with sampling techniques is that the prediction models are based on artificially rebalanced data and thus may not generalize well to future new data that arrives with a naturally occurring disparity in frequency between classes.

Cost-sensitive learning is another method that is used to deal with class imbalance. This method assigns a higher penalty to misclassifications made on the minority class, thus biasing the learner to favour the minority class. The method is effective when the costs of miss-classifying the minority class relative to the majority class is known in advance. Unfortunately, such costs are rarely known in advance, thus limiting the scope of its usage. In terms of a payment prediction scenario such costs are generally not known in advance, although some researchers such as (West, 2000) has assumed values for these cost ratios.

Yet another method is to learn from a single class (Weiss, 2004). Specialized data mining methods such as Ripper are capable of learning rules that cover a single class only. In terms of the payment prediction domain, this method can be applied to the minority class which consists of the bad customers, as incorrectly identifying such customers have a greater financial impact on the organisation than incorrectly identifying good customers. However, the main problem with this method is how to label regions which have overlap, i.e. regions where both good customers and bad customers are present together. If the dataset contains many of these overlapping regions then prediction accuracy is bound to suffer.

Research in learning from imbalanced data has also used data segmentation to partition the data and then build separate models for each of the partitions. Hsieh (2004) used domain specification information in the banking domain to segment their dataset into meaningful partitions. Shihab et al. (2003) also use data segmentation for identifying targets for ground penetrating radar. While their implementation did not use domain specific information directly, the statistical features used in determining the right segments to be used relied on extensive experimentation and feedback from the data they used to guide the process of determining the right set of data segments to be used. Our method of data segmentation, as discussed earlier does not rely on any domain specific information and thus enables it to be applied across a wide set of application domains.

Payment Prediction Methodology

Our prediction methodology is to first partition the data into segments where bad payments naturally dominate over good payments and then apply prediction algorithms that have been shown to provide good results in past research.

Data Segmentation Strategy

We first begin by defining a segment as a collection of instances that have a unique combination of credit scoring parameters where bad payments are in the majority. Such segments are termed as Bad Payment Majority Segments (MBPS). An N % MBPS means that the segment consists of at least N percent bad payment instances. We expected that prediction performance would be sensitive to the value of N, so we progressively increased its size by 5% up to the maximum value of 100% and tested the effect of each value on performance. Figure 1 illustrates the algorithm used to construct MBPS segments.

The algorithm uses as input a certain number of credit scoring parameters N, which in our case happened to be 8. These credit parameters have been widely used in credit scoring applications and have been validated extensively by the leasing company from which we obtained our data. The parameters covered factors such as Marital Status, Job sector, Age, Home ownership status, Length of home occupancy, Length in current job, Length of payment period and monthly payment to income ratio.

The algorithm scans each payment record (instance in table Z) and then counts the number of instances that correspond to good and bad payments. If the percentage of matching instances from the bad payment class exceeds the MBPS size threshold then the key, consisting of the combination of all predictor attributes is inserted into a new table T. Upon completion of the algorithm,

Figure 1. MBPS Creation Algorithm

```
Algorithm  CREATE_MBPS
// Suppose we have N credit scoring parameters (c1, c2, c3, ...cN) and
M payment histories (p1, p2, p3, ...pM) in table Z sorted by
c1,c2,c3...cN,p1,p2,p3...pM
Input Payment_Period, MBPS Size
Ouput MBPS Segments
Matrix_Rows=0, Matrix_Iteration=0
CountBad=0, CountGood=0, Percentage=0
for each row in Z
    KEY1= Z.c1+ Z.c2+ Z.c3+ ...Z.cN+ Z.p1, ...Z.pPayment_Period-1
    CountBad=0
    CountGood=0
    while KEY1=Z.c1+ Z.c2+ Z.c3+ ...Z.cN+ Z.p1, ...Z.pPayment_Period-1
        if Z.pPayment_Period="B" THEN
            CountBad= CountBad+1
            delete instance z
        else
            CountGood= CountGood+1
        end if
        next row
    end while
    Percentage= CountBad/(CountBad+CountGood)
    if Percentage >= Mbps_size then
        //only for segments that are equal or larger than MBPS size
        Matrix_Rows=Matrix_Rows+1
        Matrix_Key [Matrix_Rows]=Key1
        Matrix_Percentage[Matrix_Rows]= Percentage
    end if
end for
if Matrix_Rows>0 then
    Create_Segment_MBPS(Payment_Period)
    for Matrix_Iteration=1 TO Matrix_Rows
        Insert-Segment_MBPS(Payment_Period, Matrix_key[Matrix_Iteration])
        //Insert into table T the key that defines the current MBPS
    end for
end if
```

Table T will contain all MBPS segments. Table T is now used to train one of three data mining algorithms that we selected for this research, Logistic Regression, Bayesian Belief Networks and C4.5. The models generated are shown to be much more accurate in predicting bad payments than with the unmodified data set and the under sampling method widely used in the literature on imbalanced data set mining.

For a given payment period i, we use the actual payment status for all payments in the previous periods (1, 2,..., i-1) to enhance the predictive power. In our experimentation that we report in section 4, we show that prediction accuracy tends to progressively improve as more payments are processed and greater information on payment history is known. Thus a model is generated for each payment. At the end of the current payment period the actual payment outcome is known for each customer and this information is used to replace the estimated status in the dataset D that was produced through the credit scoring process. The updated dataset is then segmented once again and a new version of the training set T' is created which is then used for predicting the status of the next payment.

In terms of run time, the algorithm's performance can be optimized by sorting the payment records in order of the predictor attributes. The time complexity to segment the data is thus bounded

above by the sorting step and is of the order of O (N log N), where N is the total number of payment instances to be used for training. Figure 2 shows the relationships between the Credit Scoring, Data Segmentation and Machine Learning processes.

Figure 2 shows the iterative nature of the learning process. A feedback loop from the learner used actual payment status for the current payment period and adds this as another predictor for the next payment period. Data segmentation now takes place one again and the cycle continues until the last payment in the payment cycle is processed. The continuous nature of the learner process gives rise to a significant increase in prediction accuracy as our experimental results in section 4 demonstrates.

Machine Learning Algorithms used for Prediction

The three algorithms that we used were the c4.5 Decision Tree learner, Bayesian Network and Logistic Regression. Both the Decision Tree and Logistic Regression algorithms have been used before in financial credit applications. Srinivasan and Kim (1987) show that the Decision Tree has the best performance on their dataset, while Desai et al. (1996) report that Logistic Regression performs best on their dataset. We decided to include the Bayesian Network algorithm because of its ability

Figure 2. The MBPS Learning Cycle

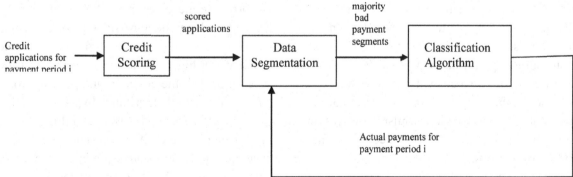

to deal with dependence between attributes. Previous research has shown that Neural Networks and Genetic Algorithms have also performed well in this domain. However, we decided against their inclusion as their model interpretability is poor, and thus their models cannot be easily used by non technical users.

Empirical Analysis

In this section we present the results of our experimentation with MBPS on a range of different performance metrics. In our first set of experiments we run the Logistic Regression, Bayesian Network and C4.5 algorithms on MBPS segments and track performance on metrics such as hit rate, coverage and the Area under the Curve (AUC) metric. We then go on in to contrast the performance of MBPS with its traditionally used counterpart, under-sampling. In all of the experiments we used the machine learning workbench Weka 3.4 (Witten and Frank, 2005) and used 10-fold cross-validation as the evaluation mechanism.

Performance Analysis of MBPS

Bad Payment Hit Rate

The Bad payment hit rate is important as it tracks the proportion of bad payments that MBPS predicts correctly and is a measure of the degree of precision in classifying bad customers. Figure 3 shows that all three algorithms exhibit a very high level of performance on hit rate across all periods. The minimum hit rate is 97.71% and all algorithms are able to reach the 100% mark at various stages in the payment cycle. C4.5 exhibits optimal performance as it reaches a 100% hit rates across all payments. Perfect hit rates are also exhibited by Logistic Regression at the first, third and sixth period, whilst the Bayesian Network gives perfect performance at the first and fourth periods.

The very good performance of MBPS on hit rate shows that the segmentation strategy has succeeded in keeping the rate of confusion between the good payment and bad payment classes down to an absolute minimum.

Bad Payment Coverage

As a consequence of segmenting the data into the majority bad payment segments and learning exclusively from such segments it is possible that a given data mining model may not be able to pick some bad payments. This is because such payments may be present in data segments which contain a minority of bad payments. In this context, it is important to assess bad payment coverage. For each payment period, bad payments coverage is defined as total bad payment records correctly predicted divided by the total number of bad payment records actually present in that particular payment period.

Figure 4 shows that generally, for all algorithms, bad payment coverage gradually improves from the first payment to the seventh payment. However, all algorithms start poorly at the first payment. All algorithms cover only 10% of bad payments in this payment period. At this period, the performance is relatively low since the prediction depends entirely on credit control parameters. As more payments are made, the bad payment coverage increases. At the second payment, payment history is used for the first time. The use of history has previously been shown to improve coverage. Zeng et al. (2007), report that by applying historical data, their collection prediction performance increases from 65.95% to 78.57%. By the fourth payment, MBPS covers the majority of bad payments, as all algorithms are able to achieve a higher than 50% coverage. At the seventh period, the coverage jumps to approximately 80% for all algorithms. In practical terms this means that sufficient historical information is now available to identify the vast majority of bad customers and action can be put into place by the company involved to recover bad debt.

Figure 3. Comparison of Logistic Regression, C4.5, and Bayesian network on bad payment hit rates with MBPS

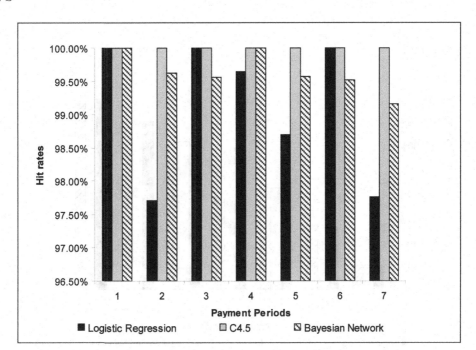

Area under Curve (AUC) Metric

The AUC metric is commonly used to measure performance of imbalanced datasets as it is not biased towards the majority class, unlike metrics such as classification accuracy. Fawcett (Fawcett, 2005) defines an algorithm *f* to be realistic if the AUC (*f*) >0.5, otherwise *f* is worse than random guessing. Figure 5 shows that realistic performances on AUC are exhibited by Logistic Regression across all payments. Its minimum performance on AUC (0.6425) occurs in the seventh period, but this is still much higher than random guessing. Furthermore, except for the first payment, the Bayesian Network performance is also realistic. The worst is C4.5, as its AUC performance across all periods is worse than random guessing.

Comparison of MBPS with Under Sampling

As shown in the previous section, the Logistic Regression algorithm is the clear winner outperforming the other two algorithms on the AUC measure and holding its own on the other metrics that we tested. As such, we decided to carry forward this algorithm to a comparative study of the performance of different data configuration methods, namely under-sampling, MBPS and the original data configuration (hereinafter referred to as the original data for brevity). The comparison was done in respect of fail prediction cost, precision and bad payment coverage.

Bad Payment Fail Prediction Cost

Two types of costs are associated with incorrect predictions with respect to bad payments. The first is when a bad payment is incorrectly classified as a good payment (False Negative) and the

Figure 4. Comparison of Logistic Regression, C4.5, and Bayesian network on bad payment coverage with MBPS

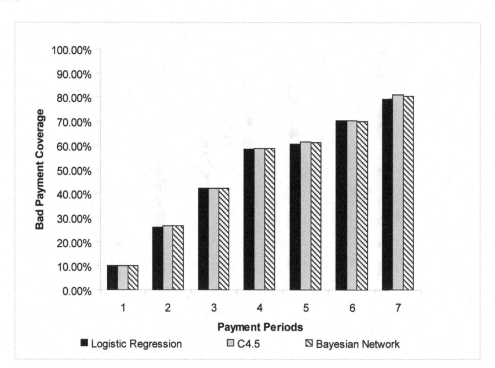

second occurs when a good payment is incorrectly identified as being bad (False Positive). The cost of a False Positive far outweighs that of a False Negative when the organization involved takes pro-active actions in respect of False Positives. Urging customers who have every intention of paying on time results in embarrassment and possibly loss of faith in the Company involved. In common with the Abdou and other studies we set the cost of a False Positive to be five times that of a False Negative. Suppose tp, tn, fp and fn denote the number of True Positives, True Negatives, False Positives and False Negatives respectively. The fail prediction cost is then given by: cost = (5*fp + fn)

$$(5*fp + fn)/(tp + fp + tn + fn)$$

The fail prediction cost for the three data configuration methods is given in Figure 6.

From Figure 6 above it can be observed that payment prediction models based on MBPS produce the lowest cost when compared with the other methods. Models based on the original dataset rank

second whilst under sampling models perform worst. The consistently poor performance of under sampling can be explained by the fact that its false positive rate is much higher than that of MBPS. This occurs due to the reverse bias introduced by removing instances of the good payment class which results in a large number of good payments being classified incorrectly as bad payments, thus impacting on the false positive rate. With the original data configuration the scale of this problem is much less as in most financial credit applications the volume of good payments dominates over bad payments. However, the true negative rate is high with such imbalanced data, thus producing higher cost models than MBPS in general. In terms of the original data configuration, both the false positives and false negative rates decrease from the fifth to the seventh periods as the ratio of good payments to bad payments become increases. This results in a decrease in the fail prediction cost.

In this research we have shown that under sam-

Figure 5. Comparison of Logistic Regression, C4.5, and Bayesian network on AUC with MBPS

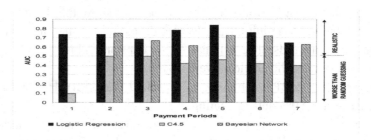

Figure 6. Comparison of bad payment Fail Prediction Cost

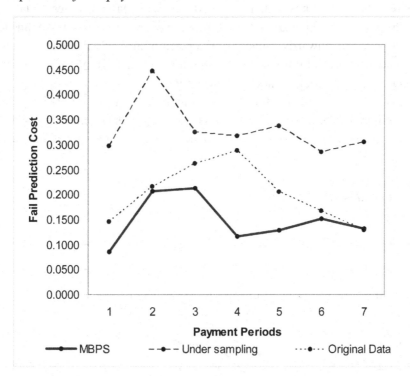

pling performs worse than the original dataset on bad payment fail prediction cost. This finding is in agreement with previous studies, such as McCarthy, Zabar and Weiss (2005) who also found that under sampling performs worse in cost sensitive learning situation.

Bad Payment Coverage

Given MBPS's superior performance on the important cost metric we now turn our attention to its coverage vis-à-vis the other two methods. We expected MBPS's coverage to be low in comparison to under sampling at the first few periods and Figure 7 confirms this expectation. However, it is apparent that MBPSs coverage continues to grow continuously with every payment period, eventually matching that of under-sampling at the sixth payment period. In contrast, the performance of under sampling although growing initially, falls from the fifth payment onwards. The original data configuration, as expected did not do as well as either under-sampling or MBPS, achieving a maximum coverage of just 50% and stagnating thereafter at this value.

The reason for the deterioration in the performance of under sampling is the increase in its false negative rate which grows from 0.28 to 0.41 from the fifth to the seventh payments. This increase is triggered by an increase in the ratio of the number of good payments to bad payments which is most marked from the fifth payment onwards. This increase in imbalance tends to reduce the effectiveness of under sampling. Although a higher under sampling rate will tend to compensate for this increase in the degree of imbalance, it will come at a severe price as Precision will tend to drop

drastically as more instances are removed from the good payment class. Our results in the next section show that Precision for under sampling drops even if the under sampling rate is held at a constant value.

Bad Payment Precision

In a credit financing scenario, accuracy in predicting bad payments is of crucial importance. This is because the correct customers involved can then be identified with a high degree of reliability. In other words in such scenarios Precision on the bad payment class assumes equal, if not more importance than Coverage. We thus investigated the performance of MBPS versus the other two data methods across the range of payments that we tracked.

Figure 8 shows that MBPS significantly outperforms the other two methods and that its performance is consistent across all payment periods.

Figure 7. Comparison of bad payment Coverage

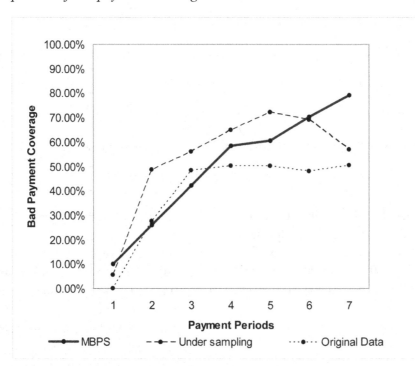

Precision on the bad payment class is governed by the true positive rate and the false positive rate. The superior performance of MBPS is due to its very low false positive rate – very few good payments are miss-classified as bad payments. This is due to the fact that MBPS consists of data segments where bad payments inherently dominate over good payments. Such data segments enable a classifier to capture more faithfully the factors that govern bad payments. In the case of under sampling, a significant fraction of good payments were miss-classified as bad payments, thus leading to poor precision.

CONCLUSION AND FUTURE WORK

In this chapter we introduced a novel method of data segmentation that was shown to outperform the standard under sampling method on key metrics when dealing with predictions on the bad payment class. Although the scope of this research was restricted to the financial credit application domain, the data segmentation strategy used is sufficiently generic to be used in any

domain where imbalanced data exists. Another significant advantage of the data segmentation strategy is that it can be applied without any modification to multiple class problems, unlike the standard re-balancing methods such as under sampling and over sampling that are tailored to binary class problems. Segmentation can be applied to each class independently of the others as the only consideration is to identify clusters where the incidence of the particular class in question naturally dominates.

As future research it would be worthwhile to investigate the use of the SMOTE method in conjunction with our data segmentation strategy. The SMOTE scheme can be used to create new instances in the neighbourhood of the minority class as a pre-processing step to applying data segmentation. The effect of this will be to increase the proportion of minority class instances within each data segment, thus giving rise to more segments where minority class instances dominate. We believe that this will help to improve coverage.

Figure 8. Comparison of bad payment Precision

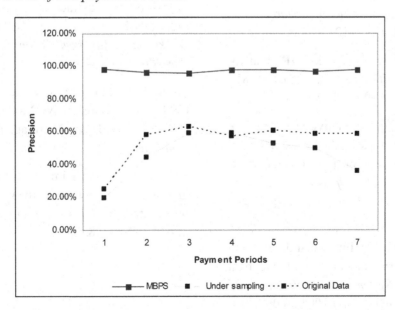

REFERENCES

Abdou, H., Masry, A. E., & Pointon, J. (2007). On the Application of Credit Scoring Models in Egyptian Banks. *Banks and Bank systems, 2*(1).

Avery, R. B., Bostic, R. W., Calem, P. S., & Canner, G. B. (1996). Credit Risk,Credit Scoring, and the performance of Home Mortgages. *Federal Reserve Bulletin,* (82), 621-648.

Boyes, W. J., Hoffman, D. L., & Low, S. A. (1989). An Econometric Analysis of The Bank Credit Scoring Problem. *Journal of Econometrics, 40,* 3–14. doi:10.1016/0304-4076(89)90026-2

Chawla, Bowyer, K. W., Hall, L. O., & Kegelmeyer, W. P. (2002). SMOTE:Synthetic Minority Over-sampling Technique. *Journal of Artificial Intelligence Research, 16,* 321–357.

Crook, J. N., Edelman, D. B., & Thomas, L. C. (2006). Recent developments in consumer credit risk assessment. *European Journal of Operational Research, 183*(3), 1447–1465. doi:10.1016/j.ejor.2006.09.100

Desai, V. S., Crook, J. N., & Overstreet, G. A. (1996). A comparison of neural network and linear scoring models in credit union environment. *European Journal of Operational Research, 95*(1), 24–37. doi:10.1016/0377-2217(95)00246-4

Fawcett, T. (2005). An introduction to ROC analysis. *Pattern Recognition Letters, 27*(8), 861–874. doi:10.1016/j.patrec.2005.10.010

Finlay, S. M. (2006). Predictive models of expenditure and over-indebtedness for assessing the affordability of new consumer credit applications. *The Journal of the Operational Research Society, 57*(6), 655–669. doi:10.1057/palgrave.jors.2602030

Hsieh, N. C. (2004). An Integrated data mining and behaviour scoring model for analyzing bank customers. *Expert Systems with Applications, 27,* 623–633. doi:10.1016/j.eswa.2004.06.007

Johnson, A. (2006). Leveraging Credit Scoring. *Mortgage Banking, 66*(6), 76–84.

Lee, T. S., Chiu, C. C., Lu, C.-J., & Chen, I. F. (2002). Credit scoring using the hybrid neural discriminant technique. *Expert Systems with Applications, 23*(3), 245–254. doi:10.1016/S0957-4174(02)00044-1

Li, Z., Xu, J., & Xu, M. (2004). ANN-GA approach of credit scoring for mobile customers. *In Proceedings of the 2004 IEEE Conference on Cybernetics and Intelligent Systems, 2,* 1148.

Maloof, M. Learning when data sets are imbalanced and when costs are unequal and unkown, *ICML2003.*

McCarthy, K., Zabar, B., & Weiss, G. (2005). Does Cost Sensitive Learning Beat sampling for Classifying Rare Classes? In *Proceedings of the 1st international workshop on Utility-based data mining UBDM '05* (pp. 69 – 77).

Servigny, A. D., & Renault, O. (2004). *Measuring and Managing Credit Risk.* New York: McGrawHill.

Shihab, S., Al-Nuaimy, W., Huang, Y., & Eriksen, A. (2003). A comparison of segmentation techniques for target extraction in ground penetrating radar data. In *Proceedings of the 2nd International Workshop on Advanced Ground Penetrating Radar, 2003* (pp. 95-100).

Smith, L. D., Sanchez, S. M., & Lawrence, E. C. (1996). A Comprehensive Model for Managing Credit Risk on Home Mortgage Portfolio. *Decision Sciences, 27*(2), 291–308.

Srinivasan, V., & Kim, Y. H. (1987). Credit granting a comparative analysis of classifactory procedures. *The Journal of Finance, 42,* 655–683. doi:10.2307/2328378

Sun, L., & Senoy, P. P. (2006). Using Bayesian network for bankruptcy prediction: some methodological issues. *European Journal of Operational Research, 10*, 1–16.

Thomas, L. C., Ho, J., & Scherer, W. T. (2001). Time to tell: behaviour scoring and the dynamics of consumer credit assessment. *Journal of Management Mathematics, 12*, 89–103.

Tsaih, R., Liu, Y.-J., Liu, W., & Lien, Y.-L. (2004). Credit scoring system for small business loans. *Decision Support Systems, 38*, 91–99. doi:10.1016/S0167-9236(03)00079-4

Weiss, G. M. (2004). Mining with rarity: a unifying framework. *ACM SIGKDD Explorations Newsletter* (pp. 7-19).

West, D. (2000). Neural network credit scoring models. *Computers & Operations Research, 27*, 1131–1152. doi:10.1016/S0305-0548(99)00149-5

Zekic-Susac, M., Sarlija, N., & Bensic, M. (2004). Small business credit scoring: a comparison of logistic regression, neural network, and decision tree models. In *26th International Conference on Information Technology Interfaces* (p. 265).

Zeng, S., Melville, P., Lang, C. A., Martin, I. B., & Murphy, C. (2007). Predictive modeling for collections of accounts receivable. In *Proceedings of the 2007 international workshop on Domain driven data mining* (pp. 43-48).

Compilation of References

Abdou, H., Masry, A. E., & Pointon, J. (2007). On the Application of Credit Scoring Models in Egyptian Banks. *Banks and Bank systems, 2*(1).

Ableson, A., & Glasgow, J. (2003). Efficient statistical pruning of association rules. In N. Lavrac et al. (Eds.), *PKDD 2003, Lecture Notes in Computer Science, Vol. 2838* (pp. 23-34). Springer.

Achtert, E., Böhm, C., Kriegel, H.-P., Kröger, P., & Zimek, A. (2006). Deriving quantitative models for correlation clusters. In *Proceedings of the ACM SIGMOD Conference on Management of Data (KDD)*, (pp. 4–13), Philadelphia, PA.

Aggarwal, C. C., & Yu, P. S. (1998). A new framework for itemset generation. In *Proceedings of the 1998 ACM Symposium Prinicples of Database Systems (PODS'98)* (pp. 18-24), Seattle, WA, USA.

Agrawal, R., & Srikant, R. (1994). Fast algorithms for mining association rules. In *Proceedings of the 20th International Conference on Very Large Databases* (pp. 487–499). San Francisco, CA: Morgan Kaufmann Publishers Inc.

Agrawal, R., & Srikant, R. (1995). Mining sequential patterns. In *International Conference on Data Engineering (ICDE)* (pp. 85-93).

Agrawal, R., Imielinski, T., & Swami, A. (1993). Database mining: A performance perspective. *IEEE Transactions on Knowledge and Data Engineering, 5*(6), 914–925. doi:10.1109/69.250074

Agrawal, R., Imielinski, T., & Swami, A. (1993). Mining association rules between sets of items in large databases. In P. Buneman & S. Jajodia (Eds.), *Proceedings of the 1993 ACM SIGMOD international conference on management of data* (pp. 207–216). New York, NY: ACM Press.

Agrawal, R., Mannila, H., Srikant, R., Toivonen, H., & Verkamo, A. I. (1996). Fast discovery of association rules. In *Advances in knowledge discovery and data mining* (pp. 307-328). American Association for Artificial Intelligence Menlo Park, CA, USA.

Akbani, R., Kwek, S., & Japkowicz, N. (2004, September 20-24). Applying support vector machines to imbalanced datasets. In *15th European Conference on Machine Learning (ECML2004), volume 3201 of Lecture Notes in Computer Science.* (pp. 39–50). Pisa, Italy.

Anderson, E., et al. (1999). *LAPACK Users' Guide.* SIAM.

Andrews, D. A., & Bonta, J. (1995). *LSI-R: The Level of Service Inventory–Revised.* Toronto, Canada: Multi–Health Systems.

Andrews, D. A., Bonta, J., & Wormith, J. S. (2006). The recent past and near future of risk and/or needs assessment. *Crime and Delinquency, 52*(1), 7–27. doi:10.1177/0011128705281756

Angiulli, F., & Pizzuti, C. (2002). Fast outlier detection in high dimensional spaces. In *PKDD* (pp. 15-26).

Angiulli, F., & Pizzuti, C. (2005). Outlier mining in large high-dimensional data sets. *IEEE Transactions on Knowledge and Data Engineering, 17*(2), 203–215. doi:10.1109/TKDE.2005.31

Angiulli, F., Greco, G., & Palopoli, L. (2007). Outlier Detection by Logic Programming. *ACM Transactions on Computational Logic, 9*(1). doi:10.1145/1297658.1297665

Antonie, M.-L., & Zaiane, O. R. (2004). Mining positive and negative association rules: An approach for confined rules. In *PKDD'04: Proceedings of the 8th European Conference on Principles and Practice of Knowledge Discovery in Databases* (pp. 27-38). New York: Springer-Verlag New York, Inc.

Apiletti, D., Bruno, G., Ficarra, E., & Baralis, E. (2006). Data Cleaning and Semantic Improvement in Biological Databases. *Journal of Integrative Bioinformatics, 3*(2).

Arenas, M., & Libkin, L. (2004). A Normal Form for XML Documents. *ACM Transactions on Database Systems, 29*(1), 195–232. doi:10.1145/974750.974757

Arunasalam, B., & Chawla, S. (2006). CCCS: a top-down associative classifier for imbalanced class distribution. In *KDD '06: Proceedings of the 12th ACM SIGKDD international conference on Knowledge discovery and data mining* (pp. 517–522). New York, NY, USA: ACM Press.

Asuncion, A., & Newman, D. J. (2007). *UCI Machine Learning Repository.* Retrieved March 2008, from http://www.ics.uci.edu/~mlearn/mlrepository.html

Aumann, Y., & Lindell, Y. (1999). A statistical theory for quantitative association rules. In *Proceedings of ACM Intl. Conference KDD*, San Diego, CA, USA.

Avery, R. B., Bostic, R. W., Calem, P. S., & Canner, G. B. (1996). Credit Risk, Credit Scoring, and the performance of Home Mortgages. *Federal Reserve Bulletin,* (82), 621-648.

Ayres, J., Flannick, J., Gehrke, J., & Yiu, T. (2002). Sequential PAttern Mining using a bitmap representation. In *KDD* (pp. 429-435).

Bailey, J., Manoukian, T., & Ramamohanarao, K. (2003). A fast algorithm for computing hypergraph transversals and its application in mining emerging patterns. In *ICDM'03: Proceedings of the Third IEEE International Conference on Data Mining* (pp. 485-488). Washington, DC, IEEE Computer Society.

Balderas, M.-A., Cubero, J.-C., Berzal, F., Marin, N., & Einsman, E. (2005). *Discovering Hidden Association Rules.* Paper presented at the SIGKDD Knowledge Discovery and Data Mining, Workshop for Anomaly Detection, Chicago, USA.

Baralis, E., Garza, P., Quintarelli, E., & Tanca, L. (2004). Answering Queries on XML Data by means of Association Rules. *Current Trends in Database Technology, 3268.* Springer-Verlag.

Barbaree, H. E., Seto, M., Langton, C. M., & Peacock, E. J. (2001). Evaluating the predictive accuracy of six risk assessment instruments for adult sex offenders. *Criminal Justice and Behavior, 28*(4), 490–521. doi:10.1177/009385480102800406

Barnoski, R. (2006). *Sex offender sentencing in Washington State: Predicting recidivism based on the LSI-R.* Technical report, Washington State Institute for Public Policy, Olympia, WA.

Barnoski, R., & Aos, S. (2003). *Washington's offender accountability act: An analysis of the Department of Corrections' risk assessment* (document no. 03-12-1202). Technical report, Washington State Institute for Public Policy, Olympia, WA.

Bayardo, R. J. (1998). Efficiently mining long patterns from databases. In *Proceedings of the 1998 ACM SIGMOD International Conference on Management of Data, SIGMOD '98* (pp. 85–93). New York, NY: ACM Press.

Bayardo, R. J., & Agrawal, R. (1999). Mining the most interesting rules. In *Proceedings of the Fifth ACM SIGKDD International Conference on Knowledge Discovery and Data Mining, KDD '99.,* (pp. 145–154). New York, NY: ACM Press.

Bayardo, R. J., Agrawal, R., & Gunopulos, D. (1999, March). Constraint-based rule mining in large, dense databases. *Proceedings of the 15th International Conference on Data Engineering (ICDE)* (pp. 188-197), Sydney, Australia. IEEE Computer Society.

Bayardo, R. J., Agrawal, R., & Gunopulos, D. (2000). Constraint-based rule mining in large, dense databases. *Data Mining and Knowledge Discovery, 4*(2/3), 217–240. doi:10.1023/A:1009895914772

Beck, J. (2007, July). Difficulties in inferring student knowledge from observations (and why you should care). In *Proceedings of the Educational Data Mining workshop, in conjunction with 13th International Conference of Artificial Intelligence in Education* (pp. 21-30). Marina del Rey, CA. USA. IOS Press.

Berk, R. (2008). *Statistical Learning from a Regression Perspective*. Springer-Verlag, New York.

Berk, R., Kriegler, B., & Baek, J. (2006). Forecasting dangerous inmate misconduct: An application of ensemble statistical procedures. *Journal of Quantitative Criminology*, *22*(2), 131–145. doi:10.1007/s10940-006-9005-z

Berzal, F., Cubero, J.-C., Marin, J., & Serrano, J. (2001). An efficient method for association rule mining in relational databases. *Data & Knowledge Engineering*, (37): 47–84. doi:10.1016/S0169-023X(00)00055-0

Berzal, F., Cubero, J.-C., Marín, N., & Gámez, M. (2004). *Anomalous Association Rules*. Paper presented at the Workshop on Alternative Techniques for Data Mining and Knowledge Discovery in the IEEE International Conference on Data Mining. From http://elvex.ugr.es/icdm2004/program.html

Berzal, F., Cubero, J.-C., Marín, N., & Gámez, M. (2004). Finding anomalies in databases. In R. Giráldez, J. Riquelme & J. Aguilar-Ruiz (Eds.), *Tendencias de la Minería de Datos en España* (p. 14), Seville, Spain: Red Española de Minería de Datos y Aprendizaje.

Besson, J., Robardet, C., De Raedt, L., & Boulicaut, J.-F. (2006). Mining bi-sets in numerical data. In *Proceedings of the 5th International Workshop on Knowledge Discovery in Inductive Databases (KDID'06) at PKDD'06*, (pp. 9–19), Berlin, Germany.

Blanchard, J., Guillet, F., & Briand, H. (2003, August). *Exploratory visualization for association rule rummaging*. Paper presented at the 4th International Workshop on Multimedia Data Mining (MDM/KDD), Washington, DC.

Blanchette, K., & Brown, S. (2006). *The assessment and treatment of women offenders: An integrative perspective*. West Sussex, England: John Wiley and Sons.

Bodon, F. (2003). A Fast Apriori implementation. *ICDM Workshop on Frequent Itemset Mining Implementations, vol. 90*, Melbourne, Florida, USA.

Bohannon, P., Fan, W., Geerts, F., Jia, X., & Kementsietsidis, A. (2007, April 15-20) Conditional functional dependencies for data cleaning. In *ICDE '07: IEEE 23rd International Conference on Data Engineering*, (pp.746-755).

Boros, E., Elbassioni, K., Gurvich, V., Khachiyan, L., & Makino, K. (2002). Dual-bounded generating problems: All minimal integer solutions for a monotone system of linear inequalities. *SIAM Journal on Computing*, *31*(5), 1624–1643. doi:10.1137/S0097539701388768

Boros, E., Gurvich, V., Khachiyan, L., & Makino, K. (2002). On the complexity of generating maximal frequent and minimal infrequent sets. In *STACS '02: Proceedings of the 19th Annual Symposium on Theoretical Aspects of Computer Science* (pp. 133-141), London, UK: Springer-Verlag.

Boros, E., Gurvich, V., Khachiyan, L., & Makino, K. (2003). On maximal frequent and minimal infrequent sets in binary matrices. *Annals of Mathematics and Artificial Intelligence*, *39*(3), 211–221. doi:10.1023/A:1024605820527

Boyes, W. J., Hoffman, D. L., & Low, S. A. (1989). An Econometric Analysis of The Bank Credit Scoring Problem. *Journal of Econometrics*, *40*, 3–14. doi:10.1016/0304-4076(89)90026-2

Brefeld, U., & Scheffer, T. (2005). Auc maximizing support vector learning. In *Proceedings of the ICML Workshop on ROC Analysis in Machine Learning*.

Breiman, L. (2001). Random forests. *Machine Learning*, *1*(45), 5–32. doi:10.1023/A:1010933404324

Brennan, T. (1987). Classification: An overview of selected methodological issues. In D. M. Gottfredson & M. Tonry (Eds.), *Prediction and Classification: Criminal Justice Decision Making* (pp. 201–248). Chicago: University of Chicago Press.

Brennan, T. (1999). Implementing organizational change in criminal justice: Some lessons from jail classification systems. *Corrections Management Quarterly, 3*(2), 11–27.

Brennan, T., & Dieterich, W. (2008). *New York State Division of Parole COMPAS Reentry Pilot Study: Two-Year Follow-Up.* Traverse City, MI: Northpointe Institute Inc.

Brennan, T., Breitenbach, M., & Dieterich, W. (2008). Towards an explanatory taxonomy of adolescent delinquents: Identifying several social-psychological profiles. *Journal of Quantitative Criminology, 24*(2), 179–203. doi:10.1007/s10940-008-9045-7

Brijs, T., Swinnen, G., Vanhoof, K., & Wets, G. (1999, August 15-18). The use of association rules for product assortment decisions: a case study. In *Proceedings of the Fifth International Conference on Knowledge Discovery and Data Mining* (pp. 254-260), San Diego, USA.

Brijs, T., Vanhoof, K., & Wets, G. (2003). Defining interestingness for association rules. In *International journal of information theories and applications, 10*(4), 370-376.

Brin, S., Motwani, R., & Silverstein, C. (1997). Beyond market baskets: generalizing association rules to correlations. In *SIGMOD '97: Proceedings of the 1997 ACM SIGMOD international conference on Management of data* (pp. 265-276), New York, NY: ACM.

Broyden, C. G. (1970). The convergence of a class of double-rank minimization algorithms. *Journal of the Institute of Mathematics and Its Applications, 6*, 76–90.

Bruno, G., Garza, P., Quintarelli, E., & Rossato, R. (2007). Anomaly Detection Through Quasi Functional Dependency Analysis. *Journal of Digital Information Management, 5*(4).

Bruno, G., Garza, P., Quintarelli, E., & Rossato, R. (2007, September 3-7). Anomaly Detection in XML databases by means of Association Rules. *Second International Workshop on Flexible Database and Information Systems Technology,* (pp. 387-391).

Burges, C. (1998). A tutorial on support vector machines for pattern recognition. *Data Mining and Knowledge Discovery, 2*, 121–168. doi:10.1023/A:1009715923555

Cai, C. H., Fu, A. W.-C., Cheng, C. H., & Kwong, W. W. (1998). Mining Association Rules with Weighted Items. In *Proceedings of Intl. Database Engineering and Applications Symposium (IDEAS'98)* (pages 68-77). Cardiff, Wales, UK.

Calders, T., & Jaroszewicz, S. (2007). Efficient auc optimization for classification. In *In 11th European Conference on Principles and Practice of Knowledge Discovery in Databases (PKDD 2007).*

Calders, T., Goethals, B., & Jaroszewicz, S. (2006). Mining Rank-Correlated Sets of Numerical Attributes. In *Proceedings of the 12th ACM SIGKDD International Conference on Knowledge Discovery and Data Mining (KDD),* (pp. 96 - 105).

Cao, L., Zhao, Y., & Zhang, C. (2008). Mining Impact-Targeted Activity Patterns in Imbalanced Data. *IEEE Transactions on Knowledge and Data Engineering, 20*, 1053–1066. doi:10.1109/TKDE.2007.190635

Caruana, R., & Niculescu-Mizil, A. (2006). An empirical comparison of supervised learning algorithms. In *ICML '06: Proceedings of the 23rd international conference on Machine learning* (pp. 161–168). ACM: New York, NY, USA.

Carvalho, D., Freitas, A., & Ebecken, N. (2005). Evaluating the correlation between objective rule interestingness measures and real human interest. In: *Proceedings of the 9th European conference on principles of data mining and knowledge discovery (PKDD),* (pp. 453–461).

Caulkins, J., Cohen, J., Gorr, W., & Wei, J. (1996). Predicting criminal recidivism: A comparison of neural network models with statistical methods. *Journal of Criminal Justice, 24*(3), 227–240. doi:10.1016/0047-2352(96)00012-8

Ceri, S., Di Guinta, F., & Lanzi, P. (2007). Mining Constraint Violations. *ACM Transactions on Database Systems, 32*(1). doi:10.1145/1206049.1206055

Chawla, N. V., Bowyer, K. W., Hall, L. O., & Kegelmeyer, W. P. (2002). Smote: Synthetic minority over-sampling technique. *Journal of Artificial Intelligence Research, 16*, 321–357.

Chen, M., Han, J., & Yu, P. (1996). Data mining: An overview from a database perspective. *IEEE Transactions on Knowledge and Data Engineering, 8*(6), 866–881. doi:10.1109/69.553155

Coenen, F. P., Leng, P., & Ahmed, S. (2004). Data Structures for Association Rule Mining: T-trees and P-trees. *IEEE Transactions on Data and Knowledge Engineering, 16*(6), 774–778. doi:10.1109/TKDE.2004.8

Coenen, F. P., Leng, P., & Goulbourne, G. (2004). Tree Structures for Mining Association Rules. *Journal of Data Mining and Knowledge Discovery, 8*(1), 25–51. doi:10.1023/B:DAMI.0000005257.93780.3b

Cohen, E., Datar, M., Fujiwara, S., Gionis, A., Indyk, P., & Motwani, R. (2001). Finding interesting association rules without support pruning. *IEEE Transactions on Knowledge and Data Engineering, 13*, 64–78. doi:10.1109/69.908981

Cohen, E., Datar, M., Fujiwara, S., Gionis, A., Indyk, P., Motwani, R., et al. (2000). Finding interesting associations without support pruning. In *Proceedings of the 16th International Conference on Data Engineering(ICDE),* (pp. 489-500).

Cornelis, C., Yan, P., Zhang, X., & Chen, G. (2006). *Mining Positive and Negative Association Rules from Large Databases.* Paper presented at the 2006 IEEE Conference on Cybernetics and Intelligent Systems.

Crook, J. N., Edelman, D. B., & Thomas, L. C. (2006). Recent developments in consumer credit risk assessment. *European Journal of Operational Research, 183*(3), 1447–1465. doi:10.1016/j.ejor.2006.09.100

Cutting, D. R., Pedersen, J. O., Karger, D., & Tukey, J. W. (1992). Scatter/gather: A cluster-based approach to browsing large document collections. In *Proceedings of the fifteenth annual International ACM SIGIR conference on research and development in information retrieval* (pp. 318–329).

Dahle, K. P. (2006). Strengths and limitations of actuarial prediction of criminal re-offence in a German prison sample: A comparative study of LSI-R, HCR-20 and PCL-R. *International Journal of Law and Psychiatry, 29*(5), 431–442. doi:10.1016/j.ijlp.2006.03.001

Daly, K. (1992). Women's pathway to felony court: Feminist theories of lawbreaking and problems of representation. *Review of Law and Women's Studies, 2*, 11–52.

Daly, O., & Taniar, D. (2004). Exception rule mining based on negative association rules. In A. Lagana et al. (Eds.), *ICCSA 2004, Lecture Notes in Computer Science, Vol. 3046* (pp. 543-552). Springer.

Dasu, T., & Johnson, T. (2003). *Exploratory Data Mining and Data Cleaning.* Hoboken, New Jersey: Wiley-Interscience.

Dawes, R. (1979). The robust beauty of improper linear models in decision models. *The American Psychologist, 34*, 571–582. doi:10.1037/0003-066X.34.7.571

Delgado, M., Sanchez, D., Martin-Bautista, M. J., & Vila, M.-A. (2001). Mining association rule with improved semantics in medical databases. *Artificial Intelligence in Medicine, 21*(1-3), 241–245. doi:10.1016/S0933-3657(00)00092-0

Denning, D. E. (1987). An Intrusion-Detection Model. *IEEE Transactions on Software Engineering, 13*(2), 10.

Desai, V. S., Crook, J. N., & Overstreet, G. A. (1996). A comparison of neural network and linear scoring models in credit union environment. *European Journal of Operational Research, 95*(1), 24–37. doi:10.1016/0377-2217(95)00246-4

Ding, J. (2005). *Efficient association rule mining among infrequent items.* Ph.D. thesis. In University of Illinois at Chicago.

Dong, G., & Li, J. (1999). Efficient mining of emerging patterns: discovering trends and differences. In *Proceedings of ACM SIGKDD Conference on Knowledge Discovery and Data Mining (KDD)* (pp. 43-52).

Dong, G., & Pei, J. (2007). *Sequence Data Mining (Advances in Database Systems)*. Springer.

Dougiamas, M. (1999). *Moodle.* Retrieved August 01, 2008, from http://moodle.org/

Dunkel, B., & Soparkar, N. (1999). *Data organization and access for efficient data mining.* Paper presented at the 15th International conference on data engineering.

Dzeroski, S., & Todorovski, L. (1995). Discovering dynamics: from inductive logic programming to machine discovery. *Journal of Intelligent Information Systems, 4*, 89–108. doi:10.1007/BF00962824

Edmonds, J., Gryz, J., Liang, D., & Miller, R. J. (2001). Mining for empty rectangles in large data sets. In *ICDT '01: International conference on database theory* (pp. 174-188), London, UK: Springer Berlin / Heidelberg.

Elbassioni, K. (2008). Algorithms for dualization over products of partially ordered sets. To appear In *SIAM J. Disctere Math.*

Elmasri, R., & Navathe, S. B. (2005). *Fundamentals of Database Systems*. Pearson, Addison Wesley.

Fawcett, T. (2005). An introduction to ROC analysis. *Pattern Recognition Letters, 27*(8), 861–874. doi:10.1016/j. patrec.2005.10.010

Fine, J. P., & Gray, R. J. (1999). A proportional hazards model for the subdistribution of a competing risk. *Journal of the American Statistical Association, 94*(446), 496–509. doi:10.2307/2670170

Finlay, S. M. (2006). Predictive models of expenditure and over-indebtedness for assessing the affordability of new consumer credit applications. *The Journal of the Operational Research Society, 57*(6), 655–669. doi:10.1057/palgrave.jors.2602030

Fletcher, R. (1970). A new approach to variable metric algorithms. *The Computer Journal, 13*, 317–322. doi:10.1093/comjnl/13.3.317

Flores, A. W., Lowenkamp, C. T., Smith, P., & Latessa, E. J. (2006). Validating the Level of Service Inventory-Revised on a sample of federal probationers. *Federal Probation, 70*(2), 44–78.

Freund, Y., & Mason, L. (1999). The alternating decision tree learning algorithm. In *Proceeding of the Sixteenth International Conference on Machine Learning* (pp. 124–133). Bled, Slovenia

Ganti, V., Gehrke, J., & Ramakrishnan, R. (1999). CACTUS: Clustering categorical data using summaries. In *KDD '99: Proceedings of the fifth ACM SIGKDD International conference on knowledge discovery and data mining* (pp. 73–83). New York, NY, USA: ACM Press.

Garcia, J., Romero, C., Ventura, S., & Calders, T. (2007). Drawbacks and solutions of applying association rules mining in learning management systems. In *Proceedings of the International Workshop on Applying Data Mining in e-learning (ADML'07),* (pp. 13-22). Crete, Greece. Retrieved August 01, 2008, from http://ftp.informatik. rwth-aachen.de/Publications/CEUR-WS/Vol-305/

Garner, S. R. (1995). Weka: The Waikato environment for knowledge analysis. In *Proc. of the New Zealand Computer Science Research Students Conference* (pp. 57–64).

Garofalakis, M. N., Rastogi, R., & Shim, K. (1999). SPIRIT: Sequential pattern mining with regular expression constraints. In *VLDB* (pp. 223-234).

Geng, L. Q., & Howard, J. H. (2006). Interestingness Measures for Data Mining: A Survey. *ACM Computing Surveys, 38*(3), 9. doi:10.1145/1132960.1132963

Geng, L., & Hamilton, H. J. (2006). Interestingness measures for data mining: A survey. [CSUR]. *ACM Computing Surveys, 38*(3). doi:10.1145/1132960.1132963

Georgii, E., Richter, L., Rückert, U., & Kramer, S. (2005). Analyzing microarray data using quantitative association rules. *Bioinformatics (Oxford, England), 21*(2), ii1–ii8. doi:10.1093/bioinformatics/bti1121

Gibson, D., Kleinberg, J. M., & Raghavan, P. (1998). Clustering categorical data: An approach based on dynamical systems. In *VLDB '98: Proceedings of the 24rd international conference on very large data bases* (pp. 311–322). San Francisco, CA, USA: Morgan Kaufmann Publishers Inc.

Goldfarb, D. (1970). A family of variable metric updates derived by variational means. *Mathematics of Computation, 24,* 23–26. doi:10.2307/2004873

Gottfredson, M. (1987). Prediction: An Overview of Selected Issues. *Prediction and Classification: Criminal Justice Decision Making.* Chicago: University of Chicago Press.

Grann, M., Belfrage, H., & Tengstrom, A. (2000). Actuarial assessment of risk for violence: Predictive validity of the VRAG and the historical part of the HCR-20. *Criminal Justice and Behavior, 27,* 97–114. doi:10.1177/0093854800027001006

Grove, W., & Meehl, P. (1996). Comparative efficiency of informal (subjective, impressionistic) and formal (mechanical, algorithmic) prediction procedures: The clinical-statistical controversy. *Psychology, Public Policy, and Law, 2,* 293–323. doi:10.1037/1076-8971.2.2.293

Guha, S., Rastogi, R., & Shim, K. (2000). ROCK: A robust clustering algorithm for categorical attributes. *Information Systems, 25*(5), 345–366. doi:10.1016/S0306-4379(00)00022-3

Gunopulos, D., Mannila, H., Khardon, R., & Toivonen, H. (1997). Data mining, hypergraph transversals, and machine learning (extended abstract). In *PODS '97: Proceedings of the 16th ACM SIGACT-SIGMOD-SIGART symposium on Principles of database systems* (pp. 209-216), New York: ACM Press.

Gyenesei, A. (2000). Mining Weighted Association Rules for Fuzzy Quantitative Items. In *Proceedings of PKDD Conference* (pp. 416-423).

Hahsler, M. (2006, September). A model-based frequency constraint for mining associations from transaction data. *Data Mining and Knowledge Discovery, 13*(2), 137–166. doi:10.1007/s10618-005-0026-2

Hahsler, M., & Hornik, K. (2007). New Probabilistic Interest Measures for Association Rules. *Intelligent Data Analysis, 11*(5), 437–455.

Han, J., & Fu, Y. (1995). Discovery of multiple-level association rules from large databases. In *VLDB '95: Proceedings of the 21th International Conference on Very Large Data Bases* (pp. 420-431), San Francisco, CA, USA: Morgan Kaufmann Publishers Inc.

Han, J., & Kamber, M. (2006). *Data Mining: Concepts and Techniques* (2nd ed.). Morgan Kaufmann Publishers.

Han, J., Cai, Y., & Cercone, N. (1993). Data-driven discovery of quantitative rules in relational databases. *IEEE Transactions on Knowledge and Data Engineering, 5*(1), 29–40. doi:10.1109/69.204089

Han, J., Pei, J., & Yin, Y. (2000). Mining frequent pattern without candidate generation. In *Proceeding of ACM SIGMOD International Conference Management of Data(ICMD)* (pp. 1–12).

Hare, R. D. (1991). *Manual for the Hare Psychopathy Checklist-Revised.* Toronto, Canada: Multi-Health Systems.

Harrell, F., Califf, R., Pryor, D., Lee, K., & Rosati, R. (1982). Evaluating the yield of medical tests. *Journal of the American Medical Association, 247,* 2543–2546. doi:10.1001/jama.247.18.2543

Hastie, R., & Dawes, R. (2001). *Rational Choice in an Uncertain World: The Psychology of Judgment and Decision Making.* Thousand Oaks, CA: Sage Publications.

Haykin, S. (1998). *Neural networks: a comprehensive foundation.* 2nd Edition. Prentice Hall.

Hipp, J., Myka, A., Wirth, R., & Guntzer, U. (1998). A new algorithm for faster mining of generalized association rules. In *PKDD'98: Proceedings of the Second European Symposium on Principles of Data Mining and Knowledge Discovery* (pp. 74-82). London, UK: Springer-Verlag.

Hodge, V. J., & Austin, J. (2004). A Survey of Outlier Detection Methodologies. *Artificial Intelligence Review, 22*(2), 85–126.

Hopcroft, J. E., Motwani, R., & Ullman, J. D. (2006*). Introduction to Automata Theory, Languages, and Computation.* Retrieved August 01, 2008, from http://infolab.stanford.edu/~ullman/ialc.html

Hsieh, N. C. (2004). An Integrated data mining and behaviour scoring model for analyzing bank customers. *Expert Systems with Applications, 27,* 623–633. doi:10.1016/j.eswa.2004.06.007

Hsu, P., Chen, Y., & Ling, C. (2004). Algorithms for mining association rules in bag databases. *Information Sciences, 166*(1-4), 31–47. doi:10.1016/j.ins.2003.05.013

Huang, Y.-F., & Wu, C.-M. (2002). Mining generalized association rules using pruning techniques. In *ICDM'02: Proceedings of the 2002 IEEE International Conference on Data Mining* (pp. 227-234). Washington, DC: IEEE Computer Society.

Huhtala, Y., Krkkinen, Y., Porkka, P., & Toivonen, H. (1999). TANE: An Efficient Algorithm for Discovering Functional and Approximate Dependencies. *The Computer Journal, 42*(2), 100–111. doi:10.1093/comjnl/42.2.100

Hussain, F., Liu, L., Suzuki, E., & Lu, H. (2000). Exception rule mining with a relative interestingness measure. In *Pacific-Asia Conference on Knowledge Discovery and Data Mining (PAKDD),* (pp. 86-97).

Hwang, S., Ho, S., & Tang, J. (1999). Mining exception instances to facilitate workflow exception handling. In *Proceedings of the Sixth International Conference on Database Systems for Advanced Applications (DASFAA)* (pp. 45-52).

Ivchenko, G. I., & Honov, S. A. (2006). On the Jaccard similarity test. *Journal of Mathematical Sciences, 88*(6), 789–794. doi:10.1007/BF02365362

Jain, A. K., Murty, M. N., & Flynn, P. J. (1999). Data clustering: a review. *ACM Computing Surveys, 31*(3), 264–323. doi:10.1145/331499.331504

Japkowicz, N. (2000). Learning from imbalanced data sets: A comparison of various strategies. *AAAI workshop on Learning from Imbalanced Data Sets.*

Japkowicz, N. (2001). Supervised versus unsupervised binary-learning by feedforward neural networks. *Machine Learning, 42*(1), 97–122. doi:10.1023/A:1007660820062

Jaroszewicz, S. (2006). Polynomial Association Rules with Applications to Logistic Regression. In *Proceedings of the ACM SIGKDD International Conference on Knowledge Discovery and Data Mining (KDD),* (pp. 586 - 591).

Jaroszewicz, S. (2008). Minimum Variance Associations–Discovering Relationships in Numerical Data, In *Proceedings of the Pacific-Asia Conference on Knowledge Discovery and Data Mining (PAKDD),* (pp. 172-183), Osaka, Japan.

Jaroszewicz, S., & Korzeń, M. (2007). Approximating Representations for Large Numerical Databases. In *Proceedings of the 7th SIAM International Conference on Data Mining (SDM),* (pp. 521-526), Minneapolis, MN.

Jaroszewicz, S., & Scheffer, T. (2005). Fast Discovery of Unexpected Patterns in Data, Relative to a Bayesian Network. In *Proceedings of the 11th ACM SIGKDD International Conference on Knowledge Discovery and Data Mining (KDD),* (pp. 118-127), Chicago, IL.

Jaroszewicz, S., & Simovici, D. (2004). Interestingness of Frequent Itemsets Using Bayesian Networks as Background Knowledge. In *Proceedings of the 10th ACM SIGKDD International Conference on Knowledge Discovery and Data Mining (KDD),* (pp. 178-186), Seattle, WA.

Jaroszewicz, S., & Simovici, D. A. (2002). Pruning redundant association rules using maximum entropy principle. In M.-S. Cheng et al. (Eds.), *PAKDD 2002, Lecture Notes n Computer Science, Vol. 2336* (pp. 135-147). Springer.

Jaroszewicz, S., Scheffer, T., & Simovici, D. (in press). Scalable pattern mining with Bayesian networks as background knowledge. *Data Mining and Knowledge Discovery.*

Jensen, C. S., Dyreson, C. E., Bohlen, M. H., et al. (1998). The consensus glossary of temporal database concepts - february 1998 version. In *Temporal Databases: Research and Practice. (the book grow out of a Dagstuhl Seminar, June 23-27, 1997), volume 1399 of Lecture Notes in Computer Science* (pp. 367-405). Springer.

Jiang, L., & Deogun, J. (2007). SPICE: A New Framework for Data Mining based on Probability Logic and Formal Concept Analysis. *Fundam. Inf., 78*(4), 467–485.

Jin, W., Tung, A. K. H., & Han, J. (2001). Mining top-n local outliers in large databases. In *KDD* (pp. 293-298).

Joachims, T. (2005). A support vector method for multivariate performance measures. In *Proceedings of the ICML 2005*.

Johnson, A. (2006). Leveraging Credit Scoring. *Mortgage Banking, 66*(6), 76–84.

Kamber, M., Han, J., & Chiang, J. Y. (1997). Metarule-guided mining of multi-dimensional association rules using data cubes. In *Proceeding of 3rd International Conference on Knowledge Discovery and Data Mining(KDD)* (pp. 207-210).

Kavvadias, D. J., & Stavropoulos, E. C. (2005). An efficient algorithm for the transversal hypergraph generation. *J. Graph Algorithms Appl., 9*(2), 239–264.

Khachiyan, L., Boros, E., Elbassioni, K., & Gurvich, V. (2006). An efficient implementation of a quasi-polynomial algorithm for generating hypergraph transversals and its application in joint generation. *Discrete Applied Mathematics, 154*(16), 2350–2372. doi:10.1016/j.dam.2006.04.012

Khachiyan, L., Boros, E., Elbassioni, K., Gurvich, V., & Makino, K. (2007). Dual-bounded generating problems: Efficient and inefficient points for discrete probability distributions and sparse boxes for multidimensional data. *Theoretical Computer Science, 379*(3), 361–376. doi:10.1016/j.tcs.2007.02.044

Khan, M. S., Muyeba, M., & Coenen, F. (2008). On Extraction of Nutritional Patterns (NPS) Using Fuzzy Association Rule Mining. In *Proc. of Intl. Conference on Health Informatics (HEALTHINF 08), INSTICC press Vol. 1* (pp. 34-42). Madeira, Portugal.

Kivinen, J., & Mannila, H. (1992). Approximate inference of functional dependencies from relations. *Theoretical Computer Science, 149*(1), 129–149. doi:10.1016/0304-3975(95)00028-U

Klemettinen, M., Mannila, H., Ronkainen, P., Toivonen, H., & Verkamo, A. I. (1994, November). Finding interesting rules from large sets of discovered association rules. *Proceedings of the 3rd International Conference on Information and Knowledge Management (ICKM)* (pp. 401-407), Gaithersburg, MD.

Knorr, E. M., & Ng, R. T. (1998). Algorithms for mining distance-based outliers in large datasets. In *VLDB* (pp. 392-403).

Knuth, D. (1997). *The Art of Computer Programming,* vol. 2, *Seminumerical Algorithms*, Addison-Wesley, Reading, MA.

Koh, Y. S. (2008). Mining non-coincidental rules without a user defined support threshold. In *PAKDD: Proceedings of the 12th Pacific-Asia Conference on Advances in Knowledge Discovery and Data Mining*, (pp. 910-915). Springer.

Koh, Y. S., & Pears, R. (2007). Efficiently finding negative association rules without support threshold. In *Australian Conference on Artificial Intelligence* (pp. 710-714). Springer Berlin / Heidelberg.

Koh, Y. S., & Pears, R. (2008). Transaction Clustering Using a Seeds Based Approach. *Advances in Knowledge Discovery and Data Mining, 12th Pacific-Asia Conference on Knowledge Discovery and Data Mining* (pp. 916-922). Springer-Verlag.

Koh, Y. S., & Rountree, N. (2005). Finding sporadic rules using Apriori-Inverse. In *Advances in Knowledge Discovery and Data Mining, 9th Pacific-Asia Conference on Knowledge Discovery and Data Mining 2005* (pp. 97–106). Berlin / Heidelberg: Springer.

Koh, Y. S., Rountree, N., & O'Keefe, R. A. (2006). Finding Non-Coincidental Sporadic Rules using Apriori-Inverse. *International Journal of Data Warehousing and Mining, 2*(2), 38–54.

Koh, Y. S., Rountree, N., & O'Keefe, R. A. (2008). Mining interesting imperfectly sporadic rules. *Knowledge and Information Systems, 14*(2), 179–196. doi:10.1007/s10115-007-0074-6

Kroner, C., Stadtland, C., Eidt, M., & Nedopil, N. (2007). The validity of the violence risk appraisal guide (VRAG) in predicting criminal recidivism. *Criminal Behaviour and Mental Health, 17*(2), 89–100. doi:10.1002/cbm.644

Kuok, C. M., Fu, A., & Wong, M. H. (1998). Mining Fuzzy Association Rules in Databases. *SIGMOD Record, 27*(1), 41–46. doi:10.1145/273244.273257

Lallich, S., Teytaud, O., & Prudhomme, E. (2007). Association rule Interestingness: Measure and statistical validation. In F. Guillet & J. H. Howard (Eds.), *Quality Measures in Data Mining* (pp. 251-275): Springer.

Lanckriet, G. R. G., Ghaoui, L. E., Bhattacharyya, C., & Jordan, M. I. (2002). Minimax probability machine. In *Advances in Neural Information Processing Systems, 14.* MIT Press.

Lee, T. S., Chiu, C. C., Lu, C.-J., & Chen, I. F. (2002). Credit scoring using the hybrid neural discriminant technique. *Expert Systems with Applications, 23*(3), 245–254. doi:10.1016/S0957-4174(02)00044-1

Lee, W., Stolfo, S., & Mok, K. (1998). Mining audit data to build intrusion detection models. In *Proceedings of ACM Intl. Conference KDD.*

Lent, B., Swami, A., & Widom, J. (1997). Clustering association rules. In *Proceeding of International Conference Data Engineering (ICDE)* (pp. 220-231).

Li Gu, L. J., He, H., Williams, G., Hawkins, S., & Kelman C. (2003). Association rule discovery with unbalanced class distributions. In *AI 2003: Advances in Artificial Intelligence* (pp. 221–232).

Li, D. H., Laurent, A., & Teisseire, M. (2007). On transversal hypergraph enumeration in mining sequential patterns. In *IDEAS* (pp. 303-307).

Li, J., Shen, H., & Topor, R. (2001, November). Mining the smallest association rule set for predictions. *Proceedings of the IEEE International Conference on Data Mining (ICDM)* (pp. 361-368), San Jose, CA. IEEE Computer Society.

Li, J., Zhang, X., Dong, G., Ramamohanarao, K., & Sun, Q. (1999). Efficient mining of high confidence association rules without support threshold. In *Proceedings of the 3rd European Conference on Principle and Practice of Knowledge Discovery in Databases, PKDD '99* (pp. 406 – 411).

Li, Y., & Sweeney, L. (2005). *Adding semantics and rigor to association rule learning: the GenTree approach* (Technical Report CMU ISRI 05-101). Pittsburgh, PA: Carnegie Mellon University, School of Computer Science, Institute for Software Research International.

Li, Z., Xu, J., & Xu, M. (2004). ANN-GA approach of credit scoring for mobile customers. *In Proceedings of the 2004 IEEE Conference on Cybernetics and Intelligent Systems, 2,* 1148.

Lin, J.-L. (2003). Mining maximal frequent intervals. In *SAC '03: Proceedings of the 2003 ACM symposium on Applied computing* (pp. 426-431), New York: ACM.

Lin, W., Alvarez, S., & Ruiz, C. (2002). Efficient adaptive-support association rule mining for recommender systems. *Data Mining and Knowledge Discovery, 6*(3), 83–105. doi:10.1023/A:1013284820704

Little, R. J. A., & Rubin, D. B. (1987). Statistical analysis with missing data. New York: Wiley.

Liu, B., Hsu, W., & Chen, S. (1997, August). Using general impressions to analyze discovered classification rules. *Proceedings of the 3rd International Conference on Knowledge Discovery and Data Mining (KDD)* (pp. 31-36), Newport Beach, CA. AAAI Press.

Liu, B., Hsu, W., & Ma, Y. (1998). Integrating classification and association rule mining. In *KDD98: Proceedings of the 4th International Conference on Knowledge Discovery and Data Mining* (pp. 80–86). New York City: AAAI Press.

Liu, B., Hsu, W., & Ma, Y. (1999). Mining association rules with multiple minimum supports. In *KDD '99: Proceedings of the fifth ACM SIGKDD international conference on Knowledge discovery and data mining*, (pp. 337–341). New York, NY, USA: ACM Press.

Liu, B., Hsu, W., & Ma, Y. (1999, August). Pruning and summarizing the discovered association. *Proceedings of the 5th ACM SIGKDD International Conference on Knowledge Discovery and Data Mining* (pp. 125-134), San Diego, CA.

Liu, B., Hsu, W., Ma, Y., & Chen, S. (1999). Mining interesting knowledge using DM-II. In *Proceedings of ACM Intl. Conference KDD*, San Diego, CA, USA.

Liu, B., Hsu, W., Mun, L.-F., & Lee, H.-Y. (1996). *Finding interesting patterns using user expectations* (Technical Report TRA 7/96). Singapore: National University of Singapore, Department of Information Systems and Computer Science.

Liu, B., Ku, L.-P., & Hsu, W. (1997). Discovering interesting holes in data. In *IJCAI'1997* (2): *Proceedings of Fifteenth International Joint Conference on Artificial Intelligence* (pp. 930-935).

Liu, H., Lu, H., Feng, L., & Hussain, F. (1999). Efficient search of reliable exceptions. In *Proceedings of the Third Pacific-Asia Conference on Methodologies for Knowledge Discovery and Data Mining(PAKDD)*, (pp. 194-204).

Liu, X.-Y., & Zhou, Z.-H. (2006). The influence of class imbalance on cost-sensitive learning: An empirical study. In *ICDM '06. Sixth International Conference on Data Mining* (pp. 970–974).

Liu, X.-Y., Wu, J., & Zhou, Z.-H. (2006). Exploratory under-sampling for class-imbalance learning. In *ICDM '06. Sixth International Conference on Data Mining* (pp. 965–969).

Lo, D., Khoo, S.-C., & Liu, C. (2007). Efficient mining of iterative patterns for software specification discovery. In *KDD* (pp. 460-469).

Lu, J. (2004). Personalized e-learning material recommender system. In Proceedings of the *International conference on information technology for application (ICITA'04)* (pp. 374-379). China.

Lu, J.-J. (2002). Mining Boolean and General Fuzzy Weighted Association Rules in Databases. *Systems Engineering-Theory & Practice, 2*, 28–32.

Lu, S., Hu, H., & Li, F. (2001). Mining Weighted Association Rules . *Intelligent Data Analysis Journal, 5*(3), 211–255.

Lykken, D. (1995). *The Antisocial Personalities.* Lawrence Erlbaum: Hillsdale, N.J.

Ma, L., Tsui, F.-C., Hogan, W. R., Wagner, M. M., & Ma, H. (2003). A framework for infection control surveillance using association rules. *AMIA Annual Symposium Proceedings* (pp. 410-414). American Medical Informatics Association.

Ma, Y., Liu, B., & Wong, C. K. (2000). Web for data mining: Organizing and interpreting the discovered rules using the web. *SIGKDD Explorations, 2*(1), 16–23. doi:10.1145/360402.360408

Maloof, M. Learning when data sets are imbalanced and when costs are unequal and unkown, *ICML2003.*

Mannila, H. (1998). Database methods for data mining, tutorial. In *KDD '98: Proceedings of the fifth ACM SIGKDD international conference on Knowledge discovery and data mining.* ACM.

Mannila, H., & Pavlov, D. (1999). Prediction with local patterns using cross-entropy. In *Proceedings of ACM Intl. Conference KDD*, San Diego, CA, USA.

Mannila, H., Toivonen, H., & Verkamo, A. (1994). Efficient algorithm for discovering association rules. In *Knowledge Discovery and Data Mining (KDD)* (pp. 181-192).

Mannila, H., Toivonen, H., & Verkamo, A. I. (1997). Discovery of frequent episodes in event sequences. *Data Mining and Knowledge Discovery, 1*(3), 259–289. doi:10.1023/A:1009748302351

Marukatat, R. (2007). Structure-based rule selection framework for association rule mining of traffic accident data. In Y. Wang, et al. (Eds.), *CIS 2006, Lecture Notes in Computer Science, Vol. 4456* (pp. 231-239). Springer.

Masseglia, F., Cathala, F., & Poncelet, P. (1998). The PSP approach for mining sequential patterns. In *PKDD* (pp. 176-184).

McCarthy, K., Zabar, B., & Weiss, G. (2005). Does Cost Sensitive Learning Beat sampling for Classifying Rare Classes? In *Proceedings of the 1st international workshop on Utility-based data mining UBDM '05* (pp. 69 – 77).

McGarry, K. (2005). A survey of interestingness measures for knowledge discovery. *The Knowledge Engineering Review, 20*(1), 39–61. doi:10.1017/S0269888905000408

Meo, R. (2000). Theory of dependence values. *ACM Transactions on Database Systems, 25*(3), September 2000.

Merceron, A. (2008). Unterstützung des Erlernens von endlichen Automaten mit Hilfe von Mustern. In J. Desel & M. Gliz (Eds.) *Proceedings Wokshop für Modellierung in Lehre und Weiterbildung,* (pp. 27-36). Modellierung 2008, Berlin, Germany. Retrieved August 01, 2008, from http://www.ifi.uzh.ch/techreports/TR_2008.html See also http://public.tfh-berlin.de/~merceron/pub/DP-DFA_eng.pdf

Merceron, A., & Yacef, K. (2003). A Web-based Tutoring Tool with Mining Facilities to Improve Learning and Teaching. In *Proceedings of the 11th International Conference on Artificial Intelligence in Education,* (pp. 201-208). Sydney: IOS Press.

Merceron, A., & Yacef, K. (2004). Mining Student Data Captured from a Web-Based Tutoring Tool: Initial Exploration and Results. [JILR]. *Journal of Interactive Learning Research, 15*(4), 319–346.

Merceron, A., & Yacef, K. (2005). Educational Data Mining: a Case Study. In *Proceedings of the International Conference on Artificial Intelligence in Education (AIED2005)* (pp. 467-475). Amsterdam, The Netherlands. IOS Press.

Merceron, A., & Yacef, K. (2007). Revisiting interestingness of strong symmetric association rules in educational data. In *Proceedings of the International Workshop on Applying Data Mining in elearning (ADML'07)* (pp. 3-12). Crete, Greece 2007. Retrieved August 01, 2008, from http://ftp.informatik.rwth-aachen.de/Publications/CEUR-WS/Vol-305/

Merceron, A., & Yacef, K. (2008). Interestingness Measures for Association Rules in Educational Data. In R. de Baker, T. Barnes & J.E. Beck (Eds.), *Proceedings of the first International Conference on Educational Data Mining (EDM'08)* (pp. 57-66). Montreal, Canada. Retrieved August 01, 2008, from http://www.educationaldatamining.org/EDM2008/uploads/proc/full proceedings.pdf

Merz & Murph. P. (1998). UCI repository of machine learning databases. http://www.ics.uci.edu/~mlearn/-MLRepository.html

Minaei-Bidgoli, B., Kashy, D. A., Kortemeyer, G., & Punch, W. F. (2003). Predicting student performance: an application of data mining methods with the educational web-based system LON-CAPA. 33rd *ASEE/IEEE Frontiers in Education Conference*. Boulder, Colorado.

Minaei-Bidgoli, B., Tan, P. N., & Punch, W. F. (2004). Mining Interesting Contrast Rules for a Web-based Educational System. In *Proceedings of the International Conference on Machine Learning Applications (ICMLA 2004),* Louisville, KY, USA, CSREA Press.

Monahan, J., Steadman, H., Silver, E., Appelbaum, P., Robbins, P., & Mulvey, E. (2001). *Rethinking risk assessment: The MacArthur study of mental disorder and violence*. New York: Oxford University Press.

Morishita, S., & Sese, J. (2000). Traversing itemset lattices with statistical metric pruning. In *Proceedings of the POD Intl. Conference*, Dallas, TX, USA.

Morzy, M. (2006). *Efficient Mining of Dissociation Rules.* Paper presented at the 8th Conference on Data Warehousing and Knowledge Discovery, Krakow, Poland.

Mun, L.-F., Liu, B., Wang, K., & Qi, X.-Z. (1998). Using decision tree induction for discovering holes in data. In *PRICAI '98: Proceedings of the 5th Pacific Rim International Conference on Artificial Intelligence* (pp. 182-193), London, UK: Springer-Verlag.

Mustafa, M. D., Nabila, N. F., Evans, D. J., Saman, M. Y., & Mamat, A. (2006). Association rules on significant rare data using second support. *International Journal of Computer Mathematics*, 83(1), 69–80. doi:10.1080/00207160500113330

Muyeba, M., Khan, M. S., & Coenen, F. (2008). Fuzzy Weighted Association Rule Mining with Weighted Support and Confidence Framework. In *PAKDD Workshop 2008, LNAI 5433* (pp. 49–61), Springer-Verlag, Berlin Heidelberg.

Nanavati, A. A., Chitrapura, K. P., Joshi, S., & Krishnapuram, R. (2001). Mining generalised disjunctive association rules. In *CIKM '01: Proceedings of the tenth international conference on Information and knowledge management* (pp. 482-489), New York: ACM.

Newman, D., Hettich, S., Blake, C., & Merz, C. (1998). *UCI repository of machine learning databases.* http://www.ics.uci.edu/~mlearn/ MLRepository.html.

NIST/SEMATECH e-Handbook of Statistical Methodsn (2007), retrieved August 2008 from http://www.itl.nist.gov/div898/handbook/.

Northpointe (2006). Compas reentry [computer software].

Ohsaki, M., Kitaguchi, S., Okamoto, K., Yokoi, H., & Yamaguchi, T. (2004). Evaluation of rule interestingness measures with a clinical dataset on hepatitis. In *Proceedings of the 8th European conference on principles of data mining and knowledge discovery (PKDD)*, (pp. 362–373).

Ohshima, M., Zhong, N., Yao, Y. Y. Y., & Liu, C. (2007). Relational peculiarity-oriented mining. *Data Mining and Knowledge Discovery*, 15(2), 249–273. doi:10.1007/s10618-006-0046-6

Ohshima, M., Zhong, N., Yao, Y. Y. Y., & Murata, S. (2004). Peculiarity Oriented Analysis in Multi-people Tracking Images *Advances in Knowledge Discovery and Data Mining* (pp. 508-518). Springer.

Omiecinski, E. R. (2003). Alternative Interest Measures for Mining Associations in Databases. *IEEE Transactions on Knowledge and Data Engineering*, 15(1), 57–69. doi:10.1109/TKDE.2003.1161582

Owen, B. (1998). *In the Mix: Struggle and Survival in a Woman's Prison.* Albany, N.Y: State University of New York Press.

Padmanabhan, B., & Tuzhilin, A. (1998). A belief-driven method for discovering unexpected patterns. In *KDD* (pp. 94-100).

Padmanabhan, B., & Tuzhilin, A. (2000). Small is beautiful:discovering the minimal set of unexpected patterns. In *Proceeding of 6th ACM SIGKDD International Conference on Knowledge Discovery and Data Mining (KDD)* (pp. 54-63).

Papoulis, A. (1965). *Probability, Random variables, and Stochastic Processes.* McGraw-Hill, Inc.

Park, J., Yu, P., & Chen, M.-S. (1997). Mining association rules with adjustable accuracy. In *Proceedings of the CIKM Intl. Conference*, Las Vegas, Nevada, USA.

Pavlov, D., Mannila, H., & Smyth, P. (2003). Beyond independence: Probabilistic models for query approximation on binary transaction data. *IEEE Transactions on Knowledge and Data Engineering*, 5(6), 1409–1421. doi:10.1109/TKDE.2003.1245281

Pearl, J. (1998). *Probabilistic reasoning in intelligent systems.* Morgan Kaufmann, Los Altos, CA.

Pearl, J. (2000). *Causality: models, reasoning, and inference.* Cambridge University Press, Cambridge, UK.

Pei, J., Han, J., Mortazavi-Asl, B., Wang, J., Pinto, H., & Chen, Q. (2004). Mining sequential patterns by pattern-growth: the PrefixSpan approach. *IEEE Transactions on Knowledge and Data Engineering, 16*(11), 1424–1440. doi:10.1109/TKDE.2004.77

Petersilia, J. (2001). Prisoner reentry: Public safety and reintegration challenges. *The Prison Journal, 81*(3), 360–375. doi:10.1177/0032885501081003004

Pintilie, M. (2007). Analysing and interpreting competing risk data. *Statistics in Medicine, 26*, 1360–1367. doi:10.1002/sim.2655

Plasse, M., Niang, N., Saporta, G., Villeminot, A., & Leblond, L. (2007). Combined use of association rules mining and clustering methods to find relevant links between binary rare attributes in a large data set. *Computational Statistics & Data Analysis, 52*(1), 596–613. doi:10.1016/j.csda.2007.02.020

Quinlan, J. R. (1986). Induction of decision trees. *Journal of Machine Learning, 1*(1), 81–106.

Quinsey, V. L., Harris, G. T., Rice, M. E., & Cormier, C. A. (1998). *Violent Offenders: Appraising and Managing Risk*, Washington, DC: American Psychological Association.

Quinsey, V., Harris, G., Rice, M., & Cormier, C. (1998). Violent recidivism of mentally disordered offenders: The development of a statistical prediction instrument. In *American Psychological Association.*

Rahal, I., Ren, D., Wu, W., & Perrizo, W. (2004). Mining confident minimal rules with fixed-consequents. In *Proceedings of the 16th IEEE International Conference on Tools with Artificial Intelligence, ICTAI'04* (pp. 6–13). Washington, DC: IEEE Computer Society.

Ramaswamy, S., Rastogi, R., & Shim, K. (2000). Efficient Algorithms for Mining Outliers from Large Data Sets. In *SIGMOD* (pp. 427-438).

Rao, C. R., & Toutenburg, H. (1997). *Linear Models: Least Squares and Alternatives*, Springer Verlag, Heidelberg.

Rice, M. E., & Harris, G. T. (1995). Methodological development, violent recidivism: Assessing predictive validity. *Journal of Consulting and Clinical Psychology, 63*, 737–748. doi:10.1037/0022-006X.63.5.737

Rizzolo, F., & Vaisman, A. (2008). Temporal XML: modelling, indexing, and query processing. *The VLDB Journal, 17*, 1179–1212. doi:10.1007/s00778-007-0058-x

Roddick, J., & Rice, S. (2001). What's interesting about cricket? – on thresholds and anticipation in discovered rules. *SIGKDD Explorations, 3*, 1–5. doi:10.1145/507533.507535

Rodger, S. (1996). *JFLAP*. Retrieved August 01, 2008, from http://www.jflap.org/

Romero, C., & Ventura, S. (2007). Educational Data Mining: A Survey from 1995 to 2005. *Expert Systems with Applications, 33*(1), 135–146. doi:10.1016/j.eswa.2006.04.005

Romero, C., Ventura, S., de Castro, C., Hall, W., & Ng, M. H. (2002). Using Genetic Algorithms for Data Mining in Web-based Educational Hypermedia Systems. In P. M. de Bra, P. Bruzilovsky, R. Conejo (Eds.), *Adaptive Hypermedia and Adaptive Web-Based Systems (Ah02).* Lecture Notes in Computer Science 2347. New York: Springer Verlag.

Rückert, U., & Kramer, S. (2006). A statistical approach to rule learning. In *Proceedings of the International Conference on Machine Learning (ICML)*, (pp. 785–792), Pittsburgh, PA.

Rückert, U., Richter, L., & Kramer, S. (2004). Quantitative association rules based on half-spaces: An optimization approach. *In Proceedings of the IEEE International Conference on Data Mining (ICDM)*, (pp. 507–510).

Savasere, A., Omiecinski, E., & Navathe, S. (1995). An efficient algorithm for mining association rules in large databases. *In Proceeding of the 21st International Conference on Very Large Databases (VLDB)*, (pp. 432-444).

Savasere, A., Omiecinski, E., & Navathe, S. (1998). Mining for strong negative associations in a large database of customer transactions. In *Proceedings of the Fourteenth International Conference on Data Engineering (ICDE)* (pp. 494-502).

Schölkopf, B., & Smola, A. (2002). *Learning with Kernels.* Cambridge, MA: MIT Press.

Schroder, B. S. W. (2003). *Ordered Sets: An Introduction.* Birkhauser, Boston.

Seno, M., & Karypis, G. (2001). LPMINER: An algorithm for finding frequent itemsets using length-decreasing support constraint. In N. Cercone, T. Y. Lin, & X. Wu (Eds), In *Proceedings of the 2001 IEEE International Conference on Data Mining ICDM* (pp. 505–512). Washington, DC: IEEE Computer Society.

Servigny, A. D., & Renault, O. (2004). *Measuring and Managing Credit Risk.* New York: McGrawHill.

Shanno, D. (1970). Conditioning of quasi-newton methods for function minimization. *Mathematics of Computation, 24,* 647–656. doi:10.2307/2004840

Sharma, L. K., Vyas, O. P., Tiwary, U. S., & Vyas, R. (2005). A novel approach of multilevel positive and negative association rule mining for spatial databases. In *MLDM '05: Proceedings of* the 4th International Conference on Machine Learning and Data Mining in Pattern Recognition (pp. 620-629). Springer.

Sharma, S. (1996). *Applied multivariate techniques.* John Wiley & Sons Inc.

Shihab, S., Al-Nuaimy, W., Huang, Y., & Eriksen, A. (2003). A comparison of segmentation techniques for target extraction in ground penetrating radar data. In *Proceedings of the 2nd International Workshop on Advanced Ground Penetrating Radar, 2003* (pp. 95-100).

Shragai, A., & Schneider, M. (2001). Discovering quantitative associations in databases. In Joint 9th *IFSA World Congress and 20th NAFIPS International Conference* (pp. 423-42).

Shyu, M.-L., Chen, S.-C., & Kashyap, R. (1999). Discovering quasi-equivalence relationships from database systems. In *Proceedings of the CIKM Intl. Conference,* Kansas City, Mo, USA.

Siebes, A. (1994). *Homogeneous discoveries contain no surprises: Inferring risk-profiles from large databases.* Technical report, Computer Science Department/Department of Algorithmics and Architecture, CWI, The Netherlands.

Silberschatz, A., & Tuzhilin, A. (1996). What makes patterns interesting in knowledge discovery systems. *IEEE Transactions on Knowledge and Data Engineering, 8*(6), 970–974. doi:10.1109/69.553165

Silver, E., & Miller, L. (2002). A cautionary note on the use of actuarial risk assessment tools for social control. *Crime and Delinquency, 48,* 138–161. doi:10.1177/0011128702048001006

Silverstein, C., Brin, S., & Motwani, R. (1998). Beyond market baskets: generalizing association rules to dependence rules. *Data Mining and Knowledge Discovery, 2*(1), 39–68. doi:10.1023/A:1009713703947

Smith, L. D., Sanchez, S. M., & Lawrence, E. C. (1996). A Comprehensive Model for Managing Credit Risk on Home Mortgage Portfolio. *Decision Sciences, 27*(2), 291–308.

Smith, W. (1996). The effects of base rate and cutoff point choice on commonly used measures of association and accuracy in recidivism research. *Journal of Quantitative Criminology, 12,* 83–111. doi:10.1007/BF02354472

Song, X., Wu, M., Jermaine, C., & Ranka, S. (2007). Conditional Anomaly Detection. *IEEE Transactions on Knowledge and Data Engineering, 19*(5), 631–645. doi:10.1109/TKDE.2007.1009

Spiliopoulou, M. (1999). Managing interesting rules in sequence mining. In *PKDD* (pp. 554-560).

Spitzer, W. (1986). Importance of valid measurements of benefit and risk. *Medical Toxicology, 1*(1), 74–78.

Srikant, R., & Agarawal, R. (1996). Mining quantitative association rules in large relational tables. In *Proceedings of the Association for Computing Machinery- Special Interest Group on Management of Data (ACM SIGMOD)* (pp. 1-12).

Srikant, R., & Agrawal, R. (1995). Mining generalized association rules. In *Proceedings of the 21th International Conference on Very Large Data Bases (VLDB)* (pp. 407-419).

Srikant, R., & Agrawal, R. (1996). Mining sequential patterns: generalizations and performance improvements. In *EDBT* (pp. 3-17).

Srikant, R., Vu, Q., & Agarawal, R. (1997). Mining association rules with item constraint. In *Proceeding of 3rd International Conference on Knowledge Discovery and Data Mining (KDD)* (pp. 67-73).

Srinivasan, V., & Kim, Y. H. (1987). Credit granting a comparative analysis of classifactory procedures. *The Journal of Finance, 42*, 655–683. doi:10.2307/2328378

Steinbach, M., Tan, P.-N., Xiong, H., & Kumar, V. (2004). Generalizing the notion of support. In *Proceedings of the ACM SIGKDD International Conference on Knowledge Discovery and Data Mining (KDD)*, (pp, 689–694), Seattle, WA.

Strohmann, T., Belitski, A., Grudic, G., & DeCoste, D. (2004). Sparse greedy minimax probability machine classification. In S. Thrun, L. Saul, and B. Schölkopf (Eds.), *Advances in Neural Information Processing Systems, 16*. Cambridge, MA: MIT Press.

Sun, L., & Senoy, P. P. (2006). Using Bayesian network for bankruptcy prediction: some methodological issues. *European Journal of Operational Research, 10*, 1–16.

Sun, P., Chawla, S., & Arunasalam, B. (2006). Mining for Outliers in Sequential Databases. In *SDM* (pp. 94-105).

Sun, Y., Kamel, M. S., & Wang, Y. (2006). Boosting for Learning Multiple Classes with Imbalanced Class Distribution. In *ICDM '06. Sixth International Conference on Data Mining* (pp. 592-602).

Sun, Y., Kamel, M. S., Wong, A. K. C., & Wang, Y. (2007). Cost-sensitive boosting for classification of imbalanced data. *Pattern Recognition, 40*(12), 3358–3378. doi:10.1016/j.patcog.2007.04.009

Suzuki, E. (2002). Undirected Discovery of Interesting Exception Rules. *International Journal of Pattern Recognition and Artificial Intelligence, 16*(8), 1065–1086. doi:10.1142/S0218001402002155

Suzuki, E., & Zytkow, J. M. (2005). Unified algorithm for undirected discovery of exception rules. *International Journal of Intelligent Systems, 20*(6), 673–691. doi:10.1002/int.20090

Suzuki, E., Watanabe, T., Yokoi, H., & Takabayashi, K. (2003). *Detecting Interesting Exceptions from Medical Test Data with Visual Summarization.* Paper presented at the Proceedings of the Third IEEE International Conference on Data Mining.

Svetina, M., & Zupancic, Joze. (2005). How to increase sales in retail with market basket analysis. *Systems Integration,* 418-428.

Swets, J. (1988). Measuring the accuracy of diagnostic systems. *Science, 240*(4857), 1285–1293. doi:10.1126/science.3287615

Szathmary, L., Napoli, A., & Valtchev, P. (2007). Towards Rare Itemset Mining. In *Proceedings of the 19th IEEE international Conference on Tools with Artificial intelligence - Vol.1 (ICTAI 2007) - Volume 01 (October 29 - 31, 2007). ICTAI. (pp. 305-312).* Washington, DC: IEEE Computer Society

Tan, P. N., Kumar, V., & Srivastava, J. (2002). *Selecting the Right Interestingness Measure for Association Patterns.* In *Proceedings of the 8th ACM SIGKDD International Conference on Knowledge Discovery and Data Mining* (pp. 67-76). San Francisco, USA. ACM Publisher.

Tan, P.-N., Kumar, V., & Srivastava, J. (2004). Selecting the Right Objective Measure for Association Analysis. *Information Systems,* (29): 293–313. doi:10.1016/S0306-4379(03)00072-3

Tao, F., Murtagh, F., & Farid, M. (2003). Weighted association rule mining using weighted support and significance framework. In *Proceedings of the Ninth ACM SIGKDD International Conference on Knowledge Discovery and Data Mining, KDD '03* (pp. 661–666). New York, NY: ACM Press.

Tata, C. (2002). The quest for coherence in the sentencing decision process: Noble dream or chimera? In *Sentencing and Society: Second International Conference*. Glasgow, Scotland.

Techapichetvanich, K., & Datta, A. (2005). VisAr: A new technique for visualizing mined association rules. In X. Li, et al. (Eds.), *ADMA 2005, Lecture Notes in Computer Science, Vol. 3584* (pp. 88-95). Springer.

Thomas, L. C., Ho, J., & Scherer, W. T. (2001). Time to tell: behaviour scoring and the dynamics of consumer credit assessment. *Journal of Management Mathematics, 12*, 89–103.

Thomas, S., & Sarawagi, S. (1998). Mining generalized association rules and sequential patterns using SQL queries. In *KDD '98: Proceedings of the Fourth International Conference on Knowledge Discovery and Data Mining* (pp. 344-348).

Thrun, S., Tesauro, G., Touretzky, D., & Leen, T. (1995). Extracting rules from artificial neural networks with distributed representations. [MIT Press.]. *Advances in Neural Information Processing Systems, 7*, 505–512.

Thuraisingham, B. (2004). Data Mining for Counterterrorism. In H. Kargupta, A. Joshi, K. Sivakumar & Y. Yesha (Eds.), *In Data Mining: Next Generation Challenges and Future Directions* (pp. 157-). MIT Press.

Toivonen, H., Klemettinen, M., Ronkainen, P., Hatonen, K., & Mannila, H. (1995). Pruning and grouping of discovered association rules. *Workshop Notes of the ECML 95 Workshop in Statistics, Machine Learning, and Knowledge Discovery in Databases* (pp. 47-52), Greece. University of Waikato (n.d.). Weka 3 – data mining software in Java (version 3.4.12) [software]. Available from http://www.cs.waikato.ac.nz/ml/weka/.

Tong, Q., Yan, B., & Zhou, Y. (2005). Mining quantitative association rules on overlapped intervals. In *ADMA'05: Proceedings of the* 1st International Conference on *Advanced Data Mining and Applications* (pp. 43-50). Springer.

TPC benchmark H. Transaction Processing Performance Council, retrieved August 2008 from http://www.tpc.org/tpch/default.asp

Tsaih, R., Liu, Y.-J., Liu, W., & Lien, Y.-L. (2004). Credit scoring system for small business loans. *Decision Support Systems, 38*, 91–99. doi:10.1016/S0167-9236(03)00079-4

Tukey, J. (1977). *Exploratory Data Analysis,* Addison-Wesley.

Vapnik, V. (1998). *The Nature of Statistical Learning Theory*. Wiley, NY.

Verhein, F., & Chawla, S. (2007). Using Significant, Positively Associated and Relatively Class Correlated Rules for Associative Classification of Imbalanced Datasets. In *ICDM'07: Seventh IEEE International Conference on Data Mining* (pp. 679-684).

Walton, R. (1989). *Up and Running*. Boston: Harvard Business School Press.

Wang, B.-Y., & Zhang, S.-M. (2003). A Mining Algorithm for Fuzzy Weighted Association Rules. In *IEEE Conference on Machine Learning and Cybernetics*, 4 (pp. 2495-2499).

Wang, F. (2006). On using Data Mining for browsing log analysis in learning environments. In C. Romero & S. Ventura (Ed.), *Data Mining in E-Learning. Series: Advances in Management Information* (pp. 57-75). WIT press.

Wang, F.-H., & Shao, H.-M. (2004). Effective personalized recommendation based on time-framed navigation clustering and association mining. *Expert Systems with Applications, 27*(3), 365–377. doi:10.1016/j.eswa.2004.05.005

Wang, J., & Han, J. (2004). BIDE: Efficient mining of frequent closed sequences. In *ICDE* (pp. 79-90).

Wang, K., He, Y., & Cheung, D. W. (2001). Mining confident rules without support requirement. In *Proceedings of the Tenth International Conference on Information and Knowledge Management*, (pp. 89–96). New York, NY: ACM Press.

Wang, K., He, Y., & Han, J. (2000). Pushing support constraints into frequent itemset mining. In *Proceeding of International Conference on Very Large Data Bases (VLDB)*, (pp. 43-52).

Wang, K., He, Y., & Han, J. (2003). Pushing support constraints into association rules mining. *IEEE Transactions on Knowledge and Data Engineering, 15*(3), 642–658. doi:10.1109/TKDE.2003.1198396

Wang, K., He, Y., Cheung, D. W.-L., & Chin, F. (2001). Mining confident rules without support requirement. In *Proc. ACM CIKM*, (pp. 89–96).

Wang, K., Xu, C., & Liu, B. (1999). Clustering transactions using large items. In *CIKM '99: Proceedings of the eighth international conference on information and knowledge management* (pp. 483–490). New York, NY, USA: ACM Press.

Wang, W., Yang, J., & Yu, P. S. (2000). Efficient Mining of Weighted Association Rules (WAR). In *Proceedings of the KDD* (pp. 270-274). Boston.

Webb, G. I. (2006). Discovering significant rules. In *Proc. of the Twelfth ACM SIGKDD* (pp. 434-443).

Webb, G. I., & Zhang, S. (2002). Removing trivial association in association rule discovery. *Proceedings of the 1ˢᵗ International NAISO Congress on Autonomous Intelligent Systems (ICAIS)*, Geelong, Australia. NAISO Academic Press.

Weiss, G. M. (2004). Mining with rarity: a unifying framework. *SIGKDD Exploration Newsletter, 6*(1), 7–19. doi:10.1145/1007730.1007734

West, D. (2000). Neural network credit scoring models. *Computers & Operations Research, 27*, 1131–1152. doi:10.1016/S0305-0548(99)00149-5

Wu, X., Zhang, C., & Zhang, S. (2004). Efficient mining of both positive and negative association rules. *ACM Transactions on Information Systems, 22*(3), 381–405. doi:10.1145/1010614.1010616

Xiao, X., Dow, E. R., Eberhart, R., Miled, Z. B., & Oppelt, R. J. (2003). Gene clustering using self-organizing maps and particle swarm optimization. In *IPDPS'03: Proceedings of the 17th international symposium on parallel and distributed processing*. Washington, DC, USA: IEEE Computer Society.

Xin, D., Cheng, H., Yan, X., & Han, J. (2006) Extracting redundancy-aware top-k patterns. In *Proceedings of the 2006 ACM SIGKDD International Conference on Knowledge Discovery and Data Mining (KDD'06)*, Philadelphia, Pennsylvania, USA.

Xiong, H., Shekhar, S., Tan, P., & Kumar, V. (2004). Exploiting a support-based upper bound of Pearson's correlation coefficient for efficiently identifying strongly correlated pairs. In *Proceedings of the Tenth ACM SIGKDD international Conference on Knowledge Discovery and Data Mining* (Seattle, WA, USA, August 22 - 25, 2004). (pp.334-343). KDD '04. ACM, New York, NY,

Xu, J., Xiong, H., Sung, S. Y., & Kumar, V. (2003). A new clustering algorithm for transaction data via caucus. In *Proceedings Advances in knowledge discovery and data mining: 7th Pacific-Asia conference, PAKDD 2003*, (pp. 551–562) Seoul, Korea.

Xiong, H., Tan, P., & Kumar, V. (2003). Mining Strong Affinity Association Patterns in Data Sets with Skewed Support Distribution, In *Proceedings of the Third IEEE International Conference on Data Mining (ICDM)* (pp. 387-394).

Xiong, H., Tan, P.-N., & Kumar, V. (2003). Mining strong affinity association patterns in data sets with skewed support distribution. In *Proceedings of the Third IEEE International Conference on Data Mining* (pp. 387–394). Washington, DC: IEEE Computer Society.

XML. Extensible Markup Language 1.0 (1998), retrieved August 2008 from http://www.w3C.org/TR/REC-xml/.

XQuery. An XML Query Language (2002), retrieved August 2008 from http://www.w3C.org/TR/REC-xml/.

Yacef, K. (2005). The Logic-ITA in the classroom: a medium scale experiment. *International Journal of Artificial Intelligence in Education, 15*, 41–60.

Yan, X., Han, J., & Afshar, R. (2003). CloSpan: Mining closed sequential patterns in large databases. In *SDM* (pp. 166-177).

Yuan, X., Buckles, B. P., Yuan, Z., & Zhang, J. (2002, July). Mining negative association rules. *Proceedings of the 7th IEEE International Symposium on Computers and Communications (ISCC)* (pp. 623-628), Taormina, Italy. IEEE Computer Society.

Yue, S., Tsang, J., Yeung, E., & Shi, D. (2000). Mining Fuzzy Association Rules with Weighted Items, In *IEEE International Conference on Systems, Man, and Cybernetics, 3*, 1906-1911.

Yun, C.-H., Chuang, K.-T., & Chen, M.-S. (2001). An efficient clustering algorithm for market basket data based on small large ratios. In *Compsac'01: Proceedings of the 25th international computer software and applications conference on invigorating software development* (pp. 505–510). Washington, DC, USA: IEEE Computer Society.

Yun, H., Ha, D., Hwang, B., & Ryu, K. H. (2003). Mining association rules on significant rare data using relative support. *Journal of Systems and Software, 67*(3), 181–191. doi:10.1016/S0164-1212(02)00128-0

Zaki, M. J. (2000). Generating non-redundant association rules. In *KDD'00: Proceedings of the sixth ACM SIGKDD international conference on Knowledge discovery and data mining* (pp. 34-43). ACM, New York, NY, USA.

Zaki, M. J. (2001). SPADE: An efficient algorithm for mining frequent sequences. *Machine Learning, 42*(1-2).

Zekic-Susac, M., Sarlija, N., & Bensic, M. (2004). Small business credit scoring: a comparison of logistic regression, neural network, and decision tree models. In *26th International Conference on Information Technology Interfaces* (p. 265).

Zeng, L. (1999). Prediction and classification with neural network models. *Sociological Methods & Research, 27*(4), 499–524. doi:10.1177/0049124199027004002

Zeng, S., Melville, P., Lang, C. A., Martin, I. B., & Murphy, C. (2007). Predictive modeling for collections of accounts receivable. In *Proceedings of the 2007 international workshop on Domain driven data mining* (pp. 43-48).

Zhang, S., Wu, X., Zhang, C., & Lu, J. (2008). Computing the minimum-support for mining frequent patterns. *Knowledge and Information Systems, 15*(2), 233–257. doi:10.1007/s10115-007-0081-7

Zhao, Y., Zhang, H., Figueiredo, F., Cao, L., & Zhang, C. (2007). Mining for combined association rules on multiple datasets. In *DDDM07: KDD Workshop on Domain Driven Data Mining*, San Jose, CA, USA

Zhong, N., Liu, C., Yao, Y. Y. Y., Ohshima, M., Huang, M., & Huang, J. (2004). *Relational peculiarity oriented data mining.* Paper presented at the Fourth IEEE International Conference on Data Mining.

Zhong, N., Yao, Y. Y. Y., & Ohshima, M. (2003). Peculiarity Oriented Multidatabase Mining. *IEEE Transactions on Knowledge and Data Engineering, 15*(4), 952–960. doi:10.1109/TKDE.2003.1209011

Zhou, L., & Yau, S. (2007). Efficient association rule mining among both frequent and infrequent items. *Computers & Mathematics with Applications (Oxford, England), 54*, 737–749. doi:10.1016/j.camwa.2007.02.010

Zhou, Z.-H., & Liu, X.-Y. (2006). Training cost-sensitive neural networks with methods addressing the class imbalance problem. *IEEE Transactions on Knowledge and Data Engineering, 18*(1), 63–77. doi:10.1109/TKDE.2006.17

Zolezzi, M., & Parsotam, N. (2005). Adverse drug reaction reporting in New Zealand: implications for pharmacists. *Theraputics and Clinical Risk Management, 1*(3), 181–188.

About the Contributors

Yun Sing Koh is currently a currently a Lecturer in Computer Science at Auckland University of Technology, New Zealand. After completing a Bachelor's degree in Computer Science and Masters in Software Engineering at the University of Malaya, she went on to do her PhD in Computer Science in Otago, New Zealand. Her current research interests include data mining, machine learning, and information retrieval.

Nathan Rountree is a Lecturer in Computer Science at the University of Otago in Dunedin, New Zealand, where he teaches papers on databases, data structures and algorithms, and Web development. He holds a bachelor's degree in Music, a postgraduate diploma in Computer Science, and a PhD in Computer Science, all from Otago. His research interests include Computer Science education, artificial neural networks, and collaborative filtering.

* * *

Marco-Antonio Balderas is a teacher within the School of Agronomy, Science, Autonomous University of Tamaulipas at Victoria City. He earned an Advance Studies Diploma (DEA) in 2005 and is pursuing a doctorate at the Department of Computer Science and Artificial Intelligence, University of Granada, Spain. He focuses on the discipline of data mining, specifically in the area of association rules, and his current research interests systems and the computer networks.

Hans Bohlscheid An executive in the Australian Public Service, Hans' present role as a senior program director was preceded by a long career in education where he held a number of teaching and principal positions. For the last four years he has been responsible for the development and implementation of Commonwealth Budget initiatives based on changes to legislation and policy. During this period he has managed a considerable suite of projects, however it is his recent involvement in a pilot which sought to determine the effectiveness of data mining as a predictive and debt prevention tool that has shifted his focus to research and analysis. In addition to his government responsibilities, Hans is currently managing a 3-year University of Technology Sydney research project which is funded through an Australian Research Council Linkage Grant in partnership with the Commonwealth. He is a Partnership Investigator and Industry Advisor to the University's Data Sciences and Knowledge Discovery Laboratory, and he has co-authored a number of publications and book chapters relating to data mining. His personal research involves an examination of project management methodology for actionable knowledge delivery.

Markus Breitenbach is a Research Analyst at Northpointe Institute for Public Management. Before coming to Northpointe, Dr. Breitenbach worked as a Research Assistant at the University of Colorado and studied methods for clustering collections of images. He has a background in pattern recognition, has worked on various OCR, information retrieval and document management projects. He earned a Ph.D. in Computer Science emphasizing Machine Learning techniques at the University of Colorado.

Frans Coenen is a senior lecturer in the Department of Computer Science at Liverpool University, UK. He received his PhD in Knowledge-Based Systems (KBS) from Liverpool Polytechnic in 1989. He has been involved in various capacities (chair, co-chair, technical programme chair, deputy technical programme chair) with the British Computer Societies (BCS) annual international AI conferences (ES99, ES2000, ES2001, ES2002, AI2003, AI2004 and AI2005)), founder and first editor of the Expert Update (the SGAI magazine) and member of the BCS Specialist Group on Artificial Intelligence (SGAI) committee. He supervises several PhD students and his research interests are in Knowledge Discovery in Databases (KDD) and Data Mining.

Tim Brennan is probably best known for his book on *The Social Psychology of Runaways* (Co-authored with Del Elliott and Dave Huizinga) and his chapters on criminological classification in *Criminal Justice Annual Reviews – Edited by Don Gottfredson and Michael Tonry*. His research interests are in classification and risk assessment of youth and adult offenders and technical procedures for pattern recognition and artificial intelligence. He is published widely in: criminological assessment, delinquency, jail and prison classification, youth runaway, adolescent loneliness and suicide, information technology and implementation processes in Criminal Justice. His work has been supported by grants from the *National Institute of Justice, National Institute of Mental Health, National Institute of Corrections*, and so on. Tim Brennan received his Ph.D from Lancaster University, England in 1972. He is an Associate Member of the Institute of Cognitive Science, University of Colorado.

Giulia Bruno received the master's degree in Computer Engineering from the Politecnico di Torino. She has been a Ph.D. student in the Database and Data Mining Group at the Dipartimento di Automatica e Informatica, Politecnico di Torino, since January 2006. She is currently working in the field of data mining and bioinformatics. Her activity is focused on the analysis of gene expression data, gene network modelling, data cleaning and semantic information discovery. Her research activities are also devoted to classification of physiological signals to monitor patient conditions for clinical analysis.

Longbing Cao is an Associate Professor in Faculty of Engineering & IT, University of Technology, Sydney, Australia. He is the Director of Data Sciences & Knowledge Discovery Research Lab. His research interest focuses on domain driven data mining, multi-agents, and the integration of agent and data mining. He is a chief investigator of three ARC (Australian Research Council) Discovery projects and two ARC Linkage projects. He has over 50 publications, including one monograph, two edited books and 10 journal articles. He is a program co-chair of 11 international conferences.

William Dieterich has over ten years experience conducting research in criminal justice and juvenile justice settings. He has worked as a research analyst on several studies at the University of Denver, including a school-based randomized trial of a prevention curriculum and a series of observational studies examining co-occurring mental health and substance abuse problems among juvenile offenders. He was the research analyst on numerous projects for the Colorado Division of Youth Corrections, including an evaluation of the Colorado Regimented Juvenile Training Program. He has worked as a research analyst on many outcomes studies, including the Denver Drug Court study. He has expertise in prognostic modeling, sampling design, data collection, and psychometrics. He has broad experience designing and implementing COMPAS pilot studies conducted for prison, parole, and probation agencies. William Dieterich received his Ph.D. in Social Work at the University of Denver in 2003.

Khaled Elbassioni is a senior researcher at Max-Planck-Institute für Informatik, Saarbrücken, Germany. He obtained his B. Sc. M.Sc. degrees in Computer Science from Alexandria University, Egypt in 1992 and 1995, respectively, and his Ph.D. degree in Computer Science from Rutgers University, USA. His research interests include the design and analysis of enumeration algorithms - for problems arising in graph and hypergraph theory, matroid theory, geometry, data mining and mathematical programming - approximation algorithms for combinatorial optimization problems, discrete mathematics, computational and combinatorial geometry, and game theory.

Adrian Fan is a graduate student of University of Colorado, Boulder and an enthusiast of practical applications of machine learning. His experiences range from Fair Isaac's Confabulation research group to AnswerOn's analytics R&D involving various machine learning and NLP techniques. His area of focus is the adaptation of machine learning knowledge and techniques to business intelligence and analytics.

Paolo Garza received the master's and PhD degrees in Computer Engineering from the Politecnico di Torino. He has been a postdoctoral fellow in the Dipartimento di Automatica e Informatica, Politecnico di Torino, since January 2005. His current research interests include data mining and database systems. In particular, he has worked on the classification of structured and unstructured data, clustering, and itemset mining algorithms.

Dino Ienco took his Bachelor degree in Computer Science in 2004 at the University of Turin, Department of Computer Science (Italy). In 2006 he took his Master degree summa cum laude in Computer Science at the University of Turin, Department of Computer Science (Italy). He started his PhD program in 2007. His research is focused on pattern mining, unsupervised learning methods for bioinformatics and feature selection for supervised learning.

Szymon Jaroszewicz received Ph.D. degree from University of Massachusetts at Boston in 2003. Currently he is with the National Institute of Telecommunications in Warsaw, Poland. His research interests include association rule mining and in particular rule interestingness and using background knowledge in the data mining process. He has also worked on rule discovery in numerical data.

Muhammad Sulaiman Khan is a member of the Intelligent and Distributed Systems (IDS) and a PhD research student in the School of Computing at Liverpool Hope University, UK. He received his MSc in Computing (Lahore, Pakistan) and another MSc in Distributed Systems from Liverpool Hope University. He has several years of industrial experience as an applications programmer. His current research is in Fuzzy Association Rule Mining with Weighted and Composite Items.

Anne Laurent has been assistant professor at the University of Montpellier 2 in France since September 2003. As a member of the TATOO group in the LIRMM Laboratory, she works on data mining, sequential pattern mining, tree mining, both for trends and exceptions detections and is particularly interested in the study of the use of fuzzy logic to provide more valuable results, while remaining scalable.

Dong (Haoyuan) Li is a Ph.D. student in the computer science department at the University of Montpellier 2 in France. He received the B.S. degree in mechanical engineering at the University of Zhejiang in China and the M.S. degree in computer science at the University of Montpellier II. His research interests include knowledge based data mining and its applications.

Rangsipan Marukatat is a lecturer at the Department of Computer Engineering, Faculty of Engineering, Thailand. She received a B.Sc. in Statistics from Chulalongkorn University, Thailand; M.Sc. and Ph.D. in Computer Science from University of Edinburgh, UK. Her research interests include data mining, data warehouse, and distributed / parallel processing. The material appeared in this chapter is part of her research project funded by the National Science and Technology Development Agency of Thailand (NSTDA).

Rosa Meo took her Master degree in Electronic Engineering in 1993 and her Ph.D. in Computer Science and Systems Engineering in 1997, both at the Politechnic of Turin, Italy. From 2005 she is associate professor at Department of Computer Science in University of Turin where she moved in 1999 as researcher. Rosa's research field is Database and Data Mining. She teaches courses at the degree level and PhD level on Database, development of advanced applications with DBMS and Data Mining. Rosa Meo served in the Programme Committees of many scientific, peer-reviewed conferences in Data Mining and Databases such as ACM SIGKDD, ICDM, ECML/PKDD, SIAM Data Mining, VLDB, ACM CIKM, ACM SAC, PAKDD, DaWaK, DEXA, and journals such as IEEE TKDE, IEEE TODS, KAIS.

Agathe Merceron received a PhD in Computer Science from the University Paris Orsay, France and is now Professor at the University of Applied Sciences TFH Berlin, Germany. Her teaching duties include foundation of computer science and data mining both for face to face and on-line students in the department for Media Informatics, where she is responsible for the on-line degrees. Her research interests include Information Systems and Knowledge Management applied to E-learning and particularly Educational Data Mining. She is a member of the editorial board of the Journal of Educational Data Mining. She is also involved in the "Information and Communication Technologies for Teaching and Learning" community and has been an active member of the European Network of Excellence "Kaleidoscope". For more information, please visit her website at public.tfh-berlin.de/~merceron.

Maybin Muyeba is a Senior Lecturer in the Department of Computing and Mathematicas at Manchester Metropolitan University, UK. He received the Msc in Industrial and Information Technology from the Department of Computer Science, Hull University and the PhD degree in Data Mining from Manchester Institute of Science and Technology (UMIST). Prior to joining Mancester Metropolitan University, he was lecturer at Liverpool Hope University, Bradford University (UK) and University of Zambia. He is a programme committee member of several conferences including PAKDD 2009, EPIA 2007, DMIN and reviews several other conferences and journals including EUROPAR 2004, DMIN, PAKDD, Annals of Information Systems journal and CAE: An international journal. His research interests are in applying Data Mining techniques to Health data analysis (Health Informatics) and how these can be used in decision making at policy level, Fuzzy logic and their applications and pervasive Computing.

Richard A. O'Keefe holds a B.Sc. (Honours) degree in mathematics and physics, majoring in statistics, and an M.Sc. degree in physics (underwater acoustics), both obtained from the University of Auckland, New Zealand. He received his Ph.D. degree in artificial intelligence from the University of Edinburgh. He is the author of "The Craft of Prolog" (MIT Press). Dr O'Keefe is now a lecturer at the University of Otago, New Zealand. His computing interests include declarative programming languages, especially Prolog and Erlang; statistical applications, including data mining and information retrieval; and applications of logic. He is also a member of the editorial board of theory and practice of logic programming.

Raymond Sunardi Oetama received his master's degree from the Auckland University of Technology (AUT). Prior to that, Raymond was an IT Manager for Semesta Citra Dana, Indonesia. He has vast experience in the finance sector and has worked as both a Quality Control Cycle (QCC) Facilitator and an IT Associate Analyst in Federal International Finance (FIF). He holds a bachelor degree in Mathematical Science from Institute Technology Sepuluh November in Surabaya. Raymond is currently in the process of starting his doctorate degree at Auckland University of Technology. His current research interest is in the area of data mining and knowledge discovery. He has keen interest in data mining tools for banking, finance and trading applications.

Russel Pears (PhD, Cardiff University UK) is a Senior Lecturer and Director of the Doctoral Programme at the School of Computing and Mathematical Sciences at the Auckland University of Technology, New Zealand. Currently he is involved in a number of research projects in Data Mining, including mining of classification and association rules in high speed data streams, mining rare association rules, financial time series modelling and prediction, and recommender systems for on line book stores. He teaches in the Data Mining and Data Warehousing areas for undergraduate and postgraduate degrees in Computer Science at the Auckland University of Technology. He has published in a number of refereed international conferences and journals in the areas of Data Mining, Database Management Systems and Data Warehousing.

Pascal Poncelet is a professor at the University of Montpellier 2 in France. He was a professor and the head of the data mining research group in the computer science department at the École des Mines d'Alès in France. His research interest can be summarized as advanced data analysis techniques for emerging applications. He has published a large number of research papers in refereed journals, conference, and workshops, and been reviewer for some leading academic journals. He is also co-head of the France CNRS Group "I3" on Data Mining.

Elisa Quintarelli received her master's degree in Computer Science from the University of Verona, Italy. On January 2002 she completed the Ph.D. program in Computer and Automation Engineering at Politecnico di Milano and is now an assistant professor at the Dipartimento di Elettronica e Informazione, Politecnico di Milano. Her main research interests concern the study of efficient and flexible techniques for specifying and querying semistructured and temporal data, the application of data-mining techniques to provide intentional query answering. More recently, her research has been concentrated on context aware data management.

Stephen S.-T. Yau (M'89-SM'94) received the M.S. and Ph.D. degrees from the State University of New York at Stony Brook in 1974 and 1976, respectively. In 1976-1977, he was a member of the Institute for Advanced Study at Princeton University. From 1977 to 1980, he was a Benjamin Pierce Assistant Professor at Harvard University. He received the Sloan Fellowship from 1980 to 1982. In 1980, he joined the Department of Mathematics, Statistics, and Computer Science, University of Illinois at Chicago (UIC) as Associated Professor. He was promoted to Professor at UIC in 1984. He has also held several visiting professorship positions at Princeton University (1981), Institute for Advanced Study (1981-1982), University of Southern California (1983-1984), Yale University (1984-1985), Institute Mittag-Leffler, Sweden (1987), The Johns Hopkins University (1989-1990), and the University of Pisa, Italy (1990). He was awarded the University Scholar (1987-1990) by University of Illinois. Dr. Yau has been the managing editor of the Journal of Algebraic Geometry since 1991, the Director of the Control and Information Laboratory since 1993, and Editors-in-Chief of Communications in Information and Systems since 2002. He received the Guggenheim Fellowship in 2002, IEEE Fellow Award in 2003, Distinguished Professor Award of University of Illinois at Chicago in 2005.

Chengqi Zhang is a Research Professor in Faculty of Engineering & IT, University of Technology, Sydney, Australia. He is the Director of UTS Research Centre for Quantum Computation and Intelligent Systems and a Chief Investigator in Data Mining Program for Australian Capital Markets on Cooperative Research Centre. He has been a chief investigator of eight research projects. His research interests include Data Mining and Multi-Agent Systems. He is a co-author of three monographs, a co-editor of nine books, and an author or co-author of more than 150 research papers. He is the chair of the ACS (Australian Computer Society) National Committee for Artificial Intelligence and Expert Systems, a chair/member of the Steering Committee for three international conferences.

Huaifeng Zhang was awarded Ph.D degree by Chinese Academy of Sciences (CAS) in 2004. Right after receiving Ph.D degree, Dr. Zhang joined UTS as a principal researcher and project leader to work on an ARC Discovery Project. In 2007, he joined UTS flagship Centre for Quantum Computation and Intelligent Systems (QCIS) to work in a joint project conducted by UTS and Australian government. He has more than 40 publications in the previous five years, including one book published by Springer, seven articles in journals, three chapters in edited books. His research interests include combined pattern mining, sequence classification, behaviour analysis and modeling, etc.

Yanchang Zhao is a Postdoctoral Research Fellow in Data Sciences & Knowledge Discovery Research Lab, Faculty of Engineering & IT, University of Technology, Sydney, Australia. His research interests are association rules, sequential patterns, clustering and post-mining. He has published more than 30 papers on the above topics, including six journal articles, one edited book and three book chapters. He has served as a chair of two international workshops, a program committee member for 14 international conferences and a reviewer for 9 international journals and over a dozen of other international conferences.

Ling Zhou received a Master's degree in Mathematics and Computer Science and Ph.D. degree in Mathematics from the University of Illinois at Chicago in 2001 and 2007 respectively. Dr. Zhou has a broad interest in the field of data mining and specifically in rare item association rule mining. She has authored papers published in Computers and Mathematics with Applications, and Proceeding of the 8th International Workshop on Multimedia Data Mining etc. Dr. Zhou used to serve as a statistical consultant at Stroger Cook County Hospital in medical research and holds a Research Analyst Role in Epi-Q Company in the area of health outcomes and economics research currently.

Index

A

absolute rare rules 76, 90, 93, 95

added value 185, 192

adverse drug reactions 205, 206

anomalies 131, 132, 133, 138, 143, 148

anomalous rule, canonical 171

Apriori algorithm 1, 2, 3, 4, 5, 6, 7, 8, 9, 10, 12, 13, 47, 53, 55, 56, 57, 59, 63, 77, 78, 79, 80, 82, 86, 87, 88, 89, 90, 91, 94, 95, 96, 216, 217, 218, 219, 220, 221, 224, 225, 226, 228, 229

arbitrary nonlinear relationships 118, 119, 128

area under the curve (AUC) 237, 255, 262, 263, 265

association rule mining (ARM) 15, 16, 17, 18, 20, 25, 27, 30, 31, 47, 48, 49, 51, 52, 53, 54, 57, 59, 61, 62, 63, 168

association rules, anomalous (AARs) 168, 169, 170, 171, 172, 173, 174, 176, 178, 179, 180, 181, 182, 183

association rules (ARs) 1, 2, 3, 4, 5, 6, 7, 9, 12, 13, 15, 16, 17, 18, 19, 23, 24, 25, 26, 27, 28, 29, 30, 31, 33, 34, 36, 37, 45, 46, 47, 48, 49, 53, 57, 62, 98, 99, 102, 105, 106, 107, 108, 109, 110, 111, 113, 114, 115, 116, 118, 119, 120, 122, 123, 129, 130, 131, 132, 133, 134, 135, 136, 137, 138, 140, 142, 143, 145, 146, 147, 148, 168, 169, 170, 171, 176, 180, 182, 183, 185, 186, 187, 188, 189, 190, 191, 193, 194, 195, 196, 198, 200, 201, 202

association rules, class (CARs) 66, 67, 68, 69, 71

association rules, high confidence 2, 3, 5, 7, 9, 10, 11, 13

association rules, informative 218, 220, 224, 228

association rules, low support 2, 3, 5, 6, 7

association rules, negative 217, 218, 222, 223, 224, 228, 229, 230

association rules, positive 217, 223, 224, 225, 226, 227, 228

association rules, quantitative 15, 17, 27, 28, 29, 30

association rules, weighted 47, 62

B

background knowledge 118, 119, 120, 121, 123, 124, 125, 127, 128, 129

base-rate 231, 233, 235, 236, 241, 243, 250

Bayesian networks 120, 123, 124, 125, 127, 129, 255, 256, 261, 262, 263, 264, 265, 269

Bayes' Theorem 33, 34, 35, 37, 38, 39, 45

belief 150, 153, 154, 155, 156, 157, 158, 159, 160, 161, 162, 163, 164, 165, 166

belief trees 156, 157, 160, 163

C

clustering 76, 77, 78, 80, 81, 82, 83, 84, 85, 91, 94, 95, 96, 97

combined patterns 71

concordance index 235

conditional support 69, 70, 71

confidence interval 33, 38, 39, 40, 45

confidence level 35, 40, 41, 43, 44

confidence measure 36

confidence threshold 37

confidence values 36

contrast rules 185, 186, 193, 195, 200

T

transactional co-occurrence matrix (TCOM) 16
transaction clustering 78, 80, 81, 82, 84, 95
t-tree 49

U

unexpectedness 150, 151, 152, 153, 154, 156,
157, 158, 159, 160, 161
upward closure 76, 89, 95

V

variable support threshold 5, 6
violent crimes 241, 242

W

Weka data mining software 217, 219, 221, 225,
230